The Mexican Kickapoo Indians

The Texas Pan American Series

Felipe A. Latorre & Dolores L. Latorre

The Mexican

Kickapoo Indians

Foreword by William Madsen

University of Texas Press, Austin & London

The Texas Pan American Series is published
with the assistance of a revolving publication
fund established by the Pan American Sulphur
Company.

Library of Congress Cataloging in Publication Data

Latorre, Felipe A   1907–
  The Mexican Kickapoo Indians.

  (The Texas pan-American Series)
  Bibliography: p.
  Includes index.
  1. Kickapoo Indians. I. Latorre, Dolores L.,
1903–   joint author. II. Title.
E99.K4L37   972'.1   75–11654
ISBN 0–292–75023–4

Second Printing, 1976

To our Indian friends,
who valiantly strive to
keep alive old moons while
facing new ones.

The people of the world are bigoted and unenlightened; invariably they regard what is like them as right, and what is different as wrong, resulting in mutual recrimination . . . They do not realize that the types of humanity are not uniform and that their customs are also not one, that it is not only impossible to force people to become different but also impossible to force them to become alike.

YUNG-CHEN
Peking, 1727

Every tradition grows ever more venerable—the more remote is its origin, the more confused that origin is. The reverence due to it increases from generation to generation. The tradition finally becomes holy and inspires awe.

NIETZSCHE
Human, All Too Human

Contents

Illustrations

Tables

Foreword

Good field work in anthropology demands two qualities: a sound knowledge of the discipline and the ability to relate meaningfully with respondents in a culture different from one's own. The Latorres have admirably demonstrated both of these qualities in this most significant study. Besides filling a notable gap in our knowledge of the Kickapoos, this book also illustrates the need for patience and understanding in the delicate task of interpreting another way of life. The Latorres combine perceptive observation with great skill and perseverance in arriving at the social realities behind the conflicting information gathered from different respondents.

The excellence of this volume is especially notable in view of the massive failure by others who preceded the Latorres in attempts to gain acceptance by the Coahuila Kickapoos in order to study their way of life. These Indians have, for many reasons, both valid and invalid from our viewpoint, been extremely suspicious of outsiders who desire to enter the confines of their world. Many have tried to penetrate the culture of the Coahuila Kickapoos in order to study them, but none met with any notable success before the Latorres. Robert E. Ritzenthaler and Frederick A. Peterson, for example, are both competent researchers; yet they totally failed in gaining Kickapoo acceptance. In fact, they met with such an increasing hostility that they were forced to abandon their attempted study after a stay of only three weeks.

The Latorres carefully researched the available literature before entering the field and planned a slow and cautious approach. Rather than appear uninvited in the Kickapoo community, they wisely settled in the nearest market town. Here they met and befriended the Indians who came to town and began to render them small but essential services. Their friendship with Chief Papícoano finally opened the way for friendly visits to the Kickapoo village. For at least six months the Latorres concentrated on gaining Indian acceptance and trust rather than attempting any in-depth study of the culture itself.

Once the actual investigation was operative, the authors realized that various factions among the Kickapoos were trying to use the anthropologists as pawns in subtle power fights. Some fed wrong information to the Latorres, and others spread rumors intended to label them as undesirables. The anthropologists skillfully and diplomatically sidestepped the conflicts and succeeded in convincing the Kickapoos that a valid study would be a thing of value to later generations of Indians. Using humor as well as friendship, the Latorres finally gained the closest relationship with the Kickapoos ever enjoyed by outsiders.

I personally witnessed the rapport that the Latorres had with the Kickapoos while visiting them in the field. The experience was delightful and instructive. Not only are the Latorres the most gracious of hosts, but they also had the ability to sensitize me in a brief period to the principal values of Kickapoo culture so that I could witness and appreciate many of the dominant themes in their daily life. My wife and I will both always remember our visit with the Latorres as a beautiful experience with anthropologists operating simultaneously as social scientists, as artists, and as very fine human beings. Throughout, the Latorres demonstrated a sincere and deep appreciation and respect for the people they were studying. The Latorre relationship with the Kickapoos finally more closely resembled that of friends collaborating on a book than the too frequent picture of super-scientists viewing human specimens.

In an age when minorities of every persuasion are seeking autonomous identities, this book will be especially appreciated. The Kickapoos have survived warfare, exploitation, geographical change, and the accelerating shock of mechanical progress. Despite this, they are still Kickapoo, and their community in Coahuila stands as a beautiful testimonial to those who choose to maintain their cultural ties with the past. The Kickapoos' mechanisms for maintaining their identity are clearly described in depth.

Readers will find this book a rewarding experience and will enjoy entering the world of the Kickapoos with the Latorres as their competent guides.

William Madsen
University of California at Santa Barbara

Acknowledgments

As we look back upon our years in Múzquiz, a long list of friends passes before our eyes, all of whom aided us in the progress of our research: Drs. Ignacio Bernal and Fernando Cámara Barbechano of the Instituto Nacional de Antropología e Historia de México, Dr. Edgardo Reyes Salcido of the Instituto Tecnológico y de Estudios Superiores de Monterrey, and Dr. William Madsen, then of the Department of Anthropology of the University of Texas at Austin (and now at the University of California at Santa Barbara), who sponsored and encouraged our project; Mr. and Mrs. Bill Kuykendall of Kyle, Texas, who introduced us to the Kickapoos; Mr. and Mrs. Roberto Spence, Sr., of Sabinas, Coahuila, Sra. Rosa R. de la Garza, Sra. Vita G. de Romo, and Dr. Jesús Pader of Múzquiz, whose cooperation, hospitality, and assistance were ever at hand; Drs. B. L. Turner and Marshall C. Johnston of the Botanical Laboratories of the University of Texas at Austin who determined the plants used by the Indians; Mrs. Hoye Eargle, for her unselfish assistance in the preparation of the manuscript; Dr. Madsen and Dr. W. W. Newcomb, who read the manuscript; our faithful servants, Azucena Villareal and Jovita Garza, whose kindness to the Indians and generosity with their folklore were of inestimable help; many others listed in the bibliography; and, last, but not least, Chief Papícoano and all of the Kickapoos, whose friendship made this endeavor a reality.

Introduction

For over a century a group of Kickapoo Indians, originally residents of Wisconsin, have been living in northern Coahuila, eighty miles by air from the U.S.-Mexican border. During a visit to Mexico in 1960 we flew over their village, El Nacimiento, and were intrigued by the anachronistic and arresting picture it presented—glistening wigwams, scattered at random at the edge of an extensive valley, much of it covered with semi-desert brush, and protected in the west by the foothills of Sierra Hermosa de Santa Rosa, at whose feet rose a crystal-clear stream which meandered through the village.

What was going on here? Why were the Kickapoos still living in this land so different from their native Wisconsin? Why had they not returned to their homeland? What had brought them to Mexico? What were they like? How did they live? The idea of finding the answers to these and many other questions was challenging.

We began to search for available publications on the Kickapoos and discovered that, although their history and migrations had been traced, information about their culture and way of life was practically nonexistent.

The latest publication was a brief preliminary study done by Robert E. Ritzenthaler and Frederick A. Peterson, whose stay among the Indians in 1954 was cut off after three weeks. Their summary dismissal from the village with only a twenty-four–hour notice and their reluctance to leave what was, in their words, an "ethnographer's paradise"[1] indicated that no in-depth study had been done on this group. John M. Goggin, who visited the village in 1949 for two days, stated that "the group's reputation for hostility has been such that few people have attempted visiting or studying them,"[2] while Margaret Welpley Fisher, editor of William Jones's *Ethnography of the Fox Indians*, made this observation: "This particular work is of great interest since the Fox have earned the distinction along with their kindred, the Mexican Kickapoo, of being ranked among the most conservative of all Indians."[3] Three other short works by Mexican writers—Carlos Basauri, Alfonso Fabila, and Roberto de la Cerda Silva—offered us brief information.[4]

Before making any definitive plans to study the Kickapoos, we made a preliminary trip to Múzquiz, trading post of the Indians, and drove to the village, some eighteen miles into the mountains, to pay our respects to Chief Papícoano. We found the chief, then about seventy-four years old, wearing the traditional dress. Through his aide, who spoke Spanish and some English, we made our plans known and presented him with a letter of introduction from the former president Lázaro Cárdenas, who had defended the Kickapoos in their land difficulties.

Although we were not overwhelmed by the chief's warmth in receiving us, he made no objections to our plans, and we further sealed our friendship by promising to bring him a pair of field glasses, which he requested, on our next trip to the village.

Seeing the village from the ground after our chat with Chief Papícoano increased our interest in studying this small group of people so isolated from modern trends.

Encouraged and exhilarated by our visit to the village, we believed that a further attempt should be made to study the Kickapoos in order to fill the existing vacuum. Approval to work in Mexico was granted upon our work's being designated as Project Number 8 of the recently established Centro de Investigaciones Sociales (Center of Social Research), with headquarters at the Instituto Tecnológico y de Estudios Superiores in Monterrey, Nuevo León, of which our advisor, Dr. William Madsen, then of the University of Texas at Austin, was president that year.

Fully aware of the difficulties encountered by others in the village, we took a house in Múzquiz and went prepared to stay for however long was necessary. Fortunately there was no language barrier, Spanish being our native tongue.

As the work advanced, we realized that we had found a unique opportunity, in which our most imperative responsibility was the simple gathering of data, avoiding interpretations or early analysis that might influence our research. Now, after ten years of close relationship with the Kickapoos, we present our field study, showing both the glorious and the inglorious aspects of Kickapoo life, for the consideration of anthropologists and the enjoyment of any reader interested in a radically different view of the human situation.

Not only have we gathered heretofore unknown information, but also our relations with these Indians have enriched our lives. Their determination to maintain their tribal identity at all costs; their selective choice of items from surrounding cultures—white as well as Indian—to facilitate and ease their lives; the apparent satisfaction they derive from belonging to a small, integrated community; the performance of the many ceremonies which keep them in harmony with the Creator, their ancestors, and their peers—all these seem to us worthy of admiration and considerable envy.

The Kickapoos are a remarkable people. We hope that each person reading this work will feel the same warm empathy toward them that we came to feel. Finally, we hope that we may have, in part, unraveled the mystery of the Kickapoos.

The Mexican Kickapoo Indians

Chapter 1

Historical Sketch

Since the purpose of this work is to present the Kickapoos from an ethnological viewpoint, no attempt will be made to give a detailed historical background. Their history has been adequately treated by several writers, in particular A. M. Gibson, who in 1963 published a painstakingly documented volume, *The Kickapoos: Lords of the Middle Border*, which is the best-delineated history of the Kickapoos thus far.

The Mexican Kickapoos belong to the Algonquian-speaking family, which once included tribes from the Delawares of the Atlantic seaboard to the Cheyennes of the western Great Plains. The Algonquian heartland, however, was in the Old Northwest, where twenty-odd Algonquian tribes were situated, all possessing a common language and, in general, the culture traits of one tribe.[1]

Specifically, the Kickapoos belong to the North-Central Algonquian group, whose members had three common cultural features: a lineage-structured kinship system with Omaha terminology, a complex system of clans regulating personal names, and division into moieties.[2]

Relations with the French and English, 1600–1765

The first mention of the Kickapoos places them in lower Michigan, between Lake Michigan and Lake Erie, in 1600.[3] When the French explored Wisconsin in 1654, they found the Sauk, Fox, Kickapoo, and Potawatomi tribes established as refugees among the Menomini and Winnebago in Wisconsin, having been driven westward to this area by the Iroquois. (The Iroquois had exhausted the fur resources in their own area and had obtained arms from the Dutch and English, with which they easily pushed the Kickapoos and others farther west.)[4]

Many writers concur that Father Claude-Jean Allouez was the first white man to record meeting the Kickapoos in the Green Bay area, in 1672. They lived in villages, raised crops, and, when these were harvested, hunted game over a large area.[5]

Fascinated by European goods and warmed by the fiery brandy dispensed by the French, most of the Algonquians became easy prey to French exploitation. The Kickapoos, however, were an exception. From the beginning of their contact with the French they showed a conspicuously independent spirit and a studied hostility toward acculturation and particularly toward the Jesuit priests. Forming a confederacy with the Mascoutens and the Fox, their neighbors, the Kickapoos became leaders of a combination which produced constant trouble for New France. As a result, the Kickapoos and their allies became outlaws in the western French territory, seriously threatening the dream of a French empire in America.[6]

Ultimately, a series of depredations brought the conflict between the French, the Kickapoos, and their allies into an open war. In 1712 a band of Kickapoos living near the Maumee River took as prisoner a French messenger returning from the Louisiana country. In retaliation, a canoe filled with Kickapoos was captured by the Hurons and Ottawas, allies of the French. Among the slain was the principal Kickapoo chief. That same year the Mascoutens plotted with the Fox and the Kickapoos for the capture of Fort Detroit and approached it in preparation for the siege. The Mascoutens were attacked by the Hurons and Ottawas until they were finally forced to retreat to Presque Isle, where they were taken as slaves.[7]

The Kickapoos, enraged over the defeat of their allies, engaged in an all-out war against the French and their Indian allies. This spurred the French to organize a massive campaign of retaliation against the Kickapoos, forcing them to come to terms.[8]

Having made friends with the French—under duress—the Kickapoos were sufficiently impressed with the European goods that they received as payment for their pelts to stay close to the trading posts, protecting the French against the Iroquois, who continued their trade with the English.[9] For two decades, the Kickapoos were allies of the French at one time, their enemies at another, at other times fighting other Indian tribes at French instigation, pawns in the French and Indian War.

The habitat of the western tribes slowly shifted eastward during the first half of the eighteenth century. This was in part due to the concentration policy of the French, because of the Fox wars, but was chiefly due to the tribesmen's desire to return to the home from which they had been driven nearly a hundred years earlier. By the end of the first quarter of the century, the French allies (including the Kickapoos) occupied the land west and north of the Wabash and Maumee rivers.[10]

After the Kickapoos, Sauk, and Fox destroyed the Illinois Confederacy in 1765, the Kickapoos fixed their headquarters for a time near Peoria. One group established themselves at about the mid-point of the Sangamon River; another group went farther east and settled on the Wabash. The first contingent became known as the "Prairie band," while the portion who settled on the Sangamon were known as the "Vermilion band."[11]

The French began their countermeasures by sending scouts to the Kickapoo villages to take women and children as hostages while the warriors were away. This threat drove the Kickapoos across the Mississippi, where they built villages on the Skunk River in present Iowa and reunited with their old allies, the Fox. The opportunity to regain their captive relatives presented itself a year after their move, when they took the explorer Pierre Boucher and the Jesuit priest Michel Guignois prisoners and later exchanged them for the hostages.[12] The exchange of prisoners resulted in a new alliance between the French and the Kickapoos and led to the renunciation of Kickapoo friendship with the Fox, bitter enemies of the French.

Between 1735 and 1763, British agents moved up the Tennessee toward the Ohio Valley in an attempt to cut the Wabash-Maumee trade route, the most direct passage between New France and Louisiana. Supplying the Chickasaw and Natchez Indians with arms and gifts, they offered bounties for raids into French territory west of the Ohio River. The French struck back by sending their newly made allies, the Kickapoos, into Chickasaw and Natchez territory on various occasions with great success —thereby reducing the British threat to the French interests north of the Ohio River. When the British saw their Indian allies defeated and the continuance of the French trade route now protected by the Kickapoos, they attempted to provoke a conspiracy among the French-allied Indians, but the Kickapoos resisted these overtures and remained loyal to the French.[13]

It was during these days of struggle between the British and the French to gain the loyalty of the Kickapoos that the French presented them with a Louis XV medal, a treasure that the Mexican Kickapoos still possess.

During the French and Indian War the Kickapoos defended the Ohio-Mississippi perimeter of New France. By 1759 the French were on the retreat in America.[14] With the Treaty of Paris in 1763, vanquished France transferred to the British title to Canada and the land of New France east of the Mississippi River; West Louisiana was ceded to Spain in compensation for Florida, which Spain yielded to Great Britain.[15]

These negotiations brought general fear to the Algonquians and led the Ottawa Indian leader Pontiac to attempt the capture of Fort Detroit. The Kickapoos, resentful toward the British and their Indian allies, the Chickasaws and the Miamis, took Pontiac's side, guarding the southern routes to Detroit during the taking of the fort by Pontiac and his Indian army.

The British attempted a reconciliation with the Algonquians by sending Capt. Thomas Morris to Fort Miami, where he found French traders and a large Kickapoo force; but when the Kickapoos learned of Captain Morris's intention of visiting other tribes, he was forced to desist from his mission. Unable to take the Illinois country in the face of mounting losses in men and goods, the British sent a second mission in 1765, headed by George Croghan. While approaching the mouth of the Wabash he was captured, and five of his fourteen men were scalped. The Kickapoos repeated the Boucher-Guignois maneuver they had so adroitly executed with the French in 1729: they held Croghan captive for thirty-five days, after which they utilized his release as their means of gaining recognition by the British on their own terms.[16]

Spanish Overtures, 1765–1815

With the ceding of Louisiana to Spain by the Treaty of Paris, the Kickapoos, among other Indians, were in a position to make friends or enemies with the Spanish. Antonio de Ulloa, distinguished naval officer and geographer, was appointed governor of Louisiana and soon built a chain of posts and settlements along the Mississippi, in the meantime establishing himself as a patron of the Indians of the Illinois country and inviting them to settle within Spanish territory. A Kickapoo chief, Serena, led his band to Spanish Louisiana in 1765, settling on the Missouri River near Saint Louis.

Relations with the Americans after 1779

After the capitulation of Henry Hamilton, British lieutenant governor, at Vincennes in 1779, the lower Northwest was attached to the United States. The Kickapoos switched their allegiance from the British to the Americans when Gen. George Rogers Clark promised that no colonizers would invade the conquered territory. However, before General Clark left Fort Massac on the lower Ohio, twenty families of settlers from Kentucky followed his army to Illinois country, soon to be trailed by many others. Strangled by the alarming encroachment of settlers and bitter over Clark's broken promise that the Americans had no designs on their land, the Kickapoos turned for counsel to the British, who still held Detroit in 1789 and whose objective, like that of the Indians, was to stem the American influx.[17]

The post–Revolutionary War period was a time of chaos in the villages

of the settlers. The Indians of the Old Northwest took up their toma-
hawks against the Americans and attacked everyone—sparing not even
the French. All Indians of that area, including the Kickapoos, were
counted as American enemies. No law existed in the land—Indians were
fighting each other as well as the settlers. The British, occupying areas of
Michigan, carried on extensive trade with the Indians and encouraged
them in their hostility to the American settlers.

After several attempts at subduing the hostile Indians, President
Washington sent Gen. Anthony Wayne, whose troops defeated the Indians at the Battle of Fallen Timbers in 1794. The result of this overthrow
was the Treaty of Greenville the following year, establishing a new
boundary line for the Indians and legally opening Ohio to settlement. For
fifteen years a relative peace prevailed throughout the country.[18] The
Kickapoos and their allies agreed to sign a land-cession treaty with the
United States relinquishing land claimed by them in Ohio in return for
land in Illinois and a five-hundred-dollar annuity.[19]

As these newly ceded lands began to be invaded by settlers, the Indians
began organizing again, this time with the secret support of the British.
The leaders in this movement were Tecumseh and his brother, the Shawnee "Prophet." Headed by Chief Tecumseh, large bands of Shawnees,
Delawares, Kickapoos, and others, who had formed a village at Tippecanoe (where the Wabash and Tippecanoe rivers meet), called on Gen.
William Henry Harrison at Vincennes and told him they no longer would
tolerate the occupation of the Indian lands by whites.[20]

Alarmed over the new movement of the Indians and fearing an upris-
ing that could become uncontrollable, General Harrison met them at
Tippecanoe in an encounter which ended in the defeat of the Indians.
Hiram W. Beckwith describes the participation of the Kickapoos: "They
fought in great numbers and with frenzied courage at the battle of Tippecanoe. As a military people, the Kickapoos were inferior to the Miamis,
Delawares, and Shawnees, in movements requiring large bodies of men;
but they were preeminent in predatory warfare."[21]

When Congress declared war against Great Britain in 1812, the Indians
of many tribes, including the Kickapoos north of the Ohio River, arrayed
themselves on the side of the British.[22] When Tecumseh and his brother,
the Prophet, fled to Amherstburg, Ontario, where a great intertribal village had been established, 150 Kickapoos and their families joined
them.[23]

After the War of 1812, Henry Clay, John Quincy Adams, and Albert
Gallatin met with the British in Ghent to negotiate the terms of the set-
tlement, one of which dealt with the Indians: "The Indian allies of Great
Britain [are] to be included in the pacification, and a boundary [is] to be

settled between the domain of the Indians and those of the United States. Both parts of this point are considered by the British government as *sine qua non* to the conclusion of the treaty."[24]

Although the American commission presented many protests, over a period of two years treaties were signed with thirty-four tribes or parts of tribes of American Indians, including the Kickapoos, who had previously fought on Britain's side against the United States. These Indians agreed to the terms of the treaties and signalized their fealty to the United States, concluding one of the most remarkable episodes of United States history, in which domestic Indian policy was dictated by diplomatic relations with a foreign government.[25]

Migration to the West, 1815–1850

During the administration of President James Monroe (1817–1825), the United States embarked on a policy of forcing eastern Indians, including the Kickapoos, to emigrate west of the Mississippi. At Edwardsville, Illinois, in 1819, the Kickapoos living in Wabash country agreed to a treaty by which they conveyed to the United States more than thirteen million acres of their land between the Illinois and Wabash rivers. The United States gave them in return a tract of land in the southwestern part of Missouri on the Osage River, near the Delaware reservation, and agreed to pay them an annuity of two thousand dollars for fifteen years.[26]

Thus began the slow migration of the Kickapoos to the Osage River, where they settled next to the Osage tribe. The Osages resented the Kickapoos, accusing them of depleting the game. The inevitable result was constant conflict between the two tribes, requiring severe interference from the U.S. authorities.[27]

While 2,000 Kickapoos gradually moved to Missouri during 1819, two renegade bands, each numbering about 250 warriors, repudiated the treaty of 1819 and remained in Illinois. It was not until 1835 that the United States government was able to induce the last of these recalcitrant Kickapoos to move west.[28]

By 1832 the Kickapoo tribe, numbering about 3,000, had split into a number of bands scattered from Lake Michigan to the Mexican territory which, four years later, would become the Republic of Texas. One Kickapoo community of 350, followers of the prophet Kennekuk, who advocated peace with the Americans, remained in eastern Illinois. Another group, under Chief Kishko, had settled on the Osage River in Missouri; to the south roamed several bands with a total population of about 900, under the leadership of various war chiefs, including Pecan and Black

Buffalo; still another band of 300, headed by Chief Mosqua, had settled in the province of Texas on the Sabine River.[29]

Unhappy with the land given them on the Osage River and constantly at war with their Osage neighbors, the Kickapoos importuned William Clark, the Superintendent of Indian Affairs in Saint Louis, to settle them elsewhere. This was finally accomplished by the Treaty of Castor Hill in 1832, by which the Kickapoos surrendered title to their Missouri domain in exchange for a home on the Missouri River near Fort Leavenworth, Kansas.[30]

During the early 1800's, Kickapoos, Shawnees, Delawares, Cherokees, and others who were located on the White River in Arkansas affiliated with one another under the leadership of Bowles, the Cherokee chief. Bowles and his people later left their land in Arkansas in protest against the Cherokee Removal Treaty of 1817 and emigrated to Texas; with the approval of the Spanish crown, they located on the Sabine River north of Nacogdoches and established themselves as frontier guards between the Mexican settlers and the "wild" Plains Indians, who were a constant menace to the colonizers, swooping down from U.S. territory into that area of Mexico. These Cherokees soon needed the aid and assistance of the Algonquians, and the Shawnees, Delawares, and another band of Kickapoos went to their assistance.[31]

After Mexico gained its independence from Spain in 1824, the Indians under Bowles, including eight hundred Kickapoos, formed a loose confederacy and were permitted by the Mexican government to remain on their lands, establishing villages and farms and raising large herds of livestock.[32]

When José María Sánchez, a representative of the Mexican government, arrived in Nacogdoches in 1832, he was impressed with the well-being of the settlers and the Indians. In describing a chance meeting with two Kickapoo warriors, he says they were mounted on excellent horses, each carrying a freshly killed deer, and had an appearance "more fierce than that of any other Indians, revealing in their manners a certain pride which is their characteristic."[33]

Unfortunately for the Indians, this state of affairs did not last long, for the Mexican government soon developed a lavish land-grant policy that attracted great numbers of American colonists. These colonists quickly became dissatisfied with the Mexican government. In 1835 they rebelled and set up a provisional government for the Republic of Texas. The rebels feared that the confederated Indians might side with Mexico in the coming struggle for Texas independence. In December, 1835, Provisional Governor Henry Smith instructed Indian Commissioner Sam Houston to make a treaty with the Cherokee Indians and their allies living in Texas near Nacogdoches.[34] In February, 1836, Houston met with Chief Bowles. They made a treaty guaranteeing the Cherokees' peaceable possession of their land in return for their neutrality during the revolution. The Indians did remain quiet, but no Texas government ever ratified the treaty made by Houston.[35]

Depredations resulting from the Indians' feeling that they had been treated unjustly, on one hand, and the settlers' hunger for land, on the other, led to continuous conflict in spite of Houston's efforts, as president of the new Republic of Texas, to allow the Indians to live in peace. Houston was followed by Mirabeau B. Lamar, who, unlike his predecessor, was a bitter enemy of all Indians. Lamar's declarations encouraged the settlers to push farther into Indian country, and the Indians retaliated by further depredations, with the result that the settlers eventually saw no solution other than the expulsion of the Indians from Texas.[36]

This atmosphere of unrest was soon exploited by the Mexicans, smarting from the defeat of Santa Anna and hoping to repossess their lost territory.[37] By 1837, Kickapoo depredations became so numerous and destructive of life and property that settlers edging into Cherokee lands fled to Nacogdoches for safety. Chief Bowles, fearing reprisal from the Texans, denied Cherokee participation in these raids, declared the Kickapoos to be renegades, and no longer recognized them as members of the Indian confederacy. When Mexican agents came to recruit an army for a counterrevolution to win Texas back, they were listened to readily by the Kickapoos.[38]

On September 8, 1838, a hunting party of Kickapoos came upon a Texan survey group near the present town of Dawson and attacked. Seventeen of the Texans were killed and five injured. This ambush, called the Battle Creek Massacre, aroused great fear and indignation among the colonists.[39]

Vicente Córdova, leading agent of the Mexican forces in the Nacogdoches area, had gathered around him about two hundred men and established a rebel post on the Angelina River, from which small guerilla bands roamed the countryside, terrorizing the Anglo-American settlements. Meanwhile the Kickapoos, led by Capitán Benito, son of the famous raider Black Buffalo, continued to harass the Texans. Gen. Thomas J. Rusk was sent to meet Córdova's forces, which, learning of the impending attack, escaped from Rusk's trap and sought safety in the Kickapoo village.

Soon after the Battle Creek encounter, the combined Mexican and Indian forces surprised the small frontier community of Killough and massacred many of its citizens. This brought further protests from the colonists and was responsible for General Rusk's attack on the Kickapoo village on October 15, 1838, where a battle raged for three days.[40]

The Battle Creek Massacre, the almost entire destruction of the Killough community, the actions of the Córdova guerillas, and the incriminating letters and orders for the Indians found on the bodies of Mexican agents killed by Texas troops—all these provided Lamar with the necessary material to overthrow Houston's tolerant policy toward the Indians. All Indians now became suspect—even the once-peaceful Cherokees were targets of Lamar's attack.

Texas Vice-President David Barnett and Secretary of War Albert Sidney Johnston were sent as emissaries to the confederated tribes to negotiate their removal to Indian Territory. The commission was authorized to purchase the Indians' improvements and to provide aid and safe conduct in removing the Indians. Chief Bowles deliberated over the proposals; and, while negotiations were under way, Capitán Benito killed several families at Mustang Prairie. In July, 1839, the Texas government charged all Indians living in the vicinity of Nacogdoches with conspiring with Mexican agents.

On July 19, Gen. Kelsey H. Douglass, heading a Texas army, marched upon the Cherokee villages on the Angelina River. Chief Bowles was slain, and his people fled in terror—not, however, before stoutly defending their homes and fields in the face of overwhelming forces.[41]

In the fall of 1839, John Bowles, son of Chief Bowles, set out to lead his followers into Mexico, but Col. Edward Burleson, on a campaign against the wild tribes, came across their trail and attacked them some seventy-five miles northwest of Austin. John Bowles and his mother were killed; and, although the Indians fought desperately, they could not long withstand the hot fire that was being poured into them by the Texans. Those who were able to escape joined their kinsmen in Indian Territory[42] or fled to Mexico.

In spite of an all-out program to rid Texas of Indians, many still roamed the state after its annexation to the United States in 1845. In 1848, Commissioner George W. Bonnell gave a survey of Indians listed as living between the Trinity and Red rivers as follows: 1,200 Kickapoos, 400 Delawares, 375 Shawnees, and 100 Cherokees, as well as others.[43]

Mexican Settlement, 1850–1864

The first historical mention of the Kickapoos' being in Mexico came from the United States consul in Matamoros, who reported that during the last six months of 1839 various small parties of Indians had arrived in that city at different times from eastern Texas; they consisted principally of Chero-

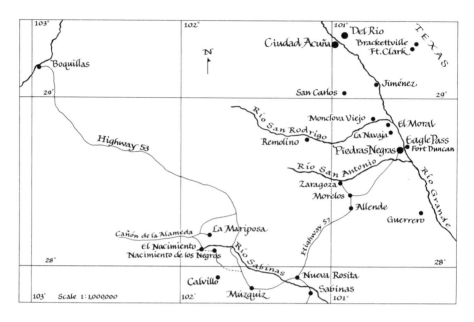

El Nacimiento and environs. (Map by Barbara Whitehead)

kees, Delawares, Kickapoos, and Caddoes, about eighty warriors altogether, all of whom had entered the Mexican military services.[44] After being mustered into the Mexican service, the Kickapoos were moved by border officials up the Río Grande to a point near Morelos, Coahuila.[45]

Jesse Sumpter, who was stationed at Fort Duncan, near the present Eagle Pass, Texas, in the summer of 1849, recalled that, when his cavalry company was ordered to escort Col. Joseph E. Johnston's survey party, the men camped near Brackettville, Texas. One day they discovered a number of Indians, carrying a white flag, coming toward them from Las Moras Mountains. They turned out to be Seminoles on their way to Mexico from Arkansas, led by Wild Cat (Coachoochee), the noted Seminole chief, and the Negro Gopher John. In the crowd, as near as Sumpter could guess, were one hundred Seminoles and one hundred Negroes.[46] Some Kickapoos were also in this group.

Wild Cat, having been moved to Indian Territory after the Seminole Wars of 1836–1842, had allied himself with Gopher John, who had assumed the leadership of the Negro element in the Seminole tribe (composed of runaway slaves), and in 1849 they led a migration to Mexico to establish a military colony.[47] Some five hundred restless Kickapoos, wandering from their home in Missouri in December, 1849, moved across the Red River and headed toward Eagle Pass to join Wild Cat's Mexican colony.[48]

Mrs. William L. Cazneau (Cora Montgomery), a newspaper correspondent who lived in Eagle Pass, colorfully described the arrival of Wild Cat and his party, who camped on the Río Grande nearby:

> We were sipping our chocolate, with every door thrown wide to welcome the breeze . . . when we were astonished to see Francesca coming up at a rapid pace . . . point[ing] . . . toward the hills. We looked out in surprise, for there, emerging from the broken ground in a direction that we knew was untravelled by any but the wild and hostile Indians, came forth a long procession of horsemen. The sun flashed back from a mixed array of arms and barbaric gear, but as this unexpected army . . . drew nearer it grew less formidable in apparent numbers, and opened upon us a more pacific aspect. Some reasonably well-mounted Indians circled around a dark nucleus of female riders. . . . But the long straggling rear-guard was worth seeing. . . . Such an array of all manners and sizes of animals, mounted by all ages, sexes and sizes of negroes, piled up to a most bewildering height, on and among such a promiscuous assemblage of blankets, babies, cooking utensils, and savage traps, in general, never were or could be held together on horseback by any beings on earth but themselves and their red brothers. The party began to break away and vanish into the little ravines that dip down to the river edge, and we understood by these signs they were encamping among us.[49]

A few days after their arrival in Eagle Pass, the Seminoles, Kickapoos, and Mascogos—as the Negroes were called by the Mexicans[50]—reported to the subinspector of the Colonia Militar de Guerrero (now Guerrero, Coahuila), a few miles south of Piedras Negras, soliciting land to establish a military colony.[51] In July, 1850, the Seminoles, allied Negroes, and Kickapoos were admitted to Mexico and temporarily settled at San Fernando de Rosas (now Zaragoza, Coahuila), at La Navaja, near Presidio Monclova Viejo, and at the Colonia Militar de Guerrero.[52]

By this time, Wild Cat, as chief of the Seminoles, and in representation of the Kickapoos and the free Negroes, had been assigned sixteen *sitios de ganado mayor* (approximately seventy thousand acres), half at the headwaters of the Río San Rodrigo and half at the headwaters of the Río San Antonio, some fifty miles southwest of present Ciudad Acuña. This arrangement, signed by the Inspector General of the Eastern Military Colonies, Antonio María Jaúregui, and Wild Cat in San Fernando de

Rosas (Zaragoza) on June 27, 1850, stipulated that the new colonizers were to obey the authorities and laws of the republic; maintain harmonious relations with nations friendly to Mexico; prevent, by all means possible, the Comanches and other barbarous tribes from continuing their incursions through the area; pursue and punish them; refrain from any commerce with these tribes; and maintain the best possible relations with the citizens of the United States.[53]

An additional clause in this agreement, which the Kickapoos have jealously guarded and maintained, reads: ". . . although the Kickapoos, Seminoles, Mascogan Negroes, and other Indians who may come to Mexico must subject themselves to the laws of the country, it is not demanded of them to change their habits and customs."[54]

The citizens of Remolino, situated near the rivers where land had been assigned to the Indians, were not pleased to have the newcomers settle among them and dispatched complaints to the provisional government in Coahuila, which issued a decree dated September 25, 1850, assuring the inhabitants that the lands would be returned to their owners and other lands would be found upon which the Indians could be settled.[55] Nevertheless, some of the Indians did eventually settle near Remolino, where they were attacked by Col. Ranald S. Mackenzie in 1873 (see below).

Meanwhile, the Indians and Negroes at La Navaja had barely established themselves and planted corn when they were called to supplement the regular Mexican forces in a campaign against the "wild Indians" in which they spent two months and during which they succeeded in turning back the marauding hordes.[56] A communiqué from the subinspector dated July 14, 1851, reported that the Kickapoos taking part in this first campaign had defected, driving with them the herd of horses that had been captured from the Comanches, and crossing the border at Eagle Pass. Of some five hundred Kickapoos who had arrived the previous year seeking asylum in Mexico, only Chief Papicua, nine men, seven women, and four children remained in Mexican territory, living near Morelos and dedicating themselves to agriculture.

In part because of this defection, the Mexican military authorities prepared to move all the Indians and Negroes to Hacienda El Nacimiento, twenty-three miles northwest of Santa Rosa María del Sacramento, and negotiations were begun to acquire the property from the owners of the land, the Sánchez Navarro family.[57]

Much confusion has resulted for historians and others from the changes in the names of towns in Coahuila, among them Santa Rosa, which, by a decree of Governor Simón Blanco on February 16, 1850, lost its old name and acquired a new one: Melchor Múzquiz, in honor of one of its sons, Gen. Melchor Múzquiz, provisional president of Mexico for a few months.[58] The name Santa Rosa persisted, however, for many decades. Today, Melchor Múzquiz has been shortened to Múzquiz.

A further reason for the removal of the Negroes from near the Río Grande to a safer place was the constant danger of raids carried out by slave hunters and filibusters.[59] Eagle Pass and its environs were the scouting area for a number of slave hunters, as this crossing had become a terminus for Negroes seeking freedom in Mexico.[60] On November 10, 1851, for example, while the Seminoles and Negroes were still established at La Navaja, Col. Emilio Langberg, Inspector of the Military Colonies, reported that a special messenger had arrived from the commander of Presidio Monclova Viejo with the alarming news that volunteers (American filibusters) were across the Río Grande from La Navaja, with the intention of attacking and capturing all the Negroes as well as the Seminole Indians living there.[61] The outcome of this particular incident is not reported, but a series of such threats to the Indians and Negroes forced them to seek more protected lands in the interior.

By July of 1852, Wild Cat and Chief Papicua were in Mexico City soliciting permission to establish themselves at Hacienda El Nacimiento, the Sánchez Navarro property already mentioned. This request was granted by the Ministry of War, replacing the land formerly occupied on a temporary basis at La Navaja with four *sitios de ganado mayor* (17,352 acres) in Hacienda El Nacimiento and an equal amount of land in the state of Durango, which the Indians never took up.[62]

In return for this new concession of land, the Indians and the Negroes were asked by the Mexican authorities to settle in villages and be ready to muster two hundred warriors on request. These lands were to be given in perpetuity on condition that the grantees obligated themselves to repel the Comanches, Mescaleros, Apaches, and all other Indians who were at war with the Mexican nation. Since only a handful of Kickapoos were in Mexico at this time, and they were living near Morelos, the Seminoles and the Negroes took up the land in Hacienda El Nacimiento.[63] This is the tract now occupied by the Mexican Kickapoos. The last of the Seminoles departed for Indian Territory in Oklahoma in 1861, while in 1859 the Negroes went to Laguna, Coahuila, returning to El Nacimiento in 1865 after the French Intervention. When a later contingent of Kickapoos arrived from Oklahoma in 1864, they occupied the land abandoned by the Seminoles.[64] The Kickapoos from Morelos presumably settled in El Nacimiento too, as there is no further record of their movements. It is likely that their chief, Papicua, was the grandfather of Chief Papícoano, but no proof of this has been found.

Indian Attacks on Texan and Mexican Colonists

While the Anglo-American settlers were having difficulties with the Indians on the Texas side, the Mexican colonists moving northward had been equally harassed by hostile Indians for more than a century. From the time of the Spanish conquest, Indian tribes that had acquired the horse made periodic raids into the interior of Mexico as far as Durango, destroying haciendas and towns, capturing women and children, and leaving in their wake a trail of blood. This constant harassment led Spain, in the early eighteenth century, to build a string of presidios along its frontier, extending from Altar in present Sonora to San Antonio de Béxar in Texas. The presidios served, in part, to defend the colonists. They proved effective against the Indian incursions until about 1832, after which the colonization of Texas, the Texans' fight for independence, and the Mexican-American War disrupted many of the Indians located in Texas, who again began to invade Mexican territory.[65]

By 1848 the Indian invasions had once more become so serious that new military colonies were decreed by the Mexican government to preserve the integrity of the new boundary and to defend the frontier states. These colonies were to be located at the old presidios and manned by 100 to 150 men each until the civil inhabitants could form a community and live in peace.

Unfortunately, the distance from Mexico City and the frequent economic and political crises faced by the young Mexican nation caused these presidios to be poorly manned and financed, making their establishment only partly effective.[66] An investigation by the Comisión Pesquisidora de la Frontera del Norte (Investigation Committee of the Northern Frontier), whose results were published in 1877, revealed that Santa Rosa (Múzquiz), one of the original eighteenth-century presidios, had suffered great depredations between 1848 and 1870: 187 incursions by hostile Indians; forty-five inhabitants killed, twenty-one injured, and twenty-three taken captive; and over sixteen hundred head of cattle and horses stolen. Although Santa Rosa was the hardest hit, nearby towns were also heavily affected by the continuous raids. It was difficult, if not impossible, for the colonists to make much progress in their endeavor to settle the new country.[67]

Under these circumstances, the Kickapoos, Seminoles, Negroes, and other "civilized" tribes were well received in Mexican territory and established in military colonies to serve as a buffer against the repeated raids on the colonists.

Either the Kickapoos who had defected from Mexico with a herd of horses in 1850 or some of those who had remained in the United States were active as middlemen between the prairie or "wild" Indians and other tribes and colonists, according to Capt. Randolph B. Marcy, who in 1852 embarked on an expedition to discover the headwaters of the Red River of Louisiana. Not far from Fort Arbuckle his party was visited by a group of young Kickapoo hunters, who for the past several years had engaged in a traffic with the prairie Indians which had a tendency to defeat the efforts of the military authorities to check their depredations upon the citizens of the northern provinces of Mexico. The Kickapoos procured articles for which the prairie Indians were willing to make great sacrifices. Since the traders desired only horses and mules for the articles, the prairie Indians raided northern Mexico to procure the animals.[68]

The Period of the American Civil War

In 1861 the only Kickapoos in Mexico were a few living in Morelos and Allende, Coahuila, under the command of Capitán Tabaco, who in 1863 was granted permission and funds to return to the United States for the purpose of bringing back many of the Kickapoos who wanted to leave the United States, in part because of the Civil War.[69]

Although the Kickapoos were indifferent to the issues at stake in the Civil War, the period proved very disturbing to them. First the North and then the South entreated them to join forces. Big Chief Machemanet of the Kickapoos, unwilling to take part on either side, set out to lead his people into Mexico. In December of 1862 they arrived at the ranch of William Tankersley, two miles from the present town of Knickerbocker, Texas. Since Tankersley had known some of the same Kickapoos from previous times, when they had assisted him in recovering stolen stock from the Comanches, he invited them to camp on his ranch.

The following day, a large company of Confederate troops appeared, inquiring about the Kickapoos. Tankersley assured the army officers that the Kickapoos were friendly and could, during the war, be a protection to his and neighboring ranches, since many of the Texan men had been recruited into the Confederate forces and this scarcity of males had encouraged the Comanches to resume their raids. But the commanding officer "replied that the Kickapoos had many fine horses, which interested him more and would be of more value to the Confederacy than Indian friendship, and he proceeded to pursue and attack the Kickapoos."[70]

When the Kickapoos saw the cavalry approaching, they sent an old man, flanked by two old women, with a white flag. These were shot down by the cavalry. Although not anticipating this attack, the Indians offered stubborn resistance, causing the Confederate forces to lose sixteen men. The Kickapoos quickly broke camp and left, thinking that the Texans had declared war on them. They forded the Río Grande and, according to a U.S. Senate Document, went into Mexico at the north end of Sierra del Carmen, in the state of Coahuila, taking up their home in Hacienda El Nacimiento, on the land formerly held by the Seminoles.[71]

A. M. Gibson reports, however, that the group under Machemanet joined the Morelos group, who had been mustered into the Mexican Army in 1839, and did not go to Hacienda El Nacimiento as stated by the Senate Document.[72]

In October, 1864, a party of about 250 Kickapoos arrived in Santa Rosa, asking to remain in the municipality while they appealed to President Benito Juárez, temporarily living in El Paso del Norte (now Ciudad Juárez) during the French Intervention, for permission to establish themselves permanently in Mexico.[73] Was this the group who arrived with Machemanet and did not find conditions satisfactory in Morelos? Unfortunately, history does not tell us.

Meanwhile, the chiefs of two other Kickapoo bands in the United States, Papequah and Pecan, were much impressed with reports of the conditions in Mexico brought by Machemanet's couriers. During the summer of 1864 more than one hundred Kickapoos from the Fort Leavenworth Agency, headed by Chief No-ko-aht, left in protest of the Kickapoo allotment treaty and arrived at the camps of Papequah and Pecan. No-ko-aht's disillusionment with the Indian agents was sufficient to stir the other two leaders into action. They accepted the invitation of the Mexican authorities to join their tribesmen in Mexican territory. In the late summer of 1864 the three bands, totalling some seven hundred, left Kansas, guided by scouts sent by Machemanet.[74]

According to No-ko-aht, the leader of the three bands, Papequah's and Pecan's groups left before he did and did not join up with him until spring of the following year.[75] It was No-ko-aht's party of 120 which, on January 8, 1865, engaged in a battle with Texas Rangers and Confederate troops commanded by Captains John (or Henry) Fossett and S. S. Totten on a branch of Dove Creek, east of Mertzon, Texas, where a marker now stands to commemorate the event. According to an account by Harry Wood, four officers and twenty men fell at the hands of the Kickapoos after their chief's daughter, accompanied by her father, went to meet the troops with a white flag and was killed.[76] J. N. Gregory justifies the many later Kickapoo raids into Texas as springing from the treatment they received at Dove Creek. The result of this encounter was to intensify their aversion to Texans and turn them into bitter enemies.[77]

No-ko-aht's version of the Battle of Dove Creek after his return to Kansas from Mexico is worth reading, for seldom do we have occasion to hear the Indian side. He does not say that his daughter was killed or that he went out to meet the enemy with a white flag, but he does mention by name a young warrior:

. . . we saw some tracks of soldiers. . . . We failed to find the soldiers, and leaving a white flag went on. A number of days after we reached another track by a stream and we camped seven days. . . . I was out hunting horses, and . . . I was fired upon by soldiers. . . . All our young men were scattered that morning hunting horses, and one or two were killed while out. Then the soldiers came upon our camp. There was a stream between the two camps. The first killed was Aski. The Indians continued firing yet. Then a woman was killed. [His daughter?] This was before we fired. The fight was but a few minutes. A good many were killed on both sides. When we drove them to one side another force came in behind us. Then we whipped the second party back and the third one attacked us and we fired on them once. We killed a good many of the first party, a few of the second and none of the third. . . . The second and third Texan forces went [?] to the mountains . . . and drove up all our stock. . . . After the Texans drove off our stock we pursued for awhile, when we returned. We saw bodies of two or three Kickapoos who had been killed before the fight. They had taken two of our boys prisoners before the fight, and they took them along with them. Afterwards they got away. We had fifteen killed altogether . . .

All our stock was taken away nearly; some families had none. We were obliged to leave most of our things. Aski tried to shake hands and make peace with the Texans, but they shot him.

We found some papers among the Texans which showed that they had followed us ten days.[78]

The three bands reunited after leaving Texas and arrived in the Múzquiz area in the early spring of 1865, in time to plant corn. They settled in Hacienda El Nacimiento, where, according to No-ko-aht, they found no other Kickapoos but did find a few Negro families and some Northern whites living there for the duration of the Civil War. The whites left in the spring of 1866. No-ko-aht and his followers learned that twenty Kickapoos were living in Mexico in or near the present city of Allende, Coahuila. The seven men in the group were soldiers in the Mexican Army and had been for a long time. No-ko-aht does not mention Machemanet and his band, who had presumably arrived earlier.

The Mexicans wanted two hundred of the Indians' young men to enlist in the army, but the Kickapoos refused to have this number taken from their ranks. Finding conditions unfavorable in Mexico for their mode of life, No-ko-aht and some of his group returned to Kansas, while others stayed in Mexico.[79]

As was mentioned above, on October 13, 1864, the alcalde of Múzquiz reported that a few days earlier more than two hundred Kickapoos, both men and women, had asked permission to remain in the municipality of Múzquiz. In the archives of Múzquiz no record appears of this petition until 1866, when the alcalde stated he had received a decree from the government of Coahuila on January 11 in which two *sitios de ganado mayor* (8,676 acres), expropriated from the Sánchez Navarro estate and abandoned by the Seminoles and Negroes in 1861, were assigned to the Kickapoos and Potawatomies by order of President Benito Juárez.[80]

By 1865 all of the Kickapoos except those living in Kansas had removed to Mexico. Thereafter these Kickapoos were known as Mexican Kickapoos, an identification which is still applicable in the twentieth century.[81]

The Mexican Kickapoos, 1865–1960

The attitudes of Texan and Mexican colonists toward the presence of the Kickapoos in their countries were almost diametrically opposed. Most Texans, despising them as marauders, wanted them removed. Most Mexicans, needing them as protectors, wanted them to stay.

After the Civil War, the U.S. government reoccupied existing military posts in Indian country or built new ones in an effort to curb the incursions of the Comanches and Apaches through Texas and force them to settle in fixed reservations. Since this new approach to the Indian problem curtailed the incursions of the "wild Indians" into Mexico, where the Kickapoos and others had been able to pursue them and capture their booty since 1864, the Kickapoos now sought other means of acquiring horses and mules, for which they had an easy market—and this meant raiding Texas ranches. For twenty years, beginning in 1865, the Mexican Kickapoos launched an offensive on Texas "unmatched for calculated viciousness, vindictiveness, and destruction of life and property."[82]

Matters between the Kickapoos and the Texans worsened to such a point that in 1872 the U.S. Congress adopted a measure authorizing an investigation into the Kickapoo war on Texas and appointed three commissioners to inquire into the matter. These men spent a year gathering depositions in frontier towns, determining that the Kickapoos were "especially distinguished for a bitter animosity to the inhabitants of Texas, and for unceasing activity in their bold raids." They also charged that the Kickapoos were under the protection of Mexican authorities. Their conclusion was that these depredations would soon terminate if the Kickapoos were removed to Indian Territory.[83]

In the meantime, the Bureau of Indian Affairs, heeding the distressed calls for help from the Texans harassed by the Kickapoos, also proposed their removal to Indian Territory before the Texans took matters into their own hands and created international problems for the U.S. government.

Although no particular land had been designated in Indian Territory for the Kickapoos, some agents believed they were ready to return to the United States. This was not the opinion of William Schudhardt, U.S. consul in Piedras Negras, Coahuila, who knew the Kickapoos. He stated that any rumors that the Kickapoos were ready to return to Indian Territory were "utterly false" and further believed that "so long as the Kickapoo have the protection of the Mexican Government and cross into Texas to loot, rob, and plunder, and as long as these acts are countenanced by the citizens of Mexico, and as long as the Kickapoo can find a ready market for their booty they will never willingly quit."[84]

In 1871, John D. Miles, agent for the Kickapoos in Kansas, accompanied by several Kickapoos, including No-ko-aht, was sent to confer with the Kickapoos in Mexico concerning their removal. In spite of the encouraging signs that Agent Miles first met, his mission was a total failure—the Mexican authorities in Múzquiz never allowed him to counsel with the Kickapoos in a direct way.[85] Upon his return, Miles stated, ". . . the people of Santa Rosa were so decidedly opposed to the removal of the Kickapoo, giving for their reason that the city and the whole community would be invaded at once by Mescaleros and other marauding bands of Indians; that the Kickapoo were their only defense; and not only this, but . . . the Kickapoo trade was a matter of no mean importance to them."[86]

After the failure of the Miles commission, the U.S. State Department sent a second commission, headed by H. W. Atkinson and T. G. Williams.[87] Seeking to avoid the disaster of the Miles Commission, which had no official backing, Atkinson and Williams called upon the governor of Coahuila, who endorsed their plan and appointed a commissioner to accompany them.[88]

While State Department Agents Atkinson and Williams were negotiating the peaceful removal of the Kickapoos, the War Department was making other plans to stop the raids into Texas. In March, 1873, General Sherman ordered Col. Ranald S. Mackenzie and his Fourth Cavalry to Fort Clark, near Brackettville, some thirty miles from the Mexican border. In a conference which included Secretary of War William Belknap, Gen. Phillip H. Sheridan, Mackenzie, and others, Mackenzie was given unwritten orders to raid the Lipan and Kickapoo villages near Remolino, some sixty miles from Fort Clark.[89] Lt. John L. Bullis, aide to Mackenzie, had had under his command during the preceding three years a number of Seminole Negro Indian scouts familiar with the Kickapoos, their customs, and their territory. This knowledge was of invaluable help to the planners of the raid.[90]

Mackenzie had neither legal authority nor permission from the Mexicans to make this raid; nonetheless, he aimed at the Kickapoo village situated near Remolino, crossing the Río Grande under cover of darkness. By dawn his men had arrived at the village, four hundred strong. The encounter was one-sided, as the Indian men had gone on a hunting expedition, leaving behind only the aged, infirm, some women, and children. The captors pursued the frightened victims and took forty of them, whom they escorted to San Antonio.[91]

While traveling from Monterrey to Múzquiz, Atkinson and Williams received the startling message that Mackenzie had attacked the Kickapoos living at Remolino. As soon as the second commission arrived in Múzquiz, they sent out word to the Indians, stating the purpose of their mission and asking them to meet in council.

Many delays faced the commission, for the Indians, scattered widely, had to be gathered in a meeting place and furnished provisions, since they were in such a destitute condition. The animosity of the citizens of Múzquiz, which had defeated Miles, was even worse after the raid at Remolino, since the Indians now feared future attacks from the Americans. The commission finally met in council with the seventy men who had escaped the Mackenzie raid in Remolino, who were willing to forget those who had been killed but demanded the return of those who had been captured and taken to San Antonio.

Atkinson and Williams telegraphed the Department of the Interior, asking that the captured Kickapoos be placed in their charge. The request was refused; and, to make matters worse, the captives were moved from San Antonio to Fort Gibson in Oklahoma. Atkinson and Williams were faced with the dilemma of explaining to the Kickapoos why they, as representatives of the U.S. government, could not return the captives.[92]

A number of the Indians finally agreed to return to the United States on condition that they were supplied with pack animals, arms, and food, and allowed to skirt Texas on the way to their new home. The Indians probably would never have left Mexico had it not been for the Mackenzie raid, for the Remolino captives now in Oklahoma were related to many of them. In 1875 Atkinson returned to Mexico and removed 114 more Indians, about half of those who had remained.[93]

The Kickapoos who remained in Mexico continued their raids into Texas; they were also defending northern Mexican settlements against the "wild Indians." In July, 1877, Apaches took possession of a Kickapoo horse herd near El Nacimiento. The Kickapoos followed on foot, discovered the Apache camp, attacked, and killed all the women and seventeen warriors, including three chiefs. The victors returned to Múzquiz with seventeen scalps and 125 horses they had captured.[94]

Lt. John L. Bullis, who had been instrumental in the successful attack on the Kickapoo village near Remolino, was stationed at Fort Clark and had a secret agent in Múzquiz, R. E. Moffitt,[95] who, in partnership with a Mr. Harris, operated a mercantile business where the Indians traded pelts for provisions. In a letter to Bullis on January 1, 1879, Moffitt wrote that Gen. Jerónimo Treviño had sent a group of Kickapoos to Presidio San Carlos, where eighty-one Mescaleros had been captured by the garrison. The Mexican authorities claimed great credit for having captured this large number of Mescaleros, who had been raiding the border ranches, and hoped the United States would now be satisfied with the Mexicans' effort to rid the border of raiders.[96]

In 1879, John Willet, an English land entrepreneur, bought Hacienda El Nacimiento, comprising 310,000 acres from the Sánchez Navarro estate. Of this land, 252,000 acres were sold to David Harkness McKellar of New Zealand and the balance to J. W. and A. E. Noble of Victoria, Texas. The portion sold to the Noble brothers included the land which had been occupied by the Seminole and Kickapoo Indians and the Negroes.

In an 1895 statement, Willet said that he visited Hacienda El Nacimiento in the year of purchase and found no Indians or Negroes on the place, and that to his knowledge the Seminole Indians, the Negroes, and the Kickapoos were "mere squatters." Willet had made inquiries before acquiring the large property but had been unable to find any title to the land showing ownership by the Indians.[97] However, as has been shown, a part of this land had been expropriated from the Sánchez Navarro estate and granted to the Kickapoos and Potawatomies by presidential decree in 1866. Although the Kickapoos and Negroes were protected by presidential order, the sale of the land to McKellar and the Nobles created a crisis for them.

In a 1967 interview, Chief Papícoano told us that the remnants of those left after the Mackenzie raid and the removal of others to Indian Territory had fled from Remolino because of fear of further attacks and had settled in a place called Calvillo, some ten miles south of Hacienda El Nacimiento. The thirty-seven families who lived at this place spent the winters there and their summers in Hacienda El Nacimiento.[98] Perhaps Willet went to Hacienda El Nacimiento during the time the Kickapoos were absent.

The Negroes must have been in Hacienda El Nacimiento in 1879, for when Willet appealed to the governor of Coahuila, Evaristo Madero, for an order to remove them, the Múzquiz authorities refused to comply.[99]

Fearful of losing their land, in 1883–1884 the Negroes and Kickapoos sent Gopher John (Juan Caballo, or John Horse), chief of the Negroes who had gone to Coahuila with Wild Cat in 1850, to Mexico City to appeal their case before President Manuel González. What luck Gopher John had with the president is not known, as he died on the return trip. However, when President Porfirio Díaz resumed office in 1884, he protected the Negroes—and presumably the Kickapoos as well—against José María Garza Galán, governor of Coahuila, who had tried to evict them.[100]

After the Kickapoo reservation in Oklahoma was allotted in severalty, while the greater portion of the land was opened to white settlement, some of the Indians, disgusted with the turn of events, returned to Mexico. When the United States government removed the restrictions to their allotments, enabling them to sell, several land swindlers from Shawnee descended upon them in Mexico, precipitating a U.S. Senate investigation.

After the upheaval of the 1907 investigation, the tranquillity sought by the Kickapoos finally came to them—but not for long. A number of their young men once more enlisted in the Mexican Army, this time to help various aspirants to the presidency during the Mexican Revolution. During the early period, when Francisco Madero was trying to win the presidency, he was aided by Pancho Villa, who went to the Kickapoo village and requisitioned all the best horses and mules owned by the Kickapoos.[101]

When Victoriano Huerta assumed power, the Kickapoos fought on his side. News was slow in reaching the Kickapoos, so that when Venustiano Carranza overthrew Huerta they were unaware of the turnover, believing they were still fighting for Huerta. Col. Emilio Acosta, commander of the cavalry post in Múzquiz, took the Kickapoos prisoners because of their fealty to Huerta. After several days of a bread-and-water diet, the Kickapoos were released, but they were so annoyed by the constant changes in command that some left the ranks and returned to their village.[102]

In the meantime, a contingent of Carranza's men, under the command of Col. Atilano de la Garza of Múzquiz, arrived at the Kickapoo village in search of arms. After they mistreated some of the men, a soldier was shot by an Indian as he was leaving. The following morning the angry soldiers returned to burn the village, and the frightened Kickapoos fled to nearby Cañón de la Alameda.[103]

During those agonizing years of the revolution, the Kickapoos hid out in the sierra at night, not daring to sleep in the village for fear of another visit from the troops. Not until 1920, when peace returned to Mexico, did the Kickapoos feel free to resume their tranquil way of life: farming, raising stock, hunting, trapping, observing their tribal customs, and hoping the Mexicans and all others would leave them alone in their isolated village.

The mid-forties' long drought; tapping of the reservoir by the American Smelting and Refining Company for their plant in Nueva Rosita, [104] which greatly affected the water table on the Kickapoos' land; the arrival of the threshing machine; continuous fencing of neighboring ranches; and tick-control programs—all combined to force the Kickapoos to seek a livelihood elsewhere.

A few at a time began going to Eagle Pass, Texas, seeking work on neighboring farms. By the time we arrived in 1960, 98 percent or more of the Kickapoos left each April to spread from California to New York as migrant workers, returning to their village in the late fall.

As has been noted, even before the Kickapoos came in contact with the white man, they had been compelled to leave their land and migrate westward because of the exhaustion of fur-bearing animals by the Iroquois. When they made friends with the French, they followed the fur traders and broke up into several bands. Rivalry between the English, French, and Spanish for their fealty and trade forced them to fragment further and to move again. When the Americans gained their independence, the Indians were victims of battles, treaties made and broken, encroachment on their lands by colonizers, and movements to Indian Territory.

When Texas gained its independence the Kickapoos were again dispersed because of the Texans' fear that they would side with the Mexicans to regain their lost territory. When at last they found a new home in Mexico they were not left in peace, either by the Anglo-Americans, who, resenting the raids into Texas, attempted to move them into a reservation in Indian Territory, or by the Mexicans, who, once they had served their original purpose of protecting them from the marauding Indians, tried to evict them.

How they have survived in the face of these many trials will be shown in the following pages.

Chapter 2

Setting, Language, and Transportation

Setting

The Kickapoo village of El Nacimiento is located twenty-three miles north by northwest of the city of Múzquiz, Coahuila, official seat of the *municipio* of Melchor Múzquiz. It is situated at an altitude of 1,500 feet above sea level[1] on the piedmont of the Sierra Hermosa de Santa Rosa, the eastern escarpment of the Sierra Madre Oriental.

Access to the village from Múzquiz, difficult for strangers without a guide, is over an extremely rough trail—somewhat improved in the Kickapoo territory—which takes about two hours to cover by automobile when dry and is almost impassable in rainy weather.

Although the village is properly known as El Nacimiento, common use now applies this name to the Negro village five miles south, while Ranchería is the name used by the Mexicans to denote the Indian village. The Kickapoos resent this name, since it connotes a small group of humble Mexican jacales, and for this reason they use the name Colonia de los Kickapoo to designate their village.

The village is located eight miles south of Cañón de la Alameda, gateway by horse or motor to many ranches in the valleys of the Sierra Hermosa de Santa Rosa, at altitudes between four and five thousand feet. This difference in elevation affords the Kickapoos a varied flora.

Adjoining the Kickapoo land is the Negro grant. It is now occupied by descendants of the Negroes who accompanied the Seminoles and others who sought refuge in Mexico.

Altogether, the Kickapoo village occupies approximately 22.40 hectares.[2] Eight homesteads and a large cleared plot where ceremonial ball games take place are located across the river from the main village. Two irrigation ditches, fed by springs which form a tributary of the Sabinas River, pass through the village and supply water for the 506.12 hectares[3] of farm land east of the village which gradually slopes into the Valley of

Aerial view of the Kickapoo village in 1964.

Santa Rosa. This land is divided into plots of varying size allotted to the original Indian settlers. No one today seems to know for sure how the land was distributed, but one theory is that each family received the amount of land it was able to clear.

This land, formerly part of Hacienda El Nacimiento of the vast Sánchez Navarro holdings, must have been cleared before the arrival of the Kickapoos, but it is understandable that in a few years of neglect nature would have taken over, and reclearing was a necessity before farming could be resumed.

At first sight, the village seems to sprawl at random, but upon closer examination one perceives that it is laid out according to a plan. Two main lanes cross it from east to west, crossed by two others from north to south. Several less well defined lanes branch off from the four main ones.

On either side of the lanes are barbed-wire gates, leading into seventy-eight compounds of one-half to one acre each, surrounded by barbed-wire fences. Within the compounds are the eighty-three homesteads, seventy-six built in the traditional Woodland style and seven in the Mexican jacal style of wattle-and-daub. The remaining land, consisting of 6,493.48 hectares,[4] is used for pasture.

For many years the village has been in its present location, but formerly the winter houses were built at the site of eleven crystal-clear springs in a pecan grove, protected from the cold west winds by a sharply rising hill. Even today the site evokes an Algonquian village as it might have been painted by George Catlin.

In the summer, the entire village moved to higher and drier ground, where it is presently located, in an area surrounded by thorn brush rather than shaded by towering pecan trees. We have been told that the permanent move was due to the ravages of succeeding floods and to the prevailing dampness, which was responsible for much illness.

The village enjoys few modern conveniences. It has no paved roads, schools, utilities, sewerage, safe drinking water, public transportation (except for the bus to Múzquiz on weekends), mail delivery, stores, places of amusement, police, or fire protection. Neither do the Kickapoos pay income or property taxes to the Mexican government.

The only modern touches to be seen are numerous automobiles (pickups predominating), two tractors, treadle sewing machines, guns, flashlights, battery-run radios, and a few stoves fueled by butane gas. Some of the house owners have dug wells within their compounds, but most of the water is still hauled from the springs. Even the water, which before 1950 was usually available except in periods of extreme drought, is now frequently scarce, since the springs have been tapped for use in the large mining towns nearby.[5] Four cemeteries are located close to the village, two to the north, one to the west, and one to the south.

The population of the village consists of approximately 400 individuals. The Kickapoos keep no tribal roll and have consistently opposed census taking in Mexico as vehemently as they did when living in the United States. Nonetheless, several counts have been made. In 1870 the population was 500.[6] The 1920 census showed that only 293 Indians lived in the village. This low figure may be due to the influenza epidemic of 1918, which caused serious ravages. The 1930 census showed an increase, with 495 Kickapoos over five years of age living in the village. When Alfonso Fabila made a census in 1940, which he describes as a major achievement, since the Kickapoos were much opposed to it, he found the population consisted of 354.[7]

After painstaking effort, we succeeded in compiling a tribal roll during the summers of 1963 and 1964; it showed a population of 425, including ten Mexicans married to Kickapoos. However, it is difficult to state the number of Indians in the village at any given time, because of their shuttling back and forth between Oklahoma and Mexico, hiring out as farm laborers during the summer and winter crop seasons in Texas, and absenting themselves on hunts or peddling trips.

Language

Spoken Language

The Kickapoos speak a dialect of the Algonquian language stock.[8] Although they began going into Mexico in 1839, their dominant language is still Algonquian. All adults speak Spanish to some degree; those who have lived in Oklahoma or attended Anglo schools for varying periods of time know some English; and one girl, who was born in Mexico but attended school in Oklahoma to the ninth grade, has an excellent command of English.

We regret that we were not trained linguists and did not learn to speak Algonquian, thereby missing many of the nuances of the Kickapoo culture. However, since both of us are bilingual, we were able to communicate with the Indians in Spanish, without the necessity of interpreters.

The Kickapoos speak a very "broken" variety of Spanish. They disregard all syntax, paying no attention to tense, gender, number, or grammatical rules. This is not due to the influence of the low-income Mexicans with whom they socialize, for these speak grammatically and employ a rich vocabulary related to their particular environment and local industries, such as mining, ranching, and farming. In our opinion, it is instead a result of the Kickapoos' nonchalant indifference to the culture around them, based on their feeling of self-sufficiency.

The Kickapoos tell us that members of the Mexican group speak a somewhat different type of Algonquian from that used by those in Oklahoma. This is understandable in view of the differences in environment and surrounding language for the two groups.

The Kickapoos in Mexico have done with the Spanish names of many objects for which they had no parallel what the Spaniards did when they encountered the novel life of the Aztecs and other Indians, with their vocabulary for flora and fauna. They simply Castilianized such Nahuatl words as *ahuacacuahuitl*, the Aztec word for "avocado,"[9] which they transformed into *ahuacate* or *aguacate*—both pronounced practically the same. The Indians have Algonquianized the word *aguacate* and transformed it into *aguacatemisi*. For the word *café* ("coffee"), they use *cafti*, and so on. They have incorporated many Spanish words into their speech and many *pochismos* (English words which have been Castilianized), such as *lonche* ("lunch").

In choosing a given name in Spanish, a Kickapoo tends to select one which sounds similar to his or her Algonquian name. Two examples are names of men we knew well: Nicolás Elizondo, whose Algonquian name is Nekanesheka, and Merced Elizondo, whose Algonquian name is Mecesiza.

One of the frustrating experiences with the Indians was learning their names—all eponyms of their clan totem and usually long, since a name may be a description of the totem, such as "Fat Bear Sliding" or "Buffalo Running through the Brush." Because of this, the Kickapoos tend to drop one or two syllables from the beginning or end of their names. For instance, in speaking of their chief, they seldom used the entire name, Papícoano, preferring the foreshortened name Pícoano.

One day an informant brought an aunt to call, and, as we had difficulty in learning her name and taking it down because of its length, our friend told us to call her Tanacoa. Only later did we learn that the aunt's name was Tecacuetanacoa.

About twelve of the Kickapoo men are able to read and write in the syllabary invented by the Cherokee Sequoyah. One woman knows how to read it but does not write it. Although this syllabary is commonly known as Ba Be Bi Bo, from the first series of sounds of the syllables, the Kickapoos assert that it should be called Pa Pe Pi Po, since they do not have a *b* sound in their language. They also tell us they do not have an ŏŏ sound (as in *book*). The Sequoyah syllabary originally had characters for eighty-five sounds,[10] but the Kickapoos presently use only forty-eight.

Those who use this form of reading and writing are aware that it was invented by a Cherokee Indian and profess great admiration for him. They early asked us to tell them about his life and to translate excerpts from sources at hand. One man was sufficiently interested to jot down notes in his little book.

A few Kickapoo men are able to write simple Spanish, with scant thought given to spelling or syntax. In order to understand a letter written by them one has to read it out loud. There is little interest in reading Spanish in any form—newspapers, magazines, or books.

Gestures and Sign Language

In order to aid their limited Spanish, the Kickapoos use many gestures, including some that they claim as Indian and others that they have learned from the Mexicans.

Indian gestures include the following:

To indicate the time of day, the index finger is pointed upward, following the path of the sun, and stopped approximately where the sun would be at the intended time.

To indicate rain, both hands are held in front of the body, shoulder high, palms down, fingers pointing down, while the hands are moved quickly up and down several times. This is one of the few gestures claimed by the Kickapoos as Indian which we were able to find in W. P. Clark's *The Indian Sign Language*.[11]

Another sign found in Clark's book is the sign for mounting a horse, which Clark calls simply "horse."[12] The left hand is extended in a circular motion in front of the speaker, while the fingers are kept close together in a horizontal position, palm facing the speaker. The index and middle fingers of the right hand are opened wide and swung over the index finger of the left hand. This gesture is also common among the Mexicans.

To tell a person, "Come here!" one cracks the ring and middle fingers of the right hand; to say, "Let's go!" the middle and index fingers of the right hand are cracked.

To greet a friend, the right hand is held high above and in front of a person while exclaiming, "Hau!"

To seal a promise with another, the person agreeing stands and points upward with the index finger of the right hand, throws back his head, and whistles as loud as possible.

To indicate that a girl has not reached her menarche, both hands are slightly cupped and placed over the breasts of the speaker.

To indicate an abortion, the right hand is brought, palm downward, toward the pubis, then thrown outward from the body with a swift motion.

To indicate a direction of the compass, either the right hand is pointed in the direction or the chin, with lips puckered, is lifted in the direction. Sometimes a slight motion of the head is used to indicate a direction.

Mexican gestures used by the Kickapoos include these:

To express the idea of killing with a gun, one goes through the motions of picking up an imaginary gun, aiming, and shooting; then, to indicate that the victim topples over, one holds the left hand in front of the speaker in a slightly cupped position while bringing the right hand, palm up, quickly over the left hand with a sharp whack.

To ask, "What's happened?" the right arm is thrown out with the hand up and the fingers extended, and the shoulders are shrugged slightly while the head is turned toward the right shoulder, lifting the chin upward and puckering the lips.

To express indolence or laziness, the right hand is held chest high, with the fingers slightly cupped, and moved up and down.

To express fornication, the buttocks are pinched or the left hand is placed on the hips so that the elbow makes a forty-five-degree angle. The fingers of the right hand are bunched together and jerked quickly back and forth through the opening made by the left arm.

To indicate that two people are "buddies," the index fingers of both hands are brought together several times, tapping each other.

To indicate a loose woman, the right hand is lifted, with the index finger pointing upward, while the entire hand is rotated back and forth.

To indicate who "wears the pants" in the family, the hands are held as though driving a car, moving them as if steering. This means that one spouse "manages" the other. In Spanish, the word *manejar* means both "to manage" and "to drive a car."

To indicate eating, the tips of the fingers of the right hand are brought together and pointed to the mouth several times in a quick motion.

To indicate drinking, the index, middle, and ring fingers are pressed into the palm while the thumb and little finger are held up straight. The hand is brought to the mouth with a motion as though tipping a glass or a bottle. This gesture is usually used to indicate that a person drinks excessively.

To indicate money, a circle is made by bringing the index finger and the thumb together. The hand is thrown outward with the circle facing the listener and is moved up and down several times.

To indicate stinginess, the left hand is brought up to the height of the ears, while the right hand is slightly cupped and tapped on the left elbow several times.

To indicate the height of a person, usually a child, the right hand, with the palm facing the left side, is extended in front of the speaker to indicate approximate height.

To indicate the height of an animal, the entire hand is extended with the palm down.

To indicate that one is "broke," the fingers of the right hand are wrapped over the index finger of the left hand and a motion as though to pull it off is made.

Some of the more Mexicanized Kickapoos, in greeting a friend, embrace them as is the Mexican custom. A few men place the right arm across a man's shoulders as a sign of affection—also a Mexican gesture.

Transportation

The safe-conduct issued to a band of Kickapoos at Fort Dearborn, Illinois, in 1832[13] has served them well. With this document, repeatedly copied, the Indians enjoy free and unmolested access to both the United States and Mexico.

In recent years each adult Kickapoo who works in the United States has been issued a card by the U.S. Immigration Service with his Algonquian name, his Mexican name if he uses one, and a photograph. This action was taken because some Mexicans acquired copies of the safe-conduct and began crossing as Kickapoos.[14] On the immigration card is printed the statement "Member of the Kickapoo Indian tribe, pending clarification of status by Congress." These words have come to be interpreted by many as meaning that Kickapoos enjoy dual citizenship. Although those born in Mexico are consequently Mexican citizens, the Mexican border authorities honor both the safe-conduct and the card issued by the U.S. Immigration Service, while the American officials are still waiting for Congress to resolve the question of whether the Kickapoos are U.S. Indians or Mexican citizens.

Because of this ambiguous situation, the Mexican customs agents allow the Kickapoos, unlike other Mexican citizens, upon paying a fee ranging from ten to twenty dollars (U.S.)[15] to take automobiles into Mexico for a period of six months on a multiple-entry permit.

Today, almost all the migrant families own automobiles. The favorite, by far, is the pickup, followed by the station wagon and the four-door sedan. In spite of the general illiteracy, a few Kickapoos know how to read a road map, but the majority seem to arrive at their jobs like homing pigeons.

Some are tireless drivers, leaving the village, 120 miles from the U.S. border, to go to Utah, Montana, or Wyoming in nineteen hours without an overnight stop. Others stop in parks or on the road, prepare their meals with utensils they carry, and sometimes spend the night.

The first public transportation came to the Kickapoo village in 1928, when an enterprising merchant from Múzquiz initiated bus service, at first making daily round trips when the road was passable. Passengers from the village were obliged to spend the night in Múzquiz at the hostelry owned by a relative of the bus owner. Today, the bus goes to the village only on weekends (Saturday afternoon and Sunday morning).

During severe rainy periods, when the road is impassable, some of the Indians go into Múzquiz, a distance of twenty-three miles, on horseback, having to ford two rivers and several streams. Others, rather than risk traveling by horse under these circumstances, walk the twenty-three miles, wading or swimming across the rivers, and return with supplies on their backs.

For those who do not own cars, transportation is still an acute problem. When money is scarce or when the bus is not running, they spend hours in Múzquiz trying to find a ride back to the village. They check in at the stores and cafés most frequented by their peers, stop at the plaza, leave word with friends, and finally walk to the road leading to the village and the mines in hope of picking up a ride with a fluorite ore truck, the sand and gravel trucks, the milk pickup truck, or anyone with whom they can hitchhike.

In an emergency, those without cars hire one of their own people to take them into Múzquiz, either paying a fee or buying the gasoline. It is easy to understand why, in spite of the expense, which most can ill afford, a Kickapoo's greatest ambition is to own a pickup.

Chapter 3

Habitation

typical Kickapoo compound contains one or more summer houses, occupied during the warm months; one or more elliptical wigwams, or winter houses, occupied during the winter months; a cook house; and a menstrual hut. Some compounds also have a Mexican jacal (hut) or a storeroom.

Formerly, the wigwam was covered with birch bark, but the absence of birch trees in Mexico made it necessary to seek a new material.[1] The Indians say that one of their people dreamed that cattails would serve adequately and would have the additional value of protecting them from storms and lightning. (George Irving Quimby reports that the Sauk and Fox, closely allied to the Kickapoos, were using reed or cattail mats as far back as the early seventeenth century.)[2]

The cook house, which we believe is an adaptation to the hot summers of Coahuila, has been built for many years, according to informants in their sixties who do not remember a time when this house was not used. Nevertheless, old Mexican informants say that years ago only a few of these houses were used.

Generally speaking, the houses belong to the women; however, of the seventy-five Kickapoo-type houses, five belong to men, who inherited them from their mothers. Female relatives of the five males build the houses with the help of the owners and make the necessary mats—the latter being strictly female work.

Besides the Kickapoo houses there are seven Mexican jacales, occupied by Kickapoos whose owners are married to Mexicans.

The Kickapoo habitation, which has persisted through 120 years of residence in Mexico with only slight adjustments due to the ecology, is inextricably woven into each phase of the culture, especially the religion, the economy, and the status of women.

One informant related an incident which happened to her several years ago and which reveals the importance the Kickapoos place on their houses. This woman has neither husband nor children, and for this reason relatives in Oklahoma urged her to live with them. While in Okla-

In the Kickapoo village, 1910. At right is the "bald" Indian mentioned by Dr. Mark R. Harrington. (Photo by Dr. Mark R. Harrington; courtesy the Museum of the American Indian, Heye Foundation.)

The village in 1965. Winter wigwam in center; unroofed summer house in background.

36   Habitation

homa she had a vivid dream in which deceased relatives, scolding her for her neglect, appeared in the winter house. The dream was sufficiently disturbing to cause her to return to the village immediately and construct her house. On the way, she had unusual luck: a free ride as far as Eagle Pass, Texas, easily found cattails, and another free ride to the village. This chain of fortune further reinforced her decision to continue building her house as long as she was able.

Another woman complained of the arduous task and cost of gathering materials for the houses and of the time consumed in their construction. Her husband, who was listening, merely pointed his index finger heavenward with the remark, "El manda [He commands]." The Kickapoos are certain that Kitzihiat, the Great Spirit, lives in a wigwam like theirs, for a myth relates how their culture hero, Wisaka, brought to his people the knowledge of how to build the wigwam on returning from a visit to his father, Kitzihiat.

Any adult woman may build and own a Kickapoo house, with previous permission from the chief if she is building for the first time. Once she obligates herself, she must continue until her death or until she passes the house to another relative, either because she moves away or because she is incapable of maintaining it. If she leaves the village and does not pass her house to a relative, she must dismantle all the houses in the compound and leave it cleared for someone else. While talking on this subject, we pointed out to our informants that a certain woman had abandoned her house to live in Oklahoma. The quick retort was that this woman was sure to be punished for her negligence.

The following incident was told as an example of the punishment that could befall a woman who neglects her duty to her house. One woman married and left to live in a nearby town where her husband found work, abandoning her houses for several years. The village was much concerned about this neglect, particularly the chief and clan leaders, who did not miss the opportunity to point out the danger involved. A few years later the woman returned with her dying husband. Her own health had suffered in the meantime due to a severe case of rheumatism. Both the husband's death and the wife's rheumatism were attributed to the neglect of the houses.

Fear of reprisal is ever-present in the minds of the Kickapoo women, should they fail in their house-building obligations. For this reason, those who are not able to return to the village in time send money to relatives to perform this task.

Although the house belongs to the oldest female in the household, who is responsible for its construction and maintenance, all able male and female relatives cooperate in building it. If a woman has no family, friends and relatives assist her; or, if the owner is custodian of a clan bundle, every member of the clan is obligated to cooperate, especially when the clan houses are enlarged for the New Year festivals. Building the houses at the stipulated times takes precedence over any other activity. Frequently, men who work in the United States at seasonal jobs fail to appear, even when urgently summoned by their employers, until their wives' summer houses have been refurbished.

A young, recently married woman does not have to wait a stated length of time before she builds a home of her own, but she usually lives two years in the home of her mother or another female relative, until the marriage seems to "jell," or until the couple have saved enough for the construction of a house. At this time, she gets permission from the chief to build. She may opt to continue living in her mother's compound, her sister's, her aunt's, or occasionally in her grandmother's, but seldom in that of her mother-in-law or sister-in-law. The Kickapoos discourage this last set-up, as too much risk is involved: if the marriage should break up, the woman would have to move her house elsewhere.

At present, ten daughters have their homes in the same compounds as their mothers; six, in the compounds of sisters; three, in those of aunts; one, in a grandmother's compound; three, in the compounds of mothers-in-law; and three, in those of sisters-in-law.

When a woman moves away, she may dismantle her houses, or she may pass them on to a daughter, a granddaughter, her brother's daughter, her sister's daughter, her sister, or any female relative except a sister-in-law or daughter-in-law. (Since Kickapoo marriages are extremely brittle, if the daughter-in-law could keep the houses, the son would run the risk of not having a haven, if he had no other consanguine female relative.) A woman may also pass her house to a son or other male consanguine relative if she chooses. Before a woman dies, she tells her consanguine relatives to whom she leaves her house. The relative to whom the house is passed may be an infant and thus unable to care for it, in which case female relatives obligate themselves to maintain it until the child comes of age.

Apart from building and maintaining a home, the owner is liable for keeping the house and compound free of litter. Trash is swept to the edge of the compound and allowed to remain there. It is also her duty to observe the restrictions and taboos associated with the house. No house may be built or refurbished until the corresponding ceremony, granting permission, is held; the house must be constructed entirely of virgin material; no nails or hardware may be used (instead, every coupling is made fast with pita); and special places designated in the house for such activities as sleeping, eating, working, cooking, and the storage of objects must be strictly observed.

Taboos are numerous. No one may eat on the west side of the house, as this location is reserved for food offerings to the spirits. No menstruating woman may enter the house; neither may a woman enter during her period of involution after childbirth. No one may groom his hair, pare his nails, or shave inside. No one may spit indoors, especially into the fire; neither may one jump over the fire, especially a woman, who, if she inadvertently does so, will bleed to death during the following menstrual period. Wood and silver craftsmen may not make any object inside of the wigwam, in particular those pertaining to the ceremonial games.

There are four "recognized" clan bundle houses, but a fifth one also exists; it belongs to a Potawatomi Indian, owner of a Buffalo bundle. Bundle houses are closely guarded and never left alone when the owner is absent. Not only a clan bundle house, but any house where a bundle is kept, even if the bundle is an individual one, must be kept immaculate. Seeking asylum in a house where a bundle is kept, after a fight or murder, is absolutely forbidden. When a young man once sought refuge in the house of a female relative, custodian of a bundle, male relatives quickly bound him and took him to Chief Papícoano, who administered the proper punishment: banishment from the village for several days. Formerly, the penalty consisted of being tied to a tree for several days.

Although the women and a few men own the houses, the compound belongs to the community, and the owner enjoys its use only as long as the house is properly maintained. At the time of our study, twenty-four compounds contained only one family (or one person) each; in thirty-six there were two families; and in eighteen there were three families. Each compound is separated from the others by a barbed-wire fence. The earth of the compound is tamped almost to the consistency of cement.

Unlike Mexican women, who surround themselves with plants either in the ground or in cans, the Kickapoo women allow no vegetation to grow around or near the house, for fear of brush fires and to avoid harboring snakes, centipedes, tarantulas, and dangerous insects. Some compounds, through which irrigation ditches flow, have an anaqua, mulberry, fig, or pecan tree growing near the water; and as late as 1949 there were a number of peach trees.[3]

In the compound is a woodpile, to which large pieces of firewood are brought from the *monte* to be cut into smaller sections. All daily ashes are taken to a certain pile, but the ashes from ceremonial feasts are deposited in a separate place within the compound.

In order to eliminate the chore of carrying water from the river, a good distance from the village, many house owners are now digging shallow wells.

Before the Kickapoos began going to the United States to work, they engaged in hunts lasting several weeks every October, which dispersed them through large areas of Coahuila and adjoining states. In anticipation of the hunts, the winter houses were readied, and aged members of the family too feeble to travel were charged with their care.

Today, most Kickapoos do not return to the village from work until late October or November. By this time, the chief has transferred his authority to a clan leader, who oversees the construction of the winter houses and performs the necessary ceremonies. When the Kickapoo New Year arrives, sometime in January or February, all winter houses must be occupied.

All the houses in the village are identical in construction. The only difference is the size, which varies in order to accommodate the extent of the family. If a woman lives alone, as several do, she builds a small wigwam; on the other hand, an extended family builds a large one. The average house is eighteen feet in length and fifteen feet in width.

Since the winter house is a temporary structure used only for about four months, the material for its framework need not be as lasting as that used for the summer house. Materials favored for the winter house are hackberry, Montezuma bald cypress, and sycamore. The winter house is oval in shape, with a roof which can best be described as a low, elliptical dome. To build the framework, two four-inch crotched posts of sycamore or other selected timber, carefully peeled and pointed at one end, are staked into the ground to support the ridgepole. Four other posts of the same wood support the rafters. Under the ridgepole and about six feet below it runs another pole, suspended from the first by ropes, used for hanging a chain to dangle the kettle over the central fire. Long saplings, two to three inches in diameter, previously soaked in the river to make them pliable, are staked in the ground to form the outside staves of the structure and are bent to meet their companion saplings from the opposite side. These are secured with pita to form the domed roof. One- to two-inch saplings are tied horizontally to the uprights to form a latticework, over which the double-thick cattail mats are placed in opposite directions, to assure a waterproof roof. These mats are battened down by slender saplings tied with pita.

The house has only one entrance, two feet wide and six feet high, facing east, and covered by a canvas flap. When the occupants leave the house, sticks are carefully laid in the opening in such a way that any tampering is easily detected. There are no windows; the entrance and the

Summer house, with ramada at left.

smoke hole in the roof, six by two feet, directly over the central fire, permit sufficient ventilation. During inclement weather, the sides of the house are covered by canvas to assure a warmer interior. The floor consists of tamped earth, neatly swept and frequently sprinkled.

Upon entering, one is struck by the simplicity of the furnishings. Along three walls, on either side of the door and in the rear, are low benches forty-five inches wide and eleven feet long, standing four inches above the ground. The benches occupy three sides of the rectangle behind the four upright posts supporting the rafters and leave a free quarter-pie–shaped area on either side of the door.

To build the benches, crotched saplings are sunk into the ground two feet apart, and over them are laid connecting saplings of black-brush acacia. Lengthwise over this framework is laid a cushion formed by joining pairs of sotol scapes with pita. Several brightly dyed mats, either of cattail or of sotol, are placed over the cushion.

On these benches the family members sleep, lounge, work, and eat. For sleeping, bedrolls, consisting of quilts, blankets, and pillows, are spread on the benches at night; they are stored during the day on the numerous trunks, suitcases, and boxes kept on the west bench. Parents sleep to the left of the door, children and other members of the family to the right of the door, and small children at the foot of the parents' bench.

Some of the houses have one or two crudely made unpainted chairs bought on the streets of Múzquiz from local artisans. These are reserved

Woman preparing saplings to build a new house.

for guests other than Kickapoos. Practically every house has a treadle sewing machine, covered with a neat casing and kept in one of the quarter-pie areas. The other side is used for storing numerous boxes with food supplies. Hanging from the framework are such articles as flashlights, bunches of keys, kerosene lamps, and a mirror.

The summer house is a rectangular structure, sixteen feet long by fifteen feet wide, covered with a hipped roof, projecting two feet over the walls. Like the wigwam, the summer house has no windows and only one entrance, facing east and covered with a canvas flap. The entire framework is made of posts, poles, and saplings of one-seed juniper or desert willow, both durable varieties of timber, for the summer house is left standing four years. Each spring, in the intervening years, all the old pita is replaced, as well as any material which is worn. At the end of four years, the house is completely dismantled, the old material discarded, new material secured for replacements, and the house rebuilt on another location in the compound.

The summer house is usually occupied by late March, after the New Year ceremonies. Shortly before the houses are refurbished or rebuilt, the clan leader authorized to oversee the construction of the winter houses in the fall returns his authority to the chief, who directs the building of the summer houses. When all the houses are ready, except for the roofing, the chief holds a ceremony, after which his wife is the first to roof her house. Next, the bundle houses are roofed, and the others follow suit.

To form the framework of the house, four crotched, peeled, and pointed posts about four inches in diameter and eight feet in height are staked in each corner in holes previously dug with a crowbar to the depth of a man's arm. About six feet of the posts remain above the ground, and the earth is firmly tamped around them. Four connecting poles are laid over the crotches of the corner posts and fastened with pita.

Four feet from the entrance and four feet from the rear wall, two eleven-foot posts are sunk to the depth of a man's arm. These are the supports for the ridgepole. Suspended by rope is another pole, six feet above the floor, from which is hung a chain to hold the kettle over the central fire. Four other crotched posts projecting eight feet above the ground and four feet from each wall form a rectangle twelve feet long and seven feet wide. The poles connecting this rectangle, the ridgepole, and the outside poles connecting the corner posts form the rafters, on which slender saplings are laid crosswise to form the latticework where the mats are spread. Between the four principal corner posts, six crotched posts on the north, east, and south sides of the house are fastened to the connecting poles with pita, but only four are staked on the west side.

In the interior, uprights for the walls are crossed by four horizontal rows of saplings. The walls of the summer house are made from scapes of sotol, tied with pita, two at a time, at top, center, and bottom. These are again reinforced by three rows of horizontal saplings on the outside of the scape walls. The roof is covered with two layers of cattail mats transferred from the winter house, one laid in an east-west position, the other north-south; they are battened down with slender saplings, which cross each other and are tied with pita. The summer house has no smoke hole, since the interstices between the scapes provide sufficient ventilation.

The interior furnishings of the house are similar to those of the winter house, except that the benches are two feet above the floor and the storage areas on either side of the entrance are rectangular rather than quarter-pie–shaped. The same restrictions and taboos observed for the winter house hold for the summer house as well.

In front of the summer house is a ramada, or open porch, elliptical in form, sixteen feet long and fifteen feet wide, open on three sides, and covered with a hipped roof nine feet high at the ridge, two feet lower than the roof of the summer house. The ramada is built of the same durable material as the summer house. Two crotched, peeled, and pointed posts about four inches in diameter are sunk into previously dug holes the depth of a man's arm, approximately six feet from both ends of the edges of the ramada and directly centered in front of the entrance of the house. These posts, nine feet above the ground, support the ridgepole. Four other crotched posts, two on the north side of the ridgepole and two on the south side, form a rectangle, on which are laid the rafters of slender saplings; over these, other saplings are crossed to form a latticework. On the outside edges of the ramada are sunk fourteen slender posts, four feet apart, standing six feet above the ground. Over these are tied connecting saplings, on which rests the edge of the roof. The four corner posts of this ellipse are connected by four saplings to the posts forming the rectangle. The roof is made in the same manner as that for the house and is covered with cattail mats battened down by saplings running in opposite directions.

On the north and south sides of the ramada, far enough from the edges to be protected from the elements, two benches like the ones in the house are built and covered with dyed sotol or cattail mats. A wide shelf for the storage of extra roofing mats is built under the east end of the roof.

As in the house, the floor is of tamped earth, frequently sprinkled. An earthenware water jar, covered with a gunny sack, is hung on the east wall of the house under the ramada, and an enameled-ware drinking cup rests above the water jar, for use by both family and visitors. Wire or sotol baskets containing eggs, vegetables, fruits, and a few ears of dried ceremonial corn are hung from the rafters. During the summer, most of the activities of the family—sleeping, lounging, sewing, moccasin and basketmaking, and visiting with relatives and friends—are transferred to the ramada.

Unlike the summer and winter houses, which are rebuilt periodically, the cook house is seldom repaired and is allowed to stand until it begins to collapse, at which time it is completely dismantled, the useless material burned or carted away, the usable material reserved, and the entire building reconstructed in another location.

The cook house, twelve feet square and similar in appearance to the summer house, minus the ramada, is located near the summer house and faces south. Framework material and construction is the same as that used for the summer house, but the cook house is roofed with the bark and leaves of beaked yucca, known in Mexico as *soyate*. This material, extensively used by low-income Mexicans to roof their jacales, is extremely durable, lasting fifteen years before having to be replaced. Like the summer house, the cook house has no smoke hole; the interstices between the sotol scapes that form the walls suffice for ventilation.

Inside the cook house are two benches, on the north and west sides, two feet above the tamped-earth floor. The bench on the north wall serves as a work table for the preparation of food. In the back are stacked several wooden orange crates used as open cabinets for the storage of dishes, tableware, and small containers for staples. On the other end are kept large wooden and tin boxes for the storage of bulky staples. Under this bench are stored the firewood and several containers for water.

On the west bench are kept such articles as saddles, harnesses, chaps, ropes, and work tools. The space on the east side of the cook house is occupied by a wooden table covered with oilcloth on which are placed cooking utensils and a meat grinder. Nearby are one or two chairs like those in the winter or summer houses. An upended orange crate, on which stand a small basin and a dish with a bar of soap, is usually placed inside the door, a small mirror above it. The traditional wooden mortar and pestle may be kept in this house, but it is likely to be found lying on the ground nearby. Clustered around the central hearth are several iron and enameled-ware cooking utensils.

Near the edge of the compound, facing east like all traditional Kickapoo houses, but away from the others, is the menstrual hut, a small, rectangular structure where the women retire during their menses and where they spend their period of involution. In inclement weather, or in an emergency, this hut also serves as a place to deliver a mother of her child, the center post serving as a brace for the parturient.

The hut is approximately six feet square. It may be built of any timber except one-seed juniper or desert willow, and the roof cannot be of cattail. It is usually covered with *soyate* like the cook house. The preferred material for the house is Texas mountain laurel, black-brush acacia, oak, sweet acacia, or other available material. This building is occasionally repaired, but at no stated times, and therefore is usually the most bedraggled of the houses in the compound. Bedding and special utensils for cooking are kept in this hut, since none of these articles may be stored in any other house; nor may they be used except on the occasions stipulated.

To build the menstrual hut, a crotched post is sunk into a premade hole

Mexican jacal in the Kickapoo village.

in what will be the center of the house, leaving about six feet above the ground. At each of the four corners of the house are sunk and securely tamped crotched posts which stand five feet above the floor. Connecting poles are laid in the crotches of the corner posts and tied with pita. Over these are laid thin saplings to support the roof. The walls are made from scapes of sotol and covered on the outside with discarded canvas.

Although construction of a Mexican-type house has always been discouraged by Chief Papícoano and the clan leaders, several of the Kickapoo women living with Mexicans have built small jacales. Some of these women have no Kickapoo houses, but others have both Mexican and Kickapoo houses, especially if the owner is the custodian of a bundle, since it is imperative that she keep it in a house with a cattail roof.

Usually, a woman who lives in a Mexican house has two small jacales, as is the custom among the lower-income Mexicans of this area. One of these is used as a cook house and the other as sleeping quarters. The jacales, ten by twelve feet, are of the simplest construction. The framework is made from any wood except one-seed juniper or desert willow; the walls are made from sotol, maguey scapes, or a combination of both, sometimes daubed with mud. The roof is made from *soyate*.

The cook house, with only one door and no windows, has a bench, two feet above the tamped earth floor, at the opposite end from the door, where boxes and tins for staples are stored. Beneath the bench are stored the wood and containers for water. A small table, two or three crudely made chairs, and several orange crates which serve as cupboards complete the furnishings. Around the central hearth are found the same cooking utensils as in the Kickapoo cook house.

The jacal used for sleeping is the same size as the cook house. To the right of the door, a bench, six feet wide, made in the same manner as those in the Kickapoo summer house, serves for sleeping. Bedding is not rolled up during the day but remains on the bench and is covered with a simple bedspread. Mosquito netting over the bed is necessary, since no fire is built in this room, and consequently there is no smoke to drive out the insects. The remaining furniture consists of one or two chairs, several trunks and boxes for storage, a dressing table made from orange crates, and a treadle sewing machine carefully covered.

Some women have wood-burning stoves in the Kickapoo cook houses; others have butane gas stoves. A few, considered highly privileged, have *trasteros* (store-bought cupboards) and iron bedsteads. When one woman brought a wood cook stove from Oklahoma, which her sister no longer needed, as she had installed a gas stove, it created a furor in the village. The stove had six *comales* (plates), a shelf above, where food could be kept warm, and a tank in which water could be heated.

The latest sensation in the village is the three-room concrete-block house which the son of one of the clan leaders is building with Mexican laborers. It boasts steel casement windows and a small concrete porch. The Kickapoos are both astonished and concerned at this innovation. There is much talk among them about the shortage of virgin building material in the sierra, *monte*, and swamps, plus the difficulties they encounter with the Mexican forest rangers, who blame the Kickapoos for the extermination of much of the one-seed juniper, sotol, and yucca. Could this house of concrete blocks be the first of many? It is saddening to dwell upon this possibility.

Before the women may gather cattails for roofing and matmaking, the clan leader designated by the chief to oversee the construction of the winter houses has a ceremony, prior to the first frost, asking Kitzihiat for a plentiful harvest and for the protection of the women on this venture.

Unfortunately, cattails have been exterminated from all the swamps within a radius of 50 miles of the village. (The Kickapoos blame this scarcity on menstruating women who entered the water, causing the springs to dry.) For the past several years, the women have had to travel long distances to find cattails. Until a few years ago, they went by bus into Múzquiz, where they caught a slow mixed train to Cuatrociénegas, 150 miles away. There, they hired a truck to take them the remaining 25 miles to the swamps and to return them with the cattails to the village. Today, the trip to these swamps has been shortened, since most families own pickups. The women who live alone form a car pool and hire the owner of a pickup to take them; or else they go with relatives or friends.

The women take their bedding, cooking utensils, and food. Arriving at the swamp, they immediately build a flimsy camp of saplings, over which they spread a canvas. Upon entering the swamps, each woman who is going to cut cattails says a prayer and offers a bit of Indian tobacco to the snakes who own the water and the cattails. They ask permission to cut only what they need and ask the snakes not to molest them. Only leaves ten feet high or more are cut, just above the rhizome. A companion holds the leaves for the cutter and ties them into manageable bundles with split pita which they have at hand for this purpose. This task takes from two to three days, as a woman needs thirty bundles to make fifteen or more mats for roofing and an added quantity if she plans to make bed mats.

When the women return to the village, the bundles are propped against the unoccupied summer house or the cook house and allowed to dry. When a woman finds time from her many chores, she takes one bundle at a time, sits outdoors on a canvas, and, with a sharp knife, begins to clean the cattails; that is, she separates each leaf from the others, cuts off the pithy bottom and the tapering end, and saves only those leaves which are nine feet long. The cleaned leaves are soaked in hot water to make them pliable and give them a tawny green color.

When a woman is ready to make the mats, if possible selecting a cloudy, damp day to keep the leaves pliable, she calls five or six of her female relatives and friends to assist her. She has at hand a lunch, plenty of bottled soda pop, and coffee to serve her helpers. In one morning six women make a roofing mat eighteen by nine feet.

To sew the mats, two rows of stakes, eighteen feet apart with one foot between stakes in each row, are pounded into the ground, leaving six inches above ground. Two slender saplings are placed on the outside of each row of stakes. A loose piece of twine is tied between the first two stakes on one row. The first step in sewing the mat consists in taking two leaves and folding the ends, one above the other, over the twine, while fastening them to it with a knot made with another piece of twine. This gives the mat the only finished end. The eight remaining stakes at one end serve as guide lines to tie eight pieces of twine eighteen feet long to

Woman cleaning cattails.

Women sewing a roof mat.

the sapling on the outside. The mat needle used is made from a piece of hammered-out iron eighteen inches long and three-quarters of an inch at its widest. An eye is perforated at the blunt end, and the pointed end is slightly curved upward. A woman threads the needle with a long piece of twine and commences to pass the twine through the upper leaves, tying knots each foot, continuing this process until she arrives at the end and ties the remaining twine to the sapling on the outside of the opposite row of stakes.

When one woman is a few feet along the first row, another begins the second row, and so forth, until all six are sewing at the same time, each a short distance behind the next. When the first woman reaches the end, she begins the seventh row, and the others follow suit. As soon as the nine rows are completed, the mat is turned over and sewed on the other side. The result is a solid, firm, light, flexible, and waterproof cover, easy to adjust over the rounded or hipped roofs of the houses and on the walls. The new mats are stored on the shelf in the east end of the ramada, to be used for the winter house the following year, or for the summer house if needed.

Today, women buy commercial twine for sewing mats, but formerly several species of pita were used for making cordage. During their long hunting expeditions the women cut the pita, boiled it until the pulp softened, scraped the pulp off by rubbing it between two sticks, and allowed the remaining fiber to dry in the sun. The task of making the cordage belonged to the grandmothers, who rolled the fibers on their shins into long strands and wound them into balls.

Not all of the women know how to make the finely woven cattail mats used for the benches. Those unable to make them either purchase them from the few who have the ability or make them from sotol leaves. Commercial dyes are used for both types of mats, and commercial twine is used for the weft of the cattail mat. Formerly, yellow dye was obtained by boiling the root of Laredo Mahonia (*Mahonia trifoliata*, also known as agarita) for, at that time, only blue and green commercial dyes were available. The leaves are prepared in the same manner as those for making a roofing mat.

A woman who wants to make a bench mat invites two or three relatives or friends, who know the technique or want to learn, to help her with the task. Near a stream or an irrigation ditch they set up a flimsy shelter to protect the material from the sun. They stake two crotched posts about eight feet apart, leaving six feet above the ground, and over these they lay a slender sapling tied with pita. This simple contraption serves as a loom. Over the sapling they throw the dyed cattail in the desired colors, which they weave and secure with the commercial twine. Nearby are several tubs of water in which the dyed cattails are dipped to keep them pliable and from which the women take water to moisten them as the work progresses. At the end of the day, the finished section is taken down by lifting it, as well as the sapling, from the two crotched posts. It is covered with dampened canvas and sprinkled frequently until the work is resumed the following morning. Three women can make a mat of this type in three days.

When a woman needs a new sotol mat for the benches, she invites a few friends to gather sotol in the sierra behind the village. They usually ride burros or horses and take pieces of canvas on which the leaves can be carried. About twenty sotol plants are needed to make four of the ninety-three–by–forty-five–inch mats. An ordinary ax is used for cutting the plant at the base. The thick, pithy, dry outer leaves are discarded; only the tender green ones are retained. Since sotol leaves have sharp fishhook thorns on both edges, bundles of twenty to thirty leaves are tied with pita and placed in the canvas for easy transport on burros or horses.

While still in bundles, the leaves are boiled, then untied, dried on canvases, and allowed to bleach in the sun for several days, with frequent turning. When ready to use, each leaf is held in the left hand, base up. With a sharp short-handled knife, about one foot along the edge, beginning at the base end, is cut. The leaf is turned over and cut on the other edge. Then, with one long continuous cut, the edges, as well as the fishhook thorns, are slit off. Lastly, the pointed end and base are trimmed, leaving the leaves about five-eighths of an inch wide and four feet long.

When ready to be dyed in the desired colors—usually green, yellow, red, and dark purple—the leaves are placed in hot water in which the dye has been dissolved and boiled about four hours, or until the desired shade is obtained. Dyed leaves are placed on a canvas, sprinkled with water, and covered with another canvas to keep them moist until used.

These mats, unlike the cattail variety, do not need a loom, but are simply made over one of the benches, which serves as a guide for size. The twilled method of weaving is used in making this type. Raw ends are covered by a long strip of sotol on both sides and secured with an overhand stitch of thinner strips of sotol. Two women can make a mat of this type in two days.

Chapter 4

Food and the Quest for Food

When a group of older Kickapoos get together, they enjoy recalling with nostalgia the old *campañas*, or hunting expeditions, in which they participated up to the mid-forties, when they began their annual trek to the United States as migrant workers.

After they harvested the summer crops and planted winter wheat and oats, and after the women built their winter houses in early fall, Chief Papícoano named three chiefs, each charged with specific duties: one man policed the village during the absence of the hunters; another directed the expedition; and the third supervised the gathering of cattails.

Before leaving the village, each hunter had a ceremony in which he asked for success. Old people, too feeble to undertake the long journey, remained in the village to look after the houses, crops, and livestock. The leader of each group rode ahead, carrying only his gun, followed by the families, driving as many as sixty horses and burros. Besides providing transportation, the animals were loaded with large, elliptical open baskets carrying cooking utensils and covered baskets with clothing and provisions. The bedrolls were placed behind the riders. On these expeditions they carried a wooden mortar and pestle, a third the size of the one commonly used. The provisions consisted of corn, dried pumpkin or squash, beans, potatoes, rice, sweet potatoes, baking soda, wheat flour, coffee, sugar, and salt.

The chief of the hunt assigned different areas to each group of two or three families, and the groups avoided trespassing on one another's hunting territories. These families ranged within a radius of one hundred miles or more from the village, camping at springs.

Although by the turn of the century the majority of the surrounding ranches had been fenced (an enterprise begun in 1890 by David Harkness McKellar, who founded La Mariposa), until the campaign for the control of tick fever was begun in 1907 at El Conejo ranch, ranchers left their gates unlocked. The Kickapoos reported at the *casco* (headquarters) of a ranch for permission to hunt. Some of the ranchers received them kindly and supplied them with provisions from their hacienda store.

Upon arriving at a site where water and cattails were plentiful, the families built temporary shelters of ocotillo (Jacob's staff) covered with tarpaulins. The men set out on daily hunts while the women gathered cattails and pita to make into mats and cordage. When the men returned from the hunts, they skinned the animals and turned the meat over to the women, who cut it into thin slices and dried it in the sun to make jerky. If the weather was overly warm, the women built a frame of green wood approximately eight feet long, three feet wide, and three feet high, on which they smoked the meat to protect it from spoilage. When the meat had been smoked sufficiently, it was aired on tarpaulins until dry and stored in deer skins.

Although turkeys were abundant, the hunters killed only enough for an occasional meal and did not smoke them. During these expeditions, each group of families killed sixty to one hundred deer and many bears—enough to supply them for several months. The one- to two-inch layer of fat on the bears was removed, rendered into oil, and stored in deer skins. The meat was either made into jerky or smoked. Deer ribs and tongues and bear ribs were smoked and reserved for the New Year ceremonies held after returning to the village; the brains were spread on gunny sacks, dried, and saved for tanning skins.

Deerskin containers for transporting meat and rendered bear oil were made by cutting off the head and feet of the animal. The skin of the hind legs was slit on the inside of the leg to the tail, and the animal was skinned from the feet toward the head, using the fist. While fresh, the slits and four feet openings were seamed with sinew. After the receptacle was filled with the meat or oil through the neck opening, it was seamed. This made a leak-proof container, easily carried on horses and burros.

While in camp, the women made a variety of pemican by pounding venison or bear jerky in the mortar and pestle and combining it with bear fat. This the men carried on their daily hunting trips.

When the Kickapoos first went to Coahuila over one hundred years ago, wild game of all kinds was plentiful. Their dependence on deer for daily fare and for ceremonies soon exhausted the supply on their land grant and forced them to range into the surrounding territory, which was divided into large, unfenced haciendas and ranches. Today, not only are there no deer or bears on their land, but such small game as weasels, beavers, badgers, otters, lynxes, mountain lions, porcupines, peccaries, squirrels, armadillos, opossums, rabbits, quail, turkeys, mourning doves, water and land turtles, and several varieties of fish and shellfish found in the streams, such as catfish and bass, have been nearly extinguished.

Some animals, like the weasel and beaver, whose pelts were in great demand by local merchants, were trapped by the thousands even after laws protecting game had been passed by the government. The quail have been almost exterminated by the youngsters, who kill them with bows and arrows and take the eggs for food. Kickapoos recall when the pecan trees in their grove attracted many squirrels; none are to be found today.

Thanks to the campaign begun in the early sixties to eradicate the screw worm, plus the termination of the severe drought of the late forties and fifties, followed by a series of rainy years, deer have become more plentiful. This has happened in spite of the failure of the Kickapoos and the Mexicans in general to observe the closed-season directive issued by President Lázaro Cárdenas in 1938. This directive, sent in answer to a request of the Kickapoos to hunt the year around, states that the solicitors "may dedicate themselves to the hunt during nine months—between the 16th of October and the 15th of July of each year, respecting the remainder as a closed season in order to encourage the increase of deer."[1]

Although the necessity of observing the closed season has been repeatedly explained to them, the Kickapoos continue to hunt whenever they need venison. During the closed season, when the fawns are about a month old, they use a deer call which imitates the plaintive cry of the young animal, attracting the doe to the location of the hunters. The Indians also have no compunction about flashing deer at night with lights fastened on their hats. The Kickapoos are able to distinguish the various animals in the dark by the color of their eyes and the movement of their heads. The deer have bright yellow eyes and do not close them. Cattle have gray-blue eyes and close them slowly. Coyotes, whose eyes are blue, move their heads from side to side as though seeking to escape. The cougar lowers his head as though trying to hide in the ground; his eyes are small and red.

The Indians have continuing difficulties with the ranchers. The latter, supported by a directive issued by President Miguel Alemán during his term of office (1946–1952) which strictly prohibited hunting on ranches without permission of the owners,[2] find justifiable reasons for not wanting the Kickapoos to invade their ranches. They accuse the Kickapoos of such infringements as entering without permission or with tick-infested horses, pulling out the clamps or cutting the fences to enter, mistaking cattle for deer, and hunting too near the ranch headquarters, endangering the personnel. The ranchers do not hesitate to call the federal police or the game and forest wardens, who arrest the Kickapoos, place them in jail, and impound their firearms and pickups.

The Kickapoos respond by asking, "How can the ranchers claim the deer or bear as their own when they do not brand these animals? Deer are for anyone who wants them, and especially for the Kickapoos, for whom the deer were placed in this world by the Great Spirit, Kitzihiat." Reinforcing these beliefs is another: that for every deer killed, three more spring up.

Mexican informants have told us that, until the thirties, some Kickapoos employed the bow and arrow to hunt deer. Today, they use Winchester .30–.30's. They are frugal with their imported ammunition, averaging two shots per deer, but are generous in sharing it with a companion who has little or none, expecting reciprocity in a similar situation.

When a man needs a deer, he asks two or three other good hunters to accompany him, and beforehand he holds an individual ceremony asking for luck and protection. All of the hunters are careful not to eat chili, which is believed to dull the sight. Prior to departing on a hunt, they bathe in the river to lessen the deer's awareness of their presence and, for double protection, chew a bit of the magical rhizome, Solomon's seal, and rub it on their bodies to attract deer and to deter rattlesnakes. If the hunt is to last several days, they take provisions and cooking utensils.

Sometimes, if the hunt takes them into areas inaccessible by motor, they go on horseback; otherwise, they travel by pickup, parking on a road or trail, where they leave one or two companions to jack up a tire or open the hood, simulating trouble, in case a rancher or a game warden passes by. In the meantime, the hunters take off through the ranch. If game is plentiful and they decide to remain several days, those on the road are notified to go home and return at a specified day and time.

The Indians are experts in tracking deer. A Kickapoo can estimate by the freshness of a hoofprint how recently one has passed: a matter of a few days, a day, only hours, or minutes. Upon reaching a likely location, the chief of the hunt climbs the highest point in the area, from which he can observe the movement of animals, carefully considering the prevailing wind. When he is sure that deer are present, he joins his companions and tells them the directions to take in order to throw the deer into each other's paths and avoid personal accidents. The Kickapoos are careful and cautious hunters. In the years we have known them, we have not heard of an instance in which one has been killed on a hunt.

Chief Papícoano enjoyed telling of an experience in which he nearly killed a Mexican hunter. One day while he was butchering a doe, he heard a noise in the brush which sounded as though a large buck were hurrying toward him, cracking branches on his way. Believing that the buck had perceived the scent of the doe, he picked up his gun and poised it in the direction of the sound, where he soon saw the huge head of an eight-point buck. As he was about to shoot, he noticed that the head was being carried on the shoulders of a man. It was a Mexican hunter, who explained that this was a technique he used to get near the deer. The chief wasted no time in telling the Mexican how near death he had been.

If a man kills a deer and, because of its size or some other reason, cannot carry it into camp, he hangs the animal on a high limb of a tree. Nearby, he places a used handkerchief where the wind will move it; the motion of the handkerchief with the scent of man keeps away predatory animals. In order to find his way back to the deer, he cuts pita into pieces, which he scatters to mark a trail, or, in a wooded area, cuts the bark on trees to indicate his path.

A hunter skins a deer in the following manner. Branches are laid on the ground, and the deer is placed on top of them, belly up. The hide is cut from the jaw to the tail, then slit around the hoofs and on the inner side of the leg, beginning with hoofs on one side, fore and hind. The hunter moves to the other side and repeats the procedure, after which he returns to the side where he began and, with his knife, begins to skin the animal —but only until he can get his fist between the hide and the flesh. He then discards the knife and continues to skin the animal with his fist. This technique is employed to avoid damaging the hide, which is used for making moccasins and other objects. Once the hunter has reached the backside, he turns the animal over and continues the same process on the other side until he reaches the hoofs.

Half of the carcass is cut off the backbone, carefully leaving the ribs intact, and then the other half, leaving the head and backbone in one long strip. Ears must be left on the head. The hoofs are cut off and carefully hidden under a shrub; the tail, the genitalia, and the matrix are hung on a black-brush acacia. The head and backbone are smoked and cooked with hominy. The ribs and tongue are smoked.

The importance of skinning a deer in the Kickapoo manner was illustrated when hunting friends, wishing to make a gift of several skins to the Indians, charged us with this mission. It was all to no avail. The skins had been salted and therefore could not be tanned in the accustomed way; they had been skinned with a knife and consequently were too damaged to be used.

The Kickapoos believe that, if a hunter has a premonition something has gone wrong at home, he may as well give up the hunt, since he will have no luck; also, the behavior of deer is interpreted as an augury. Firearms that are the property of a deceased, if taken on a hunt before being properly smoked with cudweed, will bring no luck to the user. A Kickapoo man married to a Mexican woman loses his prowess as a hunter because Mexican women do not always observe their menses or involution period in a menstrual hut. The deer, sensitive to human scent, flee from the odor which emanates from a woman during this period.

When a man brings home a deer, he has no further authority over the carcass and skin; thereafter the disposition of the meat and hide belongs to the woman. She may give away part of the meat while it is fresh or make jerky from it and smoke the ribs, the latter being saved for ceremonial feasts or for special gifts. The women prepare the hides, sell some to saddlemakers in Múzquiz, and smoke others to make moccasins.

Second to venison, the favorite meat of the Kickapoos is bear. Today, they must go far into the sierra to find bears; and, unfortunately, as with deer, they have indiscriminately killed the females and the cubs. After a bear has been killed, it is laid on the ground on its belly with paws outstretched, facing east. The hunter squats in front of the animal, lights some Indian tobacco in his hand, and rubs the ashes on the muzzle of the bear while telling him how sorry he is to have killed him and asking to be forgiven.

After this ceremony, the animal is laid on branches and turned on its back. First, the head is cut off and hidden in the woods. The animal is split down the belly from neck to tail, and the hide is separated with a knife rather than with the fist. If a bear has a layer of fat, one to two inches thick, it is taken off before the animal is dismembered. At articulations, the forelegs are cut off, followed by the hind legs; the ribs are cut in one piece, leaving the backbone and loin together. The feet, highly relished as food, are taken home with the other meat. While in camp, the hunters cut the liver in thin slices, wrap it in the fat lining of the stomach, and broil it. At home, the meat is eaten fresh or made into jerky; the ribs are smoked and saved for ceremonies; the fat is rendered and used in cooking, for grooming the hair, and medicinally.

The Kickapoos formerly tanned the skins, cut them into strips, and used them for tying and for harnesses, to cover saddles, and as coverlets for the benches, or sold them to Mexicans to use as throw rugs. Now that bears are scarce, this is no longer done.

The Indians now raise little of the food they consume. Some grow corn, beans, and pumpkins or squash or receive them on a sharecropper's basis from their land, but the greater part of the food is bought in the Múzquiz market during the brief months spent in Mexico. They buy wheat flour in fifty-pound sacks (which are good for making sheets and pillow cases), prepared cornmeal for tortillas, baking powder, lard, beans, various *pastas* (such as macaroni and spaghetti), rice, coffee, sugar, salt, potatoes, sweet potatoes, cabbage, pumpkins or squash, onions, garlic, cumin seed, cinnamon, eggs, beef, pork, pork sausage and cracklings, goat, kid, bananas, candy, and canned peaches and pears. These supplies are supplemented by venison and other available small game. During the months spent in the United States, the Kickapoos eat the same diet, to which they add chickens (less expensive than in Mexico), cakes, apples, grapes, peanut butter, strawberry preserves, fruits, and sugar-cane syrup.

In the past, they utilized many of the wild berries and fruits that grow around them, such as Laredo Mahonia berries and grapes, from which they made a jelly; the fruit of the prickly-pear cactus, eaten raw or made into a jam; and pecans from their grove. For seasoning they gathered wild oregano, peppermint, and *chilepiquín*. Salt is used sparingly by the Kickapoos, who believe that it is damaging to the muscles of the body, particularly those of the legs and arms, since salt makes one fat and the muscles less flexible.

Although the Kickapoos are adventurous eaters, judging from the variety of food they seemed to enjoy in our home, their regular diet is limited and unimaginative. Menus are monotonous and must have been more so before the Indians learned from the Mexicans the use of several vegetables and condiments. All meals are accompanied by coffee and imported tea, although the latter is a relatively recent item; in the past, the Kickapoos made their teas from local plants, such as pecan leaves, white-flowered Lippia, and crotons. If the cook has time, she prepares soups and dried beans; but, if a quick meal is a necessity, ground meat or jerky, seasoned with onions, tomatoes, and garlic, with or without scrambled eggs and accompanied by fried potatoes, may be served.

With few modern kitchen appliances other than a meat grinder, a woman prepares a meal which is tasty, abundant, and wholesome. As in cleanliness, there are many individual differences in the women's ability to cook. Some seem to throw food together as if the only purpose is to satisfy hunger; others season the food, cook it, and serve it in a way which can be enjoyed.

Before the white man came, the Kickapoos and related tribes used pottery, which was later replaced by brass kettles brought by the French.[3] As brass kettles became more difficult to get, they were reserved for ceremonial meals and replaced by black ironware and enameled-ware utensils for daily use.

A woman's utensils with which to prepare food include a tripod to place over the open hearth, on which the cookware is set; a wooden mortar and pestle for triturating corn, jerky, and formerly coffee, when it was toasted at home; and a Mexican volcanic-rock mortar and pestle for grinding onions, peppers, garlic, and spices. For mixing bread, washing dishes, and winnowing corn, she uses large enameled-ware dishpans. For cooking she has a large iron kettle hanging over the fire, in which she prepares soups, and a Mexican clay pot for beans. For breadmaking she uses, besides the large dishpan, a rolling pin, a board, and a heavy piece of galvanized sheet iron on which she bakes; she may deep fry the bread in the Dutch oven or bake it. For quick frying, she has several iron-ware skillets. She also has enameled-ware coffee- and teapots, several kitchen knives and spoons, wire baskets for storing perishables, a potato masher, a strainer, and many glass jars for storing food. Formerly, the Mexican metate and mano to grind corn for tortilla making were used, but the Kickapoos now buy prepared cornmeal. The metate was also used for grinding the stick cinnamon used for flavoring squash or pumpkin pies and corn gruels.

Eating utensils consist of a few enameled-ware flat bowls for food, deep bowls for beverages, spoons, and a few, very few knives and forks for visitors. Before enameled-ware eating utensils came into vogue, wooden bowls and ladles were used. The entire family sat around one common bowl and dipped their ladles into the food.

To prepare a meal, a woman combines the ingredients for breadmaking at the north bench, or at a table, if she owns one; triturates the jerky or corn with mortar and pestle; or grinds the meat in the meat grinder. She places these ingredients on the floor near where she sits, either on the floor or on a low stool; pulls an empty orange crate toward her to serve as a table, on which she puts the breadboard and rolling pin; and proceeds to make the bread, placing it on the galvanized griddle or frying it in a Dutch oven. While making bread, she also prepares the dish she plans to serve, usually accompanied by potatoes, if she is not serving a soup. Since she keeps her utensils, water, firewood, and supplies within arm's reach, she manages, with little effort and few steps, to produce an acceptable meal.

When family members gather for a meal, they sit on the benches, or squat around the fire if they eat in the cook house, while the mother ladles out the food into enameled-ware soup bowls. An enameled-ware spoon is used for the liquid parts and the fingers for the solids. When a Kickapoo family entertains a non-Kickapoo guest for a meal, they borrow a table and chairs if they have none. Only the men sit at the table with the guest, while the women hover over the fire preparing the food and serving it when ready, handing out freshly baked tortillas or filling the bowls with steaming coffee or tea.

Some of the old people regret that the Kickapoos are no longer as hospitable at mealtime as they were in the old days. When a casual guest arrives today, he is not invited to share the meal with the family. If a visitor who arrives at mealtime is invited to eat, he may say, "I have already eaten," or he may say, "I am hungry," whereupon he sits down to eat with the family. After the meal they say, "Thank Kitzihiat we have eaten."

Following are the methods employed in the preparation of some of the food eaten by the Kickapoos.

Bread

Fried wheat bread: Combine flour, baking powder, and a small amount of salt in a dishpan. Make a depression in the center, add water and lard gradually, and mix with the hands until the dough is of the right consistency. Form small balls and pat them out into flat cakes about eight inches in diameter. With a fork, punch two holes in the center of each cake and fry in deep fat until golden brown.

Thick white bread: Combine the same ingredients as for fried wheat bread; knead, roll into a large cake, place in greased and preheated Dutch oven, cover, and bake over coals. Spread coals over the lid of the oven.

Tortillas de harina (wheat tortillas): Use the same method and ingredients as for fried bread, but without the holes, and bake the tortillas over coals on a heated griddle.

Corn tortillas, made from "Masarina" (brand-name for prepared cornmeal): Add water to the cornmeal until the dough is of the right consistency to pat into flat, thin cakes, or flatten with a press. Bake on a griddle heated over coals.

Corn pones: Put hominy (see below) through a meat grinder. Pat the resulting dough into small, fat cakes, place them in a greased, preheated Dutch oven, cover, and cook over coals. These corn pones may also be fried, or made into one large cake and baked in the Dutch oven.

Sour-dough cornbread: Add one cup of water to one cup of prepared cornmeal. Allow this mixture to stand for a day or two until it ferments. Add one cup of wheat flour, salt, baking powder, lard, and two beaten eggs to the fermented mixture. Pour into a greased, pre-heated Dutch oven, cover, and bake over coals.

Fresh corn-on-the-cob bread: Scrape the grains off fresh roasting ears with the jawbone of a deer. Add tender green black-eyed peas, a bit of salt, and baking powder. Pat into small cakes and bake in a greased, pre-heated Dutch oven.

Migas de tortilla (literally, tortilla crumbs): This is a Mexican dish much liked by the Kickapoos and frequently served. Cut leftover tortillas into strips and fry in deep fat. Set aside in a warm place. Make a sauce by combining tomatoes, onions, garlic, chilies, cumin seed, and oregano. Spread this mixture over the fried tortillas. Scrambled eggs may be served over the tortillas, reserving the sauce to spread over all.

Meats

Picadillo (ground meat with tomato sauce): Brown meat in a small amount of fat and add tomatoes, onions, garlic, and chilies which have been ground in the *molcajete* (mortar and pestle). Add salt and cook until the meat is almost done. Add enough water to make it soupy and cook until done. This is another Mexican dish, quick and easy to prepare.

Jerky: Shred beef, venison, or bear jerky and triturate in a mortar and pestle until powdery. Soak in water for half an hour; drain. Brown in a small amount of fat; add salt, pepper, and water; and cook until tender. Add ground tomatoes, onions, garlic, chilies, and cumin seed, and cook until all ingredients are blended. When ready to serve, the jerky may be eaten alone or added to scrambled eggs.

Jerky with cornmeal: Brown cornmeal in fat; add jerky and sauce made with tomatoes, onions, etc., as described above.

Fresh fried venison: Slice venison into thin strips and fry in bear oil or store-bought lard.

Pork with squash: Cut pork ribs into bite-size pieces and brown in fat. Add sliced tomatoes, onions, garlic, chilies, oregano, and salt; cook until almost done. Add sliced fresh squash and steam until tender but not overcooked.

Soup: Boil triturated corn until tender. Add deer bones with meat, ripe squash or pumpkin, a bit of salt, and any other ingredients at hand, such as soaked dried beans, fresh beans, macaroni, rice, potatoes, cabbage, or sweet potatoes. Cook until the beans and meat are tender, usually an hour or more.

Fried kid's viscera: This dish is called *fritada de cabrito* in Mexico. Chop the liver, kidneys, lungs, heart, and, if desired, intestines of a kid. Brown in fat and season with onion, garlic, oregano, cumin seed, and black pepper. If the kid is butchered at home, save the blood and cook separately. Chop fine and add to the viscera mixture before serving.

Blood sausage: For the Mexican dish called *morcilla*, chop pork viscera and coagulated blood; season with oregano, garlic, rue, cumin seed, salt, and pepper. Stuff the mixture into a pork gut and boil until done.

Corn

Chicales (dried fresh corn): Remove the shucks from fresh roasting ears, scrape off the grains with a deer jaw, and dry in the sun. As needed, soak the grains in water and ashes. Drain, and cook in fresh water until tender when pressed between the thumb and index fingers. This style of corn is often used in dishes which call for triturated corn. *Chicales* may also be ground in the meat grinder.

Hominy: Pour wood ashes into a bucket of water until a thick mixture is obtained. Strain. Allow the ashes to settle at the bottom of the container, and drain off the water. Add more fresh water to the ashes and boil for a few minutes. Add dry corn, previously checked for impurities, and boil until the hulls slip off the grains easily when pressed between the thumb and index fingers. Drain, and add more fresh water. Rub the grains together until all hulls are removed. Rinse in fresh water until the grains glisten. Hominy may be used immediately or spread on gunny sacks or canvas to dry in the sun for two or three days. Take it indoors at night to avoid moisture from the dew. When it is sufficiently dry, store it, and, as needed, soak it in water overnight before using.

Toasted dry corn: This is called *pinole* in Mexico. Toast dry grains of corn in a heavy skillet, triturate with the mortar and pestle, cook in water or milk, and add sugar and cinnamon for flavor.

Fresh boiled corn-on-the-cob: Boil the corn in the shucks.

Fresh roasted ears: Place the corn among coals in the shucks.

Sopa de helote (literally, stewed fresh corn): This is another Mexican dish popular with the Indians. Scrape the grains from fresh roasting ears. Fry in fat. Add tomatoes, onions, garlic, salt, and oregano; and cook until tender.

Hominy and meatballs: Triturate hominy after soaking and add to meatballs.

Green tamales: Grate the kernels off fresh corn. Cook with a bit of salt until thick. Wrap in green shucks and steam until done.

Beans

Dry beans are soaked overnight. They may be added to soups or cooked alone with the condiments at hand, such as oregano, garlic, cumin seed, and chilies.

Beans and cracklings: Soak beans overnight, drain, and cook in a *jarrito* (Mexican earthenware bean jar) with fresh water; add oregano, garlic, cracklings, and, toward the end of the cooking period, salt to prevent toughness.

The varieties of beans with thick skins are cooked in wood ashes in order to remove the hulls. Then the beans are mashed and fried in lard.

Black-eyed peas are preferably eaten while green or in the pod, thickened with a bit of flour.

Squash or Pumpkin (Cucurbita moschata *and similar varieties*)

In order to preserve the part of a ripe squash or pumpkin not immediately used, either of the two following methods may be employed. (a) The pumpkin is cut crosswise, peeled, and seeded. It is cut into round slices about one-eighth of an inch thick. These rings are hung on a pole to dry in the sun for a day or two, interlaced, and again sunned until completely dehydrated. (b) The second method consists of cutting the pumpkin rings into halves. At the end of each half, a slit is made, into which the next half is inserted. These are hung on a line and dried until dehydrated. As needed, the pumpkin is soaked in water for a short time.

Pumpkin pies: Cook pumpkin, either dry or fresh, in water until tender; drain and mash. Add grated *piloncillo* (brown sugar cones), sesame seed, and pecans. Set aside. Make a dough of the consistency for wheat tortillas; but, instead of water, add beer. Knead, spread on a board, and cut in circles six inches in diameter. Place the pumpkin filling on one side, fold over, and pink the edges. Bake in a Dutch oven. Place coals on the lid of the oven.

Irish potatoes

Irish potatoes are much used by the Kickapoos. They may be put in soups, boiled in their skins, baked in the coals, mashed, or fried.

Sweet potatoes

Sweet potatoes may be fried like Irish potatoes, boiled in water with *piloncillo* and cinnamon, cooked in their skins in the coals, added to soups, or made into pies.

Other Foods

When a person is ill, he is given hominy soup containing squirrel, or potatoes baked in their jackets in the coals.

Skunk, killed with a bow and arrow, may be substituted for squirrel. The hair is singed, the skin is scraped, and the stink gland is removed.

Chapter 5

Crafts

Basketry

Basketry among the Kickapoo women is almost a lost craft since they began going to work in the United States. In the early sixties, many of the women were still making a few baskets for their own use and for sale or trade. Formerly, great numbers were made and peddled from Piedras Negras to Monclova, Coahuila.

Ritzenthaler and Peterson believe that the craft was adopted from the Mexicans;[1] however, Mexicans in Coahuila do not make baskets of any kind. What is more likely is that the women, lacking birchbark to make containers, adapted the desert materials for the baskets and containers which the Woodland people have made from time immemorial.[2]

Old informants relate that at one time they did not use dyes to color the baskets but began the practice because the Mexican public liked the colors and suggested their use. The baskets are handsomer without the aniline dyes, as sotol acquires a golden color more pleasing than the dyes, which tend to fade.

Informants also recall that their grandmothers made baskets from the stalks of Indian mallow which grew profusely in the pecan grove where the village once stood. The leaves were stripped off the stems and discarded. The bark was peeled, tied together, and soaked in the river for four days. It was then pounded between two sticks to loosen any remaining pulp and sunned for several days to bleach it. When grandmothers sat around the fire in the evenings, they rolled the fibers on their shins and made them into balls. Once dyed, the bark was ready to make baskets or bags, or to be used as cordage before the Kickapoos began to buy istle twine.

The favored material used today for basketmaking is sotol. The gathering and preparation of the material is the same as for mats. While the baskets are being made, the material is kept moist to make it pliable. The bottom of the basket of undyed material is woven in a twilled pattern about three-quarters of an inch wide. Bottom leaves are bent upward to form the sides in a checkered pattern, with the dyed elements crossing horizontally, alternating with rows of narrower sotol, either dyed or plain. To make the handle and rim, thin withes of catclaw are used. These are bound with an overcast stitch of narrow sotol.

Baskets are made in many different styles and sizes and for many purposes. The largest is oval-shaped, with or without a cover, twenty inches long by fourteen inches wide and ten inches high. This basket was formerly used for carrying household utensils on the annual hunting expeditions, for general storage in the house, and as a unit of measure for shelled corn or wheat.

The most common type is the circular basket with a handle over the top. This variety is made in all sizes from four to fourteen inches in diameter. The circular basket, with a cover, is used as a sewing basket, to keep piece goods, threads, buckskin, beads, needles, and beeswax. Without the lid, such baskets are used for storing a variety of objects, such as bread, vegetables, and eggs.

One unique type of basket, used as a catchall for women's trinkets, is a tiered basket that can be hung from the framework of the house. The background is a woven mat of sotol, twenty-four inches long and seven inches wide. Three baskets without covers, six by three inches, are woven into the mat five inches above one another.

Wood, Bone, Stone, and Metal Work

A visitor to the Kickapoo village, observing the many uses to which wood and fibers are put, cannot help but understand why theirs is called a Woodland culture. With wood, fibers, animal skins, hair, antlers, stone, and clay, they produce most of their utilitarian needs—or did, until the white man brought them European goods. Although they live surrounded by a Mexican culture whose building material is primarily adobe and stone, the Kickapoos continue to use wood and fibers for the construction of their homes and many of their household articles. The change of flora from Wisconsin to Coahuila, a semidesert, is vast; yet they have ingeniously found new materials to replace those they had used for centuries.

While the hunters now use modern firearms, the wooden bow and arrows continue to be an important part—if only symbolically—of their culture. From infancy, a male child gazes at the miniature bow and arrows suspended from the hoop of his cradle board. By the time he is four, he receives his first real set of bow and arrows and dedicates many hours of the day to the practice of marksmanship.

Basketmaking. This is considered woman's work by the Kickapoos, but this man—of Mexican, German, and Negro ancestry—was persuaded to help.

A boy's self bow, or one-piece bow, is usually undecorated and crudely made of sycamore or catclaw. The bow is thirty inches long and the arrows, twenty inches. The shafts of the arrows, usually made from kidneywood, may have either blunt or sharp heads. Turkey feathers are attached to the arrows with sinew thread and glue made from the scum of boiled deer antlers.

Although a child's bow and arrows may be crude, the self bow and arrows for an adult or youth are finely made. The bow is undecorated but highly polished and shellacked. The favorite wood for bowmaking is bois d'arc, found on only one ranch in the area, which is now closed to the Kickapoos, but also brought from Oklahoma and Texas. Handsome bows are also made from the local Texas black walnut.

The man's bow is fifty inches long, flat, with rounded edges and tapering at the wings. The arrows are twenty inches long, including the lanceolate head, which is made of finely sharpened steel or brass. The shaft, made from Apache plume or sticky Baccharis, is circled with crayon in three different areas, with lines in the colors indicating the owner's distinguishing design. Turkey feathers are fastened on with sinew and antler glue. Buckskin is used for the string for all bows. When using the bow, the hunter places a protective leather band on his left wrist and releases the arrow by the primary method.

Yacapita, a Comanche woman who had lived among the Kickapoos since girlhood, with Kickapoo baskets, ca. 1929. (Photo by Mrs. Sarah S. McKellar; courtesy John Woodhull.)

Wood, Bone, Stone, and Metal   67

Quivers are double and ordinarily made of undecorated buckskin; those used as gifts are fringed and painted with the giver's distinguishing marks.

Second only to the bow and arrows as indispensable equipment for hunting are the wooden saddle and the deer call. The design of the saddletree used by the Kickapoos is almost the same as that used by the Blackfoot Indians, called "prairie chicken snare saddle";[3] the difference lies in the fact that the pommel and cantle of the Kickapoo saddletree are made of wood rather than elkhorn or black-tailed deer antler.

Formerly, the saddletree was completely covered with buffalo, deer, bear, or peccary hide; but today a blanket is thrown over the seat and held in place by the cinch and the leather straps for the narrow iron stirrups. The saddle is used by men, women, and children, on both horses and burros. Formerly the Kickapoos made a packsaddle with two cantles and no pommel. Their favorite wood for saddle-making is hackberry.

The deer call is seven inches long and two inches in diameter. It consists of two pieces. The upper one is cone-shaped, ending in a small orifice on which the lips are placed. The upper piece fits snugly over the lower half, containing a thin piece of steel wedged against a small cone, one side of which has been cut so that the metal fits tightly against it. Below the small cone with the piece of metal is another opening. By blowing through the upper orifice and opening and closing the bottom aperture, one produces a call imitating that of a young fawn. The deer call is carried around the neck by means of a buckskin thong attached to both parts. The preferred wood for making deer calls is chinaberry, Texas black walnut, Texas madrone, or pecan. The decoration depends on the ingenuity of the maker; some are plain, while others are painted and embellished with simple incised designs.

The majority of household utensils have been replaced by iron and enameled ware, but still much in use are the wooden mortar and pestle, bowls, and ladles, the latter two being used today almost exclusively for the bowl-and-dice game and for ceremonial feasts.

The mortar is thirty inches high and nine inches in diameter at the top. The upper part tapers slightly toward the bottom, whose lower three inches form a base eleven inches in diameter. The top of the mortar is hollowed to a depth of ten inches. To hollow out the bowl, the maker marks the thickness of the bowl and, with an adz, makes a small depression and fills it with live coals, which burn the wood slowly. Care must be taken that the coals do not burn into the sides. Each night the ashes are removed and replaced with new coals until the desired depth is obtained. The burnt residue is scraped with an adz.

The pestle is forty inches long and made from a single piece of wood.

The middle twenty-five-inch section is two inches in diameter, while the two ends are three inches in diameter. Woods favored for the mortar and pestle are sycamore, one-seed juniper, and Montezuma bald cypress. Wood for this article, as for all others, must be cut when the moon is full and the weather is cold. This assures that the material is at its full strength and maturity and is not apt to be destroyed by borers.

Although any Kickapoo man can make the wooden objects they use, only one gifted craftsman remains who makes beautiful objects, ladles of all sizes being his specialty. They are simple in design, but his choice of wood and his clever use of the grain, plus the high polish, make them unique pieces. Woods liked for making ladles are pecan, Texas black walnut, chinaberry, Montezuma bald cypress, anaqua, Texas madrone, desert willow, Texas ash, honey mesquite, and sycamore.

Wooden bowls are made in all sizes, from round ones four to fourteen inches in diameter, to oval ones of eight to eighteen inches. The majority of the bowls are plain, but the old ones sometimes had a fluted border or a base.

Another article still in daily use is the wooden cradle board. The main board, well polished and with rounded edges, is twenty inches long, one inch thick, and nine inches wide. A narrow board eleven inches long, one inch wide, and three-quarters of an inch thick is placed crosswise under the main board, three inches below the top and extending one inch on either side. The narrow board is fastened to the main board above with thongs run through two sets of perforated holes on either edge of the main board. The hoop, with rounded edges, one inch wide and half an inch thick, rises ten inches over the main board and is doweled to the ends extending on either side. It is further reinforced by three thongs which run through larger holes perforated at the edge of the top and holes five inches up the hoop and on top of it. Thongs on the sides and foot of the cradle board are tied over the swaddled infant after he is placed in it. The cradle board has no footboard, and no nails are used in its construction.

Formerly, children played with tops made by their elders; today, these are bought in the store.

Both the pipe and the flageolet used in ceremonies are finely made, the latter in two different styles. One is thirteen inches long by one inch in diameter. A carefully selected piece of wood is cut lengthwise through the center, hollowed out, and glued together. At the orifice which is brought to the lips is a small slit in the upper part, three-eighths of an inch long. On top of the flageolet, two inches from the mouthpiece, is an inclined, square aperture, and two inches below the inclined opening is a series of seven holes, three-eighths of an inch in diameter, spaced one inch apart.

The end opposite the mouthpiece has an opening one inch in diameter. Another type of flageolet is only nine inches long and one inch in diameter. It is also split, hollowed out, and glued together. Either for adornment or for reinforcement, it is tied with six thongs, each made into a neat bow. This flageolet, except for the carved slide, is similar to the one illustrated by Alanson Skinner.[4] The favored wood is lime prickly-ash (*Zanthoxylum fagara*).

The tools now employed for wood carving are all modern: saw, adz, chisel, awl, wood rasp, ax, wedge, and drill. Coals are used for hollowing out mortars, and heat and buckskin thongs are employed to bend and hold wood in place. Occasionally one sees an awl with a deer-antler handle, but the most common articles made from antlers are the dice for the bowl-and-dice game.

Formerly, the mat-sewing needles were made from bison or bovine ribs, but today the Indians hammer out a long iron nail and bore a hole at one end to thread the twine.

Bowls for the ceremonial pipes are made of various stones found locally. The favorite is a pinkish-red rhyolite which takes a high polish. The majority of the pipes are unadorned, but some are embellished with angular geometric incised designs. The bowl, at right angles to the stem, is placed almost in the center of the stone, which is five inches long and one inch in diameter, flat at the bottom with a rounded front tip. The wooden pipe stem is eight inches long, including the doweled part which fits into the stone section. The stem has a small orifice, an eighth of an inch in diameter, which couples with the orifice perforated into the stone section. The wood favored for pipe stems is Texas black walnut. The pipes are encased in finely made buckskin jackets, fringed at the ends and embroidered with glass beads.

For the few old men and women who like to smoke a pipe, a simple and crude elbow type, seven inches long, is completely made of wood. It is seldom seen today, cigarettes having become popular among Indians of all ages.

Silversmithing is now practiced by only one man in the village, who is also the best wood carver. Women and men are both wearing less German-silver jewelry. This has created a hardship on the craftsman, who has difficulty making a living from silversmithing, with the result that he has extended his work to include making ax handles, gun butts, and new parts for guns. The articles formerly worn by the men and women were bracelets, brooches, buckles, buttons, combs, earrings, kerchief and queue rings, and finger rings. Today, the men wear no jewelry except at ceremonies, and then very little. The women wear only bracelets, rings,

Silversmith at work in the ramada, with a woman customer.

and earrings. All decorative designs are angular and geometric and are incised. Abalone shell bought in Mexico is much used for settings in both rings and bracelets. The tools used for silversmithing include several hammers, cold chisels, etching tools, an iron anvil, a grinding wheel, various grades of polishing cloths, solder, and a small propane gas tank for welding.

The Kickapoos are clever at making useful, if crude, tools out of tin. One of these is a beaming tool used for shaving deer hair in the winter, when it is at its thickest. The top of a can, eight inches in diameter, is folded over, and the edges are welded and sharpened. Another tool made from tin is a pumpkin slicer. A piece of tin one inch wide and ten inches long is bent into a loop held together with a piece of buckskin thong. When sharpened, it makes a practical tool for slicing pumpkins or squashes into long, thin rings or half rings.

Formerly, when the women wore shakers around their calves at dances, they also were fashioned from tin. Triangular pieces of tin were folded over a piece of buckskin and tied to a band which encircled the calf. Informants recall with nostalgia what a pretty sound the shakers made when the women danced.

The Kickapoos formerly used a Jew's-harp introduced as a trade item by the Europeans.[5] The silversmith made one for our collection; it is a replica of one shown in Webster's Dictionary.

Skins and Fabrics

After wood and vegetable fibers, the material most extensively used by the Kickapoos has been deerskin, which, until the arrival of the white man, they used for clothing and many other purposes.

The preparation of the skins is a woman's work. The hunter skins the animal and turns over the meat and hide to the woman who heads a household. If the hide is not to be tanned immediately, it is allowed to dry in the shade, but it is never salted. When a woman is ready to tan, she awaits a spell of calm, sunny weather so that the skin will dry evenly. If the hide has been dried, she soaks it in water for three days; if it is fresh, soaking for one day suffices. The water is wrung out of the hide by wrapping it around a post and, with a stout stick used as a tourniquet, twisting it until almost dry.

The second step is to remove the hair. A stout semiflattened and crudely finished board fifty inches long and seven inches wide with a tapering end is staked obliquely into the ground. A woman sits in front of the board on a low stool, throws the skin over it, and, with both hands holding the beaming tool, shaves off the hair.

The ordinary beaming tool consists of a cylindrical piece of wood, twelve inches long and one and three-quarters of an inch in circumference at the ends, where it is held. The center portion, where the blade is imbedded, is four inches wide and an inch thicker than the ends. (The tin-can beaming tool described above is used instead in the winter.)

After the hair has been removed, the skin is thrown over a line and allowed to dry until the following day. Brains of deer, cattle, or goats are dissolved in a container of water, in which the skin is soaked for several hours. (If fresh brains are not to be used immediately, they are rubbed on a gunny sack and dried in the sun. When needed, the impregnated sack is placed in the container with the skin. If the weather is warm, and fresh brains at hand are in danger of spoiling, they are cooked before being dried.)

After several hours of soaking in brain water, the skin is again wrung out, tautly laced with buckskin to a rectangular wooden frame, and the frame propped. When the skin is partly dry, it is vigorously rubbed with a scraper to remove the fat, stretch the skin, and break down its fibers until it begins to crackle. When this state is achieved, the skin is taken from the frame and may be further softened by rubbing it briskly in a seesaw motion over a fleshing stake. It is then stored in a cool place until such time as it is smoked, sold, or given away.

To smoke the skin, an old bucket in which soil has been poured is half filled with triturated pieces of corncobs or rotted pecan wood, covered

Girl softening buckskin.

with hot coals. Pecan wood gives the skin a rich dark brown color; corn-cobs give a softer buff color. After a thick, smouldering smoke begins to rise, the skin, temporarily sewed together lengthwise and loosely tied at the top, is placed over the bucket, which is covered with a wet cloth around the edge to prevent the skin from burning. When the skin is suf-ficiently smoked on one side, it is turned over and smoked on the other. The Kickapoos claim that smoking makes the skin impervious to water and that a wet or soiled article made of smoked skin will return to its original softness after being washed.

Formerly, when the Indians did not have as many galvanized buckets as they have today, they dug a hole in the ground, a foot in diameter, in which they placed dried pieces of corncob or rotted pecan wood with live coals. Around the hole, they staked four slender green saplings to support the skin while it smoked.

For winter wear, the Indians prefer moccasins made from deer killed during the cold months, since the hide is thicker and fluffier, thus making the moccasins warmer and softer. The skins from animals killed in the summer are much thinner and wear out quickly.

The Kickapoos, in spite of the shortage of deer, still find many uses for the tanned skins. Some wear the moccasins daily. They are frequently used as gifts, not only among themselves, but for non-Indians as well. Every adoption ceremony requires a pair of unsewn moccasins and a pair of new leggings for the adopted male and a new skin for the drum. In the case of a man's or a woman's dance, a skin is spread out, with cigarettes on it for all those attending. The men go to the New Year clan festival wearing handsomely beaded moccasins, gifts from their aunts or nieces. In fact, all attendants at the New Year clan festivals, regardless of sex or age, wear moccasins.

The skins are a sure trade item. In Múzquiz, various stores display the moccasins in their windows, and people come from as far as Mexico City to buy them, in the belief that wearing them will relieve the user of annoying corns and calluses.

The Indians make two types of moccasins. The most popular is the one made from a single piece of skin, slightly puckered at the front and heel, cut in such a way that the skin turns like a cuff in the back and on either side of the instep, forming a flap. The other variety is made of two pieces, with uppers of buckskin and a sole of bovine leather. These are used strictly for hard wear or when going into the *monte* or sierra, where thorns and rough stones are a hazard. The one-piece moccasin is decorated on the instep with beading in angular geometric designs; the two-piece one is unadorned but has a thong intercalated in the upper part which can be tightened around the ankle for better security.

Although every Kickapoo woman early learns to prepare the skins and make the moccasins, not all are equally gifted in the cutting or the beading. Today, only the instep is beaded, whereas formerly the flaps also were beaded. Because of the higher cost of beads and the difficulty in finding them, the instep design is becoming narrower. One woman is particularly outstanding in her design and quality of work and is the admiration of all the others. An informant, in describing her work to us, exclaimed, "She can even make letters with beads!"

We have noted with interest that a young Mexican woman, who is legally married to a Kickapoo man and observes the Kickapoo ways, has learned to make beautiful moccasins and equals the best of the Indian women in beading them.

In applying the beads, the women use two different techniques. The handsomer of the two is the overlay or spot stitch, which makes a flat, smooth surface, resembling French *pavé*. The second technique is the "lazy" stitch, which gives a ridged or corrugated surface. In the overlay method each bead is threaded and sewed onto the buckskin separately; in the "lazy" method three or four beads are threaded at a time and sewed onto the buckskin, forming a loose pattern.

Formerly, excellent and sturdy moccasins were made from porcupine skin after removal of the quills. We have seen only one pair, on an old man who told us they had belonged to his father. He wears them only in dry weather, in order to conserve them.

Although few of the men today wear the buckskin leggings, they are frequently made as gifts for the adoption ceremony. Some men, especially those owning a dance, wear them when acting as hosts. They also use an unadorned variety as chaps to protect them from the thorn brush when hunting or herding in the *monte*.

The Kickapoos make numerous articles from buckskin, such as small tobacco pouches for ordinary smoking tobacco, coin purses, and pipe and flageolet cases. The articles in the bundles are all wrapped in pieces of buckskin. Each mature Kickapoo carries a small, round piece of buckskin containing his or her portion of Indian tobacco. Although rope is commonly used, buckskin thongs take the place of string in many instances.

We have seen only one bison-hide trunk, whose top had been lost. This trunk had once belonged to a Shawnee Indian.

No woman in the village today knows how to weave the yarn sashes formerly worn to support the leggings. Until recently, an old woman in Oklahoma made them. Neither do the women make the fiber or yarn bags that were used before they began buying the istle variety seen in Mexican shops and the more recent nylon type now replacing the brightly colored fiber *morral*.

Chapter 6

Dress, Personal Care, and Adornment

The traditional attire of the Kickapoo man consists of a frontier-style calico print shirt, with a finely tucked bib and ruffled cuffs, adorned with narrow ribbons of contrasting or matching colors; buckskin leggings, ornamented on the sides with beads and pompoms of wool yarn; a breechcloth; a European vest, adorned with German-silver brooches or beads; and moccasins. A Pendleton blanket, a wide-brimmed hat, and a kerchief at the neck complete the dress. If the man is a chief or one of the clan leaders, he is privileged to wear a feather in a vertical position on either his queue or his hat. If he is not a chief but has a responsible position, such as being the owner of a dance, he is entitled to wear the feather at an angle.

The only person in the village who wore this attire habitually was Chief Papícoano; on others it was seen only on ceremonial occasions. Even Chief Papícoano did not adhere entirely to the old-style clothing, usually wearing khakis under the leggings rather than a breechcloth, oxfords or tennis shoes instead of moccasins, and, for warmth, a heavy sweater or a camel's-hair coat. Little adornment, other than a feather in his hat or a few beads on his vest, was worn by the chief.

Formerly, the men used long, dangling earrings; many strings of glass, bone, or metal beads; large silver brooches on their vests; bracelets; rings; and beaded garters worn below the knees.

Today the majority of the older men wear nondescript work clothes. Trousers may be either Levis or wool slacks; shirts may be anything from T-shirts to heavy flannel plaids. To protect themselves from the cold, the men wear sweaters, leather or plastic jackets, Eisenhower jackets, and U.S. Army coats. They wear long wool or cotton underwear and socks in winter but discard these items as soon as warm weather arrives. For footwear they use high work boots, oxfords, or cowboy boots. The wide-brimmed straw or felt hats worn in northern Mexico are popular with the majority of the older men, but occasionally one appears with distinctive headgear, such as a chauffeur's cap with insignia or an army camouflage cap. Many return from the United States with clothing bought at Army and Navy stores or with castoffs given to them by proselyting religious sects in Oklahoma and Texas.

The young men tend to emulate the northern Mexican cowboys, who wear tightly fitted beige Levis belted low on the hips, wide-brimmed hats with the sides turned up, beige denim shirts to match the Levis, and cowboy boots. Over the shirts they wear leather or plastic jackets. Youths and small boys copy their older brothers and young fathers.

The Kickapoos say that long ago their ancestors wore their hair in a roach. Today, men's hair styles are an interesting study in variety. The older men, particularly the clan leaders, wear a long bob to the earlobes and, in the back, a thin queue, sometimes two feet long, tied at the end with a narrow ribbon. Formerly, the queue was encased in a beaded band from which several strings of beads dangled. Wives are charged with keeping the queue braided; if a man does not have a wife, he goes to an aunt or cross-niece to have her braid it. The men who wear their hair in this fashion tend to look disheveled, as many tuck both hair and queue into hats when in Múzquiz.

A few young men and boys wear their hair in the long bob with a queue, but this style is fast disappearing among the young set because of the teasing they receive from the Mexican boys. When the Beatles became popular, with their shoulder-length hair, the boys and youths began to copy them. Grandmothers frown on this fashion, observing that the youths' hair length far exceeds the traditional bob. Shortly before the Beatles' hairdo became popular, one mother complained because her thirty-year-old son would not wear the long bob and queue; but, after he copied the Beatles, she accused him of having hair the length of a horse's mane.

Young men who wear Mexican cowboy clothes tend to have long sideburns, with hair combed toward the back and down to the nape. Some also wear moustaches, which are popular among the Mexicans.

The Kickapoo adults go to Múzquiz to get haircuts, but the youngsters and children have their hair cut by any member of the family who qualifies. Hair may be cut in a short bob reaching the earlobes, in a crew cut, or anything between, depending on the ingenuity and ability of the home barber.

The men do not shave but pull out the scant hair on their faces with the discarded magazine spring of a .30–.30 Winchester rifle. They place the spring between the right-hand thumb and index finger, passing the spring over the face while closing and opening the loops. This motion catches the hairs and pulls them out. It is a handy and convenient gadget, easily carried, and can be used anywhere—that is, anywhere except in the cattail-covered house.

Dress, Personal Care, and Adornment   77

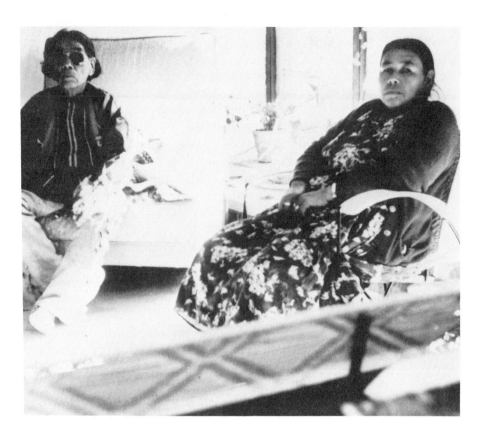

Chief Papícoano and his wife in the Latorres' home in Múzquiz.

Bear oil is highly regarded for keeping the hair lustrous and preventing baldness, but many now use such commercial products as Brilliantine. Formerly, they used the raw medulla extracted from deer bones to make the hair lustrous. One never sees a bald Kickapoo. Could it be because of the use of bear oil? When Dr. Mark R. Harrington visited the village in 1910 he observed only one bald Kickapoo, whom he described as a novelty.[1]

The traditional woman's dress of today, consisting of a flounced skirt and a loose overblouse of printed or solid cotton, is seen much more than the man's traditional clothing. This dress was probably copied from that of the American pioneer women of the nineteenth century.[2] Several changes have taken place in the woman's dress in the past few years, such as the elimination of the shawl collar on the blouse, formerly adorned with many German-silver brooches. Also gone is the beaded headband to encase the single braid, the German-silver comb worn on the back of the head, and the many strings of beads worn around the neck. The blouse and skirt are now embellished only with rickrack of a

Kickapoo man.

matching or contrasting color. The skirt is made with two to four flounces, while before it had only one flounce at the bottom.

For adornment, the women wear a single choker-type string of beads around the neck; German-silver bracelets, usually in pairs; earrings, brooches, and rings of the five-and-ten-cent-store variety. The older women pin one or two large safety pins on their blouses for use in an emergency—for instance, to remove a thorn or replace a loose button.

The women display as much variety in footgear as the older men do in clothing. They may be seen in moccasins of their own making, moccasins made by Indians from the United States, oxfords, loafers, tennis shoes, slippers, or boots. They are particularly fond of wearing long wool stockings in bright solid colors or argyle plaids during the cold months, but they go barelegged in the summer.

In warm clothing they show as much variety as in footwear. One sees sweaters, plastic and leather jackets, short car coats, occasionally a long coat; and sometimes the older women bring out their Pendleton blankets

Kickapoo woman.

during inclement weather. Old faded skirts are used for petticoats, and a few women wear brassières, called *chicheros* from the Mexican use of the word *chiche* for "breast." Usually they wear nothing on their heads, except in extremely cold weather, when they place a silk scarf over their hair, tied under the chin. The women are totally unconcerned about matching their clothes, and sometimes this attitude results in unique and bizarre combinations.

Although handbags are becoming popular among the women, most are seen carrying Mexican istle satchels or the newer plastic versions which are lighter in weight. But by far the most favored place to carry valuables is in the bosom. One of our informants regularly kept us in suspense while she dug down into her ample bosom, from which she extracted prized miscellany. This, of course, is where the women keep the protective Solomon's-seal rhizome.

Some women, who have become acculturated to Mexican or Anglo ways, discard the two-piece dress and wear the type of clothing used by Mexican or Anglo women of their economic class. One day, one of these

Woman wearing a Pendleton blanket, at the Latorres' home in Múzquiz.

women, who had just returned from the United States, came to call on us for the first time. We took her for a Mexican until she spoke, for she was dressed in a tightly fitting pink cotton dress, nylon stockings, and white kid slippers. She was using lipstick and nail polish, and her hair, very kinky from a permanent, hung to her shoulders. A few weeks later, the same woman returned; we hardly recognized her as the former visitor. It had taken only a few days in the village for her to revert to the acceptable dress of a woman her age. This time she was wearing the two-piece flounced dress, with her hair pulled back from her forehead and caught in a single braid. There was no sign of lipstick or nail polish.

Younger women often combine store-bought blouses with homemade flounced skirts, over which they wear sweaters and cardigans; others dress like Mexican or Anglo girls of comparable age and economic class. Some of the more daring wear capri pants, jeans, or short skirts and boots, with their hair in the latest fashion after having been set in plastic curlers.

The usual style of hairdo is a long braid down the back, tied at the end

Kickapoo girl.

Small girl.

One of the chief's daughters, very "mod."

with a narrow ribbon. Some of the women have permanents and even dye their hair. One informant, developing a becoming streak of white hair on the top of her head, asked us to bring her some dye from Texas. After we told her that many Anglo women paid several dollars to achieve the same effect artificially, she never renewed the subject.

One still sees some small girls wearing the old-style dress, as well as the topknot formerly worn up to the time of the menarche. The dress consists of a tight-fitting bodice, buttoned down the back, attached to a long, full skirt. Boots, about eight inches high, the lower part made from buckskin and the uppers from fawnskin, buttoned down the back, were worn with this dress. These boots are no longer seen. Most of the little girls now wear store-bought Mexican or Anglo clothes, but some mothers make them two-piece dresses, replicas of those worn by older women.

Although the infants are now clothed with rubber pants, corduroy playsuits, and other modern articles, one old item is not forgotten. Each infant, until he is able to walk, wears a pair of buckskin moccasins with a hole in each sole. This is done to show the spirit of a deceased person, wandering about the village before being dispatched to the hereafter, that the child is inadequately shod to accompany him on the journey the spirit will make.

The women gather many pounds of *chilepiquín* in the fall to sell on the market. For this task they have a special dress, consisting of a bodice sewed to a full skirt without flounces. The skirt is pulled up toward the body and secured with safety pins on each side, thus forming an ample bag in which the chilies, stems, and leaves are deposited.

Until the Kickapoos began going to the United States to work, the woman's most prized technological possession was her treadle sewing machine, with which she made all of her clothes and those of her family. Women continue to make their own and the children's garments; but, with the exception of the man's traditional frontier-style shirt, all of the men's and boys' clothing is store-bought.

The majority of the Kickapoos are clean, with well-groomed hair and neat clothes, but the few who are filthy seem to linger in one's memory to the detriment of those by whom one's senses were not offended. The Indians rationalize the few cases of disregard for bodily cleanliness by pointing out that the culprits are descendants of the Comanches. They say, "What can you expect—they are Comanches!" When it is pointed out to them that one member of a Comanche family may be dirty while another is clean, they conclude that it boils down to individual differences.

The Kickapoos bathe frequently, specifically prior to the numerous ceremonies throughout the year. Women finishing their menses and parturient women must bathe before returning to the cattail-covered house.

On one occasion, having spent the night in the village, when we were called by our hostess to the cook house for hot coffee in the morning, she pointed out an unforgettable sight. The day was just beginning to break, but through the interstices of the walls, we discerned the figure of Chief Papícoano, passing in the lane with his inimitable limp. He was returning from the river, wearing only his Kickapoo-style shirt, reaching halfway down the upper leg, followed by his wife, carrying towels and clothing.

The Kickapoos bathe in the river while partly dressed; they dry and change into clean garments by clever legerdemain, never exposing themselves to others. Their modesty equals that of the Puritans. The water from the springs is tepid and, in winter, warmer than the surrounding air. They say that only full-blooded Indians can tolerate bathing in the river during the winter. Half-breed children are bathed indoors at this time to prevent their catching a cold. If the weather is unusually inclement, adults heat water in the cook house in galvanized wash tubs and bathe indoors. Children are frequently bathed in this manner, winter and summer.

When we first became acquainted with the Indians, the word quickly spread that we had a guest bathroom in which baths, including free soap, towels, and plenty of hot water, were available. One day Chief Papícoano sent his aide to call on us; and, as we had chatted lengthily, well past the lunch hour, we invited our guest to join us, euphemistically inquiring whether he did not wish to wash his hands in the bathroom. Upon assuring himself that we had hot water, soap, and towels, he stuck his head out of the bathroom and stated nonchalantly, "I will take a bath." Half an hour later, when he had not reappeared, we became concerned, fearing we had offended him by implying that he should bathe before sitting down to a meal with us. But when he emerged from the bathroom to join us and we explained our euphemism, his casual answer was, "No, you did not offend; the chance of a hot bath presented itself and I took it."

The Kickapoos suffer from bad teeth, like others of their economic class. Few brush their teeth; they merely wash out their mouths or use a homemade toothpick.

The women, in particular, suffer in the winter from chapped hands, with deep cracks that become infected, and, because they use no lipstick, from chapped lips. The hands are primarily damaged while cleaning the cattails, whose razor-sharp edges cause numerous cuts. To relieve the chapped hands, they use cooking lard, and, for the lips, mentholatum.

Because the Kickapoos spend much of their time, especially in the winter, around an open wood fire, their clothes, bodies, and hair become impregnated with the smoke, causing them to have a characteristic odor. Unless offensive body odor is also present, the smokiness is not unpleasant after one becomes accustomed to it.

By far the most disagreeable sight is the runny noses of the children, which are seldom wiped and, in winter, seem to run like open hydrants. When impetigo sores, frequently seen on children whose mothers exercise little care in cleanliness, are added to a runny nose, it takes will power not to pass out paper handkerchiefs.

The Kickapoos consider long hair and plumpness a sign of beauty for women. Reinforced by this belief and unconscious of the dangers of obesity, women, after they begin to have children, gain excessive weight, some tipping the scales at 250 pounds.

Chapter 7

Economy

Income

When the French met the Kickapoos they were living in southern Wisconsin among the Menomini and Winnebago, having been driven there from Michigan, along with the Sauk, Fox, and Potawatomi, by the Iroquois.[1] At this time, as for centuries earlier, the Kickapoos lived in permanent villages occupied during the summer. Their economy was based primarily on farming, hunting, and some fishing, augmented by the collection of wild rice, roots, berries, and nuts. The women, like the closely related Sauk and Fox women, cultivated corn, beans, and squash with a digging stick and a hoe made of wood, shell, or bone. The women and children also protected the crops from birds and harvested them, storing the surplus food in underground pits lined with bark.[2]

The men hunted deer, elk, bear, and such small game as beaver, squirrel, skunk, otter, and lynx, either with bows and arrows tipped with flint points or with snares, in the nearby deciduous forests during the summer. They fished with hooks made of bone or with nets and snares of woven fibers.

After the crops were harvested in early fall they began a three- to four-month-long hunting expedition into the prairies in search of buffalo.[3] All able-bodied persons went on the hunts, carrying the children along and leaving in the village only those too sick, old, or weak to travel the long distances on foot. The women were assigned to carry bedding and clothing on their backs, by means of headbands, to the location of the temporary shelters built during the hunting season.[4]

The usual method of killing the buffalo was to surround the herd with a ring of fire by igniting the dry prairie grass. An unfired opening was left in the ring; and, as the buffalo ran through the opening, as many as two hundred could be killed with bows and arrows in one day.[5] The meat, divided among the families, was thinly sliced by the women and smoked or sun-dried to preserve it. The skins were made into robes, trunks, and bedding.

The fur trade greatly altered the Kickapoo economy. While continuing their agricultural, hunting, and collecting pursuits, they increased the trapping of fur-bearing animals, whose pelts were traded to the French for such European goods as steel traps, knives, and scissors; iron fishhooks, hoes, and hatchets; flintlock guns; ammunition; cloth; beads; silver ornaments; ribbons; blankets; rum; brass pots for cooking; and brass to replace the Indians' flint points. The stone tools, the clay pottery, and the skin clothing were soon exchanged for the new imported French articles.[6] The watermelon, melon, apple, peach, and other European fruits were readily incorporated into the Kickapoo diet.[7]

The first account of the Kickapoos' coming into possession of the horse dates from 1801.[8] However, Peter Pond, a fur trader who traveled through the area where the Kickapoos were living on the Wisconsin River between 1765 and 1788, reported that the Sauk already had the horse by this time and added, "Sauk men often join war parties with other nations and go against the Indians on the Missouri and west of that. Sometime they go near San Fe, New Mexico and bring with them Spanish horses."[9] Although he did not include the Kickapoos, it is safe to assume that they also had the horse by this time, for they were neighbors of the Sauk.

In 1820, while Maj. Morrell Marston was U.S. Army commanding officer at Fort Armstrong, Illinois, he reported on the Sauk, Fox, and Kickapoos who had villages on the Rock River nearby:

> They leave their villages as soon as their corn, beans, etc., is ripe and taken care of, and their traders arrive and give out their credits . . . and go to their wintering grounds, it being previously determined on in council what particular ground each party shall hunt on. The old men, women, and children embark in canoes, the young men go by land with their horses; on their arrival they immediately commence their winter's hunt, which lasts about three months. Their traders follow them and establish themselves at convenient places in order to collect their dues and supply them with such goods as they need. In a favorable season most of these Indians are able not only to pay their traders, and will supply themselves and families with blankets, strouding, ammunition, etc., during the winter, but to leave considerable of the proceeds of their hunt on hand.[10]

The disturbances of the American Revolution forced a shift of the fur trade from the upper Great Lakes to the Far Northwest.[11] As the American colonists began to move westward and cut down the forests for farms, the game diminished or moved elsewhere. The economy of the Indians came to be dominated by the annuity payments for the lands they ceded to the Americans after the Treaty of Greenville.[12] Sometime after 1806 the Kickapoos began to split up. Some moved to the land allotted them in Kansas, others went to Missouri, and various groups moved to Texas, at that time Spanish territory.[13]

In 1852, when Capt. Randolph B. Marcy was exploring the basin of the upper Red River, he reported that

> A number of Delawares, Shawnees, and Kickapoos, from Missouri and the borders of Arkansas, have for several years past been engaged in a traffic with the prairie Indians, which has had a tendency to defeat the efforts of the military authorities in checking their depredations upon the citizens of the northern provinces of Mexico. These traders, after procuring from the whites an outfit of such articles as are suited to the wants of the prairie Indians, visit all the different bands, and prosecute a very lucrative business. The goods they carry out consist of a few articles of small value, such as tobacco, paint, knives, calico, wampum, beads, &c., &c., which are of the utmost importance to the Indians, and which, if necessary, they will make great sacrifices to procure; but as they have no commodity for exchange that the traders desire except horses and mules, they must necessarily give these for goods, and large numbers are annually disposed of in this manner.[14]

As can be seen from the events described above, in a period of less than two hundred years the Kickapoos had greatly expanded their range of economic activities, progressing from trading with the French, to living on annuities from the Americans, to trading with the prairie Indians, while maintaining their original agricultural-hunting economy in addition. When they arrived in Mexico each head of a household had from one to two hundred horses and mules. These were sold or traded and were the tribe's largest source of income. The Kickapoos were not averse to adding stolen cattle and horses or catching mustang ponies to increase their herds.

When they settled in their present village in the 1860's, parcels of irrigable farm land were allotted to the heads of households. These sufficed to provide the families with crops of corn, beans, squash, watermelon, and melons. From their Negro neighbors they acquired a taste for sweet potatoes and sugar cane, which they also raised; but they did not build sugar mills, preferring to take their cane to the Negro village, where syrup and *piloncillo* (brown sugar cones) were made. Game of all kinds was abundant, including several varieties of fish, which the youths killed with bows and arrows.

The provisions they needed to buy in Múzquiz or from itinerant peddlers were few: coffee, tea, rice, wheat flour, tobacco, and mescal. Their taste for European goods continued in Mexico, where they bought, or traded pelts and skins for, guns and ammunition, steel traps, knives, scissors, iron cooking utensils, plowshares, hatchets, axes, and tools for wood carving. The women bought calico, ribbons, blankets, and sheeting; but buckskin leggings, children's winter boots of fawn skin, and moccasins continued to be made and used.

In Mexico the Kickapoos established the same routine they had known when they lived along the upper Great Lakes, staying in the village in their summer houses during the time the crops needed attention, while availing themselves of nearby game for food and pelts; then spreading out by families in various directions for the annual hunts in the late autumn and early winter.

This nearly idyllic state of affairs continued until David Harkness McKellar fenced La Mariposa hacienda adjoining the Kickapoo grant.[15] Fencing at first was no obstacle to the wide-ranging Kickapoos during their annual hunts, for many of the ranchers were indebted to them for locating water holes or springs and, when deer were abundant, especially in the dry years, were glad to have them killed to preserve the pasture for the cattle. Nevertheless, the fencing of the McKellar hacienda was the beginning of the decline of the great hunts, the Kickapoos' main source of meat, skins, and pelts.

Whereas ranchers previously had raised the half-wild Longhorns, by 1900 Shorthorn cattle were introduced, followed by Herefords, both necessitating better and safer fencing.

The year 1907 saw the first tick-control program begun by Messrs. Jennings, Moore, and Blocker at the ranch of El Conejo. Other dipping vats were built from 1913 to 1915, and the ranches adjoining the Kickapoo land built them in the 1920's.[16] This program greatly affected the Kickapoos' hunting. Ranchers, after this, did not permit the entry of horses unless they had been dipped. Access to ranches was limited to three or four Kickapoo hunters to whom the ranchers were indebted and who were willing to dip their horses in the ranchers' vats.

Until the 1930's, although the Mexican Revolution damaged their village and fields, the influenza epidemic of 1918 decimated their number, and the tick-control program limited their hunting more and more, the Kickapoos continued to live fairly comfortably.

One Mexican informant, descendant of a half-breed Negro woman from the adjoining grant, remembered that when he was a lad during the early 1930's he often accompanied his mother to the Kickapoo village on her weekly trip to peddle tamales and sweet-potato pies. At this time, the Kickapoos were exceedingly hospitable and generous to anyone who arrived in the village, whether Mexican, Negro, or Anglo. Visitors were immediately invited to partake of a meal, if one was being served, and no visitor left empty-handed. All were given pumpkins, corn, venison or bear meat, and pecans, of which the Kickapoos had an abundance.

When Dr. Mark R. Harrington paid a visit to the Kickapoos in February, 1910, to collect specimens for the Heye Foundation's Museum of the American Indian in New York City, he found the Kickapoos overly generous with food. After calling on several Indians to buy specimens, each of whom served him a bowl of food, he returned to the wigwam where he was to spend the night, later recalling that "We came waddling in, full—almost to overflowing—with Kickapoo food."[17]

In the late thirties and forties, several events occurred which forced the Kickapoos to abandon their village each spring—not to participate in an annual hunting expedition, but to migrate to the United States in search of farm work. Although President Cárdenas had decreed that the Kickapoos must observe the closed season to avoid killing does and fawns, they continued to ignore the new law; thus, by 1940, they had exhausted all of the fauna on their land and much on the land that surrounded them.[18] The following president, Miguel Alemán, decreed stronger conservation laws and expanded both the federal police and the forest and game wardens, the first to control cattle rustling and the second to prevent the extermination of endangered flora and fauna.

For a few years after President Cárdenas's attempt to encourage the Indians to raise more wheat by providing the seed, some raised substantial crops, thus balancing the loss of income from venison, bear, and pelts. One man raised twenty-seven tons in 1945—the last large crop before the drought. Up to this time, many Mexicans went to the village to buy both wheat and corn for food and seed. Prior to the Cárdenas dotation, the Kickapoos had raised small crops of wheat and, when these were gathered, had hired out as families to harvest the crops of Mexican farmers, ranging from Zaragoza to San Blas, Coahuila. With the arrival of the threshing machine about this time, income from this labor came to an end, but the Indians continued to harvest corn crops and gather pecans for Mexican farmers.

Several of the men found work in Múzquiz and at the American Smelting and Refining Company zinc plant in Nueva Rosita; others worked as cowherds or shepherds. The women made baskets and moccasins, which they traded or sold, and cooked stems of the century plant to peddle on the streets.

In the mid-forties began a prolonged drought which lasted almost a decade. The water table fell so low that the springs no longer provided sufficient water to irrigate. To aggravate the situation, the American Smelting and Refining Company, in order to supply its plant and personnel with sufficient water, began taking it a few miles south of the village springs, draining the water table even more.[19]

Not long after Chief Papícoano began to rent Kickapoo land to small-time ranchers, also affected by the drought and seeking new pastures to save their herds, the Kickapoos realized that their land was quickly being overgrazed. This situation endangered their herds of horses, mules, and burros, which had fed on high grasses but were now forced to eat such desert plants as black-brush acacia, an unaccustomed forage that formed hard balls in their stomachs, resulting in death. The Kickapoo herds were decimated.

It was during the decade of the 1940's that the first of the Kickapoos began seeking work as migrant laborers in Texas, since practically every other avenue of income had been closed to them: fencing, tick control, and the closed season on deer had put a serious limit to their supply of food and skins; the power threshers had robbed them of a more recently found source of income; the leasing of their land and the drought had killed off their herds and dried their fields. Again, the Kickapoos were faced by seemingly unsurmountable odds; but again, as before, they sought a solution.

Fortunately for the Kickapoos, the safe-conduct issued them by Major Whistler at Fort Dearborn could be used again, as we have seen. Both U.S. Immigration Service in Eagle Pass and the Mexican authorities in Piedras Negras allowed them access to either country, although legally they are Mexican citizens according to the terms under which, in 1850, land was first assigned them: "The individuals belonging to the mentioned tribes as well as others who may follow to establish themselves in the Republic will be considered Mexican citizens."[20]

With the paving of Mexican National Highway 57 in 1949, regular bus service was established between Múzquiz and Piedras Negras, giving the Kickapoos added mobility. As they acquired their own transportation, they spread in every direction throughout the United States, from Texas to Arizona, Oklahoma, Colorado, Wyoming, Idaho, Montana, Nebraska, Wisconsin, Michigan, Illinois, Ohio, California, and New York, following the seasonal crops.

In the following pages we shall describe the economic situation during the decade of the 1960's.[21]

Soon after the Kickapoos began to work as migrants, producers of beet sugar in Montana, cherry and apple growers in Utah, cucumber growers in Wisconsin, tomato growers in Indiana, and cotton growers in the Southwest, among others, began to seek out the Kickapoo workers by sending their contractors to the Texas Employment Commission in Eagle Pass or by going to the village, where the Indians were advanced funds for transportation and food. The demand for the Kickapoos increased as the introduction into the United States of Mexican *braceros* (farm laborers) became more restricted.

Since dealing with individual Kickapoos was difficult for employers because of the language barrier, little time was lost by the more astute Indians, who spoke better Spanish, in becoming contractors, each guaranteeing the growers a certain number of hands for the crops. In turn, the growers guaranteed the Kickapoo contractors a percentage on each basket of vegetables or fruit picked or row of beets thinned by individual workers. This percentage relieved the contractor of doing menial labor or added to his income if he was not above working like the others.

During the months of January and February, in the 1960's, a few single men were employed to irrigate spinach fields near Crystal City, Texas, owned by large packing companies which harvested by machinery. At the time of our study, the men were paid one dollar per hour, worked from eight to ten hours a day, and were covered by Social Security.

In late April, entire families traveled to Eagle Pass, where they set up flimsy camps under the International Bridge or rented substandard houses in the ghetto area of the city. Since the majority of families during the sixties availed themselves of some type of automobile, they commuted daily from Eagle Pass to Crystal City and surrounding towns for the onion harvest. Some of those who did not own cars paid their contractor a fee to transport them; others rode in company-owned buses. All children over four years old accompanied their parents and helped in the harvest, while grandmothers were left in charge of the infants and toddlers in camps or houses in Eagle Pass.

The contractors received two cents for each bushel of onions collected by their crew. In 1965, workers averaged seventeen cents per bushel, depending on the size of the onions. A man and wife could gather about one hundred bushels a day. Other onion growers paid the workers seventy-five cents per hour, but the Kickapoos preferred working by the job, frequently as a family enterprise, rather than by the hour. The onions, previously loosened from the ground by machinery, were gathered into piles by the children, while the parents cut off the roots and stems and put them into baskets.

Some of the Indians, particularly those who planted wheat and other crops on their land, preferred to work out of Eagle Pass the greater part of the year in the onion, spinach, carrot, string bean, tomato, lettuce, table beet, and melon crops, as this allowed them to make quick return trips to the village to supervise their crops.

One woman reported on a visit to her sister and her family, who were then staying in Eagle Pass while working in beet fields out of Crystal City. For those who did not have transportation, the growers provided bus service, departing from Eagle Pass at 5:00 A.M. The Indians worked ten hours a day, were provided with short-handled hoes to thin the beets, and were paid seventy cents per hour. Three Mexican-American overseers stood nearby all day, urging them to hurry and commenting on the quality of their work. They were allowed a short rest period to eat the lunch they carried with them. At 4:00 P.M., work came to a stop and they were returned to Eagle Pass, an hour's ride away. Our informant had earned seven dollars, but sixty cents was withheld for Social Security, although she got no receipt for the amount.

By the end of May, with the termination of the onion harvest in Texas, many of the Kickapoos would move on to Colorado, Wyoming, Utah, Montana, Idaho, Nebraska, and Minnesota to thin sugar beets. Employees of one company were provided with sparsely furnished camps with such modern comforts as electricity and butane gas. The majority of the women, however, were afraid of using the gas stoves and preferred cooking outdoors. Many asked that the bedsteads be removed and used their own bedrolls instead. The employers covered these workers with Social Security and gave them receipts.

This work lasted only a few weeks during May and June, depending on the weather. The Indians earned from $15 to $26 per acre for thinning beets, depending on the type of soil. One Indian told us that he and his wife and adolescent son were able to thin fifty-four acres in one month, earning $1,350 at the rate of $25 per acre.

In some years the Kickapoos arrived when snow was still on the ground, and before commencing work they went into debt to their employers; in other years, the rains were heavy and the ground was difficult to dig, thereby slowing the work.

After the beets had been thinned, some Kickapoos went to Provo, Utah, and surrounding cities for the cherry harvest; others moved on to Michigan and Wisconsin for the cucumber harvest or worked in the pickle factories; still others remained in Colorado to harvest onions, carrots, and bell peppers. The few who went to California to irrigate and harvest lettuce in Salinas and Montview were paid $1.80 per hour and were covered by Social Security.

The majority of the cherry orchards had machines to harvest the fruit, but the Indians were needed to sort and box it. The cherry harvest lasted only about three weeks. Some workers consumed their earnings while waiting two or three weeks for the harvests of pears, peaches, and apples which followed. At the end of the summer, they had little, if anything, to show for their labor. During the years when a late freeze nipped the buds and the crop was small, they went into debt.

One Kickapoo man and his family from Oklahoma spent the whole year working for the owner of a fruit orchard on the outskirts of Provo and returned to Oklahoma annually during his vacation, scheduled to coincide with the Kickapoo spring ceremonies.

Some of the fruit growers in Utah tried to convince their workers to stay during the whole year, but none of the Kickapoos from Mexico stayed away from the village after November, as they complained that the cold and snow were injurious to their health.

On a trip to the Pacific coast in 1968, we stopped in Provo to observe the type of living quarters provided for the workers. Each family was given one room in a long house. Conditions were crowded, and sanitation was at a minimum. The workers were receiving $1.25 per hour. In Utah, growers have helped the Indians with health problems, specifically tuberculosis.

In August many Kickapoos moved on to Indiana, Illinois, and Ohio for the tomato harvest, which in some years, depending on the weather, lasted until October. Each adult was given an allowance of ten dollars for travel from Mexico or elsewhere in the United States to the farms. The Indians averaged eighteen cents for a twenty-five-pound crate of tomatoes, while the contractor retained three cents per crate. A family of four adults was able to earn thirty-seven dollars a day. They were provided with sparsely furnished houses, gas stoves, electric refrigerators, and free utilities. One of the tomato growers provided a day nursery with young Kickapoo girls as attendants in order to free the mothers of young children to work, but all children old enough to pick tomatoes were employed.

After these crops were harvested, the Kickapoos, on their return home, stopped in Oklahoma and Texas for the pecan harvest or in Arizona, New Mexico, and Texas to pick cotton. In Texas they were paid four cents per pound of pecans if the trees had already been threshed by machine; if the pickers had to thresh the trees, they were paid ten cents per pound. An individual could gather between one and three hundred pounds of nuts, depending on the size, the variety, and the picker's agility. Cotton pickers in Texas received between $1.25 and $2.00 per hundred pounds of cotton. A steady and agile worker could pick as many as eight hundred pounds in one day.

Around June, some Kickapoos chopped cotton, for which they were paid seventy-five cents an hour; and some men worked in the gins during the harvest season. One blind youth earned ten dollars a day emptying cotton sacks.

One of the clan leaders, a highly respected and intelligent man, worked with his family on a farm in Texas during seven to eight months of the year. This farm produced wheat, sorghum, potatoes, lettuce, cabbage, carrots, chilies, and onions. The clan leader was also the overseer of the eight Mexican-American families who worked on the same farm. Each adult member of the families averaged around $1,200 per season. They were provided with two rooms per family, running water, electricity, and butane gas, but no sanitary provisions other than an outdoor privy; however, the owner had promised to improve housing and sanitary conditions.

The Indians had many complaints about the Mexican contractors and overseers. They said that the contractors advanced them money until they arrived at their jobs; but, once there, rather than being paid weekly, they had to wait until the season ended. In the meantime, the workers had to buy their provisions on credit at designated stores. At the end of the season they would find they had earned only a few dollars. They resented having the overseers stand nearby all day, not giving them a minute to rest or attend to their needs. Others complained that the scales were "fixed" and they were cheated out of ten to twenty pounds of cotton per sack.

By and large, the greatest source of income of the Kickapoos today is migrant labor, although by the end of the season much of the money has been spent on food, transportation, the purchase of automobiles, clothing, and sundry items to peddle in Mexico when their cash is exhausted.

The next source of income is derived from what the Indians call, in Spanish, *comerciar* (trading). The Kickapoos no longer trade pelts for necessities; nor do they trade cloth, utensils, and trinkets for horses as was observed by Marcy in 1852; but they do continue to trade. Today, with part of their earnings from migrant labor, they buy sewing machines, transistor radios, rifles, wrist watches, automobiles, costume jewelry, blankets, clothing, yard goods, and housewares. Then, as they need cash, they begin their trading expeditions to the surrounding ranches, *ejidos*, mining camps, and towns. As cash is not always readily available, they are often paid with chickens, food, corn, a small pig, or a goat. In the mines, where the workers are paid twice a month, the Kickapoos are paid in cash but sometimes prefer to trade a garment or other item of small value for a deer hide, which, when made into moccasins, can bring two or three times the value of the article traded. At other times, they trade an article for the privilege of killing a deer.

The Kickapoos are not allowed to take automobiles into Mexico from the United States on a permanent basis, but only for six months. Nevertheless, some Kickapoos have no scruples about selling a car if they find a Mexican buyer who can "fix" things with the authorities. Sometimes the Kickapoos trade an automobile for wheat seed or to settle a debt with a local merchant. Mexicans in and near Múzquiz often ask the Indians to bring them such items as transistor radios, car parts, sewing machines, and other articles difficult to get locally.

The third most important source of income for the Indians is the sale of wheat, oats, corn, beans, and squash or pumpkins in years when rainfall is sufficient to permit irrigation. In a good year, as many as two hundred hectares may be planted in wheat. Some of the Kickapoos plant their own wheat; others hire the one man who owns a tractor to plow, or use the communal tractor. Several employ Mexicans, with whom they share the crop, and others go halves with relatives who either have no land or are sufficiently ambitious to plant their own plots and those of others.

Since wheat is planted in the fall and harvested in April and early May, it is the one crop that can be planted, irrigated, and harvested during the months the Kickapoos are in the village or working in the harvests out of Eagle Pass, whose proximity permits them to return to supervise the threshing, now done by machine. In a good year those owning wheat can pay off their debts to local merchants. The merchants either harvest the wheat themselves or supervise the work in order to be paid first; consequently, little cash is received after the indebtedness is paid off.

If the prospects are good, corn, squash, and beans are planted. Corn is planted in March, April, May, or June, depending on the rainfall. Some years the Indians harvest enough to sell part, keep some for seed, and store the remainder for their use. Some of the squash is eaten while tender, and the remainder is allowed to ripen. The ripe squashes are stored on the floor in the kitchen for future use.

The four varieties of beans planted by the Kickapoos are *ojo de cabra* (nanny-goat-eye), a dark striped bean; a beige bean called *bayo* by the Mexicans; the pinto bean, the most favored by the Indians and the Mexicans in that area; and black-eyed peas, which the Kickapoos call beans. Since beans mature in sixty days, they may be planted as late as September if the rains have not been sufficient during the earlier planting season.

When the beans ripen, the entire plant is pulled out of the ground, allowed to dry in loosely made stacks, and threshed on a platform approximately ten feet long by five feet wide. The platform is built by sinking four crotched posts into the ground, leaving two feet above ground. The end posts are connected with saplings and tied with pita. Sotol scapes are laid lengthwise, resting on the connecting saplings at the ends and tied with pita, loosely enough that the center sags downward. A canvas is placed under the rack formed by the sotol scapes. The dried plants are spread on the rack and beaten with sticks until the beans separate and fall upon the canvas.

When a sharecropper is used, the Kickapoo entitled to the land provides the parcel of land and the water due each tract; the sharecropper plows the land with his team of mules, provides the seed, and harvests the crop. Other Kickapoos rent their tract of land outright to a relative or a Mexican who pays a fixed rate. Those who own teams of mules hire out to work on the irrigable parcels after finishing their planting. The man who owns the tractor also hires out to work for others; in the 1960's he charged $4.80 for a day's work, including the use of his machine.

Although raising stock, particularly horses, mules, and burros, formerly was an important source of income, today it is negligible, as a result of the ravages wrought by the drought, from which the Indians never recovered, and the introduction of the custom of renting out the land. Nonetheless, a few Kickapoos receive small incomes from the sale of animals.

After the arrival of the renters and the beginning of their annual trek as migrant workers, few of the Kickapoos made any effort to buy additional stock. One woman bought twenty head of cattle after selling an inherited allotment of land in Oklahoma in 1962. Another, a widow who had inherited money, bought fifteen head of cattle and five horses. She occasionally sells a steer, which brings her about fifty-six dollars. One of the blind men has a small herd of brood mares and sells one or two ponies each year for twenty to forty dollars. An old woman has a few goats, tended by a Mexican goatherd.

Although the majority of the Indians have resisted keeping hogs, chickens, and goats, little by little, more are finding that these animals can be a source of income. Some buy a small pig, fatten it with table scraps and corn, and, when in a pinch, sell it, as do many of the Mexicans.

Some of the women earn additional income by building winter houses for relatives who prolong their work in the United States. Other women receive pay for helping in the construction of houses or in mat-making. One particular woman, clever at both of these tasks, is often called upon to give a hand. She is not paid in money but is given lunch, several cups of coffee during the day, provisions, building materials, and mats for her house.

One couple—she is a Kickapoo and he is a Mexican—who do not work in the United States add to their income by constructing jacales for the Indians who want them, or by tending the houses and livestock of those who are away at work. For building a jacal, they are paid sixteen dollars. Sometimes they are paid in kind, receiving men's clothing, dress lengths, provisions, a transistor radio, ammunition, or the use of a team of mules to do their plowing and planting.

The same single woman who is adept at house building and mat-making also hires out as a cook and seamstress, making Kickapoo-style dresses for her peers and Mexican-style dresses to sell in Múzquiz. She receives from two to three dollars for each dress or is paid in kind, with provisions, a dress length, clothing, shoes, or stockings.

A number of Kickapoo curers, both men and women, are frequently called upon by their peers or by Mexicans to care for the sick. They receive either cash, if the patient is a Mexican, or the traditional Kickapoo gift of a dress length, unsewed moccasins, a blanket, or a kettle of stewed corn.

One of the jobs which the Kickapoos take seriously is that of *intépete* (from Spanish *intérprete*, "interpreter"). When an Indian who is unsure of his Spanish needs to deal with a Mexican, he calls on a relative or friend whom he judges to be more conversant with the language. It is often a case of the blind leading the blind, but the interpreter is considered indispensable. He is usually invited to a free lunch, a few beers, and a movie for his services.

There seems to be no limit to the lengths some of the women will go to earn a living. It is common knowledge that at least one of them was, in her heyday, a prostitute in *la zona de tolerancia* (the red-light district) near Múzquiz.

When the wild *chilepiquín* is ready to harvest in the late fall, women and children gather it by the hundreds of pounds. At the same time, they harvest wild oregano and pennyroyal. All of these are sold in Múzquiz and in the nearby cities, as well as in Eagle Pass, Texas. The women are paid $.80–$1.50 per kilo of chili. Some prefer to sell it from door to door, since this piecemeal transaction brings a better price. When a bumper crop is harvested, the price tumbles. In 1967, a particularly good year, the women sold their chili in Eagle Pass for $1.00 per pound at the beginning of the season; but, as the market became glutted, the price fell to half that.

After the chili, still on the stems, is gathered and taken home, the stems are broken into smaller units and placed on a canvas to dry in the sun. When dry, the stems are rubbed together to loosen the pods and, during a strong breeze, the chili is winnowed. The few remaining leaves and stems are picked off by hand and the chili is sunned until it is a brilliant red, ready to market.

The Kickapoos use peyote, not ceremoniously but for medicinal purposes. They also gather large quantities to sell to the Oklahoma Kickapoos and other Indians who practice the peyote cult. After the peyote is gathered, the root is severed, and the button is sliced and dried in the sun.

When deer were abundant, the women had a good income from the sale of moccasins and skins. These were either traded for provisions with local merchants or sold from house to house. The two saddlers in Múzquiz constituted a ready market for the skins. Many car owners bought them as a substitute for chamois. Moccasins sold to merchants brought from one to two dollars, and skins brought about five dollars in the 1960's.

During the dances and games of the adoption ceremony and the woman's and buffalo dances, one enterprising young man does a thriving business selling soda pop, popsicles, fruit, candy, and similar items, dispensed from his pickup. This same young man, who can best be described as a go-getter, has a small store supplied with a few necessities.

One bachelor who is partially blind has been granted begging permits from several municipalities in northern Coahuila. Throughout the year he dons his professional begging rags and goes from house to house, displaying his permits in glass frames. Although his pickings are slim, he accumulates a substantial amount by the end of the year, aided by the Mexican belief that a blind beggar must not be turned away, since the Almighty will bless those who are generous to such people. During the harvests out of Eagle Pass he gathers onions and string beans and picks cotton. While in the village he makes additional income by selling soda pop.

A number of Kickapoos have gone to Oklahoma, lured by welfare benefits. Several women with children discovered in the sixties that by placing their offspring in American schools they could receive from thirty to thirty-five dollars for each child and forty dollars toward rent. These women were also entitled to surplus commodity foods, such as milk, cornmeal, beans, rice, butter, flour, raisins, rolled oats, and peanut butter.

Fortunately for the Indians, many of their employers carry workmen's compensation. When a man pruning fruit trees with a power saw cut off the index and middle fingers of one hand, his employer's insurance covered the hospitalization and gave him $150 for his lay-off time and $56 weekly for five months, plus an additional lump sum.

Many of the Kickapoos have been given and carry Social Security cards, but they have no concept of their meaning, and none received benefits in Mexico during the period of our study. If they worked for an employer or company that withheld a part of their wages and issued them a receipt, they were apt to throw away the receipt without realizing its significance. We tried to explain the importance and value of Social Security and to report any instances of spurious withholding of wages to the Texas Employment Commission.

A number of the Kickapoos receive from a few dollars to several hundred as annual rent from the lease of their land allotments in Oklahoma and Kansas. Some are Kickapoos who were assigned the allotments while living in Oklahoma but later moved to Mexico, while others are first- and second-generation heirs. Some of the lease money is received directly from the renters, whose contracts are supervised by the Bureau of Indian Affairs; others, second- and third-generation heirs, receive their minuscule rent directly from the bureau.

Little by little, the Mexican Kickapoos are selling their allotments to Anglos, singly or with other heirs. One woman sold hers, inherited from her father, for twenty thousand dollars. A woman from Oklahoma sold her allotment and moved to Mexico to be near her father and her daughter by a former marriage. She had been a patient in a tuberculosis sanitarium for several years and continued to need medication. After the final payment, shortly after moving to Mexico, she was forced to seek work as a migrant laborer. This work worsened her condition until her Oklahoma relatives convinced her to return to receive medical aid and welfare.

Up to 1940, the U.S. consul in Piedras Negras annually took the oil-lease checks to the Kickapoos.[22] A few of the Indians continue to receive oil-lease checks, either singly or with other heirs. Only one check amounts to over one hundred dollars; the others are less than ten dollars each.

Income Received by Chief Papícoano from the Colonia (Original Land Grant)

Chief Papícoano began renting the land of the *colonia* to small-time Mexican ranchers in the thirties. In payment, the first renter gave the tribe forty rolls of barbed wire, with which they fenced some of the compounds. Once the word spread that the chief was willing to rent, ranchers who needed additional pasturage or who simply wished to exploit the rich lands of the Kickapoos appealed to the municipal authorities to influence the chief in their favor.

It was not long before there were ten renters, each with twenty to one hundred head of cattle and many goats and hogs. At first, the chief and his aide requested payment in Mexican pesos, but soon they got into arrears and asked for advances. The ranchers, counseled by officials of the Agrarian Department, began to pay in kind and, by way of explaining the change, told the Indians that in this way they could build up a herd of their own. Since the Kickapoos had never been interested in cattle, and certainly not in goats—preferring horses, mules, and burros, which require less vigilance—the animals received were soon sold.

The rental paid in 1956, according to an informant who was the *vigilante* (a post which required him to make a census of the stock owned by the renters), was five yearlings and seven mature goats for each hundred head of cattle or goats grazed on the land. That year the renters had seven hundred head of cattle on the Kickapoo land, and hundreds of goats. The chief's aide received one yearling from each renter for acting as negotiator and interpreter. Upon acquisition, the yearlings were branded with the chief's personal brand.

Although the chief occasionally spent some of the rental money for needed improvements in the *colonia* or to help a needy family, he used the greater portion for personal expenses. One year the chief and his aide sold stock amounting to $400, but it took much persuasion on the part of the Indians to convince them to share this income with other members of the tribe. Finally they distributed $120 among the eighty-two households in the village at that time.

As might be expected, this usurpation of income derived from communal land created many hard feelings. On one occasion the chief ordered one of the men to kill a yearling and distribute it among the families, but his aide rescinded the order. The village immediately divided into two factions: those who were relatives and friends of the aide and those who wanted to deal him his just rewards. The aide was almost killed by strangulation and was saved only by the assistance given him by the chief's mother-in-law. The aide took his case to the Múzquiz authorities, who jailed the assailant, thereby worsening a situation already electrically charged.

Older Kickapoos pleaded with their chief to evict the renters. At times, he vacillated between listening to them and to the renters—always supported by the municipal authorities and the agrarian officials. Some of the renters took the opportunity during these weak moments to offer themselves as sole renters if the others were evicted.

On the other hand, some of the Indians believed that the aging chief had the right to rent the *colonia* land, since he was too old to work and his position demanded unusual expenses; but they did expect him to share some of the income with the tribe and occasionally butcher an animal to distribute among them.

Chief Papícoano died in 1970, and his successor had not been named when we left Múzquiz in 1972. At that time the renters were still using the Kickapoo land. Further discussion of the Indians' problems with the renters will be found in the final section of Chapter 8.

Living Costs

The Kickapoos are spared many of the expenses common to others, such as property, school, and income taxes; utility bills; and fire, life, and automobile insurance. Since they lack such modern conveniences as piped gas, water, sewerage, telephone, electricity, and paved streets, they are spared the expense of these. Road and irrigation-ditch maintenance is performed under a communal plan, each individual contributing his time, energy, and tools for the benefit of the group. The concept of fire and life insurance is foreign to them; and, although they have acquired automobiles in greater numbers each year, none carry insurance on the vehicles. Church tithes may be considered analogous to the expenses incurred in performing and contributing to the many annual ceremonies.

Although it is impossible to ascertain the exact average income earned by a family during a year because of variation in many factors—the size of the family, the number of months spent working in the United States, and income from such other sources as land, livestock, trading, curing, etc., an average of $1,800 per year (between 1960 and 1970) is an approximate estimate.

The largest portion of this income is spent on food. Informants say that, although they earn "good money" while working, a large portion of it is spent on food. A couple needed about twenty dollars per week to buy supplies in the United States in the sixties. In Mexico, on the other hand, if a man could supplement his income by growing crops and could kill an occasional deer, he needed to spend no more than thirty dollars monthly during the same period.

The second largest item in the budget is the cost of constructing the houses, since, although these are so simple and functional that they can be built by the owners, the tribal dictates require that a new winter house be built yearly and that the summer house be refurbished annually and rebuilt every four years.

Today, more women are acquiring tables, chairs, butane-gas stoves, cupboards, iron bedsteads, and treadle sewing machines. Since none of these furnishings, except the sewing machine and one or two chairs, may be kept in the Kickapoo-style house, these women have simple, *soyate*-roofed jacales built to house their new treasures. This entails the cost of an additional house but is compensated by the fact that a jacal has a relative degree of permanence and is more burglarproof.

Soon after returning to Mexico in the late fall, the most urgent task facing the women is the gathering of cattails before the first freeze blights them. The cost of this trip averaged between forty and fifty dollars per woman in the sixties. As soon as the cattail mats have been made and stored, the women go to the *monte* and sierra to cut saplings and pita for the construction of the winter wigwam. Unfortunately, the Kickapoos have exhausted the required timbers from their land and now have to buy them from nearby Mexican ranchers or surreptitiously invade the large ranches for them, risking arrest by the game and forest wardens. In the sixties, by the time a woman occupied her winter house and held her house dedication ceremony, she had spent around eighty dollars.

In the spring, before going to work, when funds are at their lowest, she must take down the winter house and refurbish or rebuild her summer house. The one-seed juniper required for this house has also been exhausted in the Kickapoo territory and must be purchased elsewhere or secured by invading neighboring ranches.

The third largest bite out of Kickapoo income is the cost of a pickup and its maintenance. Of the 121 males over sixteen years of age in 1968, 50 had purchased automobiles; of the 110 females over sixteen, only 2 owned cars. The majority of the Indians buy used pickups, which cost from one to several hundred dollars. Usually, their employers help them to finance the vehicles, which, relatively speaking, guarantee the return of the buyers to the employer's farm or orchard the following year.

When purchasing a vehicle, a Kickapoo buys the license plate of the state in which the sale is made, but he obtains his driver's license in Múzquiz, where no test is required. Before returning to their jobs in the spring, the Indians request one of their employers to send them new license plates and charge these to their future income.

Having had little experience with automobiles, the Indians are frequently sold cars needing continuous repairs—a constant drain on their limited income. For this reason, a car owner often disposes of his vehicle. One Indian, asked why he had not bought a car while working, replied, "Why would I want two women? I have enough expense with one!"

Anxious to continue enjoying their mobility, the Kickapoos are learning to repair their cars rather than give them up. On a visit to the village one sees young men tinkering with cars. One youth removed a radiator when it developed a leak and took it to Múzquiz to be repaired. But, when it is necessary to have a major repair done by a local mechanic and the owner is low on funds, he is compelled to ask one of his employers for a loan, again charging this to future wages.

Gasoline and oil, which in the sixties cost approximately the same in Mexico as in Texas, are a constant drain on income, because of the distance between the village and Múzquiz, to which the Kickapoos go several times a week. At other times, they go a hundred miles or more on hunts or trading expeditions.

Many of the Indians still have to avail themselves of public transportation, which, luckily, is cheap in Mexico. The women who rode the train in a third-class car to Cuatrociénegas to gather cattails paid two dollars for a round-trip ticket in the sixties. The bus trip to the village from Múzquiz cost forty cents in 1961 but had doubled by 1970. The most expensive type of transportation is the taxi. When the Kickapoos had money and were anxious to arrive home, rather than wait for a bus, they had no compunction about spending twelve dollars for a taxi from Piedras Negras to Múzquiz, a distance of one hundred miles. If, upon their arrival in Múzquiz, no bus was available, they paid another taxi to take them to the village for an additional six dollars.

Although the Kickapoos pay no tithes, the ceremonies they are obligated to hold are a steady drain on their income, especially if an adoption ceremony is on their calendar. The cost of this ceremony may run as high as one hundred dollars for food. In addition, they have the expense of several dress lengths and special gifts for the person representing the deceased. The New Year clan festivals call for all new clothing and a contribution of food. Each of the smaller ceremonies, including arrival, departure, the triannual feast for the dead, house dedication, and many others, calls for a feast for the guests. The Kickapoos who work in the United States and are unable to go to Oklahoma or return to the village during the time of the summer feast for the dead send money to a relative at either location to hold the ceremony for them, since it is taboo to observe this ceremony in a non-Kickapoo house.

At the time of our study, a physician usually charged $1.50 for an office visit and prescribed several medicines to be bought at the drugstore next to his office. The fee for delivery of a baby in the local hospital with a two-day stay was $30.00. Setting a broken arm or leg bone cost the same amount, and a blood transfusion from a professional donor amounted to $20.00, plus an additional $9.00 for the equipment. The cost of a laboratory blood and urine analysis was $3.50, and blood serum was $.40 a liter. The biggest medical bargain in Múzquiz was the cost of an injection done by the local male nurse with the approval of the city physicians. He would go to the patient's house for a fee of twenty-five cents.

The fees charged for medical services in Mexico are low in comparison with those paid in the United States. One young man paid a fee of $160 for the delivery of his child in a Colorado hospital while a woman whose family was slightly injured in a car accident was presented with a bill for $500 by the clinic where her family was treated. A number of the Indians are taking advantage of the public-health hospitals in Oklahoma to have their teeth extracted and replaced with dentures. For this service they paid $85 in the sixties.

Although modern medical care in Mexico is cheaper than in the United States, it is still high in comparison with the cost of a visit to a Mexican *curandero* (curer) or *componedor* (folk chiropractor), who charges no fixed fee—the patient paying what he can afford. The usual contribution was eighty cents at the time of our study. Some of the *curanderos* accept food, clothing, or an imported item in payment for their services. If herbal teas are prescribed, the additional cost is slight; but if the *curandero* prescribes drugs, the bill may run into several dollars.

Clothing among the older Kickapoo men is not a costly item, since they wear only work clothes, blue jeans or khakis. The older women make the greater part of their clothes, but they either buy or secure used coats, sweaters, and shoes.

Among the younger Kickapoos, both men and women, clothing becomes a more serious expense, for the young men like to wear cowboy-style boots and hats, with jeans and jackets to complement them, while the young women follow the latest fashions worn by the Mexican or Anglo girls. Mothers make the greater part of their children's clothing but spend substantial amounts on coats, sweaters, and shoes.

The Kickapoos have adopted a number of Mexican amusements, which occupy many hours of their time and often prove expensive. Practically all adult Kickapoos and many youths enjoy playing *paco largo* and *paco chico*, two varieties of poker played with Mexican cards. Stakes may run high in this game; sometimes as much as twenty dollars may be lost or won in an evening. If the players become enthusiastic and wish to continue the game after their currency is exhausted, they gamble clothing, jewelry, guns, watches, knives, transistor radios, and ammunition.

Now that parental supervision has weakened and many young people have automobiles, they enjoy going to the Negro village to dance in the Mexican style. Whenever the local schoolteacher plans a carnival to raise money for a school project, she sends special invitations to the young Kickapoos, who flock to the dances and are lavish spenders.

When the Kickapoos go into Múzquiz, the men who drink immediately go to their favorite saloon, where only men are allowed. If the women wish to get a beer, they go to a café or restaurant, or buy beer through the side door of a saloon. Some of the heavy drinkers go on three- or four-day sprees and dissipate a large part of their earnings. After a drinking session, some of the men go to the *zona de tolerancia*.

The Kickapoos keep themselves informed of the Mexican holidays by transistor radio and appear in Múzquiz in large numbers for any celebration. They enjoy parades, speeches, buntings, dances, rodeos, bullfights, and crowds as much as the Mexicans. The plaza on these occasions is abuzz with local people and visitors from the ranches, mines, and farms, all strolling, seeing and being seen, stopping at the refreshment stands, and chatting with friends and acquaintances.

On ordinary weekends when they go to Múzquiz to do their marketing and trading, the Indians usually end the evening at one of the local open-air movie houses, which cost them sixteen cents in the sixties. The movies, usually second or third rate, deal primarily with Indians and cowboys, a subject that the Kickapoos thoroughly enjoy.

Many of the Indians own transistor radios. They enjoy listening to the local news and particularly to the cowboy songs of northern Mexico. Some of the younger Kickapoos buy cameras in the United States and are seen strolling on the plaza or streets of Múzquiz with a camera flung over the shoulder and a transistor radio in one hand.

For the Kickapoos who had to stay overnight in Múzquiz during the 1960's, there was a small hostelry consisting of six rooms with one outdoor cold-water shower and toilet. They were allowed to park their vehicles in the yard and camp free of charge. For the more affluent, a room containing a double bed and mattress, but no bedding, was available for one dollar per person. Those who wished to prepare their food in the yard could do so, and there were several restaurants and cafés where a meal could be had for fifty cents.

Banking

Illiteracy, combined with a general distrust of any impersonal institution, makes modern banking too difficult for most Kickapoos to handle; nonetheless, they do engage in certain aspects of banking, such as loans and deposits of money on a personal basis.

Fabila wrote that when he visited the Kickapoos in 1940 there were several "rich" Indians among them who lent money at exorbitant rates.[23] Interest in Múzquiz in the sixties was high, ranging from 8 to 36 percent per annum. The smaller the loan and the shorter the term, the higher the rate of interest. During the past three decades, the chief's aide who handled the rental income from the *colonia* also lent money to the Kickapoos, in case of emergency or illness. In Múzquiz, several merchants in the past have been moneylenders to the Indians, including, at one time, the owner of a store at which the checks for land and oil leases arrived. Before delivering the money to the owners, the storekeeper withheld the amount they owed him. More recently, two merchants lent money to the Indians or allowed them to charge provisions; but after suffering numerous losses, they decided to lend to or allow to charge only those who planted wheat with the understanding that the merchants would thresh the crop and withhold an amount of wheat equal to the debt owed them. These same merchants were also custodians of the earnings of many of the Indians, who, unable to bank, sent their savings to them for safekeeping.

One Mexican farmer who lived near the Indians told us that he was owed over two hundred dollars that he had lent to some Indians in small amounts and that he never expected to collect any of these debts. In view of the risk involved, he had long ago stopped making loans.

As noted earlier, the Kickapoos today depend almost totally on advances from their employers to tide them over from one work season to the other. The employers do not charge them interest, as it is to the latters' advantage that the Indians return to work the following season.

Some of the employers also keep in custody part of the Indians' wages and release them as requested by the worker. This is particularly helpful to those who are heavy drinkers, since a lump sum of money at the end of the work season would soon be dissipated in the saloons.

Many Kickapoos are inveterate borrowers, and during the first year of our work we fell victim to several hard-luck stories. They generally employ a borrowing technique which we learned to recognize early. A man we had never seen before would come to the house, praising our goodness while being friendly and talkative. He would then begin to extol his own virtues—particularly his honesty—and tell how much he earned in the United States and the amounts he sent the local merchants to whom he had charged his provisions. After this build-up he would ask for our address, to send us money for safekeeping while he was working. Then the final hook was cast: could he borrow twenty-five dollars to cover expenses for traveling to his job?

The majority of the Indians paid their debts as soon as they had cash, and others sent money during their periods of work. Others gradually paid, a few pesos at a time; the women brought moccasins or artifacts until they had canceled the small debt. Some loans, however, were a total loss, for we never again saw the borrowers.

A number of the Kickapoos sent us checks during their working season to be kept in our custody until their return. These were mainly from women who wanted to have cash on hand with which to cover the expenses of building the winter houses. Heavy drinkers sent money to be kept for them, asking us to release specified amounts per month. Others, still wary of banks and afraid of thievery in the village, preferred to have us keep their savings or rental money, requesting small amounts on weekends to do their marketing.

For many we exchanged dollars at the official rate of 12 ½ pesos for one

U.S. dollar. As this rate was better than that given at the banks, the Indians came to our house for this service.

We helped three Kickapoos open savings accounts in a local bank, where they earned 4½% per annum. One enterprising young man told us that he had a savings account of several hundred dollars in an Eagle Pass bank. Another young man borrowed two hundred dollars from a local bank, after asking a Mexican friend to underwrite him, to finish construction of the first modern Mexican house in the village.

Some of those who had exhausted the privilege of loans from the local merchants and from us hit upon a gimmick that soon got out of hand. One young man, of whom we were fond but who had been a poor risk, one day brought his .30–.30 carbine, on which he wanted to borrow sixteen dollars in order to cover the traveling expenses to his job. We weakened, aware of the sacrifice he was making in denying himself the use of such a prized possession.

Soon we were established in the pawnshop business, much against our will and better judgment. As the word spread, others brought more guns, transistor radios, new auto accessories, electric irons, and other gadgets bought to sell to the Mexicans. The one closet in the house with a lock soon began to look like an arsenal.

Our new "business" was not all easy sailing, however. One Indian outwitted us by bringing his gun, on which he borrowed sixteen dollars, retrieving it several months later and substituting another in its place. A few days later we learned from a close relative that the substituted gun, belonging to a grandson of his father's by another marriage, had been "borrowed." Although he had committed a breach of Kickapoo ethics, he seemed to feel no guilt. It was several years before we were relieved of the "borrowed" gun, and then only after writing the Indian a registered letter, notifying him that the gun would be sold for the indebtedness unless he retrieved it.

Another Indian also left his gun in pawn. Months later he came to ask for it to go hunting, promising faithfully to return it to our safekeeping as soon as he had bagged a deer.

Chapter 8

Political and Legal Organization

The Tribal System

Chief Papícoano, who died on February 20, 1970, at the approximate age of eighty-seven, was the third hereditary leader of the Kickapoo tribe in Mexico. The past three chiefs have belonged to the Water clan, and it was thought at the time of our study that the chief must be a member of this clan; however, Chief Papícoano's son and successor belongs to the Buffalo clan.

Chief Papícoano had the title of *capitán* and was recognized by his people and the Mexican authorities as the civil, political, and religious leader of the Kickapoo tribe. He and his aide received a monthly salary of two hundred pesos for performing the duties of peace officers in the village. They were the official representatives of the Kickapoos at Mexican government functions, the aide serving on these occasions as interpreter for the chief. During prolonged absences of the chief, authority to replace him was transferred in writing to his aide.

The death of Chief Papícoano posed a problem for the tribe, as his son, who was only twenty years old at the time of the chief's death, was not immediately recognized as chief by the authorities in Mexico City because he was one year short of legal age. Since he had been spending the greater part of the year working in Oklahoma, he had had little time for learning the ceremonies performed by the chief. This situation caused considerable speculation as to who would assume the role of chief. Chief Papícoano had two living daughters in Oklahoma who would have been eligible to be chief but wanted nothing of it. In the village lived a crossniece who also qualified.

For a woman to be chief of the Kickapoos would not be as strange as it may seem, for in 1901 the Kickapoos in Indian Territory were governed by two chiefs, one a man and the other a woman whose name was Wahpahhoko, under whom the jealousies within the tribe were reconciled. The Indian agent said of her, "While she is doubtlessly the only woman Chief in America, yet she rules her people with an iron hand and is a woman of great determination; her wish and will are absolutely irrevocable, though her actions are usually founded after mature deliberation."[1] One of the men living in the village claimed that this woman was his grandmother and was in Remolino during the Mackenzie raid in 1873. She could have been the chief in Mexico had she not returned to Oklahoma after the raid.

According to information we received after leaving Múzquiz, Chief Papícoano's son was eventually accepted as chief and in 1972 was going through a period of training to learn the chief's ceremonies. Menaquah, the leader of the Berry clan, was performing the ceremonies for him during the training period.

In addition to performing many religious ceremonies, the chief judges and pronounces sentences among his people for minor offenses, such as drunkenness, marital difficulties, family quarrels, and water and land disputes.

Minor disagreements between the Kickapoos and the Mexicans in the village or nearby are handled by a Mexican Justice of the Peace who resides in the vicinity of the Negro village. Such crimes as murder, robbery, and cattle rustling and some marital problems, specifically those involving property or distribution of money, are handled by the Mexican authorities in Múzquiz. Brushes with the federal game wardens are assigned to courts in Monclova and Saltillo.

The statement by Ritzenthaler and Peterson that the chief had the authority to distribute land to newcomers[2] lacks foundation. According to the presidential decree of September 21, 1938,[3] there are only 506.12 hectares of irrigable land, all distributed to the families who came to the village before the turn of the century. Newcomers who want to plant must either rent land held by the old families, marry those holding land, or act as sharecroppers with those who already have land.

Neither is the chief legally entitled to rent any part of the land to outsiders or to sell the natural resources of the land, according to the above-mentioned decree. Failure to comply with this regulation jeopardizes the ownership of the land. The Código Agrario (Agrarian Code) also strictly prohibits the renting of the land.[4]

The renting of the pastures came about through the manipulation of the local Mexican authorities, who, petitioned by Mexican ranchers seeking new grazing land, prevailed upon the chief to rent. Today, the Indians' land is overrun by the renters' stock, leaving little pasturage for the Kickapoos' own livestock.

Although the chief had been responsible for leasing the Kickapoo land to Mexican ranchers, much to the annoyance of his people, and although they were aware that he had misappropriated rental funds, seldom sharing any with those in need or making much-needed improvements in the village, the Kickapoos showed an almost reverential respect and loyalty toward him and believed that, upon his death, irremediable disaster would befall them and the world. Chief Papícoano was extremely reactionary, tenaciously adhering to the old beliefs and keeping himself and his people as far away from the current stream of change as possible.

The Council of Elders seldom functioned after 1938 because of the bitter disagreement over renting the land. Formerly, when the council was functioning, its primary obligation was to meet with the chief to deliberate on tribal matters. A secondary obligation was that of policing the village. The council, appointed by the chief's aide, consisted of the leaders of the four main clans and an assistant from each. Among them were secret police, whose identity was unknown to the villagers, but who reported to their colleagues any misconduct that took place. The old people say that, when this group functioned, everything in the village ran smoothly and properly. One of the duties of the police was to act as disciplinarians to the young, who then were not permitted the liberties of today—especially the girls, who were not allowed out after dark.

Besides the Council of Elders and police, the village had a town crier, responsible to the chief and the elders, who went about the village announcing important events or news.

In the early thirties, young Mexican men began to slip into the village for trysts with Kickapoo girls. The chief's aide petitioned the authorities to prohibit this intrusion, but nothing came of his request. Four girls had liaisons with Mexicans in spite of the strict vigilance, including a daughter of the chief and two daughters of the police. The four were exiled from the village for several years.

After the Council of Elders police system ceased to function, disorders began to increase and discipline relaxed. Today, in lieu of their old system, the Kickapoos call upon either the police from Múzquiz or members of the local cavalry regiment to forestall any disturbances during night dances.

Political Relations with the Mexican Authorities

The Kickapoos revere President Benito Juárez, who they believe gave them their land grant. Actually, he only confirmed their ownership, as did President Venustiano Carranza later on. When President Cárdenas gave the Kickapoos an additional 4,335.28 hectares, they transferred part of their reverence and devotion to him.

At the time of our study, the Múzquiz authorities regularly invited

Chief Papícoano and a few of the older men to the annual celebration of Flag Day, February 24. They were not, however, invited to the banquet held in conjunction with this celebration, attended by the municipal authorities, the high-ranking officers of the cavalry regiment, and the influential townspeople. The municipal authorities also invited the chief and a few older men, attired in Indian dress, to attend the annual celebration (on March 26) of the signing of the Plan de Guadalupe at the hacienda of that name, sixty miles east of Saltillo, Coahuila.

When the president or the governor arrives to inaugurate a library, a school, or the opening of a new *ejido* in the area, the Indians are sometimes asked to perform some of their dances—the Mexicans not understanding that the Kickapoo dances are meant for religious occasions.

The governors of Coahuila have been sympathetic to the Indians, granting them audiences and listening to their problems. Little has come from these talks, since any measure of reform tends to be dissipated in the course of its passage through a series of agencies. On repeated occasions, delegations of Indians have gone to Mexico City, seeking assistance for a project, justice regarding the renters, hunting permits, or clarification of their *ejido-colonia* status; but, again, these petitions have been diverted—more so since the death of President Cárdenas, who, even in retirement, had time to listen to the Indians' complaints.

Kickapoo Law and Justice

The Kickapoos are affected by two types of law and justice—that which they have evolved in their own culture and that of the surrounding culture, Mexican or American.

The Kickapoos conduct themselves according to a set of laws which they believe their ancestors received from the culture hero, Wisaka, who had obtained them from the Great Spirit, Kitzihiat. Punishment for breaking these rules is ultimately in the hands of the Great Spirit—making it more dreaded and uncertain—but the chief and the Council of Elders once had the authority to execute many specific punishments.

Heading the list of offenses to be avoided by the Kickapoos, according to seriousness, is suicide. It is believed that the suicide forfeits all hope of a future spiritual life. The second offense is the murder of a tribesman, followed by the murder of an Indian from another nation, and, finally, that of a Mexican. Formerly, the Council of Elders set the punishment for a murderer. In some cases, according to stories our informants had heard from their parents, a pit was dug in the ground, leaving the center unexcavated and higher than the ground around it. Four stakes were placed on the edge of the pit, and the extremities of the accused were tied to these with wet buckskin thongs, while his body, humped in the middle, faced downward. A rattlesnake was put in the pit. If the snake eventually left without biting the murderer, he was released; if the rattler bit him, that was penalty enough. A less severe punishment consisted of tying the murderer to a tree with his arms around it, forcing him to stand in this position from four to six days. The culprit was also obligated to pay the expenses of the adoption ceremony of his victim and to spend many hours in fasting and prayer to atone for his deed.

The Kickapoos no longer mete out punishment to murderers. Informants tell us that, as far back as they can recall, murder among them has been handled by the Múzquiz authorities, who, after a verdict by the local judge, send the culprit to the state penitentiary in Saltillo for a term of three to five years.

The degree of stigma attached to a murderer seems to depend on whether the victim was Indian or Mexican. One of the clan leaders, highly respected by the Indians, killed a Mexican who, in spite of numerous admonitions, continued to steal his horses. The Indian turned himself in, served his term in the state penitentiary, and returned to the village, where he spent many days fasting and praying to atone for his crime. He soon resumed his role in the village with no apparent loss of status. On the other hand, another Kickapoo, who killed one of his own (for pay, it is rumored), is hated by the entire village. Although this man participates in the ceremonies and is considered one of the best chanters, on occasion we have heard Kickapoos mutter under their breath, "Ese matón [that murderer]!" When he returned to the village after serving his time, he was advised by the chief to absent himself for a number of years to avoid revenge from the son of his victim.

Excessive drinking is much condemned. The worst punishment that can befall a drunkard is to be killed while under the influence of alcohol, for it is believed that his spirit stays in the place where he is killed and cannot be dispatched to the hereafter. Formerly, an inebriate who disturbed a ceremony was tied to a tree until he cooled off. Today, this punishment is no longer administered. In its place, the Múzquiz police or police from the cavalry regiment are called to keep order. This is a sufficient deterrent to keep drunkards at a respectable distance from a ceremony. If a drunkard discharges a gun, particularly inside a cattail-covered house, or injures another, he is tied up to prevent escape, and the Múzquiz police are called to arrest him and send him to the local jail, where he is confined for a few days on a diet of bread and water. If there are physical damages to another, he must pay the medical expenses.

Stealing, another serious offense, is not common among the Indians, probably because they give relatively little importance to material possessions and are all more or less on the same economic level. Formerly, stealing of livestock was punishable by the Kickapoo police, who whiplashed the culprit and forced him to return the animal or replace it.

Infidelity, considered a serious offense, is treated in Chapter 10.

A man or woman who abandons his or her spouse during a serious illness, particularly the last illness, is punished by the consanguine family of the deceased by their dispensing with the customary mourning period of the surviving spouse, thus depriving him or her of a new outfit of clothing and additional gifts of jewelry.

Although the Kickapoos believe that the Great Spirit will punish those who lie and gossip, we cannot truthfully say that they do not indulge in these most human frailties. The chief and the clan leaders in particular are supposed to refrain from gossiping and lying, for they, more than others, are subject to punishment. Once, when an old man—not a clan leader, but one who knew how to perform certain of the lesser ceremonies—became seriously ill, one of the clan leaders told us that this man's life had not been exemplary, as he had cheated, lied, and gossiped; now he was receiving his just deserts. When we asked if a curing ceremony would help, the clan leader replied that it would be of no avail, since the man was being punished by the Great Spirit.

Practicing or threatening witchcraft is believed to bring misfortune, as in the case of an old woman, suspected of being a witch, who threatened the members of her daughter-in-law's family after a quarrel between the daughter-in-law and the old woman's son. Shortly afterward, the old woman's house burned to the ground; it was only through the help of neighbors that her life was saved.

Although the Kickapoos have no established punishment for incest, anyone engaging in this act is considered by the others as a pariah and is subject to punishment by the supernatural in the form of a serious illness or a disaster affecting the village. Even a Mexican indulging in this act while living on Kickapoo land can bring bad luck. When a sharecropper, brother-in-law of one of the Kickapoo women, was surprised in *flagrante delicto* violating his fourteen-year-old daughter, the clan leaders were much distressed, expressing the opinion that this was the cause of the severe drought which had ruined their crops. Kitzihiat, the Great Spirit, was punishing the villagers.

One of the clan leaders married the daughter of the man he represented at the latter's adoption ceremony. This is considered an incestuous relationship, since, after the adoption ceremony, he should play the role of father to the daughters of the deceased. Since their marriage, it is pointed out, the couple has had a streak of bad luck. In the first place, they have not been blessed with children; and, second, on several occasions the husband has been in serious accidents which have brought him to death's door.

The Kickapoos have strict rules for conduct between relatives. A mother-in-law, although not avoided as in many other cultures, is treated with exceptional respect and is usually addressed through a third person. Disrespectful behavior is considered a serious fault. When one young couple engaged in a quarrel, the mother-in-law tried to pacify them, but so irate was the young husband that he turned to her and said, "If you were younger, I would fornicate with you." The mother-in-law, indignant at this lack of respect, replied, "You shall pay for this!" Shortly afterward, the husband was injured in an automobile accident, from which he did not recover. Some informants told us that the mother-in-law, a well-known witch, was responsible for his death, while others stated that the young man had been punished by Kitzihiat.

Failure to hold the prescribed ceremonies or to attend them is punishable by Kitzihiat through illness, misfortune, or a disaster. The serious illness and physical incapacity of one old man is thought to be the result of his attending only the ceremonies of the clan in which he was cured, while failing to participate in those of the clan in which he was named. When a woman returned from work in the United States with a broken arm, it was rumored that the accident had occurred because she failed to be back in time to hold her summer feast for the dead.

One year the village was in an uproar because the owner of one of the buffalo dances announced that he could not hold it for lack of Indian tobacco. Immediately, offers of tobacco came from clan leaders and other individuals. Everyone feared that if he failed to hold the dance—a curing ceremony—the village and the owner would suffer some disastrous illness.

When one of the most highly respected women in the village fell ill, we inquired whether it could have been caused by witchcraft. Our informant, her niece, replied that witchcraft was not involved in this case. Her aunt had observed the summer feast for the dead in an Anglo house in Utah rather than go to Oklahoma or return to Mexico to perform this ceremony in a cattail-covered house. This failure was particularly damaging to the aunt because she is the custodian of a bundle, a position of responsibility which makes her more vulnerable to punishment.

It is considered extremely hazardous to plan and speak of having an adoption ceremony and later renege. For this reason, the Kickapoos are habitually secretive in announcing an exact date for this ceremony. One man talked about having an adoption ceremony for his deceased daughter but failed to carry out his plans. The following year, when he announced it again and made preparations, the hunters were not able to find any game. A second and a third time the hunters were sent out, returning empty-handed. The man was forced to borrow smoked ribs from a clansman and buy goat and beef to feed the guests—a most deplorable situation and one which made him the laughingstock of the village.

Before a Kickapoo dies, he usually notifies his family of the game or dance which he wishes to have performed during his adoption ceremony. Failure to comply with such a request may bring a string of bad luck. An old woman who had enjoyed playing or watching the woman's double shinny ball game requested that it be performed at her adoption ceremony. Nevertheless, for some unaccountable reason, when the ceremony was held, a woman's dance was substituted for the ball game. When the dance was scheduled to begin, there were torrential rains, making it impossible for the women to dance in the thick mud. By midnight, before the end of the dance, a heavy snow began to fall. Many of the dancers and spectators who stayed until the last fell ill with colds and influenza. Informants explained that the dance had been ruined because the family had failed to comply with the deceased's wishes, causing the spirit to depart in anger.

When a Kickapoo woman died, a Christian sister in Oklahoma sent an Indian blanket and a dress length for the interment. Unfortunately, the Oklahoma woman, having long ago forgotten her Kickapoo customs, sent a red dress length, taboo for the burial of a member of the Berry clan, to which her deceased sister belonged. A third sister, living in the Kickapoo village, rather than give the dress length to one of the dancers, sold it on the sly. Only a few months later the sister who had sold the dress length followed the other to the grave. Her death was thought to be a punishment for selling the ceremonial dress length.

A man, while extremely intoxicated, began to chant songs used only during certain ceremonies. To make matters worse, he was chanting them in a cattail-covered house. Neighbors believed the man had lost his mind. That same evening as he re-entered his house, he stumbled and fell on the fire, burning himself severely; this was described as a punishment for his impiety.

The killing of animals that are kept, in whole or in part, in the clan or personal bundles is strictly taboo for the Kickapoos. Only certain persons may kill these animals, and only after a ceremony. Killing rattlesnakes at any time or spiders except under certain circumstances is also strictly forbidden.

Several degrees of vulnerability exist in the observance of food taboos. To mention two, it is thought that, if the chief breaks the taboos, it will not rain and all plant life will wither; if a member of the Buffalo, Thunder, or Eagle clan breaks them, the guilty one will become deathly ill and will recover only through prayer.

Failure to observe the menstrual, pregnancy, birth, and confinement taboos may be disastrous. A young woman, while working in Utah, gave birth to a child in a hospital where, having no one to prepare the prescribed herbal teas used during this period, she drank plain water. This failure to comply with the prescribed requirement of herbal teas was considered to be the cause of her death a few months later.

Accidents, drownings (a rare occurrence), and other disasters are thought to be a warning to the relatives of the victim to mend their ways. One anecdote told by several informants illustrates this point. A childless woman was given a small girl by a friend. The mother of the child did not know that the adoptive mother was a cruel woman who beat and neglected her daughter and often deprived her of food. One time when a large group of Indians were on a hunting expedition, this woman left the child alone while she accompanied others to gather firewood for the camp near a creek. During her absence, the little girl wandered off to wade. Unfortunately, she stepped into deep water and drowned. Upon returning to camp the Indians searched for the little girl, who was found floating on the water. The adoptive mother wept bitterly, but too late. This sad accident had been a warning to mend her cruel ways. The creek was named for the little girl, and the Kickapoos recall this incident each time they camp near the spot—as a reminder to be kind to children.

When the Kickapoos came into possession of horses and other livestock, they added punishments to fit this newly acquired element in their culture. When an animal invades the planted field of a neighbor, the owner is notified to remove it. If the animal invades a second time and destroys the crop, the owner must compensate the damaged party by paying him or giving him the animal that caused the harm.

The problem of miscegenation must have confronted the Kickapoos from the time they encountered the French. What the punishment was at that time, we do not know; but today women who have children by a Mexican run the risk of not having them named in a clan, thereby making second-class citizens of them.

A difficult barrier to overcome in gathering data was the informants' fear of punishment for "teaching us their inheritance." Giving information to strangers is discouraged by the old people. The informants fear not only ostracism from their peers but punishment from the Great Spirit as well. One informant, while "teaching" us, revealed that she was praying to Kitzihiat to forgive her for this transgression.

Mexican and American Law and Justice

Although the Kickapoos, for many years after their arrival in Mexico, tried to live as an autonomous nation within another, with laws of their own sufficient to meet their needs, it was not long before they had to bow to Mexican law. Today, such crimes as manslaughter, robbery (between Mexicans and Kickapoos), cattle rustling, invasion of ranches without permission, and traffic violations are handled by the Mexican authorities.

As far back as older informants remember, any murder committed in the village either between Kickapoos or between Kickapoos and Mexicans has been handled by the Múzquiz authorities. Quite a number of murders have taken place in the village, the majority committed when the participants were intoxicated. One of the best remembered is the murder of Chief Papícoano's father, who was killed by one of his tribesmen during a quarrel over water rights. One Kickapoo was murdered when he accused another of stealing two of his cattle. Another Kickapoo killed a young man during a drinking session, was imprisoned, but managed an escape with five Mexicans. He fled to Oklahoma and was never seen in the village again.

Since most of the Kickapoos enjoy the same economic level, with minor exceptions, robbery of one Indian by another is uncommon. It does sometimes occur, however, in the summers, when the villagers are working in the United States and fail to leave a caretaker in charge of their houses.

The most common cases of theft are between Mexicans and Kickapoos. Recently, for example, a Kickapoo brought charges against his Mexican cowherd, who, during his employer's absence, took a fine saddle and sold it for a pittance to buy liquor. The Múzquiz judge sentenced the Mexican to work out the original cost of the saddle.

In another case, a Mexican first stole a plow from an Indian, who warned him not to steal anything else. The Mexican, not heeding the advice, soon stole a horse from the same Indian. The Mexican was warned for the second time but again paid no attention and stole a second horse. With this, the Indian took matters in his own hands and went to see the Mexican to retrieve his plow and horses. The Mexican told the Kickapoo that he had stolen the plow and the two horses because he was *macho* enough to do it; whereupon the Indian told the Mexican that he was *macho* enough to kill him after his patience had been sorely tried. He did kill him and was eventually sentenced to three years in the penitentiary but was paroled the last two for good conduct.

One of the few destitute Kickapoo women went to a small ranch nearby, where she threatened a teen-age girl with a knife while her parents were absent. Frightened, the girl turned over the family's savings, as demanded by the Kickapoo woman. Although the woman disclaimed all guilt when brought before the Múzquiz judge, she spent several days in the local jail.

Cattle rustling or horse stealing from Mexican or American ranchers occurs not infrequently. One interesting case occurred many years ago, when an Indian entered the pasture of an adjoining ranch and killed cattle for the hides, which at that time brought a high price on the local market. When he was surprised in the act by the owners, he was charged with the crime and placed in the local jail. In order to make an example of him, he was paraded, half-covered with a stolen hide, around the plaza, accompanied by the cavalry regiment band.

As was explained in Chapter 7, the Kickapoos refuse to observe the closed season on deer (July 15–October 16), stubbornly insisting that they have traditional rights to hunt at any time. This has brought them into many difficulties with the *resguardo forestal* (game and forest wardens), a dependency of the Department of Agriculture and Colonization.

In September, 1965, a group of Kickapoo hunters were surprised by the game and forest wardens on the road fronting the San Jerónimo ranch. Although the hunters had hidden the deer in their pickup with tarpaulins, they were soon discovered. The meat and firearms were seized and the hunters told to claim them in Saltillo or Mexico City. It was only through our intervention and that of other friends that the men recovered their firearms many months later.

On a visit by the Kickapoos to the state capital, Saltillo, shortly afterward, in an effort to retrieve their arms and petition the governor to recognize their traditional right to hunt at any time, they were warned that any further invasion of ranches or hunting out of season would be considered just cause to impound their vehicles and firearms.

In December, 1966, a group of Kickapoos were given permission to hunt and camp in an *ejido* some fifty miles south of Sabinas, Coahuila. Noting that the adjoining ranch had many more deer, they invaded it without permission, unaware that it belonged to a former governor, who had forbidden hunting for many years in order to increase the deer population.

The invasion was reported to the *policías judiciales* (federal police), a dependency of the state's attorney general, organized to control cattle rustling. At suppertime, the police arrived at the Kickapoo camp, where the Indians were enjoying the braised livers of the four deer they had bagged on the former governor's ranch. All the hunters were arrested, the meat and firearms were seized, and the men were taken to Monclova, the nearest city, where they were jailed for two days. On this occasion their firearms were retained for more than two months.

After this incident, whenever we explained to the Indians that invasion of property without permission was a serious offense according to Mexican law, their reply was, "Kitzihiat made this land for the Indians; since you white men arrived, everything has gone wrong."

After several brushes with the federal police and the forest and game wardens, the Kickapoos had had their fill of these men and found the opportunity to avenge themselves in an encounter reminiscent of the wild West. In April, 1970, a group of Kickapoo youths were hunting in the sierra from a *callejón* (a fenced public alley between ranches) and had bagged a deer when they saw another, which they stalked, leaving their pickup in the *callejón*. The federal police arrived unexpectedly, seized the pickup, and took it to the ranch headquarters of an American, to which the youths went in search of it and from which, during a moment of confusion, they escaped, with the police in hot pursuit. The hunters left their pickup at the foot of a hill and dispersed in a circle at the top, while the police stopped on the road, trying to locate the Indians. From their vantage point out of sight of their pursuers, the youths began firing at the feet of the men below, who, fearing for their lives, dropped their Tommy guns and pistols and raised their arms in surrender. Keeping the police covered, the youths descended, seized the firearms, emptied them, and ordered their captives to disrobe. The young Indians carried off their clothes and told them to get them at the next ranch gate. On learning of the incident, the state attorney general sent the state chief of public safety and the Múzquiz police chief to El Nacimiento to deliver a warning to the young men who had been involved, but no further action was taken.

Invasion of planted fields by livestock was at one time amicably settled between the two parties in the Kickapoo fashion. Today, if the livestock of a Mexican renter invades a planted field, the Kickapoo brings charges against him for damages before the Múzquiz judge, who appraises the loss and establishes a compensation.

On weekends, many Kickapoos go to Múzquiz to market, see a movie, drink, or stroll in the plaza. On more than one occasion, men and women have been jailed for disturbing the peace because of obstreperous conduct resulting from drinking too heavily in the cafés and restaurants.

Today, the increasing ownership of automobiles results in numerous violations of traffic regulations.

On more than one occasion the Kickapoos, while harvesting crops in Texas or driving through the state on their return home, have been arrested and fined for killing deer without a license.

Once, while a group was harvesting pecans near Comanche, five of the men went hunting. They killed one deer from the road and "found" two others which, according to their story, had just been killed by passing cars. Elated over their luck, they stopped to celebrate at a beer joint before returning to camp. Becoming more euphoric with each beer, they demanded to be served past the legal closing hour. Unable to dislodge his guests by persuasion or reason, the owner had no recourse but to call the state highway patrolmen, who discovered the deer. Four of the men were jailed for two days, while the fifth was escorted to the camp, where the other Kickapoos had to ante up $250 to bail out their kinsmen and pay the fines.

Property: Real and Personal

Kickapoo property may be generally divided into three categories: real, personal, and ceremonial. Ceremonial property is discussed in Chapter 14.

The Kickapoos now own a total of 7,022 hectares of land in Mexico. This land, consisting almost entirely of pastures, is for communal use except for 506.12 hectares adjoining the irrigation ditches and 22.40 hectares occupied by the village.[5] The land near the irrigation ditches, divided into parcels of ten to twenty hectares, was assigned to the original families, who may enjoy its usufruct. A parcel may be exchanged for a similar parcel in the same area; it may be rented or let out to a sharecropper; but it may not be sold, mortgaged, or divided among the heirs, who share the land or work it in alternate years. The Kickapoos do not know with certainty the exact amount of land in each parcel, since they measure land by the total a man is able to plow with a team of horses or mules in one day, known in Mexico as a *tarea*, approximately one-quarter of a hectare.

As was explained in Chapter 1, the land now occupied by the Kickapoos was once part of Hacienda El Nacimiento but was abandoned by the Mexican settlers because of Indian incursions. While the Sánchez Navarro family owned the hacienda, or perhaps even earlier, the two main irrigation ditches were constructed and the land cleared for farming. In

1907, a Potawatomi Indian, who arrived from Oklahoma and remained in the Kickapoo village, built, with the assistance of others, a second series of irrigation ditches.

Water rights are a constant source of dispute, not only among the Kickapoos, but with their neighbors, the descendants of the Negroes who arrived with Wild Cat and who, by government decree, are entitled to use some of the irrigation water captured near the springs on Kickapoo territory. Other nearby farmers also get some of the irrigation water. The Kickapoos themselves receive four *días de agua* (days of water) per month, two at the beginning and two at the end of the month. A *día de agua* is the amount of water that runs through the canal in a day, measured from sunrise to sunset or vice versa. From this, each Kickapoo who owns a parcel of land is entitled to two *claros de agua* a month. A *claro de agua* is the amount of water that passes through a ditch approximately two feet wide and two feet deep between sunrise and sunset (or vice versa).

A few of the Kickapoos in Mexico still own eighty-acre allotments in Oklahoma or Kansas, which they lease to Anglos. Some of them also derive small incomes from oil leases.

Both Kickapoo men and women formerly owned herds of two hundred or more horses, mules, and burros; a few owned cattle. Today, a few own small herds of cattle, brood mares, and goats. Nearly every family owns one or two burros used for hauling.

Although the Kickapoos, as a tribe or as individuals, have not registered their livestock brand in Múzquiz, they have used one for many years. Until the forties, all of the Kickapoos owning livestock used the same brand, a circle with a hook. This circle may be placed in various positions. The hook may be upright, downward, to the left, to the right, or in four other positions between these. The brand may be placed on the animal's jaw, shoulder, rump, or leg. This ingenious scheme gives the Kickapoos thirty-two different versions of this one brand. After the forties, some began to personalize their brands by inserting in the circle an initial of one of their names; one man placed two crossed arrow shafts in the circle.

As of 1970, only one Kickapoo owned a tractor. He did not have the usufruct of a parcel of his own, since he was a latecomer to the village; but he married a woman who had several parcels. In 1970, the president of the *ejido* was able to obtain a communal tractor for the *ejido* with the help of the Agrarian Department. Any Kickapoo who owns a parcel may use this tractor by paying a small fee, which goes into the *ejido* treasury, and buying the fuel.

Today, many of the Kickapoos, both men and women, own automobiles, especially pickups and station wagons. Women own most of the household equipment, trunks, bedding, personal clothing, jewelry, sewing machines, and such small objects as flashlights, kerosene lamps, and transistor radios. Men own guns, knives, saddles, farming equipment, and their own bedding, personal clothing, jewelry, and transistor radios.

The *Colonia* and the *Ejido*

Historical Background

In the early 1930's, the Kickapoos became aware of ever-increasing limitations on their hunting expeditions due to the extensive program of fencing implemented by the neighboring ranchers and noted that their land was almost depleted of game, pastures, and firewood. They revived an old suspicion, which had rankled among them for years, that they had been despoiled of some of their land. Not only did the neighboring ranchers refuse them hunting privileges; they refused them privileges on land taken away from them and given to the adjoining ranches of La Mariposa and Las Rusias. This belief—justifiable only in part—came about in the following manner, as far as we can determine after appraising both the archival material available to us and information from the Kickapoos.[6]

In 1852, as explained in Chapter 1, Wild Cat and Papicua, leaders of the Seminole and Kickapoo Indians, went to the capital to exchange their military colony, La Navaja, for Hacienda El Nacimiento and an equal amount of land in the state of Durango which they never took up.[7]

With the passing of time, the Kickapoos fantasied that the Mexican government had given them eight, rather than four, *sitios* in Hacienda El Nacimiento. In an interview, Chief Papícoano told us that "President Benito Juárez had given eight *sitios* to the three nations, the Kickapoo, Seminole, and Potawatomi. During the Mexican Revolution the Kickapoos fought on the side of Francisco Madero, while the Seminole Negroes fought on the side of Carranza. Carranza took four *sitios* away from the three nations and gave two to La Mariposa and the other two to Las Rusias."[8]

Chief Papícoano had the facts somewhat scrambled. It was Gen. Victoriano Huerta who overthrew Madero, and Carranza fought against Huerta. Neither La Mariposa nor Las Rusias was responsible for the loss of the Kickapoo land. The chief was correct in saying that eight *sitios de ganado mayor* had originally been granted (but not confirmed) to the Kickapoos and the Seminoles: four in Hacienda El Nacimiento and four in Durango. However, we found only one proof of legal possession at El

Nacimiento, consisting of two *sitios de ganado mayor* ordered in favor of the Kickapoo and Potawatomi tribes in 1866.[9] Nowhere and at no time have we seen any document that shows eight *sitios* given to the Kickapoo, Seminole, and Potawatomi nations in El Nacimiento, as stated by the chief.

On October 25, 1919, Carranza ratified the Indians' possession of four *sitios de ganado mayor* in Hacienda El Nacimiento by presidential decree, ordering the Agrarian Department to confirm the rights of the descendants of the *"indios Seminoles, Kikapoos y Mascogos"* who in 1850 were given land in La Navaja and in 1852 were given four *sitios* in Hacienda El Nacimiento.[10]

This 1919 decree failed to explain (a) that two agreements had been made between Mexican officials and foreign tribes, (b) that only one tribal land grant had been approved by President Benito Juárez, and (c) why this tribal land grant right was changed into individual rights requiring confirmation. First, there had been the June 27, 1850, agreement between Gen. Antonio M. Jaúregui, representing Mexico, and Wild Cat, representing the Seminole and Kickapoo tribes and the freed Negroes, in which the Indians and Negroes were offered sixteen *sitios* near the headwaters of the San Rodrigo and San Antonio rivers.[11] Second, apparently the headwaters land was not used (although some Indians did turn up at nearby Remolino twenty-three years later; see Chapter 1). Instead, the Indian tribes and Negroes settled near and in *colonia* La Navaja, which did not please them either; thus a new agreement was reached on August 18, 1852, with Seminole Chief Wild Cat and Kickapoo Chief Papicua, in which the Mexican government offered to exchange the land at La Navaja for four *sitios* in Hacienda El Nacimiento, for the Seminole, Mascogo, and Kickapoo tribes, and four *sitios* in the state of Durango in the event other Indians arrived.[12] Third, the government of Coahuila officially granted two *sitios* in El Nacimiento to the Kickapoo and Potawatomi tribes on October 18, 1866. This land grant was approved by President Benito Juárez on November 8, 1866. Transmitting the president's approval, the Coahuila governor instructed the Múzquiz authorities to appoint an experienced land surveyor and to take all the necessary steps to insure the Indians' possession of the two *sitios*, expropriated from Don Carlos Sánchez Navarro's hacienda El Nacimiento.[13]

Because of the 1852 agreement, Mascogo Chief Gopher John requested, on February 20, 1867, an equal land grant for the Mascogos in El Nacimiento.[14] Whether this grant was issued and approved we were unable to determine.

Disregarding the Juárez land grant to the Kickapoo and Potawatomi, the 1919 Carranza decree massed Seminole, Kickapoo, and Mascogo lands, mentioning neither areas nor boundaries of partial allotments but only the total of 7,022.44 hectares, with boundaries "in accordance with the existing plat in the Agrarian Department made in 1892 by Engineer Luis Mijar y Haro," and—what was more important for future developments—changed the communal tribal rights into individual rights by ordering confirmation of the rights of Seminole, Kickapoo, and Mascogo descendants as well as "new elements that had been admitted into the *colonia* sponsored in that place by the Agrarian Department and to whom no apportionment of land and water had been made."[15]

On February 6, 1920, the government of Coahuila sent official order number 538, instructing the municipal president of Múzquiz:

> in order to extend the titles to prove the legal possession of the Mascogos, Kikapoos, Negroes, Cuarterones [half-breeds], and Mexicans who are availing themselves of the *colonia* called El Nacimiento of that municipality, it is indispensable that said Mascogos, Kikapoos, and Negroes show in a statement which you will obtain . . . their conformity to cede to the half-breed Mexicans 429 hectares of land which was assigned to them by the engineer named by said Secretariat, plus four days of water per month since said *colonia* occupies 7,421 hectares. The remaining water to be divided among the Mascogos, the Kikapoos, and the Negroes.[16]

It will be noted that in Carranza's 1919 decree the four *sitios* correctly comprise 7,022.44 hectares, each *sitio de ganado mayor* equaling 1,755.61 hectares, but in the order mentioned above the amount of land is 7,421 hectares, an increase of 398.56 hectares. No mention of the type of land or plat location was indicated. However, it is safe to infer that, at best, 398.56 hectares of pasture land were exchanged for 429 hectares of farm land plus four days of water and that the exchange applied to and despoiled only the Kickapoos, since Mascogos and Negroes are one and the same and "half-breed Mexicans" are their descendants.[17]

Apparently, the principal objective of the 1920 order was to legalize an action that had already occurred, since the engineer mentioned (but not named) in the order was Manuel López Moctezuma, who, twenty days earlier (in an official statement dated January 17, 1920), had communicated the following message to the municipality of Múzquiz: "In accordance with the disposition of the Secretary of Agriculture and Development, the land which the former *colonia* El Nacimiento occupied has been divided in three sections: the first for the Kikapoo Indians, the second, for the Mascogan Negroes, and the third, for the half-breeds and Mexicans married to women descendants of the original founders of said *colonia*." Engineer López Moctezuma then proceeded to establish the rights to parcels of land and the water rights, but nowhere did he establish the areas of the three sections into which the land was divided.[18]

On November 12, 1926, the director of the Department of Water, Land, and Colonization, a dependency of the Secretariat of Agriculture and Development, ordered Carlos Ramos, the Inspector of Colonies, to *colonia* El Nacimiento on November 15

in order to establish in that land, the boundaries of said property. Four *sitios* were ceded to the Mascogan Indians and the Kikapoos and confirmed in 1919 by the Executive of the Union and that said lands are contained within the boundaries as noted in the enclosed plat surveyed by Engineer Manuel Pastor.

At present, those who live in the *colonia* are the Mascogan Negroes, the Kikapoos and those individuals who are not full-blooded-Negroes but half-breeds.

Since this Secretariat has a real interest in solving completely the problem of the *colonia* El Nacimiento presently occupied by the Kikapoo and Mascogan tribes, you will carry out the following instructions:

1. Erect landmarks in the *colonia* El Nacimiento.
2. Make a detailed census of the number of families which comprise the Kikapoo tribe.
3. Make a detailed census of the Mascogan tribe.
4. Classify the types of soil.

Enclosed are two plats, one made by Engineer Pastor and the other by the commission from this Secretariat in 1923.[19]

It is odd that boundaries which should have been established in 1852 were ordered established for the two Kickapoo *sitios* in 1866, and were obviously established for the four *sitios* according to the plat made in 1892 by Engineer Mijar y Haro needed to be established again but according to different plats.

In fact, the use of the Mijar y Haro plat in the 1919 decree rivets the established property and landmark boundaries. The property boundaries for the 7,022.44 hectares stated in the decree were as follows: "to the north, the Rancho de los Ciruelos and the Hacienda La Mariposa, to the east, the Hacienda Las Rusias, to the south, the Hacienda El Calvillo, and to the west, the same Hacienda El Calvillo, according to the plat made by engineer Luis Mijar y Haro."[20]

The 1938 decree of President Cárdenas,[21] increasing the Indians' lands, is divided into two parts, the first for the Mascogos and the second for the Kickapoos. The introductions to both parts are similar to the 1919 decree, the only difference being that President Juárez, who was not mentioned in 1919, emerges in 1938 as having given approval to the total grant. The properties' boundaries are exactly the same as those above, but there is no mention of Engineer Mijar y Haro's plat, nor of Engineer López Moctezuma's division into three sections.

With regard to landmark boundaries the 1919 decree states:

> It is declared that the land which forms the *colonia* El Nacimiento located in the municipality of Múzquiz, state of Coahuila, has been taken out of the domain of the nation. This land has an area of 7,022.44 hectares within the following boundaries beginning with the landmark called La Cabecera, embracing the springs, following the course of the Sabinas River to the landmark known as Buena Vista near the hill of the same name. From there in a straight line of 5,566.6 meters to the landmark "in the middle," at the foot, and toward the north of the hill. From this point in a straight line of 3,049.8 meters to the landmark called El Cedrito. From there in a straight line 3,613.3 meters to the landmark called La Baca [*sic*] at the southeast of the hill called La Cuchilla or Los Cojos. From this point in a straight line 3,590 meters to the landmark called El Borrego. From this point in a straight line 6,346.6 meters to the landmark La Cabecera, the starting point. All of this is in accord with the plat existing in the Agrarian Department, Secretariat of Agriculture and Development, made in 1892 by Engineer Luis Mijar y Haro.[22]

The 1938 decree indicates, without mentioning a plat, the same landmark boundaries as above, up to the one called "in the middle," where changes in distance and directions are apparent. The decree further states that, in order to determine if, when, where, and how despoliation had been committed,

> technical personnel from the Agrarian Department proceeded to survey the communal lands of El Nacimiento thereby proving that the total area of 6,818.36 hectares, consisting of 4,316.40 hectares of pasture land, 506.12 hectares of farm land belonging to the Kickapoos, 1,961.44 hectares of farm land owned by the Mascogos and Cuarterones, 22.40 hectares occupied by the Kikapoo camp and 12 hectares by the Mascogan village. These figures show 203.64 [*sic*; should be 204.08] hectares less than the original 7,022.44 ceded to them. From the information given by the surveyors, it was shown that this area of 6,818.36 hectares is what the aforesaid tribes have owned since 1866 and that the restitution was motivated by the fixing of boundaries of the neighboring properties and the formation

of Hacienda Las Palmas, for, when the tribes received the land their boundaries were not established and, since the adjoining land and properties were abandoned, the tribe became used to roaming great extensions of land freely, and felt their interests injured when the haciendas landmarked their holdings in accordance with their titles. This has been the cause of the belief that their land has been despoiled—a belief falsely based.

The properties adjoining the communal lands are La Mariposa, Las Rusias, and Las Palmas. The latter is a *colonia* formed according to the Federal Law of Colonization. Hacienda La Mariposa is the property of The Mariposa Company.[23]

In the resolution part of the same decree, the land holdings of the Mascogos and the Kickapoos, before the additional land given to them by Cárdenas, add up to the totals given in Table 1. Thus it can be seen that

TABLE 1
Kickapoo and Mascogo Land Holdings in the 1938 Decree

Type of Land	Mascogos	Kickapoos
Farm	1,961.44 hectares	506.12 hectares
Pasture	2,158.20 hectares	2,158.20 hectares
Village	12.00 hectares	22.40 hectares
Total	4,131.64 hectares	2,686.72 hectares

the Mascogan and Kickapoo pasture holdings are exactly the same; the village lands are not too different; but the farm holdings, which should be 1,341.02 hectares for the Mascogos and 1,330.62 hectares for the Kickapoos (to add up to the 3,511.22 hectares supposedly allotted to each group), are inordinately different, the Kickapoos' share being 506.12 hectares to the Mascogos' 1,961.44 hectares. Even if the Mascogos' claim was as valid as that of the Kickapoos, it is hard to account for that difference and for the fact that the Mascogos' two *sitios* are 620.42 hectares larger than the original 3,511.22, while the Kickapoos' two *sitios* are 824.50 hectares smaller than the original amount.

The considerations and decisions of the Mascogo and Kickapoo parts of the 1938 decree state that a line between the landmark La Vaca (called La Baca in the 1919 decree) and vertex 28 should divide the Mascogo land from the Kickapoo land. Several questions arise at this point. If a supposedly straight line can divide the tribes' land, why does the same decree mix the holdings of the Kickapoos with those of the Mascogos? Why does it fail to mention that half of the 4,316.40 hectares of pasture land belong to the Mascogos and half to the Kickapoos (i.e., 2,158.20 hectares belong to each)? Why does it not mention the plat on which the location of landmarks depends? Why does it not mention the 429 hectares given to the *cuarterones*? And why did the authorities inhibit our access to all plats (see note 6)?

It can be seen that, through small and subtle changes, wise omissions in dates and plats, fickle use of Juárez approval, and the arbitrary mixture of partial contents of the land holdings of the Kickapoos with those of others, the agrarian functionaries had achieved a miracle of stratagem, for apparently President Cárdenas, who signed the 1938 decree, was not aware of the following facts:

1. Although it is probable that, when the tribes were offered the El Nacimiento land in exchange for La Navaja land in 1852, landmarks were not established nor plats made of either place, it is hard to believe that this was the case with the 3,511.22 hectares for the Kickapoos and Potawatomis approved by Juárez in 1866, when the government of Coahuila pointedly ordered that an experienced land surveyor be named and that the Indians' possession of the land be insured, especially since President Juárez was re-elected in 1867. Certainly, landmarks, distances, and directions were established in 1892 for the 7,022.44 hectares in accordance with the plat made in 1892 by Engineer Mijar y Haro, which is the core of the 1919 decree and is used deceitfully in the 1938 decree.

2. Bounding haciendas like La Mariposa landmarked their holdings in 1882 and began to fence in 1890.[24] This took place more than thirty years before the Kickapoos complained of being despoiled of their land, a complaint which apparently began in 1920 when the 7,022.44 hectares inexplicably increased 398.56 hectares to a new total of 7,421 hectares and Engineer López Moctezuma divided the land into three sections: one for the Kickapoos, another for the Mascogos, and the third, comprising 429 hectares, for the *"cuarterones y Mexicanos"* married to Indian women. One of the *cuarterones* who received a parcel in this last section, Don Aurelio Vázquez Hidalgo, justice of the peace of the district, confirmed the existence of the section and its location.[25]

3. The properties' boundaries established in the introductions to both the 1919 and the 1938 decrees had been replaced in another part of the 1938 decree by the misleading statement: "The properties adjoining the communal lands are La Mariposa, Las Rusias, and Las Palmas."[26] Colonia Las Palmas was created adjoining the Indians' lands, although it had existed as such neither in 1892 nor in 1919. We were told by a number of people that it was really not a *colonia* but a ranch, in which Gen. Emilio

Acosta and others were obliquely cast as colonists to comply at least in appearance with the Federal Law of Colonization.

4. In some way which the agrarian functionaries did not bother to explain, the original 7,022.44 hectares, surveyed and landmarked in 1892, which had increased to 7,421 hectares in 1920, had shrunk in 1938 to 6,818.36 hectares with two thriving *colonias* in their midst. The authorities simply stated that this last land area was what the Indians possessed since 1866.[27]

If President Cárdenas, before increasing the Indians' land, had had the time and patience to add up the partial areas of land given for each group in the text of his decree, he would have discovered that the Kickapoos had only 2,686.72 hectares of the 3,411.22 to which they were entitled, having been despoiled of 824.50 hectares—429 hectares to form the *colonia* for the half-breeds and perhaps the remaining 395.50 hectares to form the *colonia* Las Palmas. On the other hand, the Mascogan Negroes had had an addition of 620.42 hectares to their original 3,511.22, giving them a total of 4,131.64 hectares.

The agrarian functionaries resolved the problem by giving to the Kickapoos 4,335.28 hectares taken from La Mariposa and to the Mascogan Negroes 2,892 hectares taken from Las Rusias, owned by "Weller Lettie W."[28] Thus, according to the 1938 decree of President Cárdenas, the Kickapoos are now in possession of 7,022 hectares, or four *sitios* less forty-four ares, while the Mascogan Negroes own 7,023.64 hectares, or four *sitios* plus one hectare and twenty ares. However, the Kickapoo land is nearly all pasture, rather than farm land, which would be much more valuable.

President Cárdenas, who signed the 1938 decree, was second only to Juárez as a defender of all Indian groups. He distributed more land among them than had any previous president and was responsible for the creation of the Departamento de Asuntos Indígenas (Department of Indian Affairs). His generosity to the Kickapoos dated from 1936, when a delegation from the tribe, including Chief Papícoano and his aide, Nimácana, called on him to request his help in their efforts to obtain more land. Cárdenas listened to the Kickapoos attentively and returned their visit the same year.

According to Don Aurelio Vázquez Hidalgo, justice of the peace of the district which includes the Kickapoos, who was present during Cárdenas's visit to the Kickapoos, the president arrived with a large staff of aides, photographers, and Gen. Emilio Acosta, so-called friend of the Kickapoos, who had commanded several of them during the Mexican

Revolution. The president and his staff went to the home of Yacapita, a Comanche Indian woman who had voluntarily gone to live with the Kickapoos as a girl. She was dressed in her shabbiest and dirtiest clothes, an unhealed gun wound on her leg wrapped in filthy rags. She pleaded for help. Chief Papícoano, his aide, Nimácana, and other Indian elders, also dressed in their poorest clothes, lined up in front of the president. The chief's aide told the president they had too many brood mares and not enough land on which to pasture them and added that, during Carranza's presidency, land had been stolen from the Indians and given to La Mariposa and that the Indians wanted the return of this land. President Cárdenas promised to secure more land for them as soon as he returned to Mexico City from the tour he was making of several Indian villages and to send them money in order that a group could be his guests in Mexico City.[29]

Nimácana explained that they were destitute and needed immediate help. The president, much impressed by the deplorable condition of the Indians, signed an agreement on the spot stating that the Kickapoos could harvest their pecan crop and utilize their timber without paying taxes and could hunt on their land without observing the closed season.[30] They were not satisfied with these special privileges, which gave nothing new to them: they had always used their resources, including game, without observing a closed season.

Nimácana begged that they be given food. The president immediately signed an order to Almacenes Montemayor, a general store in Múzquiz, to deliver 2,500 pesos' worth of provisions to the Indians.[31]

Shortly afterward, the president sent the Indians the following items: two Argentine stallions, sixty mules equipped with harnesses, sixty plows, twelve wheelbarrows, six shovels, two wagons, 120 pairs of shoes, twelve kerosene lanterns, one riding saddle (a special gift to Chief Papícoano), and several sewing machines.[32]

A few months later, he also sent them a windmill and a threshing machine. Many Kickapoo and Mexican informants have told us that the Kickapoos sold some of the mules and plows. Chief Papícoano sold the fine saddle to a Mexican. Later, the saddle was seen by an officer of the local cavalry regiment who bought it. Chief Papícoano himself admitted that he sold the windmill and the threshing machine.

In August, 1936, a group of Kickapoo men, women, and young people were the guests of the president in Mexico City for ten days. In recognition of the president's hospitality, the Kickapoos performed some of their dances.[33]

The Kickapoos were not pleased with the mules that had been sent to them and requested they be exchanged for larger and less stupid ones. In

1937 President Cárdenas ordered that twenty larger and not so stupid mules be sent the Indians.[34] The following day the president ordered another sewing machine to be sent to the Kickapoo feminine cooperative and included a reminder to the men that wheat or any other seed they wished to plant in the forthcoming season would be made available to them.[35]

President Cárdenas took to heart the Kickapoos' tale of woe and, true to his promise, on September 22, 1938, he notified them that the question of restitution of the land they had solicited had been resolved by the Agrarian Department, which had found for them land of the same extension and quality as that which, because of sanctions of previous governments, had passed into the ownership of other *colonias*.[36] This was the new land granted in the decree of September 21, 1938.

When Alfonso Fabila went to the Kickapoo village in 1940, he noted that the following items had been sent to the Kickapoos by the president:

28 mules equipped with harnesses
14 steel-pointed plows
6 Egyptian-type plows with wooden points
7,500 kilos of wheat seed
2,100 Mexican pesos
2 one and one-half ton wagons
2 harrows
6 shovels
4 sewing machines
3 carbines
150 pairs of cotton overalls
50 pairs of *huaraches* [sandals]
7 bolts of heavy sheeting
3 stallions
1 saddle, worth 500 Mexican pesos, a gift to Chief Papícoano
500 fig trees
500 peach trees
25 apple trees.[37]

Fabila says that the sandals were sold, since the Indians preferred their own type of moccasins. Neither did they use the overalls, preferring their buckskin leggings. The bolts of sheeting were used to make curtains for the entrances of their houses.[38] At first, they began to sell, gamble, or pawn the fine horses, but, thanks to the timely intervention of the attorney general of the Department of Indian Affairs, who recovered the animals from the new owners, on the premise that they were federal property, the Indians refrained from further operations of this nature.[39]

The new land given to the Kickapoos was all pasture. The wheat seed given them was planted on the 506.12 hectares of irrigable land that they already owned. During the year 1939–1940 the Department of Indian Affairs lent the Indians 7,500 kilos of wheat seed, and they planted an additional 13,500 kilos. During the year, the Kickapoos incurred a debt of $1,000 in merchandise in Múzquiz, but their crop of wheat brought them $7,150, so that they netted $6,150, which was deposited in a local bank from which it could be withdrawn for communal needs.[40]

Government of the Ejido

In compliance with the Código Agrario, the expropriated land was given to the Indians not in the form of a *colonia*, as the original grant had been, but under the new type of land distribution known as *ejido*—a communal landholding in which holders enjoy only the usufruct of the land. Failure to comply with all provisions of the code automatically causes the land to revert to the government in two years.[41]

Furthermore, in compliance with the Código Agrario, the *colonia* became extinct to all intents and purposes[42]—not, however, in the minds of the Kickapoos, who, unable to comprehend the complicated laws, still consider the *colonia* an autonomous nation. Thus the foundation for a future schism, accompanied by much dissension, was laid, as the Indians, under the direction of the Agrarian Department officials, persisted in running the *colonia* and the *ejido* as separate entities.

The men who formulated the Código Agrario with its legal wording did not take into consideration the lack of preparation of Indians or low-income Mexicans to cope with such an involved procedure. The tremendous gulf between sophisticated law and the illiterate Indians lent itself to much "wheeling and dealing" on the part of some functionaries of the Agrarian Department and a few astute men who could readily assume the management of the *ejido* as caciques.

The *ejido*, according to law, is supposed to have a slate of officers, elected every three years by democratic process.[43] In 1940, officials of the Agrarian Department supervised the election of Chief Papícoano as the first president of the *ejido*. A secretary, treasurer, and alternates to these posts were also elected, as well as *vigilantes* whose duty was to keep check on the livestock and make an annual census. Whether all able-bodied men and women signed as *ejidatarios* (members of the *ejido*) on this occasion, as was prescribed by law, we have not been able to ascertain. The only list of *ejidatarios* with which we are familiar is one given us twenty-four years later by the established cacique.

No sooner had Chief Papícoano assumed the presidency of the *ejido* than he rented the expropriated land to its original owner, La Mariposa.

This arrangement continued for four years. Then the Kickapoos terminated the contract, went to Mexico City and called on their friend and protector, Former President Cárdenas, who, through the Department of Indian Affairs, issued them enough fencing to separate their land from that of La Mariposa.[44]

When Fabila visited the Kickapoos in 1940, Oscar Sukwe and one or two others already owned small herds of cattle, but the remaining Indians, combined, owned only 400 horses, 40 mules, and 150 burros.[45]

From 1940 to 1955, *ejido* officers were elected every three years, each election supervised by officials of the Agrarian Department. In 1955, the official who supervised the election of Sukwe as president found that the latter had already been operating the *ejido* to suit himself. He had been alternate treasurer during the period prior to his election as president and had signed rental contracts with six Mexican ranchers.[46]

Oscar Sukwe was the son of a Potawatomi Indian who had remained in the village after the failure of the Sonora group to settle permanently in that state. Informants, both Mexican and Kickapoo, have said that, when Sukwe's father died in 1940, Sukwe went to Eagle Pass, where his father kept his large savings, brought them to Múzquiz, and put them in the care of a local merchant, who acted as his advisor. During the following decade he acquired some fluorite mines, three trucks to haul the ore, and the bus line between Múzquiz and the village. However, hard times befell Sukwe, along with the Kickapoo tribe in general, when the drought began to assume serious proportions during the late forties. At this time he lost his mines, his trucks, and the bus line.

But, by 1955, he was rapidly metamorphosing into a cacique, as noted above, and had taken the law into his hands, not consulting other officers of the *ejido* and not abiding by the Código Agrario.

Sukwe was taken aside by the official who supervised his election and lectured about his trespasses, but later Sukwe, the renters, and the official reached an "understanding." From then on, Sukwe became entrenched as head of the *ejido* and Chief Papícoano as head of the *colonia* with the blessings of the Agrarian Department officials; each could rent the land over which he had assumed domain—not, however, without creating such dissension between those who were loyal to the chief and the followers of the Potawatomi cacique that the village split in two factions.

So entrenched did he become as president of the *ejido* that Sukwe came to think of himself, his ten sons, and his numerous grandsons as rightful owners of the land. He was recognized by the local authorities as the "legal" president of the *ejido* and, like Chief Papícoano, began to receive a salary for functioning as a peace officer.

Sukwe, to keep up appearances, allowed a nephew and a grandson to be elected presidents of the *ejido* on two occasions between 1955 and his death in 1966. Also for appearances' sake, a roll of *ejidatarios* was made,[47] which included Sukwe's ten sons, a son-in-law, and a few followers, making a total of thirty-four males, thus arrogating to a few the *ejido* rights of the majority of the Kickapoos. This roll underwent no change until 1966, although six of the members had died by then and two had moved to Oklahoma.

Sukwe placed himself in an unfavorable position with the Kickapoos by usurping the *ejido*—nothing but hate resulted from this manipulation. The Kickapoos had many complaints and grudges already against this "outsider."

They believed Sukwe responsible for the death of a Kickapoo who was killed by one of Sukwe's followers, who had quarreled with him over the exploitation of the *ejido*.

Sukwe owned an allotment in Oklahoma and received a substantial income from it, although it was later revealed to us by an Oklahoma informant that he had borrowed heavily against it. He bought a new station wagon every two or three years. This display of wealth, plus knowledge of his previous inheritance, now dissipated, gave him the unpleasant distinction of being considered rich—a situation much frowned upon by the Kickapoos.

He lent money to Kickapoos and Mexicans, demanding interest of 3 percent a month or more—not an uncommon rate in Mexico. Fabila tells us that Sukwe not only lent money at usurer's rates but also "exploited gambling among the Kickapoos."[48]

Sukwe was the only Indian who fraternized with the functionaries of the Agrarian Department and the local authorities, who, in turn, regarded him as the only "civilized" Indian capable of being president of the *ejido*. Sukwe was more illiterate than many other Indians, for he signed his name with a cross and a thumbprint, while a few of the others could read and write both Ba-Be-Bi-Bo and Spanish. But he managed to impress the Mexicans with his show of wealth and had learned the lesson of greasing the palm of officials to rise in the world.

Sukwe was an ambitious man—another trait scorned by the Kickapoos. Not content to be the cacique of the *ejido*, he fantasied that one day he might be the head of the tribe after the death of Papícoano. To prepare for this eventuality, he persuaded the chief's aide, Pisacana, to sign a statement according to which the chieftainship would be passed to him—a totally improbable situation, since the chief must be approved by the heads of the clans. When the Kickapoos learned of this stratagem, they appealed to the Múzquiz authorities to prohibit any such event. Sukwe admitted to the authorities that he owned this agreement but explained it was in safekeeping in Oklahoma. He was ordered to return it to Múzquiz, where, before the municipal authorities, Chief Papícoano terminated the authority given to Sukwe by his aide and Sukwe acknowledged the fact.[49]

Sukwe refused the Indians permission to cut firewood on *ejido* land and attempted to force them to pay rent, in kind, for using the land as pasture. But when he tried to collect a yearling from one of the most respected and prominent widows, feelings were pitched to a near explosion. Although the Kickapoos are rarely all in accord over any matter, they are as one in believing that the *ejido* was given for all of them to enjoy as communal pasture land.

Though he refused to allow the Indians to cut firewood from the *ejido*, Sukwe sold firewood to Mexican venders who supplied the demand in Múzquiz. Because of this depletion of their firewood, the Kickapoos now have to buy it from neighboring ranches.

In 1955, when Sukwe was first elected president of the *ejido*, he distributed a few yearlings among the *ejidatarios* by means of a drawing. He gave none to those who were not on his list of *ejidatarios*.

This series of incidents caused him to become so unpopular in the village that, between 1955 and 1960, he moved across the river with a few of his followers. He seldom ventured into the village proper without the company of one of his sons or followers. Although he feared the Kickapoos and they returned this feeling—some believing that he was a witch —he felt secure of his position, as he was backed by the Mexican authorities.

In 1961, a good year, the *ejido* netted $3,440 from the sale of yearlings paid in rent, and the money was deposited in the Banco Ejidal. When the Kickapoos learned that this large sum of money had been banked, they again appealed to the local authorities, who, after much persuasion, convinced Sukwe to distribute $32 to each head of a household. On this occasion Sukwe was asked by the municipal president to "contribute" $400 to the fund for a new city school.[50]

Having learned his lesson in 1961, Sukwe changed tactics. For the following two years, he did not sell the 110 yearlings and the large number of goats he received as rent, claiming that they were too thin. The official who supervised his re-election in 1964 told us that Sukwe had received only 45 yearlings and 150 goats that year. Since no renter had left, it was evident to us that Sukwe was manipulating the figures.

In 1964, renters paid 6 percent of their cattle herd and 8 percent of their goat herd in kind, the animals being selected by Sukwe. A yearling, at this time, sold for around thirty-six dollars, and a mature goat brought ten to twelve dollars.

As Sukwe became more confident in his position as cacique, he became more arbitrary with his renters, dismissing those who refused to pay increased rental and taking in new ones. According to Don Jesús Garza Salazar, he did not hesitate to ask renters for an advance when he needed ready cash, to ask them to provide fencing where necessary, or to demand a certain number of animals regardless of the size of the herd, accusing the renters of hiding their stock at the time of counting.[51]

Three of the ranchers who had availed themselves of the Kickapoo land were able to buy their own ranches in 1964, but found it profitable to continue grazing their cattle in the *ejido* or *colonia* to save their pastures.

Since the 1930's, when a Mexican moved in with a Kickapoo woman, the Kickapoo men had tried unsuccessfully to keep strangers out of their land.[52] In spite of their efforts, Mexicans have gradually moved in by one means or another: consorting with Kickapoo women as in the above case, renting the farm land or acting as sharecroppers, tending livestock and houses during the summers, or renting the pastures.

In 1954, when an official from the Agrarian Department, petitioned by the Kickapoos, went to the village with the intent of evicting the renters, the renters collected $240 among themselves and passed it to the official.[53] Instead of an eviction, the renters gained a ten-year lease, with both Chief Papícoano's and Sukwe's thumbprint signatures, on the premise that the Kickapoos did not have enough livestock to justify their amount of land, whereas the Mexican ranchers had livestock but no land. The lease specified that the income, to be paid in kind, would be the basis for a communal herd.[54]

The Kickapoos had no recourse but to wait until the contract terminated. When it did, they appealed to the Múzquiz officials, asking them to prohibit Chief Papícoano, his aide, and Sukwe from further renting the communal land, because the pastures were being depleted, the stock was soiling their only supply of drinking water, the pigs were uprooting the small trees in the grove, and the Brahman cattle frightened the women and children when they ventured to gather wood, haul water, or harvest *chilepiquín*.[55]

Receiving no satisfaction from the municipal president, the group representing the Kickapoos requested that the matter be appealed to the Agrarian Department in Saltillo, petitioning that Chief Papícoano and Sukwe desist from renting the communal land and that new elections be held with a new and up-to-date list of members.[56] The petitioners, after waiting patiently for several weeks, during which no action was taken by the authorities, called on the state official of Agrarian and Colonization Affairs, who promised that an inspector would be sent to supervise new elections and notify the renters to leave. A few days later, a notice was posted in the village informing the Kickapoos of new elections to take place on April 30. We were asked by the petitioners to act as observers.

Upon our arrival at Sukwe's home, where the elections were to take place, we were surprised to find no more than twenty Kickapoos present, including Sukwe; none of the women attended. Among those present were the renters and two caciques from nearby *ejidos*. We were coolly received by our host, who demanded the reason for our presence but, when told, allowed us to remain. Sukwe brought out the list of *ejidatarios*, in which he, ten of his sons, a son-in-law, two men who had moved to Oklahoma, and six deceased men were named. None of the heirs of the deceased had been notified that they qualified as participants.

Looking at this list of Algonquian names, in use since 1955 or earlier, the Agrarian Department official had no way of knowing which were active and which were deceased. Not counting the two who had moved to Oklahoma and the six deceased, there were twenty-six *ejidatarios*. Of these, twelve were members of the Sukwe family. With the addition of four followers, also *ejidatarios*, Sukwe had been able to control a majority since 1955. On this occasion, having been informed of the resentment among the Indians, he had one of his grandsons, only eighteen years old and not on the list of *ejidatarios*, elected president. Sukwe remained the power behind the throne; the authorities seemed willing to continue to cooperate with the cacique.

This state of affairs continued until 1966, when Sukwe and one of his sons were killed in an automobile accident in Oklahoma. This seemed a propitious time for the Kickapoos to try once more to regain the *ejido* from the renters. While the Kickapoo leaders deliberated, again unable to take concerted action, regional officials of the Agrarian Department lost no time installing one of Sukwe's sons as president of the *ejido*.

The Kickapoo leaders were so outraged that they immediately called on the state governor, Braulio Fernández Aguirre, who listened attentively to their case and promised that the state official of Agrarian Affairs and the state's attorney general would be present to supervise new elections, for the last time dispense with the *colonia*, form one entity, evict all of the renters, and place all men over sixteen and all women heads of households on a new *ejidatario* list, thereby declaring the old one null and void.

In the meantime, between the summer of 1966, when Sukwe died, and the day of the new elections, eighteen months later, Sukwe's sons sold some of the yearlings given as rent and transferred the rest to their mother.

On February 26, 1967, new elections, at which the majority of the Kickapoos were present, were held under the supervision of the head of the Agrarian Department in Saltillo, his assistant, the state's attorney general, the municipal president and the judge, and various other minor officials, with us as observers, upon the request of the Kickapoos. After two candidates were disqualified because of ill health and age, Adolfo Anico, one of the most respected men and a clan leader, was elected president. Among the other officers and alternates were three of Sukwe's sons. Fortunately for the Kickapoos, the new president was a man of integrity, an honest and dedicated leader.

The state official from the Agrarian Department announced to the Indians, first, that the *colonia* and the *ejido*, for so long two entities, would henceforth be only one. They could call their land *ejido* or *colonia*, but it must all be administered according to the Código Agrario. Chief Papícoano would continue in his role of *capitán* of the Kickapoo tribe. Second, renters would be evicted, but time must be given them to find other land. Third, all of the Kickapoo heads of households, both men and women, would be expected to appear on the new *ejidatario* roll, and a credential card would be issued to each by the president of the Republic, Gustavo Díaz Ordaz.

On the following day, the regional agrarian official dropped by and informed us that the renters had been given ninety days in which to leave and that, if they did not comply by the specified time, 50 percent of their stock would be requisitioned and given to the Kickapoos, and those who were delinquent would be jailed.

After several weeks, the new president of the *ejido* received from the state official of the Agrarian Department papers signed on the day the *ejidatario* roll was made. At that time the livestock, documents (including the presidential decree granting the *ejido* land in 1938, a plat of the *ejido*, and certificates of possession and boundaries), minutes of the officers, list of *ejidatarios*, correspondence of the *ejido*, treasurer's books, official seal for the president and officers, ink pad, and Mexican flag had not been transferred to the president by the Sukwe heirs. Two months later he had received only the official seal.

In the meantime, rumors spread in the village that the Sukwe family were fast selling all of the stock formerly owned by their father, that some of the Kickapoos were unhappy over combining the *ejido* and *colonia* and wanted to revert to the former division, and that the renters had sworn they would not leave. All these rumors had reached the president, who was justifiably disturbed over the turn of events. On a visit to us, during which he was feeling depressed, he succinctly observed, "We are like small children with a band over our eyes in the hands of the Mexicans."

It came to light that among the papers signed by the new slate of officers without prior reading were receipts for the eleven items to be transferred from the Sukwe family to the new president and the pledge of the former treasurer claiming that five head of cattle had been transferred to the new treasurer.

The five head of cattle never showed up, and, when questioned about the delay in transferring the items, the Sukwe heirs, advised by a neighboring cacique and a municipal official, claimed that they were now in their mother's possession. This posed a delicate situation for the president. He hesitated to demand them, first, because the custodian was a woman and, second, because she was his cousin.

In the meantime, Chief Papícoano, completely ignoring the new set-up, continued to rent the *colonia* and sell the stock received.

By June 3, 1967, over three months after the elections, the sixteen renters scheduled to leave within a three-month period of grace were still on Kickapoo land. In the meantime, several renters had attempted to force the rent on the president, who remained adamant. Personal notification was delivered to each renter to appear at the home of the president to sign a statement that each was aware they had been given a ninety-day period to find other land.[57] None appeared.

During these months, the president had forfeited his wages since he had not been able to report for work on the Texas farm where he normally spent several months each year. We lent encouragement and assistance to him, as determined as he to make a success of his new office and rise above the machinations of the interested parties. The other officers left to work in the United States, leaving him with all the responsibility, including keeping the treasurer's books, with which he had to be assisted, since he had never previously done this work. He was encouraged by the lively sale of sand and gravel from the river, which was beginning to provide a substantial amount of income. Previously, this income had been pocketed by Sukwe. With the earnings, the president bought barbed wire to fence off the area surrounding the springs and thus prevent the renters' livestock from soiling the Kickapoos' only source of drinking water.

By August 27, three months from the date when the renters should have vacated the land, only one had complied. The official from the Agrarian Department sent a notice to the president to collect the rent now due, but the latter stood his ground and refused to accept any pay.

In September, an engineer sent by the Agrarian Department called on us to explain that he had been ordered to make a census of the livestock on Kickapoo land in order to have a base on which to tax the owners. He added that the renters had obtained an injunction from a court in Piedras Negras prohibiting anyone from evicting them from Kickapoo land until other land could be found for them. This last news meant that the renters could continue indefinitely. The official finished his call by stating that he was interested in making a census of the livestock in order to estimate whether more renters could be allowed on the *ejido*.

The census showed that a total of 2,869 cattle, horses, mules, burros, and goats were pasturing on the 7,022 hectares of semidesert land, the goats alone amounting to 1,958. This allowed approximately 2.44 hectares of land for each animal, one-third of the land needed to maintain a good pasture. Not in the census was the stock of two ranchers who rented land from both the Kickapoos and the Negroes, shifting their animals from one to the other whenever it was beneficial to them to do so. This little game became possible simply because the agrarian functionaries discouraged a fence between the two pieces of property, with the result that fencing was only partly finished by 1971. Of the total livestock, 479 animals belonged to the Indians. Twenty of these were goats. The Indian owning the majority of livestock was Sukwe's widow, with a total of 158 animals.[58]

In January, 1968, the president assembled the Kickapoos in a meeting, during which he read the first annual report. The *ejido* had not collected one cent of rent, and no cattle had been transferred to the Kickapoos. Of the eleven items supposed to be handed over by the Sukwe heirs, only the official seal had been received, and a total of $90.40 had been collected from the sale of sand and gravel. A balance of $1.20 was in the treasury, the remainder having been spent on wire for fencing, repairs to the dam, and trips by the officers to Saltillo on official business.

In February, 1971, a new slate of officers was elected under the supervision of the Agrarian Department. The new president immediately began to accept the delayed rent and distribute it among his relatives. As of 1972, no further improvements had been made on the land. The old status quo had been resumed, and the renters were further entrenched on their land.

Chapter 9

Social Structure

T o a Kickapoo his "blood" relatives, or those he calls *los de la casa* (close relatives), from both his father's and mother's side are the most important individuals in his life. A typical Kickapoo has many relatives among the group in Mexico, many others among those in Oklahoma, and some among those in Kansas. Although his ties may sometimes be stronger with either his father's family or his mother's, this is simply a matter of circumstance. If he has been reared in a family in which his parents stayed together for many years, he will feel a strong attachment to both families, but if he is brought up only by his mother or a maternal grandmother, as is often the case, he will naturally feel closer to his mother's family. If he is reared by his paternal grandmother or an aunt (father's sister), he will be more at home with his father's family.

The Family

Two types of families are found among the Kickapoos: nuclear families, of which there were fifty-one in the 1960's, and extended families, of which there were seventeen. Besides these, there were five households consisting of childless husbands and wives, and eight women and two men who lived alone.

Matrilocality (living in the mother's home or compound after marriage) is the predominant residence pattern. Thirty-two mothers had one or two married daughters and children, with or without husbands, living in their houses or compounds at the time of our study. Seven sets of sisters lived in the same compounds but not in the same houses. Three nieces lived in the compounds of their aunts (father's sisters). Three daughters lived in the compounds of their mothers-in-law, and one granddaughter lived in the compound of her grandmother. The other women lived in single units in single compounds.

As a rule, the family is a closely knit and economically cooperative unit;

although the members have their differences, these are soon forgotten and family solidarity continues to function. One of the older men told us that he liked his big family, although each year it was harder to supply them with provisions. He added that he was an unusually fortunate man, since all of his family went to work in a group, unlike other families, in which the young people were apt to work alone, leaving the old people to fend for themselves. Another man explained the closeness of his family with these simple words: "Among us, we share everything."

Not all families keep so close together, especially if the mother dies and the father remarries. In this case, the children live with a sister of the mother or with a grandmother; and, often as not, the father stops his support of the first family, sometimes usurping their small inheritance.

Members may be added to the family through adoption. When a child is given to a person who has asked to name him, or when a child loses his parents and has no close relatives, he is adopted by someone who wants him, usually within the family. Grandmothers tend to adopt one or two grandchildren, especially the first-born of a daughter or a son, while childless couples or childless single women adopt children or grand-children of their sisters or brothers.

The Kickapoos, however, seldom give their children up for adoption to nonrelatives, as is a common practice among the Mexicans. One childless Oklahoma Kickapoo woman who was financially comfortable inquired about the possibility of adopting a child from the village. The message was relayed to several of the Indians, who were surprised at the request and observed: "I don't think that woman will get a child here. No one wants to give up a child for adoption."

A more frequent type of adoption is that which takes place when a family loses one of its members and this person is replaced by an unrelated individual of the same sex and approximately the same age, preferably one who has been a declared friend of the deceased. This individual, through the adoption ceremony, becomes a member of the consanguineal family, assuming the same role as the deceased, including behavioral patterns.

A third type of adoption occurs when two individuals of the same sex become "declared friends." This is also formalized by means of a ceremony. Thereafter the two individuals are like brothers or sisters and are treated as such by members of their respective families. This situation was brought to our attention at a dance. The man who accompanied us called to a woman, "Hi, baby!" Seeing that we were puzzled at hearing such an expression of familiarity directed to this woman, he explained that she was his wife's declared friend and therefore his wife's sister. As such, she was his sister-in-law, with whom he had a joking relationship, bordering on the ribald. He added that, had we not been with him, he would have said something bawdy to her.

Kinship

The great pioneer ethnologist of the nineteenth century, Lewis Henry Morgan, made a detailed study of kinship systems. He divided the Indian groups of North America into two categories: those who reckoned their descent through their fathers (the Omaha kinship system) and those who reckoned their descent through their mothers (the Crow kinship system).[1] The Kickapoos belong to the Omaha system, as do the Sauk, the Fox, the Shawnees, the Menominees, and other Central Algonquian groups.[2]

The Omaha kinship system is classificatory, meaning that remoteness of blood relationship does not lessen its importance. This system is non-generational—a woman calls the children of her father's sister her sons and daughters, although they may be older than she, and consistently differentiates the children of a brother from those of a sister, calling her sister's children sons and daughters and her brother's children nephews and nieces. The reverse is true for a man.[3]

Under this system, it is more important to stress kin solidarity than exact genealogical relationship. Thus, the term *father* indicates not only the male parent but also his brother, as well as the husband of his mother's sister. If a child's biological father should die or should be separated from the mother, the child will still have several fathers if his own father had brothers or half-brothers. If his mother has sisters, their husbands will be the child's fathers also. If he is an only child, he will still have sibling relationships, for the children of his father's brothers and his mother's sisters will be his brothers and sisters. He calls his mother's sister by the term *second mother*. He calls his mother's brother *uncle*, and this term is also used for the uncle's son and grandson, and so on indefinitely. The child calls both his mother's brother's wife and his father's sister *aunt*.

In a small community of less than five hundred in which each member is probably related to at least one-fourth of the other members, behavior toward the entire community is governed by strict rules requiring that everyone be polite, friendly, and helpful to others. There also are personal rules of behavior toward all members of an individual's kin, by blood or by marriage.

Omaha kinship terminology and the behavior associated with it are confusing to the uninitiated. On one occasion we asked an informant if a certain widow was seeking matrimony. Our informant and the widow were approximately the same age and often came to see us together. The reply was that if the widow were looking for a new husband, the informant would not know about it, as the widow was her daughter and daughters discuss love affairs not with their mothers but with sisters or declared friends. It came as a surprise that our informant had a daughter almost her own age, and we first considered it a joke. However, upon further questioning, the informant explained that the widow was the daughter of one of her father's sisters, and therefore her daughter. In our kinship system, the two women would be cross-cousins.

Kinship behavior may be divided into two main classes: that involving respect to one's parents, parents-in-law, and siblings, and that involving teasing or joking with blood relatives with whom such behavior is approved or with siblings-in-law—the latter often cause for much horseplay and ribaldry. The relationship between grandparents and grandchildren lies between the former two types and involves indulgence, affection, and respectful teasing.

Parents, in general, are entitled to advise, correct, and train their offspring in numerous tasks. Children are ideally expected to help their parents and be respectful toward them, but there are many exceptions in practice. On one occasion the chief's mother-in-law came to call on us in the company of a five-year-old grandson, carrying a large bundle of clothing and trinkets on her back. She laid the bundle on the floor beside her while we chatted. During her call, two of her daughters and their husbands arrived, and, after some exchange of pleasantries, the old woman bid us goodbye. When we asked if she could carry the bundle alone, she requested that we take it to the door and hoist it over her back. Neither her daughters nor their husbands made a move to help her.

Children early learn to know their parents' weaknesses. One fifteen-year-old, who earned more than his father, warned his mother not to be generous with the allowance she gave his father, as he would undoubtedly spend it drinking beer, for which he had a special propensity.

Mothers, when separated from their children, are apt to feel very sad. One woman, who left her children with their Mexican paternal grandmother so that they could continue school while she worked in the United States, reported that she had been very concerned about their welfare. (True to her fears, upon returning, she found her son with an advanced impetigo infection. All three were thin, had not been properly fed, and wore soiled clothing.) Her face beamed with joy as she told of the pleasure of being reunited with the children and her Mexican husband for the Christmas holidays.

Admonishments do not stop with the real parents, since anyone called *father* or *mother* may reprimand and advise all those whom he or she calls *son* or *daughter*. One informant told of the time she had called an old Mexican renter "a stingy old man" when he told a tale of woe to avoid being evicted. One of the woman's fathers (her father's brother or mother's sister's husband) was present and called her aside to tell her she had been disrespectful to the old man. When our informant retorted, "Why, he is only a Mexican!" her father insisted that this had nothing to do with the case and that she must always be respectful to old people, regardless of the "nation" to which they belonged.

As a rule, fathers do little of the disciplining, but they teach their sons the intricacies of the hunt, a craft, herding, agriculture, the communal maintenance of roads and irrigation ditches, and ceremonial lore. In lieu of a father, these manly tasks are taught by the father's brothers, the mother's brothers, an older brother, or a grandfather. In return, a son is expected to help his father, or anyone he calls *father*, during the latter's lifetime with services, money, or gifts. Daughters show their fathers deep respect, often having them live with them if they are separated from their wives. Fathers expect their daughters to look after their welfare, sew, cook, and wash for them. In case of an illness, the daughter, if the father is alone, is the one obligated to care for him. When death approaches, sons and daughters who are absent are called to his side so that he may verbally divide his allotment, irrigable land, and his stock; otherwise, the absent children of either sex may lose out on the inheritance.

The mother, who owns the house and is responsible for its construction, plays an important and independent role. She furnishes shelter for her children, often provides for them financially if she is separated from her spouse, cooks, washes, sews, prepares skins, makes moccasins, harvests *chilepiquín*, helps in the crop harvests, and teaches her daughters the duties of women. A mother often takes care of her daughter's offspring born of a premarital union and is usually the person who assumes the responsibility of the grandchildren in the event of her daughter's death, whether the daughter was married or not.

Mothers are apt to be indulgent with the children, spoiling their sons more than their daughters, sacrificing some personal need to buy them gifts or supplying them with money on demand. In return, sons are usually generous with their mothers. Several mothers in the village receive checks from their sons who work in the United States.

Some of the men are exceptionally devoted to their mothers. One older widower who lived with his mother left a permanent job in Múzquiz because his mother missed him and asked him to give up the work. The son's only commentary was, "I have to obey my mother's wishes."

On the other side of the coin was a man whose old mother had become a burden to him. One day while chatting with one of the Mexican renters, he remarked that his mother was "never going to die." She did die soon afterward—a horrible death, as she was burned, along with the son of the man who had wished her dead. We were told that he suffered acute feelings of guilt and remorse.

If the mother is a widow or is separated from her husband, she expects her sons to provide her with game and to work in the fields while they are children. She disciplines them while small, and, if the children are difficult, she calls upon a brother or her husband's sister to discipline them more vigorously.

Brothers are friends, the younger ones respecting their older brothers and following their advice. However, sex matters are not usually discussed between them, but with unrelated friends instead. Even as adults, brothers are likely to look after each other's welfare. With respect to giving advice to a younger brother, one man stated, "I am older than he and therefore know more than he knows."

Sisters are companionable, helping their mothers in household duties, aiding in the care of younger siblings, and learning to perform the duties assigned to women. Sisters talk among themselves about their sweethearts. Older sisters receive the same deference and respect bestowed on older brothers. On one occasion we had two small gifts for two sisters. Momentarily forgetting that we should ask the older one to make the first selection, we asked the younger one, who chose a small pink bag which the older one also wanted. During a perplexing moment in which we wished for Solomon's wisdom, the mother deftly solved the problem by giving the pink bag to the older sister, without one word of protest or comment from the younger one.

Although brothers and sisters play together without much restraint before puberty, they tend to associate mostly with their own sex group after puberty. This change, however, does not erase the respectful consideration between them. A brother is his sister's protector; she is expected to look after his clothes, making his Kickapoo-style shirts, leggings, and moccasins. In return, brothers bring small gifts to their sisters and may dispose of them in marriage.

After reaching adulthood a sister often looks after the welfare of a brother with more compassion than his own wife. One woman, a member of an herbal society, stayed at home from her annual trip to work in order to cure her brother, who was seriously ill, and remained at his side until he recovered.

But some brothers are not above taking advantage of their sisters in money matters. A man whose sister kept part of her earnings in our custody came to our home one day, telling us she had given him permission to draw out a part of her funds. Not wishing to doubt the man's veracity, we gave him the money—fortunately, only a small amount—with which he had a gay evening in a local saloon. Later we learned he had no authorization to ask for the money.

The youngest male child in the family is treated with much permissiveness, to the point of spoiling, pampering, and allowing him to have his way about everything. He is called by the affectionate Mexican term *coyote*, used to describe the baby boy in the family whose every whim is consented to.

All of the behavioral patterns for real siblings (as defined by our culture) also apply to all those whom one calls brothers and sisters, including the children of one's father's brothers and one's mother's sisters. As a result of the frequent turnover of spouses, children often have many half brothers and sisters, who are treated in the same way as full brothers and sisters.

Although children's uncles (mother's brothers) and aunts (father's sisters) are frequently disciplinarians, they are equally ready to advise, train, and guide; furthermore, uncles and aunts play practical jokes on nieces and nephews, and vice versa; and both sides must accept these jokes in good spirits. Both nephews and nieces are freer in their behavior with their uncles and aunts than with their parents. Not infrequently, a woman rears her brothers' children. This relationship is one of unusual devotion. As the nephews and nieces reach adulthood and have their own homes, they continue to help and aid their uncles and aunts.

One day we accompanied a Kickapoo couple to the door at the precise moment when a girl of about fourteen arrived with her grandmother. The man put his nose between his fingers in the gesture of discharging mucus and wiped his hand on the girl's dress. Instead of becoming angry, she giggled and replied with a quick riposte that she would wear his snot on her sleeve until she washed the dress. Asking for an explanation later, we were told that the girl was the man's niece, and he could tease her in this manner. The man added that he could also reprimand the girl anytime he believed she merited it, and she, in turn, could admonish him.

Nephews and nieces often prove more humanitarian during the advanced years of their uncles and aunts than the latters' own children. We knew one old man whose daughter treated him shabbily; in fact, she had thrown him out to make room for a new Mexican consort. Later, when he became ill, he refused to live in her home. One of his nieces came to the rescue by asking him to stay with her, although she had to leave her children and husband, who were working in Texas, in order to care for the old man. When we inquired why she did not hire someone to look after her uncle in order to join her family, she replied simply, "I cannot leave him; he is my uncle."

Disciplining between uncles and aunts and their nephews and nieces is lifelong. While watching a drunk man's dance one day, a small boy walked into the dance area and began to shake the pole set up in front of the chanters. At first, no one seemed disturbed by his behavior; but, shortly, one of the dancers spoke to the child, took him by the hand, and led him off the floor. We were sitting by the side of one of the dancer's aunts, to whom we looked questioningly. She immediately said, "He is in his right to get the boy off the floor, as he is the child's mother's brother." The uncle later came in for a reprimand from his aunt, as he became obstreperous after imbibing too much mescal. She turned to us and explained that she was in her right to call attention to his behavior, as she was his aunt.

If a man has no wife, mother, sister, or daughter, it is the duty of a niece to invite him to live in her home, look after his welfare, and braid his queue. Nephews and nieces are entitled to ask for money and gifts; but, in return, they must reciprocate. In case of illness, if the uncle or aunt does not live with a nephew or niece, the latter will take them such delicacies as the loin of a deer, some freshly made hominy, squirrels, or a skunk, all considered ideal food for a patient.

In ceremonial and religious matters, nephews are often left a sacred bundle, songs, and dances, and taught the accompanying ritual. Nieces are frequently named custodians of bundles, since it is they and not the nephews who are the owners of the houses.

When a man's dance or game takes place, it is the uncles who invite their nieces to be the recipients of the dress lengths they receive; in the case of a woman's dance, the nieces are asked to be the second chanters. The dress lengths received by the women dancers are given to uncles or nephews. A woman told us with a note of sadness in her voice, after the death of her last uncle, that now she no longer had anyone to invite her to be the recipient of a dress length at a dance or game, or to be the second chanter.

It is the duty of uncles to make the bows and arrows, the double shinny, and the lacrosse sticks for ceremonial games. If there is no uncle, the brothers perform this duty. Uncles are also the scorekeepers of these games.

The relationship between grandparents and grandchildren is one of respect and indulgence, laced with a certain amount of teasing. The grandparents are the repositories of the tribal knowledge, and it is they who pass the myths, stories, and much of the religious and medicinal lore to their grandchildren.

A woman informant told us that as a child she asked many questions and enjoyed being told stories about the culture hero, Wisaka, and about animals. Her grandmother and stepgrandfather were often happy to postpone their labors to answer her questions; but, if they were too busy, this information was withheld until after supper when the family gathered around the hearth. Her grandfather had a frustrating habit of getting to the most important part of a tale and saying, "We shall continue this another day; it is now time for you to go to sleep." This same informant received her herbal knowledge from her grandparents and today is considered one of the most proficient of the curers.

One of the most touching sights at a dance is the way small boys and girls, clutching the hands of their grandparents, learn the dance steps.

Grandchildren are usually left the personal belongings of their grandparents, such as firearms, saddles, jewelry, shawls, and other items not given away at the burial or adoption ceremony.

Not only are grandmothers ready to sacrifice small pleasures for their grandchildren; they are even willing to face the disapproval of the village and the supernatural in order to look after the welfare of a grandchild. A woman, custodian of a bundle, left her house at the time for rebuilding to be at the side of her only grandson, who had suffered a serious automobile accident that left him permanently disabled. She was the object of much gossip for abandoning her house and the bundle, since it was believed that this negligence might bring disaster to the village.

But not all grandparents and their grandchildren are as respectful and devoted to each other as they should be. We were told about a seven-year-old boy who, on the death of his mother, went to live with his grandmother. The child had temper tantrums during which he threw plates of food at his grandmother. When she was outdoors, he pelted her with rocks, forcing her to seek protection in the house; on other occasions, he disappeared, causing her much concern. The man who told us about this child remarked sadly, "If you could see with what little respect some of the children treat their *nanas* [grandmothers] today!"

Kickapoo children have many grandparents besides the parents of their father and mother. All of the siblings of their grandparents are also called by that name, and the same behavior exists toward them.

Husband and wife act toward each other much as in our society. The wife has considerable prestige, since she owns the house and its belongings and from childhood has been trained to earn her living. In spite of the brittle nature of Kickapoo marriages, some are successful and last many years; others last many years but are embittered by quarrels, recriminations, and physical assaults.

One woman, whose last marriage had survived some fifteen years, reported that her husband was working in California, but she was expecting him soon. In the meantime, she had remained in the village to build her house and would be returning to California with him later. She showed us four letters he had written her and exclaimed with a deep and wistful sigh, "My home is very lonely and I am sad; he is a good man."

On the other hand, another woman told us how her sister-in-law abused her aged and frail brother, sometimes chasing him from their home with a stick. A younger wife was noted for the shabby treatment of her spouse; whenever they quarreled, which was frequently, both she and her grown daughter by another marriage beat the man until he fled to his mother's home.

Among the Kickapoos there is no mother-in-law or father-in-law avoidance, but the relationship between these individuals and their children-in-law is one of great respect. The fact that the Kickapoos are matrilocal would, of necessity, obviate the practice of avoidance. As one woman expressed the situation, "We live together; we cannot avoid each other." Nonetheless, they seldom engage in conversation unless it is of the utmost urgency, speaking through a third member of the family when possible.

Not all mothers-in-law and sons-in-law get along, in spite of the respectful behavior which ideally exists between them. One young husband, irritated with his mother-in-law beyond his endurance, solved the problem by finding himself a permanent job in Texas.

The relationship between siblings-in-law is one of joking, in which sex is the predominant subject. Obscenity, risqué jokes, rowdy tricks, and horseplay go to great lengths. Siblings-in-law of the opposite sex may slap each other on the backside, grab at each other, and make such ribald threats as "Let's go bathing together naked," or "I am coming to bed with you tonight." This type of joking relationship exists one generation up in the case of the father's sister's husband, who is also called *brother-in-law*. There is one song in a dance held during the feast of the first fruits in which siblings-in-law of the opposite sex are partners, but without physical contact. The song begins with these words: "There comes your brother-in-law, wearing only his breechcloth."

Besides the kinship within the bilateral family, the Kickapoos enjoy an extended kinship derived from membership in the clan to which each belongs. Members of the same clan call each other *brother* and *sister*, and all call their clan leader *grandfather*.

Other extensions of kinship are primarily terminological, implying the expected behavior, and sometimes manifesting it, as in the case of old and young people. A young person calls any aged person *grandparent*, regardless of kinship, and the old people reciprocate with the term *grandchild*. Although there are no stated obligations between these individuals, young people often aid the needy or helpless old in various ways, such as taking them a piece of venison, inviting them to a meal, sharing a crop, hauling firewood, water, and construction material, and assisting in the building of their houses.

A still further type of kinship is that with the supernatural. The Kickapoos have many supernatural "grandparents" who look after their welfare or through whom they may intercede for blessings. Some of these include fire, Indian tobacco, the thunderers, Grandfather Sun, and Grandmother Earth. The culture hero, Wisaka, is considered to be the son of all Kickapoo women and the nephew of all Kickapoo men.

Clans

In 1970 the Mexican Kickapoo tribe was divided into fourteen clans, listed in Table 2 in descending order of membership. Formerly, the White Bear, Turkey, and Badger clans were also represented, but all their members had died by 1970.

TABLE 2
Clan Membership in 1970

Name of Clan	Number of Members
Man	118
Berry	80
Thunder	54
Buffalo No. 1	44
Tree	25
Black Bear	24
Eagle	15
Brown Bear	14
Buffalo No. 2	8
Fire	6
Water	5
Raccoon	1
Coyote	1
Fox	1
Total	396

Only Man, Berry, Thunder, and Buffalo have leaders qualified to officiate at the ceremonies connected with the clan bundles. Because of this situation, parents belonging to the clans that are becoming extinguished through loss of membership and lack of leadership tend to ask members of the larger clans to name their offspring.

TABLE 3
Associated Clans

Name of Clan	Number of Members
Man	118
Fire	6
Water	5
Raccoon	1
Coyote	1
Total	131
Berry	80
Tree	25
Total	105
Thunder	54
Black Bear	24
Fox	1
Total	79
Buffalo No. 1	44
Eagle	15
Brown Bear	14
Total	73
Buffalo No. 2	8

There is a belief among the Indians that members of the Man and Berry clans are long-lived, and for this reason these clans are today large and popular in comparison with the smaller ones. The four clans with the greatest membership and able leadership are increasing in size to the detriment of the ten smaller ones.

Chief Papícoano's clan membership was Water, to which the hereditary chiefs were required to belong; however, his clan is dying out and at the time of our study had only five members, all over fifty. Sons born to the chief were named in the Water clan, but they died. In order to circumvent further losses, he named his last and only surviving son in the first

Buffalo clan, hoping by this expediency to break the chain of bad luck.

Since there are only five leaders, including the leader of the second Buffalo clan (see discussion below), qualified to officiate at the New Year clan ceremonies, the members of clans lacking leadership have associated themselves with the larger clans and attend their ceremonies. The alignment is as shown in Table 3.

As noted, there are two Buffalo clans, designated as Buffalo No. 1 and Buffalo No. 2. One or two years elapsed after our arrival in Múzquiz before we discovered that the second Buffalo clan and its bundle and bundle house existed. No one spoke of it, not even the man who had inherited the bundle from his father. The Kickapoos insisted that they had only four bundle houses.

The truth of the matter is that the second Buffalo bundle is not a Kickapoo bundle but was brought to the village in 1907 by a Potawatomi from Oklahoma, who left it in care of his seventeen-year-old son, named in this clan. He remained in the village and married a Kickapoo woman. The membership is small. The bundle owner does not know how to officiate and asked a Kickapoo from the Buffalo clan to assume the leadership.

There is a tradition among the Fox Indians that their clans were supposed to be exogamous—no one should marry within his clan—but this practice is not observed today.[4] An informant of Truman Michelson's described exogamy among the Fox in these few words: "It was against their laws to marry within their own gens [clan], but now they haven't this rule."[5] The Kickapoos also formerly observed this practice but no longer do so. They marry within the same clan or any other where they find an acceptable mate.

The Kickapoos use the term *religion* in explaining their clans and say they are analogous to the many religious denominations among Protestants. Affiliation in a clan, next to membership in a bilateral family, is the strongest social tie governing the individual throughout his life.

At the naming ceremony the Kickapoo is given a name which is an eponym of the totem of the clan to which he will belong; he will be known by this name by all members of the tribe. He attends the New Year clan festivals, where he is taught ethics, the proper conduct related to ceremonialism, some herbal knowledge, and information as to the colors of clothing and ornaments he may wear. Every activity for which he must observe a ceremony—including hunting, house construction, interment, the feast for the dead, the adoption ceremony, and many others—will be affected by the particular practices of his clan.

In fact, the most unsatisfactory situation for a Kickapoo child is to be barred membership in a clan because a leader refuses to officiate at his naming ceremony. Many half-breeds sired by Mexicans have been made outcasts because of intransigent leaders. These children have no Kicka-poo name, do not belong to a clan, may not participate in clan activities, may not receive instruction, cannot be buried in a Kickapoo cemetery, and will not be dispatched to the Kickapoo hereafter by means of an adop-tion ceremony.

Membership in certain clans bestows specific privileges or duties on its members. For instance, for the past three generations, the chief of the tribe had to be a member of the Water clan. When the Kickapoos had police, they were named by the chief's right-hand man, who had to be a Berry. He, in turn, called on men who were Berry, Buffalo, and Bear to perform the duties of police. Food tasters at dances or ceremonial games must belong to either the Fire or the Tree clan.

The buckskin-covered balls used in playing the ceremonial man's or woman's ball games must be made by a man of the Eagle clan. He also makes the ball with which youths and girls play a nonceremonial game after the spring festivals. A woman of the Berry clan was, at the time of our study, the one privileged to ask Chief Papícoano's permission to play this nonceremonial game; earlier this privilege also had belonged to the Eagle clan.

Those belonging to the Berry clan have separate ceremonies and feasts for the dead, one for the male and one for the female members, while other clans may have them at the same time. Not all clans permit women to attend the New Year clan festivals. Women may attend the Berry and Tree ceremonies, but female members of the Man, Thunder, Buffalo, and both Bear clans are barred from participation.

If a deceased member of either Bear clan is honored with a ball game at his adoption ceremony, the game must be played at daybreak; all other clans play ball games in the late afternoon. When a dance is held for a member of the Man clan during an adoption ceremony, nine instead of ten dancers are invited, and the dance does not last as long as those of other clans. In this clan, games for adults must be held before sundown; games for children must be held just before noon. The Man clan requires from one to three fewer participants than the others in everything.

Members of the Black Bear clan may wear only one or two black arti-cles and never dress in all black. Female members of the Berry clan may not wear red lipstick or red nail polish, though they may use another color. They may not use red earrings. They are permitted to wear one or two red articles, but never an all-red dress. Members of the Thunder clan are not permitted to wear jewelry of any kind.

It is taboo for some clans to kill certain animals. In general, no Kicka-poo may kill spiders, but members of the Buffalo clan are permitted to kill them if they invade the compound or house.

Some anthropologists propose the idea that in societies that have clans, certain clans are subservient to others, since their members act as waiters or cooks in the others' ceremonies. In reality, no Kickapoo clan is subservient to another, as all clans at some time or another call upon members of their "reciprocal" clans to assist them in giving a ceremony. The Kickapoos call the members of their reciprocal clans *nicanaki* (clan friends). They consider it an honor for the men to be waiters and the women, cooks, at a ceremony. It is analogous to the honor extended by a hostess to her best friends to be in the house party when she entertains.

Reciprocity between clans is a fixed thing, but since the lesser clans are associated with the larger ones, this gives them much leeway. When Buffalo (No. 1 and No. 2) and the associated clans, Eagle and Brown Bear, hold a ceremony, they call on Berry, Man, Thunder, and Fire to help them. Similarly, Man and the associated clans, Fire, Water, Raccoon, and Coyote, call on Thunder, Berry, and Tree; Berry and the associated clan, Tree, call on Buffalo, Thunder, and Fire; and Thunder and the associated clans, Black Bear and Fox, call on Man, Berry, Buffalo, and Tree. (See Table 5, in Chapter 15.)

Membership in a second clan may be acquired by being "cured" in a ceremony of a clan other than one's own. A person who is cured does not acquire a new name; but he may, if the clan leader who treats him belongs to the opposite moiety, acquire a second moiety designation. In other words, if he is already a Kisko and is cured by a leader who is Oskasa, he may take the latter's designation. It is the obligation of this individual to attend the New Year clan festivals of the clan in which he was cured and contribute food and services. He may call upon and be called in a reciprocal capacity by the second clan and those with which the second clan has reciprocal agreements. He may even become so active in the second clan that he eventually becomes its clan leader. He is expected to be loyal to both his new clan and his original clan and participate in the ceremonies of both.

Moieties

All the Kickapoos belong to one of two moieties, or dual divisions, Kisko and Oskasa, to which affiliation is acquired at the naming ceremony. Occasionally, as noted above, a second moiety is acquired at a curing ceremony.

The child receives the moiety of his namer and keeps this, as well as his name, for the duration of his life, barring unusual circumstances. The Kickapoos, when speaking of the moiety, call it *partido*, or "team," an appropriate name, since one of its purposes is to divide the tribe into two more or less equal teams that can oppose each other in ceremonial games and food competitions.

Kisko is understood to mean "paints with white clay," while Oskasa means "paints with charcoal."[6] Oskasas are expected to finish any and everything they begin, while the Kiskos are under no such obligation. In ceremonies held indoors, moiety affiliation determines the side of the house on which one sits: Kiskos always on the south bench and Oskasas on the north bench. Formerly, when the Indians were active in wars, this division functioned in that activity.[7]

When competing in games or food-consuming races, the Kiskos paint their faces and sometimes their torsos with white clay from the river bottom, while the Oskasas blacken themselves with the burnt end of a piece of firewood.

Today, all members of the Berry clan are Kisko, although the present clan leader told us that formerly some of the Berry members were Oskasa. All members of the Buffalo and Fire clans are Oskasa; but, here again, at one time there were some Kisko members in the Buffalo clan. The one-member Fox and Coyote clans are Oskasa, while the Raccoon is Kisko. The remaining clans are a mixture of both moieties. Of the 396 Kickapoos named in the fourteen clans, 192 are Kisko and 204 are Oskasa.

In games and food-consumption races the moiety is all-important; clan affiliation is ignored. All of the Kiskos and Oskasas form cheering sections for their sides. Sometimes harsh words and insults are exchanged, resulting in a few fights; but when the game terminates, all is peace and joviality. Knowing that all Kickapoos are taught to be polite, kind, and friendly to each other in their daily contacts, one wonders if the wisdom of the Indians did not create this dual division to give them an opportunity to express aggressiveness and hostility in a socially acceptable way.

Lineage

Lineage among the Kickapoos is of a different type from that employed in our culture. No surnames are used by the Algonquians. A father or namer does not pass a family name to his offspring or godchild, but only his clan and moiety affiliation. Each person has a different clan name—each an eponym of his clan's totem, such as "A Fat Bear Climbing a Tree," "Running Buffalo," "Ripe Berries," or "Man Standing," to mention a few.

Repeatedly, we have been told that it is the father's right to name his children in his clan. The concept of patrilineal descent is strong in the minds of the Kickapoos, but the reality is not consistent with the ideal. It is true that, in 1970, of the seventy-five living fathers, fifty-four had from one to eight children named in their clans. The other twenty-one living fathers may have had children named in their clans, but the children were dead, and the Kickapoos will not speak of their dead and especially will not mention their names. This made it impossible to determine any figures on these last twenty-one fathers. Of the 252 living children, only 119 had been named in their fathers' clans, while 133 had been named by others who had given them their clan names.

Many factors enter into the weakening of patrilineality and will be explained in detail in the discussion of the naming ceremony, in Chapter 15.

Miscegenation is becoming more prevalent each year in spite of the Kickapoos' efforts and mechanisms to discourage it. According to Kickapoo men, the woman is only a tray on which the man deposits his seed. Therefore, if a Kickapoo man cohabits with a woman of another "nation," Mexican or Anglo, the child born of this union will be a Kickapoo; but if a Kickapoo woman cohabits with a man of another "nation," the child will not be a Kickapoo but will belong to the "nation" of the father.

A second belief which reinforces the first is that, when Kitzihiat, the Great Spirit, made the Indians, Mexicans, Anglos, Chinese, and all the peoples of the world, he also provided each with a certain place to live and a place for their spirits to dwell in the hereafter. Many children of Kickapoo mothers and Mexican fathers in the past have been named into the tribe and will, upon dying, be sent to the place where the spirits of the Kickapoos are dispatched by means of an adoption ceremony. Nevertheless, there is always a question in the minds of the Kickapoos when an adoption ceremony is held for such a half-breed. Will a spirit who is half-Kickapoo, half-Mexican be accepted by the ruler in the spirit world of the Kickapoos? They fear that when such a spirit arrives and is questioned, he will find that he does not qualify. He may be turned away and try to reach the spirit world of the Mexicans, only to be turned away from there also. Where, then, will his spirit find a resting place? He could be forced to travel without end and might take revenge upon his living relatives for the wrong perpetrated upon him.

These beliefs have caused much soul searching among the tribe, to the point that several of the more orthodox clan leaders have, in the past, refused to name a child born of a Kickapoo mother and Mexican father.

In 1970 there were twenty-seven Kickapoo women in the village who had or had had Mexican spouses and one who had had an Anglo spouse. Of these, eight were living in the village with their Mexican husbands. One of these women had been legally married, while the others were common-law wives. Of the twenty-seven unions there had been thirty-nine children known to be half-breeds. Only fifteen of these had been named into a clan and thus into the tribe. Eight had died. The remaining sixteen lived in or near the village, but had not been named into the tribe, were not active participants in the activities of the clans, and could not be buried in the Kickapoo cemeteries. A few of these children had been christened in the Catholic church and did not participate in the village life at all. The mothers of those who had been neither christened nor taken into a clan lived in the hope that some day the clan leaders would soften their ways and accept their children into the tribe.

Some women whose children were sired by Mexicans have succeeded in having them named by the simple expedient of taking up with a Kickapoo man when they learned of their condition, pinning the paternity of the child upon the Kickapoo spouse. The women enjoy telling of one case, in which the Mexican paramour of the Kickapoo woman was well known by the Indians. Soon after becoming pregnant, the woman left him and began living with a Kickapoo man. The child was named in a clan, but she grew up to resemble her father and his family to such a degree that not only the mother but the village came to call her by her Mexican father's name.

Other women with half-breed children take them to Oklahoma, where there are many half-breeds and the clan leaders are less orthodox than those in Mexico. (The naming ceremony is also easier in Oklahoma, where turkey has been substituted for the large number of deer ribs required for a naming ceremony in Mexico, thus obviating the expense and time incurred in securing venison.) Once a child has been named in Oklahoma, even the most orthodox clan leader in Mexico will recognize and accept him.

Living in the village in 1970 were three Kickapoo men legally married to Mexican women. The children of all three had been named in clans. Earlier, eleven Kickapoo men had taken Mexican or Anglo wives. Two of these lived with them in a nearby town, where the offspring were christened in the Catholic church and were never named in a clan. Three of the eleven men who had offspring outside the village had no difficulty in having their half-breed children named *in absentia*. At any time, these children will be welcomed by the Kickapoos and may participate in the activities of the clan and the tribe.

Only one case in which Indians from another "nation" were taken into the tribe and renamed has come to our attention. Sometime in the 1880's two young Comanches, a youth (Conejuca) and a girl (Yacapita), appeared in the village, claiming that both had dreamed they would be well received and find lifelong friends among the Kickapoos. It was later learned that the youth had disobeyed orders from his chief and, rather than face up to the consequences, had run away from his people. Both of these young persons were renamed in a clan and given a moiety designation so that they could participate in the activities of the tribe. (Their Kickapoo names were Nenaiquita and Penipaiyecoa.) They had several children; later, they separated, each marrying a Kickapoo, by whom they had several more offspring. In 1970 many of their descendants were still living, among them the chief's wife. At the time we were told of this case, we were assured that any Indian from another "nation" wishing to live with the Kickapoos in good faith would be welcomed and given the same treatment; this, however, did not hold true for Anglos, Mexicans, or anyone not Indian.

Another case of name changing occurred not many years ago. A Kickapoo woman left the village to live in Oklahoma, where she married a half-Kickapoo, half-Sauk man. The child of this union was named in the father's clan, the Bear-Potato, but soon afterward, when the father died, the mother returned to her people in Mexico. Unfortunately for the child, there was no Bear-Potato clan among the Kickapoos. The child had no affiliation with any existing clan and thus could not participate in the activities of the tribe. To circumvent this anomalous situation, she was renamed in the Buffalo clan.

With the exception of two Indians, one of whom is Chief Papícoano, the Kickapoos have also adopted Spanish surnames and first names; but all prefer their Indian names, which are the ones used among themselves and, to a great extent, in dealings with the Mexican authorities and the Bureau of Indian Affairs in the United States. Just when the custom of acquiring a Spanish name began is difficult to ascertain. One of the first to have such a name was a young Kickapoo who fought in the Mexican Revolution in 1910. At the end of the war, his superior officer took him to Monterrey, placed him in school, had him christened, and gave him a Spanish name.

Today such names as Valdez, González, Treviño, Aguilar, Salazar, Garza, and Elizondo are commonly used as surnames by the Indians. Popular first names are Miguel, Juan, José, Tomás, Juanita, Sara, and Margarita. For his Spanish name, the child often uses the surname of his father, thus establishing a patrilineal pattern. There is a tendency to identify with these surnames or family names, particularly by the more Mexican-acculturated Indians. One of the informants who helped us compile the tribal roll was annoyed because a family not related to hers had used the same surname. She brushed them off with the crusty remark, "I don't know why they use that name; they do not belong to our family." Some Kickapoos use their father's clan name as a surname, preceding it with a Spanish first name; others use their own clan name with a Spanish first name. A few of the young men are now using the proper Spanish form for a name; that is, the given name first, the father's surname next, and the mother's surname last. A Kickapoo woman does not acquire her husband's Spanish name. This is understandable in view of the brittleness of their marriages.

Class

The Kickapoos often state that no one in their tribe is better than anyone else, that all live in the same type of house and enjoy the same privileges and responsibilities. This is true except in the case of the chief, who, as *capitán*, has many privileges not enjoyed by others. The chief may attend any of the ceremonies held in the village without being invited and officiates at his own personal ceremonies with his bundles. He is recognized as head of the tribe by the Mexican authorities and receives a small salary from the local municipality. He is honored, respected, and feared by all members of the tribe.

The chief's wife is the first woman to roof her summer house. This, as far as we know, is her only distinction other than the honor of being the wife of the chief.

When the chief dies, his son may become the chief, provided he is legitimate; otherwise a female relative, either a daughter or a niece, may become chief of the tribe.

Clan leaders, chanters, dancers, men and women skilled in certain crafts, and those whose clan affiliation grants them certain privileges, are subjects of special respect for their personal achievement and abilities but do not form a distinctive class apart from the less gifted or privileged. All members of the herbal societies are highly feared for their ability, according to nonmembers, to transform themselves into witches and concoct powerful potions and brews. Old people, likewise, are humored, not only because of their status in the community as repositories of tribal knowledge, but also because they too can turn themselves into witches.

Chapter 10

Life Cycle

Daily Routine

A Kickapoo woman head of a household (i.e., any woman who owns a house) rises before daybreak and goes to the cook house to start the fire with coals she banked the night before. If the fire has died out, she makes a new one with a piece of flint, a piece of steel, and dry shavings—or with matches. She is economical with firewood, beginning a fire with only three sticks and adding one or two others at a time as needed. After the fire is underway, she places a tripod or trivet over it and on this sets the hot-water kettle to brew coffee or tea.

After finishing her preliminary duties in the cook house she returns to the winter or summer house, depending upon the time of the year, rouses her family, dresses the younger ones, who have taken off only their outer garments for sleeping, and rolls up the bedding, storing it over the trunks, valises, and boxes on the west bench. If it is summer and some of the family are sleeping on the benches in the ramada, she rolls up that bedding and stores it with the rest. This transforms the house and the ramada from bedrooms into sitting rooms where the family may lounge or work.

The family goes to the cook house for a cup of hot tea or coffee, generously sweetened. The Kickapoos use canned milk in their coffee, as they do not keep dairy cows. In the meantime, the mother begins to prepare the wheat tortillas, which she bakes on the *comal* or fries in a Dutch oven, and warms something left over from supper or cooks a new meal of fried potatoes, meat, and eggs.

Ideally, the Kickapoos do not eat leftovers, but food has become too costly to waste. Any leftover food must be tightly covered to avoid tempting the spirits which have not yet been dispatched to the hereafter from dipping their fingers into it, should they become hungry.

While the mother prepares the meal with the assistance of the older girls, the other family members wash their faces in the basin near the cook house door, comb their hair outdoors, or go to bathe in the river. Between eight and nine o'clock, the family gathers around the hearth for a hearty breakfast. At noon, they have lunch, which consists of a soup. The evening meal is much like breakfast, always accompanied by large quantities of coffee or tea and tortillas, either fried or baked.

After a woman washes the dishes and puts them away, aided by the older girls, they sweep the trash of the houses and compound to the edges under the barbed-wire fence, where the accumulated litter remains. If a family owns a pickup, it is employed to carry wood, cut by the younger members, from the *monte*; otherwise, women, sometimes men, and children ride horses and burros to gather wood, the most favored being sweet acacia and catclaw acacia because of the intense heat they produce. Water may be brought from the springs in drums by pickup; otherwise children, especially girls, are sent on this errand, on foot, horse, or burro; if on foot, they carry the water in two five-gallon tin cans suspended from a pole over their shoulders.

The men spend the day tending to their livestock, working in the fields, tinkering with autos, hunting, working on the roads or irrigation ditches, repairing fences, and selling merchandise which they bring from the United States. The men sometimes make wooden artifacts, such as mortars and pestles, ceremonial ladles, cradle boards, or bows and arrows for small boys. Much of a man's time is spent in conversation and in ceremonies. Much time is consumed by both men and women in going to Múzquiz to market, sell their products, see a movie, get mail, or simply sit in the plaza to enjoy the sights, while some of the men spend their leisure time in a local saloon.

A woman has many chores ahead of her each day and finds little time for diversion except in the late afternoon and evening. Besides preparing the three daily meals, she chops firewood, washes clothes, irons, mends, and sews. Grandmothers and older siblings are charged with the care of infants and toddlers while the mothers engage in household tasks.

On sunny days they wash at the river, using commercial bar soap, pounding the clothes on the rocks to loosen the dirt, and spreading them to dry on the ground or nearby shrubs. While the mothers are washing on the banks, the children play in the water until they are bathed. During inclement weather, water, in which detergent is dissolved, is heated in the cook house in galvanized tubs and the clothes are boiled and rubbed on a washboard and hung on wire or fiber lines indoors, under the ramada, or outdoors. When clothes need to be pressed, the woman spreads an old blanket and sheet on one of the benches of the ramada and uses either a flatiron heated on the hearth or an iron inside of which she places a few coals.

Bingo game in winter. Note the tarpaulin covering the summer house to protect goods stored inside.

The women, with their husbands or in small groups of female relatives or friends, often go to the sierra to sell merchandise to the miners, or peddle articles among the poorer families who live at the edge of Múzquiz and other nearby towns.

In the late afternoon, if the weather permits, men, women, and children can be seen sitting on tarpaulins outdoors playing *lotería*, a variety of bingo in which pictures are substituted for the numbers on the cards. Discarded soda pop tops are placed on the pictures when these are called. After the younger children are put to bed and the teenagers go to the river to dance, play records, or court, the older men and women get up games of *paco*, a variety of poker, or poker itself, in which considerable amounts of money exchange hands. The bowl-and-dice game may also be played, except in the prohibited season, as well as the boys' and girls' ball game, which is not ceremonial but requires permission from the chief and may not be played during the period between the New Year and the occupation of the summer houses. Formerly, the game was played either by boys or by girls, but now both sexes play together.

When a group of young people wish to get up a game, they decide on a time and tell the woman named by the chief to act as intermediary. She calls on the chief for permission to play. He prays that no one will be hurt and dispatches a messenger to the man in the Eagle clan privileged to make the buckskin ball. (The intermediary should also belong to the Eagle clan, as is the case in Oklahoma, but when a Berry relative of Chief Papí-coano wished to have this role, it was granted to her.)

Years ago, there existed an open, unfenced area in the village where the game was played, but when a relative of the chief wished to build her house on this site, she was granted permission. This change created much friction between the intermediary and the new occupants; for, after this, since no other sites were available, the game had to be played in the same clearing across the river where the ceremonial games take place. Since this location is at a considerable distance from the village, it meant a major inconvenience for the intermediary, who had difficulty in walking due to her obesity. For this reason, the game was seldom played in the 1960's.

Two stones are set two hundred feet apart to serve as goals for the teams of ten boys and girls. The intermediary sits on the edge of the field with her eyes blindfolded. Each individual wishing to participate in the game takes a small object, recognizable by touch, and places it on a pile in front of her. When the number of objects reaches twenty, no more players are allowed, but those who do not make a team are given permission to enter the game after it gets underway. The intermediary divides the objects into two piles, while each donor watches carefully to see which team he will be on.

When the game begins, the intermediary (no longer blindfolded) stands equidistant from the two goals and throws the ball into the air. Whoever catches it runs to his goal to score a point, if he can avoid being tackled by the members of the opposing team. The other members of the ball carrier's team try to block the interceptors. Boys may kick the ball, but girls must carry it in their hands. There are no scorekeepers, score sticks, or referees; and the game is fast and rough.

Small boys spend many hours practicing marksmanship by shooting at fixed objects. As soon as they acquire some skill at this, they begin to shoot at a hoop made of willow withes, which is rolled by a playmate. This method of training for marksmanship was widely used by the Indians when they depended upon their bows and arrows for a livelihood, but now it is employed only by the small boys. Besides practicing marksmanship, small boys ride sticks while carrying their bows and arrows swung on their backs, dismount from their "horses," and shoot at each other or at objects. Small girls in theory are not supposed to play with bows and arrows, but some borrow them from their brothers and playmates and learn to be good shots.

One sees small boys adept at spinning tops. Boys and girls often play tag. The child who initiates the game breaks off a twig and divides it into several shorter segments, one for each player. Holding them tightly in one hand so that the lengths are not visible, he distributes them among the players. The child who picks out the shortest segment is "it" and has to chase the others until he touches one, who then becomes "it." Items that seem to have been adopted from the Mexican children are the sling-shot, made with a piece of inner tube, and marbles. Any child who has a tree in his compound can easily have a swing by throwing a rope over a limb. They do not put seats in the swings, but cling to the rope and swing themselves back and forth while standing on a knot tied at the bottom of the rope.

Girls are frequently seen playing house. It is fortunate that their elders sweep discarded kitchen utensils only to the edges of the compound, since these serve as objects with which to play house. On one occasion we almost stepped into one of these "houses." Girls had selected a shel-tered spot near a low bush and had outlined an elliptical area with twigs, inside of which they had laid a fire with three small sticks, where they had placed several discarded pieces of kitchenware.

Until a few years ago, female relatives made stuffed rag dolls, dressed in the traditional Kickapoo style and with horsetail hair, for the little girls. Favorites were made of animal pelts, such as lynx or beaver, stuffed with deer hair. Today, little girls play with plastic dolls and other modern toys.

Informants in their sixties remember seeing the cup-and-pin game when they were children, but it is no longer played. It was a game for males. According to the myth in which the culture hero brought the bundles and games to his people, the cup-and-pin game was one of the five given to the Kickapoos; however, this game was not a ceremonial game like the other four (the bowl-and-dice, lacrosse, double-shinny, and bow-and-arrow games).

Unless they stay up for a game of poker or *paco*, the Kickapoos retire early. The bedding is spread on the benches, the flap of the door is let down, the central fire is banked, and the kerosene lamp is extinguished for the night.

Training and Education

The majority of Kickapoo parents desire children and rear them with love and tender care in a natural way remembered from their own experiences and from observing other parents around them. That is not to say that some parents do not neglect their children to the point of allowing them to die of hunger, but these are a very small minority. One young woman with eight children, when asked if she planned to have more, replied

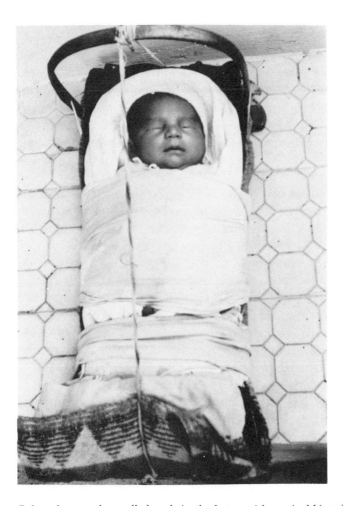

Baby asleep on the cradle board, in the Latorres' home in Múzquiz.

that all children would be welcomed, since they were a gift of Kitzihiat. Her own mother had seventeen. Men seem to be as proud of large families as women, though providing for them today has become a hardship.

The Kickapoos, as well as the Mexicans, believe that if an older child is neglected when a new one arrives, the former pouts, frets, mopes, and becomes generally unhappy, a condition known as *chípil*, which may be translated as "sibling jealousy." Once, when a woman was telling us that her sister-in-law had recently been delivered of a fine boy, she added that the older child had given it one look and told the mother to throw it out. When we inquired if the child could be *chípil*, she firmly replied, "Her children are never *chípil*; she loves and cares for all equally."

Parents are sometimes unduly reluctant to have a child treated in a hospital for a physical defect, fearing the separation, if only for a few months.

One case in particular comes to mind. After much persuasion we were able to convince the grandparents of a small girl whose mother had died at childbirth to take her to an orthopedic hospital in Oklahoma, where she could be treated for a back injury and a fistula. The grandparents permitted the child to stay in the hospital a few weeks, and she was showing much improvement; but unfortunately, unable to withstand the separation any longer, they took her out before complete recovery.

Other parents have a more realistic attitude and are willing to undergo separation when a child's life is endangered. One bright small boy was discovered to have tuberculosis when tested in Utah. The parents came to us for aid, and we assisted them in placing the child in the public health hospital in Talihina, Oklahoma; after a few months' stay there, he was able to rejoin his parents.

A child born in the winter spends many hours a day in his cradle board, which the Kickapoos believe will cause him to have a straight back and a well-shaped head. A child born in the hot summer months spends little time in the cradle board and more on a hammock made by doubling a rope around two upright posts in the house or ramada, folding a blanket over it, securing it with safety pins, and placing two short pieces of wood at each end to keep the rope separated. As soon as the baby begins to fret, he is fed or vigorously swung by the nearest relative. Sometimes the baby is placed in the cradle board and then in the blanket hammock. A child is placed daily in the cradle board until he begins to take a few steps or until he frets continuously about his confinement.

The cradle is carried not on the mother's back, as among other Indians, but in the arms and is propped up against a wall or placed in the blanket hammock as a mother goes about her chores. If a baby frets while on the board, the mother seems to find no difficulty in breast feeding him. The penis of a male child strapped into the cradle is left exposed and loosely covered with a cloth to prevent chafing after urination.

As infants, children begin to eat adult food. It was something of a shock to us to see tiny, toothless babies "gumming" on a corn tortilla, or being given tea, coffee, or soda pop.

There are no specific old men and women who gather small children around them for regular instructions, other than the clan leaders, who teach clan members the matters mentioned in Chapter 9. Grandparents and parents tell children myths about their culture hero, Wisaka, and about other manitous, people, and animals. The myths serve to teach them, not only information about their past, but practical lessons in care and consideration toward others. These myths, stories, and anecdotes are told only in the winter after the family have finished their evening meal and gather around the hearth. The children must fast in the morning if they wish to have stories told to them in the evening.

Children learn by doing and observing from early infancy. By the age of four, boys are practicing marksmanship with a bow and arrows; and, by the time they are ten, they are taken on hunts and permitted to use .22-caliber rifles. They learn at an early age to trap small game, spear fish with arrows, swim, mount a horse, work in the fields, cut wood, and carry water.

By the time a girl is ten she knows how to prepare a meal, make bread, sew a simple garment by hand or by machine, prepare skins, bead moccasins, make baskets, help care for younger siblings, carry wood and water, and help in the harvests.

At a tender age, children learn to carry heavy bundles of clothing and other articles which their elders barter or trade with local Mexicans. On one occasion, an old grandmother came to call with an adopted granddaughter carrying a large bundle, which she dropped on the floor by her chair. As we were curious to see its contents, the child obliged us by unfolding and refolding the neat bundle. First, she placed their personal bedding cater-cornered on the blanket that served as a cover, and over this she laid the articles they had brought to sell. She then folded the opposite corners of the blanket over the pile of goods, lifted the bundle by the other two corners, swung it over her back, and tied the ends over her chest, thus leaving her hands free.

By the time children are four years old they help their parents in the onion and carrot harvests in the vicinity of Eagle Pass, Texas. Youngsters, by the time they are ten, help thin beets in Montana and Wyoming, harvest fruit in Utah, and pick cotton in West Texas. Children do not consider themselves imposed upon, and neither do the parents feel they are abusing their children; instead, they believe this is part of their schooling: learning to work. A child turns over his pay to his mother—not to his father—and is given only a small part to spend at will.

Children early accompany their parents and grandparents to collect wild plants used for food, medicine, and construction, thus learning to distinguish them. One old woman, a prominent member of an herbal society, no longer able to ride her burro to the *monte* or sierra, sent her twelve-year-old son to gather the herbs she needed.

From the time they are toddlers the children participate in certain parts of tribal ceremonies, such as dancing and chanting; by the age of six or seven they are able performers. On one occasion, when a small boy of three was visiting us in the company of his grandmother, we played some Kickapoo songs recorded in Oklahoma. On hearing the familiar music, without any encouragement or entreaties, the small lad began to dance animatedly, to the delight of his audience.

If a clan leader is fortunate enough to have a son or nephew interested in learning the ritual of the ceremonies, he is soon initiated into the most secret matters.

Kickapoo children early learn the facts of life. Once we prevailed upon a woman to sing us a song which told of a young woman trying to get her lover out of the house before her parents awoke. Her twelve-year-old son, who was present, seemed to enjoy the ribald little song as much as the adults, chuckling and giggling all the while. This woman, who was an endless source of information on matters dealing with childbirth, insisted that Felipe leave the room when she discussed such matters—but not her granddaughter of eight, before whom she described a birth in vivid detail, with accompanying gestures.

Kickapoo parents are permissive with their children—to a degree. Several types of punishment are administered by the parents, usually by the mother, the mother's brother and his wife, or the father's sister. The most common punishment is to smear a child's face and mouth with soot and send him outdoors without his breakfast—his blackened face serving as a warning to neighbors not to give him water or food. If his conduct is worse than a misdemeanor, he is made to fast for one or two days. Mothers and grandmothers sometimes switch the legs of children, but slapping their faces is done infrequently. The mother's brother and his wife or the father's sister may also punish a child by throwing him in the river, keeping his head under water for a while, or throwing a pail of cold water in his face. Throwing water on a child or throwing him in the river is believed to cool off his anger. Girls are punished in this way only up to the time of their menarche.

To make them behave, children are often threatened. They are told that an ape or a monkey will "get" them. Before calling on us, they were told we might whip them if they tore the magazines or damaged a toy.

From childhood to death, an individual is subject to punishment, admonition, and unsolicited advice from parents or relatives entitled to this privilege. Children are particularly respectful and obedient to the clan leaders, whom they call *grandfather*, and to the chief. A glance or a "shush" from any of these men will quiet a fretful child immediately.

Formerly, when the Kickapoos had their own police, they patrolled the village and environs, armed with a long pole to which was affixed a sharp metal point or sharp pins. Young people caught outdoors after certain hours were pricked on their necks and delivered to their parents. One woman still bears the scars of this treatment. An informant told us that when she was being courted by her present Mexican husband her father was one of the police. He caught her out late one night and beat her with a rope until she bled.

Whenever a Kickapoo child loses a baby tooth, his mother or grandmother tells him to run around the house four times and throw the tooth over the house while saying, "I want the garter snake to swap this tooth for one of his."

If a parent wishes to summon a child who is out of sight, he whistles in such a way that he imitates the sound of the child's name. If the child is within sight or nearby, he is called by his name. Children are not summoned by whistling during the night, however, for fear a spirit might be lingering nearby and come on hearing a familiar call.

Up to adolescence, children are reprimanded if caught indulging in masturbation or sex play with either sex. Boys are taught not to molest girls wearing the distinguishing topknot hairdo which indicates that they have not reached their menarche.

Kickapoo children, taught to sleep lightly and to awaken at the least noise, must be out of bed before sunrise. They are told that if Grandfather Sun sees them lying down, this could mean they wanted to be stretched out in the cemetery. They must also be fed before sunrise and before sunset and put to bed before sunset. They are also taught that they must never be measured for height or width, since this is only done when the body is laid out in order to know the dimensions of the grave. To be measured would indicate one wanted to die.

The majority of the children seem uninhibited, sweet, and docile; but some are exceedingly shy, and others are irascible and ill-tempered. Many have lovely manners, but others act as though they could tear the house apart. No matter what the conduct of a child in public, only once did we see a mother lose her temper sufficiently to spank her son. One small boy who accompanied his mother on a visit to us sulked, pouted, and pounded on his mother during the entire visit; his mother never once reprimanded him.

One little girl who had previously behaved sweetly and gently in our home injured one of her legs and consequently had to be carried in the arms of her female relatives for several days. During a visit to our home at this time we hardly recognized the child's behavior. She acted as though everything belonged to her; she wanted to hold all of the toys in the basket and all of the dolls at the same time. When we gave her a small plastic doll and her older half-sister a small basket with miniature kitchen utensils, the younger girl wanted not only the doll but her sister's basket as well. When the latter showed determination to keep her gift, the younger sister ripped the clothes off the doll, dismembered it, and continued to whine and pout. Neither the mother nor the grandmother made one gesture of disapproval; neither did they reprimand her. After her leg had healed, the child returned to her previous good behavior.

With very few exceptions, the Kickapoos are as strongly opposed to formal schooling today as they were in 1883, when a Quaker school teacher, Elizabeth Test, was sent to their reservation in Oklahoma and was unable to enroll a single student during a period of six months.[1] Middle-aged Kickapoos today tell stories about their experiences in Indian boarding schools in Kansas, where boys and girls were carefully segregated, they were not allowed to speak their language, efforts were made to strip them of their culture, and the girls were denied the pleasure of seeing any male relative, even though he might be attending the same school. As a result, these pitiable children soon sickened and had to be sent to relatives to recover from their traumatic experiences.

Although the Mexican government has made two attempts to set up schools in the village, once during the tenure of President Porfirio Díaz, at the turn of the century, and again when President Lázaro Cárdenas was in office, no child attended either of the schools, both of which burned mysteriously, while the teachers fled in panic. Chief Papícoano and the old people, all highly respected, were still strongly opposed to any formal schooling when we were in Múzquiz. Some of the men would like to see their sons learn the rudiments of reading, writing, and numbers, but they strongly object to having their daughters instructed in these matters. Part of their resistance to formal schooling is based on the fear that it would impose taxes on them and that the salary of a teacher and school supplies would be a financial burden. Moreover, they reason, attendance in school would deprive the parents of the labor of their children both at home and in the fields. Some also believe that schooling is bad for the formation of character; others claim that persons who have attended school are quarrelsome. One man, whose son had some years of school in Oklahoma and is an inveterate alcoholic, blames the school for his son's drinking problem.

Years ago, when some Mexicans tried to teach a handful of Kickapoo youths working in Múzquiz to read and write in Spanish, Chief Papícoano immediately ordered the young people to return to the village, convinced that those who acquire the white man's ways are no better than coyotes, a term used by the Mexicans to denote sharpers.

The majority of Kickapoo parents believe that their children are so intelligent that they need only to fast to receive knowledge of reading and writing, bestowed upon them by the Great Spirit, or that they will be able to learn by watching others read and write. A few parents, however, are not satisfied with this heaven-sent method of learning and have enrolled their children in schools of nearby Ejido Morelos or the Negro village. Two half-breeds attend school in Múzquiz. Understandably, even these children spend little time in school, since the motivation is almost non-existent. Why go to school when your peers are playing at home and the adults disapprove of you?

Some parents send one or two children to live with Oklahoma relatives in order that they may attend school. In Utah, schooling is provided for migrant children; but, because of their frequent moves from one job to the next, attendance is sketchy, to say the least. A few parents whose jobs keep them in one location in Utah allow their children to attend the local schools with more regularity.

When we first began our study, the chief's aide came to us with the startling news that Chief Papícoano and the Council of Elders had decided the time was ripe for them to have a school and asked us to write to this effect to the Department of Education in Saltillo. We took the letter to the chief for his approval, official seal, and thumbprint signature, and dispatched it. A few weeks later the Department of Education sent a committee to the village, rejoicing over the expectation of schooling the Kickapoos after the two previous futile attempts. They were received coolly by the chief and his aide and told that they had no intention of having a school and that the idea had originated with us. We realized that a delicate trap had been set for us and that the Indians were trying to undermine our relations with the Mexican authorities by placing us in a ridiculous position—perhaps with the hope that we would be sent out of the country and leave them alone.

Some parents are beginning to want a school in the village, but, as of 1970, no decisive steps had been taken in that direction. The Mexican Department of Education had offered to train two or three of the brightest youngsters and return them to teach the others, as is being done throughout Mexico in a program to educate the Indian population; however, this inducement had brought forth no action on the part of the Kickapoos.

In spite of having no formal schooling, some of the Kickapoos have learned from others the syllabary invented by Sequoyah. Others have learned rudimentary reading and writing in Spanish, either from each other, from Mexican cowherd friends who rent their pastures, or from other migrant workers they meet in the United States.

The word has spread among the women that single mothers are being aided by welfare programs if they enroll their offspring in public schools in Oklahoma. Several, including Chief Papícoano's daughters, have taken advantage of this opportunity. Gradually, by one means or another, and in spite of protests and objections from the old people, the children are, by slow stages, receiving some formal education.

Sexual Development

Although most Kickapoo men and women have had several marriages and some have had numerous affairs, when the subject of sex is broached, they are exceedingly timid, giggling and blushing when asked the simplest question. When a grandmother and her daughter brought a male child in his cradle board and we noticed that the penis was left exposed to prevent the urine from soaking his body, we asked the name of the member in Algonquian. Both women and another female relative, one of our most generous informants, began to giggle, and the grandmother, after much hesitation said to us, "That is an ugly word." It was not until later, when we were alone with our informant, that we learned the word.

This same shyness reveals itself in the clothes they wear, in the fact that both men and women wear garments during intercourse, and in the women's fear of being examined by a male physician. This modesty is not present among children, certainly not among small boys, who run around totally naked or, at most, with only a brief shirt while bathing and playing in the river and irrigation ditches during the summer. Little girls are bathed in the presence of their families and friends and, until their menarche, bathe in the river with boys, wearing only a skirt.

It is easy to distinguish a Kickapoo girl before her menarche, as her hair is dressed in a particular fashion to indicate that she is still a child and not a *señorita* (young lady). The hair is braided in three sections: one on either side of the head and another in the center. The three braids are brought to the top of the head to form a little topknot, secured with a ribbon.

Small girls are early encouraged to play with dolls and feminine toys; boys practice marksmanship and shooting at "bad" Indians while using sticks for riding horses. Prior to puberty, a boy has helped his father in the care of the livestock, is an expert horseman, has helped in the fields, has been taught some ceremonial ritual, and has been told stories about "bad women."

There are no puberty rites, as such, for boys, but as soon as a boy's voice changes he is called "a young man," ceases to accompany female members of his family, attaches himself to his father, an older brother, or an uncle (mother's brother), and begins to associate with boys of his age group.

On the other hand, a girl undergoes a severe rite at her menarche. As she approaches this age, usually between eleven and fourteen, she is warned by her mother or other female relative with whom she lives: "You are soon going to lose blood. When you notice this, hide your face with your hands and conceal yourself in the *monte*; I will go to take care of you.''

In preparation for this event the mother shows the girl the new set of cooking utensils which she will use during her stay in the *monte*: a small skillet, coffeepot, casserole, cup, spoon, and knife. By this time the girl has learned to prepare some of the simple foods, such as wheat tortillas, beans, soups, and coffee or tea. When the day arrives and the girl is missed, her mother seeks her out, builds a tiny hut with a grass roof, takes bedding, food, water, cooking utensils, and firewood to her, and explains how she is to conduct herself. She must stay inside the shelter, except to take care of her toilet needs; she must not speak to anyone, particularly to a male, as she is unusually dangerous at this time; she may not scratch her head or her body with her hands, or her hair will fall out; she must stay in the shelter for ten days, the last four without food or water. She may spend her time meditating, sleeping, lying down, sewing or making baskets, and preparing her meager food. If she suffers from cramps she is given teas to relieve them. On the sixth day the female relative calls on her again, blackens her face with soot from her fire, takes away all food, water, and cooking utensils, and tells her to fast until her relative returns for the last time.

Before daybreak on the tenth day, the female relative visits her again and, depending on her clan membership, administers the appropriate ordeal. For instance, if she belongs to the Bear or Man clan, she will be made to undress and will be beaten with a willow switch until blood flows from her back, legs, and arms; if she is a member of the Berry or Tree clan, she will be made to stand straight with her arms by her sides, and her arms and legs will be slashed with a hollow-ground knife until the blood flows, when the wounds will be treated with gunpowder.

Although women remember this experience as an extremely painful one, they claim they did not cry and were willing to submit to the treatment stoically in the belief that it would give them strong arms and legs to withstand the arduous tasks they perform, prevent them from being lazy and shiftless, and ensure them a moderate menstrual period. After the ordeal, accompanied by her relative carrying new clothes, the girl goes to the river to bathe and wash her hair. After she dresses in new garments, her hair is combed in a long braid down her back. Her companion washes the bedding in the river and sets it out to dry in the sun; later, the same relative returns to the *monte* to burn the shelter. In the meantime, the girl proudly returns to the village; she is now a *señorita* and is ready for marriage.

The Kickapoos believe that, in the old days, women did not have menstruation; but the moon, herself a woman and still alive, sent them the period. This, they reason, is why the menses appear every twenty-eight days—the same as the moon. They believe their menses occur at one of the three phases of the moon: new, full, or old. Because of its association with the moon, the period is usually called *la luna* (the moon), but some call it *la enfermedad* (the sickness). During each period a woman must seclude herself in the menstrual hut, and under no circumstances may she enter a house covered with cattails. In the hut are kept bedding, dishes, and clothes used exclusively for this occasion. She prepares her own food and abstains from eating such fruits as citrus in the belief that these may arrest the flow.

Today, laxness is evident in the observance of the strict taboos. Girls complain that they are afraid to spend the nights in the *monte* during their menarche and return to the village at dusk to stay in the menstrual hut. Women, during their menses, if they have no one else to prepare food for their families, perform this task outdoors. They are no longer confined to quiet activities, such as sewing, but go to gather firewood and material to build their houses, and travel, if necessary, with their husbands and children. Many complaints are voiced by the older and more orthodox members of the tribe that women during this period spend too much of the time lolling in the compound and not enough confined to the hut.

After a woman ends her period, she leaves the hut before daybreak and goes to the river, carrying clean clothing, a towel, and soap. She bathes thoroughly, washes her hair, and only then may return to the cattail-covered house. One woman in the village is known not to observe the taboo of the cattail-covered house during her menses. Her home is called "the menstrual hut." Chief Papícoano and the clan leaders blamed her laxness as the cause of the severe droughts of the past years. The chief would have liked to see this woman move to Oklahoma, where the Indians are not as orthodox as they are in Mexico.

Kickapoo women are of the opinion that the onset of menopause should occur in the fiftieth year or thereabout; if the change happens earlier, they become concerned. With the onset of menopause, a woman feels that she is "old"; that is, she will no longer be interested in sex, and her husband will thereafter seek younger women. Among the various women with whom we talked about menopause, there were few complaints of malaise other than the fear of losing their husbands to younger women. When we asked one if she had ever experienced hot flashes, she replied that she had never heard of such a thing. Perhaps the fact that women spend a great deal of time outdoors and are active precludes discomforts during this period and leaves them little time to dwell on their aches and pains. Not all women escape the ailments associated with menopause, however, for several cases of excessive and prolonged bleeding have come to our attention. The curers usually take care of this condition with the use of herbs; but sometimes, when these have not proven effective, they resort to Mexican *curanderas* or physicians.

The women enjoy the freedom and privileges the menopause brings. They no longer have to observe the strict taboos; they are now able to handle plants and herbs heretofore forbidden to them; and they may be invited to participate in many ceremonies taboo to women during their menstruating years.

Formerly, girls up to sixteen or eighteen were carefully chaperoned; they were virgins to the day of their marriage and were supposed to be completely innocent about sex. Now, sexual experimentation is common among the Kickapoo girls after their menarche—and perhaps even earlier; if one is to give credence to an informant, known as a Don Juan, who believes there is not a single virgin over ten in the village. Some of the boys are particularly gifted in amorous ways and are much sought after by the girls. The increased parental slackness, the absence of the former police, who kept young people, especially girls, under control, and the increase in car ownership all contribute to create many unchaperoned opportunities for sex play.

Although the old people bemoan the increase in premarital offspring, particularly those of unknown paternity, others have told us that children born out of the acceptable Kickapoo wedlock have always occurred—with more frequency between Kickapoo girls and Mexicans. In compiling the tribal roll we discovered that as far back as sixty years ago a child was born in the village as the result of a dalliance between a Kickapoo girl and a Mexican.

Though there is no particular stigma attached to a girl who has one child by an unknown father, a repetition of unknown paternity gives a girl a bad name. She is expected to settle down with one man at a time and establish a home. If a young man knows he has sired a child, he will gladly bag the necessary deer to hold the naming ceremony and will give the child his clan name; however, if he suspects that he is one of several with whom a girl has had relations and she claims him as the father of her child, likely as not he will confront her with the truth and she will have no recourse but to ask some relative to name the child—if she can find a clan leader who will perform the ceremony. Otherwise, she will have to take the child to Oklahoma or rear a nameless child. If a girl has relations on the sly with a Mexican, she may deliberately attach herself to a Kickapoo man on whom she can pin the paternity of her child. This is an old trick, often tried, sometimes successfully.

Not only is premarital permissiveness common; extramarital license is equally so. The Kickapoos may be shy or modest, but they are not straitlaced in their sexual relations. We do not know of a spinster over eighteen. All the older women have been married several times, and the majority have had numerous affairs. When a woman separates from her husband, she may indulge in a series of dalliances until she finds another spouse. Women who are still married are also apt to have lovers. Unquestionably, there are cases of nymphomania among the Kickapoo women. We know of one woman who has had eight husbands and numerous lovers. She is known as being *muy troteadora* (a "trotter").

Prostitution is not unknown among the women. It is practiced not with their own men but with Mexicans. Particularly on Saturday evenings, Kickapoo women are often seen strolling along the streets of Múzquiz where great numbers of saloons are located, frequented by ranch hands and miners fresh from their isolated work who go into town with an eye for possible "dates." The women are given little for their favors—one or two dollars, perhaps a meal in a cheap restaurant, or sometimes the price of a dress length.

No cases of male homosexuality or lesbianism came to our attention. We did observe two cases of transvestitism, both among children. Once, while we were watching a woman's dance, our attention was called to a five-year-old boy attired in a girl's dress, consisting of a full skirt and blouse, with his hair combed in the premenarche topknot. We were told that this child liked to dress in a girl's clothing and his parents indulged him in his wishes. We took the information with a grain of salt, but later in the day while he was climbing a fence we saw that he was indeed equipped with male organs. Upon inquiring about him three or four years later, we were told he no longer liked to dress like a girl. On another occasion, a young mother came to call on us with her three-year-old son dressed in a girl's clothing. We have not heard of any cases among adults. Perhaps the permissiveness in childhood settles the problem forever.

We have known of two cases of fondling. Both involved adult males who enjoyed young girls; both were the laughingstock of the village; and, although one was a gifted craftsman who used his wares to lure the young girls and the other owned one of the most important dances, they were almost pariahs. This act is considered highly irregular among the Indians—and rightly so, they say, since marriage or dalliance is easy among them. Neither of these men, however, was considered a desirable husband, for they were not hunters.

Among the Kickapoos both in Mexico and in Oklahoma[2] there exists the custom of "declared friends" for both sexes. When two individuals of the same sex, whether married or single, feel a great attraction for each other in a friendship which transcends that of siblings, they seal it with a small ceremony in which they announce to Kitzihiat and to the villagers their plighted troth until death. Thereafter, they will be each other's confidants, especially in illicit love affairs; exchange gifts; and share their worldly goods as well as their sorrows. The men help each other in chores and go on hunts together. The women dress alike, especially at dances, where they stay together, and share in the performance of many labors. As noted in Chapter 9, the friends assume the various kinship roles in relationship to members of each other's families. The spouse of either is entitled to sibling-in-law conduct, which borders on the ribald. At the death of one friend, the survivor is chosen to be the representative for the deceased at the adoption ceremony. When polygyny was practiced, the surviving friend was entitled to take the widow of his deceased friend as his wife, provided that the other prerequisites for marriage were met.

Pregnancy, Birth, Lactation, and Abortion

In order to bring forth a normal, healthy child, a Kickapoo woman must observe many taboos connected with her activities and even those of her husband, for how she sleeps, what she eats, and what she looks at may affect the child in one way or another and ease or complicate the delivery. As soon as a woman is aware of her pregnancy, she begins to observe the many rules laid down for her. She believes that the breaking of these may be the cause of injury and defects to her offspring, a difficult delivery, or even death. Ideally, a pregnant woman must limit her activities to light tasks and forego riding a horse or burro, chopping wood, lifting heavy objects, and tiring herself unduly.

A pregnant woman must not sleep too many hours, for this is thought to make the delivery difficult. When she goes to bed, she must sleep on a hard surface and use a low pillow to strengthen her body. She must not sleep on her side, or the child's arms may be injured. She must not sleep crosswise on the bed, or the child will assume a breech position in the womb and be difficult to deliver. She must always lie in bed in an east-west position with her head to the east in order to facilitate delivery. Under no circumstances may a pregnant woman stand in a door, as this will cause the child to stay in the opening of the womb and delay delivery. She must never peep through the interstices of the walls of her house, for this will cause the child to be born with a squint.

Looking at a snake, dead or alive, or watching the killing of one—done by the Mexicans but never by a Kickapoo—can be exceedingly harmful. The child may be born with the fontanelle "too open" or with the umbilical cord around its neck, thereby choking during delivery. The Kickapoos fear a coyote crossing the road or trail in front of them as a certain sign of death. If this occurs to a pregnant woman, it is thought that her child has little chance to be born alive. To counteract this danger, a knot is tied in a scarf or handkerchief. This invalidates the coyote's evil spell, since one has "tied" him up. A pregnant woman must not look at a badger, or her child will be subject to earache. A child born with this propensity must be taken to the burrow where a badger lives and his head stuck into the opening while the adult prays to the animal to remedy the condition. The pregnant woman must never watch a bull calf, colt, kid, or lamb being castrated, nor may her husband castrate any animal during his wife's pregnancy, or the child will be born sterile. To make matters worse, the animal castrated by the husband will not heal and screwworms will set in. The husband must not kill or eat puppy served in a ceremonial feast.

A pregnant woman must never look at a dying person; if she does, her child will be born emaciated. She must not look at a mentally afflicted individual, or her child will be born in the same condition. She must not look at an eclipse, or the child will die, since the Kickapoos believe this is what is happening to the moon. She must not look at a rainbow, or the child will be born with a harelip. She must not look at a tree being struck by lightning or at one which has been struck by lightning, or her child will be born with itching sores on its body.

When the husband of a pregnant woman goes on a hunt, he must take a lunch to placate the crying spirit of his child and leave it at a place distant enough so that the deer will not be alarmed by the cries.

From the onset of pregnancy, a woman must observe many food taboos. She must avoid eating the intestines of any animal, or the child will become entangled in them. She must not eat nuts of any variety, or the placenta will thicken and be difficult to expel. She must not eat blood sausage, as this will cause the child to be born with a thick cover of wax in his ears and will cause her to hemorrhage at childbirth. She must avoid eggs, as they prevent the flow of milk; nor may she eat any of the citrus fruits, or her child will be born dry and puckered. She must not drink too many liquids, especially soda pop, as this causes too much fluid in the placenta. Members of the Fire clan may not eat fawn, or they will abort.

Otherwise, a woman may indulge in any food whim, and her husband may do likewise, in the belief that the child is asking for these particular foods. A pregnant woman may also eat reasonable portions of meat and drink small amounts of water.

The women reckon the months of pregnancy by the moon, and the approximate number of days by the phase of the moon (new, full, or old), dating from the last menstrual period. Kickapoo women believe they can tell the sex of the child by the shape of the mother's abdomen: if the abdomen is pointed, the child will be a boy; if round, a girl.

A woman, as soon as she recognizes her pregnancy, binds her abdomen with a heavy, coarse cloth. Rarely does a woman have prenatal medical attention unless she is under the care of a physician for another reason—a rare occurrence. A Kickapoo midwife, however, may be called in to correct a child in a breech position by manipulation and massage.

When a woman approaches the time for her delivery, she, her mother, or another woman who has had children makes the necessary preparations. The mother provides a new pair of scissors, a gift to the woman who cuts the umbilical cord. Older Kickapoo women believe that the only place and way to deliver a child is in the *monte*. One informant in her sixties told us she had never been sick a day with her seventeen children— all of whom she had delivered in the *monte* with the assistance of female relatives. She pooh-poohs the habit of younger women going to the hospital in Múzquiz for this event. Even when a woman goes to the hospital she stays only twenty-four hours, returning to the village for the period of seclusion in the menstrual hut or, in the case of an abortion, for the prescribed period in the *monte*, accompanied by her husband or lover.

Except in extremely inclement weather, when delivery takes place in the menstrual hut, the assistants go to a secluded place in the *monte* where no man is apt to pass, build a temporary shelter, and stake into the ground a single post or a crossbar, which the parturient, in a squatting position, will grasp in order to bear down and induce a quicker delivery. A rough bed of grass is spread on the ground, over which are placed old quilts, to receive the child. A fire is built nearby, and herbal teas are heated if the woman has a difficult delivery and it is necessary to administer these as an aid. The parturient is massaged to ease delivery and given teas to hasten the afterbirth.

When the moment for the delivery arrives, the mother squats on the grass and grips the pole, while the assistant kneels in front of her to receive the child, whose cord is cut with the new pair of scissors. The child is not slapped on the buttocks, as is customary in our culture, but is allowed to lie on some old clothes while the assistants look after the mother and the afterbirth. This is rolled up into a ball, tied around several times with Johnson grass, and placed out of reach on a black-brush acacia, where it will disintegrate.

If the delivery is difficult and slow or if the afterbirth is slow, one old woman who owns a special herb for this contingency is called to assist. One of the women assistants takes her a gift of Indian tobacco, and the old woman goes to the aid of the patient. An afterbirth that is slow is much feared, as it is thought that this may spell death for both the child and the mother. As soon as a woman delivers and the afterbirth is hidden, her abdomen is tightly bound, and she is made to walk back and forth until she goes to the menstrual hut, in the belief that this activity will prevent hemorrhaging.

The child's umbilical cord is tied with a twisted cloth string. Skunkbush sumac is finely triturated, moistened with saliva, and applied to the cord and surrounding area to keep it moistened. The child's abdomen is also tightly bound in several cloths, and he is swaddled in a cradle board, after which he is taken with his mother to the menstrual hut. If the child is a boy, the mother spends thirty days in the hut; if a girl, forty days. If her seclusion period is thirty days, she must observe another ten days of sexual abstinence; any indulgence before the completion of the pre-scribed forty-day period may bring death to the mother. If a woman has an abortion, either spontaneous or induced, or if the child dies at birth, she must observe the same precautions as in a normal birth.

In the hut she cares for the child in a kneeling position and does not lie down for the first ten days, during which she eats only corn gruel that she prepares in special dishes and drinks only herbal teas, in order to re-duce the uterus and produce milk. She sleeps in a sitting position during this period. If she has too much milk, her breasts are rubbed with com-mercial soap to decrease the flow; in the event they cake, they are washed with the same soap, massaged, and rinsed with warm water. After the tenth day, she may add to her diet.

She bathes the child daily in herbal water and returns him to the cradle board. The mother does not bathe until the child is four days old, nor does she wash his clothes until after the tenth day. Old rags are used for re-ceiving the discharge and are burned each day by a female relative.

A mother keeps a daily count of her days in isolation by notching the hoop of the child's cradle. After her designated period of seclusion and before sunrise, she takes a bundle of clean clothes provided by a female relative, soap, and a towel and bathes in the river, regardless of the weather. Only then is she ready to return with her child to the cattail-covered house.

Although few mothers deliver their children in the Múzquiz hospital unless some complication arises, the women frequently have their chil-dren in hospitals while working in the United States. One young mother, in relating her experience, said that the things she liked best in the hos-pital were the clean and comfortable bed and the three big meals. She did everything she was asked to do except bathe until her child was four days old.

In former days, both menstruating and parturient women were con-sidered particularly dangerous; now, women in these conditions are not as apt to seclude themselves carefully as they were formerly; but they still must under no circumstances enter the cattail-covered house. On various occasions we have been with women in the company of their husbands before their menstrual or involutionary period had terminated. The fear that a woman during this period could harm her husband seems to have lost its importance.

The Kickapoos do not practice circumcision. When we asked an old woman if this was customary, she looked at us incredulously and replied, "We don't do those things!"

When the navel stump is ready to fall off, it is closely watched, since it is thought that, if it is lost, the child will be mischievous—constantly prying into things. Once the stump falls off, it is encased in a small beaded bag and hung on the hoop of the cradle board. Once the child has outgrown the board, the beaded bag is stored until he reaches the age of seven or eight and "has acquired understanding and is able to reason." A girl is then given the small bag and told to bury it in the family's farm plot when no one is watching. Here she digs a hole about ten inches deep and, while burying the bag, tells Grandmother Earth, "I bring you this; keep it carefully for me." A boy buries his navel stump in the *monte*; he also charges Grandmother Earth with the safekeeping of his gift.

Soon after a male child is placed on the cradle board, a male relative makes him a miniature bow and arrows, which are hung on the hoop so that he will be aware of his most important role: that of a hunter. A female child has three small metal bells placed on the hoop to entertain her.

Until recently, a Kickapoo woman who could not breast feed her child was an object of pity. It was said of her that she had brought a child into the world but could not provide for him. In the rare instances when this occurred, the child was fed by another nursing mother. Today, many of the mothers bottle feed their children, sometimes with disastrous results, owing to their lack of cleanliness. Unboiled water, unwashed bottles, and clogged nipples are the culprits which carry many children to the grave.

As we noted earlier, a parturient woman while in the hut takes only herbal teas to produce milk, abstaining from drinking water, soda pop, coffee, or tea; but once she completes the involution period she discontinues the herbal teas, drinks large quantities of coffee and beer and eats many peanuts—all thought to produce abundant milk.

The Kickapoo mothers never observe a schedule of breast feeding but nurse the child when he whines. This they do in private or in public, the loose blouse they wear lending itself well to this act with no apparent loss of modesty. Children are permitted to take the breast until they no longer seek it; sometimes this stretches into the fourth or fifth year. When a child is able to walk, he goes to his mother, whines for the breast and, while standing, suckles until satisfied, when he runs off to other activities.

When a mother tires of giving the breast to a child, she rubs a bit of *chilequipín* on her nipples.

Though some women deny that the Kickapoos induce abortions, others have told us that induced abortions are frequently done among them. We know the case of a young woman, several months pregnant, who, in a jealous rage, threw herself from the summer bench to the hard-packed earth floor, falling on her abdomen in order to kill her child. (She succeeded in her efforts but nearly died herself during delivery.) Other women use certain herbs provided by the Kickapoo curers or the Mexican *curanderas*. One informant told us how, many years ago, shortly after her marriage, her husband began having an affair. At the time, she was eight months pregnant, but so great was her rage when she discovered her husband's infidelity that she went to a Mexican *curandera*, secured the herbs, and induced an abortion. She hemorrhaged to the point of almost dying and finally had to put herself under the care of a local physician, who restored her to health.

Other women abort from natural causes, such as indulging in too strenuous labor, riding a horse, or lifting heavy objects. In either case, whether an abortion is natural or induced, the woman and her husband must go to the *monte*, build a temporary shelter, prepare their food in separate utensils, and remain there, one on either side of the shelter, for a period of five days for the husband and ten days for the wife. If the woman is separated from her husband or lover, he is sought out and obligated to observe this period of isolation. On the sixth day of seclusion, a female relative goes to the shelter and takes away the remaining food, leaving only herbs, with which the woman prepares herself teas for the remaining days and returns to the menstrual hut to complete the forty-day period of involution.

Marriage and Separation

Sol Tax states that traditionally the clans of the Fox, to whom the Kickapoos are closely related in language and culture, were exogamous, but that today there is no sentiment in favor of clan exogamy.[3] Charles Callender notes that marriage within the clan among the Central Algonquians was prohibited around 1800,[4] while Betty Ann Wilder Dillingham says that one of the criteria for marriage among the Kickapoos of Oklahoma is that the couple be of different clans but adds that she found twelve clan-endogamous marriages among the group.[5] Ben J. Wallace says that an Oklahoma Kickapoo man can marry a woman from any clan.[6]

Among the Kickapoos in Mexico, clan exogamy seems to be of no consequence today, although formerly it was observed. When we asked an old woman if a man from the Bear clan could marry a woman from the same clan, she snorted slightly and replied, "Me, Tree; my man, Tree!"

The most important prerequisite for marriage is that there be no "blood" relationship on either side of the family of the contracting parties. Thomas Forsyth mentioned this requirement as far back as 1827.[7] This observation is difficult to reconcile with that of Callender, who infers that at one time cross-cousin marriage existed among the Central Algonquians, the group to which the Kickapoos belong.[8] One case of cross-cousin marriage among the Kickapoos was brought to our attention, with the criticism that it did not last long and was considered irregular.

Second, the persons marrying must in no way be related through an adoption ceremony, since a relationship acquired through this ceremony is considered the same as a blood relationship. Dillingham makes it clear that this is also true among the Oklahoma Kickapoos.[9]

Age is not an important factor. Although the majority of couples are approximately of the same age, there are several marriages between old men and young women, there being no desirable set number of years between the ages of those contracting matrimony. (Dillingham, however, indicates that among the Oklahoma Kickapoos an age difference of more than ten years is considered undesirable.)[10]

Among the Kickapoos there is still another criterion which in the past created much turmoil but today is less well enforced: namely, the prohibition of marriage with Mexican men or with descendants of the Negroes who accompanied the Seminole Indians and who still live only five miles from the Kickapoo village. Although mixed marriages occurred as far back as sixty years ago, the women, if caught, were subject to exile from the village and were beaten with ropes or disowned by their parents. Today, one woman and three men are married by law to Mexicans. There are several common-law marriages between Kickapoos and Mexicans and one between a Kickapoo woman and a quadroon descendant of the Negroes.

When a Kickapoo man marries a Mexican woman, she is usually indoctrinated by his sisters or other female relatives into the Kickapoo ways, especially in the observance of the menstrual taboos. She dresses like a Kickapoo woman, learns the crafts, and participates in the women's dances.

The Kickapoos are not averse to marriages with other Indians, especially those of related tribes, such as the Shawnee, Sauk, Fox, Potawatomi, Cherokee, and Chickasaw, or even Comanche. In the past this occurred frequently, as can be seen from their genealogies. It is assumed that the Kickapoos believe the progeny from these unions, upon arriving in the hereafter, will be received either in the Kickapoo heaven or in an adjacent one.

Marriages with Anglos are rare. One woman was married to an Anglo by a Justice of the Peace a few years back while working in Texas, but he treated her so shabbily that she soon left him. One young man who shuttles back and forth between Oklahoma and Mexico has an Anglo wife. Several Kickapoos boast of their French ancestry and support their claim to this early mixture by their fair skin and blue eyes.

A man, even today, may demand that his bride be a virgin; otherwise he may return her to her parents. (This was more likely to be done formerly than now.) After marriage a man expects his wife to rear his children in the ways of the Kickapoos. She must be able-bodied to perform the many tasks and crafts for which she is responsible and is expected to stay in the cook house, which, according to many men, is the woman's place, rather than socialize with relatives and friends in other compounds. In public, she must let him do the talking and never interrupt. Incidentally, the Kickapoo women are, by far, better informants than the men—but only when the latter are not around.

A wife must not be the jealous type, since a Kickapoo husband feels it is his prerogative to come and go as he pleases without taking her into consideration. One old woman whose son married an extremely jealous wife, who beats him when he has a night out with the boys, protested that her son is still young and therefore entitled to his peccadillos. She kept her own long marriage serene and smooth by never questioning the evening activities of her spouse.

A woman who is a tippler or a heavy gambler or who has a bad temper, a sharp tongue, or a roving eye is not considered good marriage material. In spite of the permissiveness in premarital relations, if a girl does not settle down after one or two children out of wedlock, she gets a bad name and becomes public property.

In choosing a mate, a woman first of all requires that he be a good hunter. Anyone blind, crippled, or mentally afflicted is thus disqualified. Of the four men over thirty-five who were still bachelors at the time of our study, two were blind, one was a cripple, and the fourth was a mentally retarded deaf-mute.

Although looks have never played an important role in the choice of a mate, one young man complains that the girls are now far more interested in a handsome lad than in a good hunter.

A man should not only provide the family with plenty of venison and skins but should also keep his farmland producing and his animals increasing; and today, working as a migrant laborer from seven to eight months out of the year, he should be able to earn, with his family's assistance, enough to keep them in supplies for the remaining months, when the expenditures for house building and ceremonies reach a peak.

A man who is a heavy drinker is considered a bad risk. One handsome young man, a good hunter and an excellent dancer but a heavy drinker, was unable to find a wife until after he had reached the age of twenty-six. A moderate amount of drinking is expected. A patient woman told us her husband does not spend much on himself. When he gets a strong urge to drink she accompanies him in their pickup to Múzquiz, where she goes about her shopping while he stops at his favorite saloon until his allowance is consumed. He returns to the pickup, where his wife waits for him, sleeps off the worst part of his drunk, and returns to the village.

Forsyth said that the Sauk and Fox girls were seldom unmarried by the time they were sixteen.[11] This holds true today among the Kickapoos. Of the 130 females over fourteen in 1970, only 10 were unmarried. A late menarche could be responsible for these 10 unmarried girls, or their parents might be strict—some still are—and waiting for a more desirable marriage. It is not uncommon for a girl to be married by the time she is twelve and with child before she is thirteen. Boys also usually marry by the time they are thirteen or fourteen.

The Kickapoos do not marry by Mexican law, except in a few cases of mixed marriages. Since in their culture there is no formal marriage ceremony other than the betrothal announcement, which actually comes after the marriage has been consummated and which is now usually omitted, just what constitutes marriage among them? The Kickapoos make a fine distinction in their choice of Spanish words in describing whether a person is married by the accepted Kickapoo standards or not. When a young man, after the courting period, spends a night in the house with a girl and is discovered there by the family in the morning, he is considered, for all intents and purposes, married, whether the betrothal announcement is observed or not. The couple usually live with her family until the first child is born. They may then continue on this basis, build their own home, or move into a house which has been passed to them by a female relative of the bride. To describe such a relationship, the Kickapoos use the Spanish verb *traer*, meaning, among other things, "to bind" or "to have someone subject to certain obligations." To describe a set-up in which the couple have not complied with the acceptable customs, they use the expression *andar* ("to go here and there") with someone. This denotes a state of impermanence, a temporary situation.

In the old days, according to our informants, when a young man fancied a girl, after ascertaining that there existed no blood or adoption relations between them, he began to court her when she went about her tasks of carrying firewood and water for the family. After some time, if she gave indications of accepting him, the youth informed his parents, who provided him with an equipped riding horse, which the suitor tied to the outside of the girl's compound. If she brought the horse inside the compound, unsaddled it, and fed and watered it, it was a sign of acceptance; if she ignored it, it was a rejection. If accepted, that same night the young man slipped into her house, slept with her, and was there in the morning for the family to see.

Alanson Skinner notes that, among the Potawatomi, if a girl was considered a good marriage prospect, the boy's parents approached her father and asked for her hand.[12] At one time, this custom also existed among the Kickapoos. If the girl was particularly attractive, according to Forsyth, the parents of the suitor "bought her with gifts of horses, wheat, skins and money."[13] This custom is no longer in vogue.

Today, young Kickapoos have lost many of the restraints of yesteryear, but they still must inquire from their elders about blood and adoption relationships to a girl before they consider courting her. A young man begins to meet with a girl he likes and, if he is given encouragement, they learn each other's whistle in order to communicate and later meet at night, either singly or in groups, by the river, where they engage in lovemaking, play Mexican records, and dance or drink. Although the old people frown on many of these goings-on, they seem to do little to restrain them. If a youth is serious about a girl, he will go to her house and spend the night with her; otherwise, he may carry on an affair indefinitely with one or more girls.

No Kickapoo youth or girl has told us about the actual courting techniques, but an older Mexican man, who has been married for many years to a Kickapoo woman and who, before the marriage, had several Kickapoo sweethearts, told us that the Kickapoo girls—unlike Mexican girls, who are gentle and sweet and allow their sweethearts to caress them—will not let a man touch them in the early stages of courting. A Kickapoo girl is apt to knock a man five feet away if he attempts such familiarities. Lovemaking to the Kickapoo girls consists of much pinching, biting, scratching, pulling, jostling, shoving, and general horseplay. When he returned to his home from courting, this same man's family scolded him, as all the buttons were pulled off his shirt and he was black and blue from bites, thumps, and scratches. The man's wife, who was listening, could only giggle and agree.

The betrothal announcement is still sometimes observed. After a youth has spent the night with his sweetheart and has been seen by her family, he goes to one of his aunts (father's sisters), sisters, or nieces and tells her he "is married" to a certain girl. The female relative calls on all of the groom's aunts, sisters, and nieces and selects from them acceptable gifts, such as dresses, dress lengths, unsewed moccasins, skins, jewelry, shawls, ribbons, and other finery, which she takes to the home of the bride, while another female relative accompanies her, leading a fully equipped riding horse by the rein, a gift from the groom to the bride. The bride invites all her aunts, sisters, and nieces and at least one female relative of the groom to select the gifts of their choice. All must be taken, as the bride keeps nothing. The horse she presents to one of her uncles (mother's brothers) or brothers.

On the following day, an old aunt of the bride—the latter is too shy to speak—will say to the bride's female relatives who received the gifts, "She is now married; let us send gifts to the groom's female relatives." Each offers gifts to be taken to the home of the female relative of the groom who initiated the gift-giving. She, in turn, calls all of the groom's female relatives who contributed gifts to select what they wish. By this announcement the village knows that the couple are now man and wife.

Few Kickapoo couples stay married many years—a marriage of thirty or more years' duration is a record. Most people over forty have been married from two to eight times. Quite frequently, couples quarrel, separate, and later, even after an intervening marriage, go back to each other. As men and women reach old age, they separate, the man drifting from the home of one child to that of another, those of former wives, or that of the recent ex-wife. The woman maintains her own home, either alone or with a daughter or granddaughter or other child she may have adopted for succor and companionship in her later years.

One young man, himself married several times, reflected that it was *muy bonito* (very pretty) that his brother and sister had had only one marriage each, both lasting over fifteen years. Another young man, when we commented on his third marriage in rapid succession, remarked that he did not like to change, but that the girls soon tired of one man and sought another.

Although there is a belief that having too many spouses, as well as overindulgence in lovemaking, wears out the participants, the Kickapoos seem not to take this too seriously, to judge from the turnover in the marriage market and the number of affairs constantly surfacing.

Infidelity formerly was severely punished "by cutting off the ears, or cutting or biting off the nose of a woman," according to Forsyth.[14] Our informants told an anecdote about the oldest woman in the village, who had recently died in her nineties. When young, she was a *troteadora*. At the time of the incident, she was married to an extremely jealous man, by whom she had had two daughters. In those days, when a man was working in his fields which were some distance from the house, he built himself a flimsy shelter where he stayed during the day or for several days at a time. One day the husband, suspecting his wife's peccadillos, returned, after he had told her he would be away for several days, and found her in *flagrante delicto* with her lover. The lover escaped and left the country, but the wife was almost killed by her husband's fury. He took an ax and split her skull as well as her upper lip and left her for dead. Relatives who came to her rescue called a curer, who took her to a secluded place in the *monte*, where she was nursed back to life.

Today, infidelity is taken with a more philosophical attitude. A woman married by law to a Mexican, by whom she had three children, discovered a letter in a pocket of her husband's clothes. Her twelve-year-old daughter, who was attending school, read the letter to her illiterate mother and burst into tears. Alarmed, the mother brought the letter to us. It was written by a Mexican woman friend professing great love for the woman's husband; but upon learning that the city from which the letter had been mailed was far in the interior of Mexico, she shrugged her shoulders and said, "Ugh, very far, why worry! Furthermore, we are married by the law and for keeps!"

Though incestuous relations between blood or adoptive relatives are looked upon by the Kickapoos with disgust, three cases have been called to our attention. One occurred many years ago between a father and his two daughters during the lifetime of his wife. One daughter had two children but both died. At the time of our study, there were two cases in the village, also between fathers and daughters. In Oklahoma, there is a well-known case of a Kickapoo woman who has had nine children by her father. How can this happen when incest is so repulsive and disgusting to the Kickapoos? Why are these people not punished, since their misdeeds are public knowledge? The reply is that all parties involved are bewitched and are unable to take any action.

The Kickapoos until recently openly practiced polygyny. Several of the older men, including Chief Papícoano, have admitted that they, at one time, had two or three wives. If the wives were sisters, or those the Kickapoos call sisters, which was often the case, they usually lived in the same house; otherwise, they lived in different houses in the same compound or elsewhere in the village to avoid quarreling. One old man told us how he maintained two wives who were not sisters living in the same house for many years. When we inquired how he had kept them from quarreling, he grinned and confided, "Ha, I had a special herb which kept them under control."

If a man with two wives who were sisters lost one through death and the family considered him a good risk, he was offered another sister if any were left in the family. This custom of the sororate continued even after plural marriages were dropped. It was also customary for a younger brother to inherit the wives of a deceased older brother.

When we asked an old woman whose father had had two wives simultaneously if she had ever heard of a woman having two husbands at the same time, she looked at us quizzically—somewhat taken aback—but quickly regaining her composure, she said simply, "Eso no se hace [that is not done]."

Formerly, whenever a man represented a declared friend at the latter's adoption ceremony, even though he had one wife, he was entitled to take, as second wife, the widow of the friend whom he had represented.

Today, a modified form of polygyny is practiced. A man and woman marry. During her pregnancy or several pregnancies, he leaves her and marries someone else. When the second woman becomes pregnant, he leaves her to return to the first one and continues to shuttle between them during several pregnancies. An old woman to whose daughter this had happened advised her to run the husband off for good, remarking, "No me gusta esa clase de mugre [I don't like that kind of dirty work]." She is one of the women who remember when their fathers had two wives simultaneously.

Since the Kickapoos have neither a religious nor a legal marriage, except in a few mixed marriages with Mexicans, it cannot be rightly said that they "divorce" their mates, as this word implies a legal dissolution of the marriage relations. A more appropriate word is separation.

When a couple marry in the traditional Kickapoo way, they usually live with the wife's mother, or with a female relative with whom she lived prior to her marriage. If the union is not successful, the man leaves or is thrown out and returns to his mother's home or that of a female relative with whom he has lived, unless he has another prospective wife in mind, in which case he goes to live with her. He has taken to his mother-in-law's home only his personal belongings. If he owns any livestock or enjoys the usufruct of a plot of irrigable farmland, he does not share it with his wife—it is his.

If an older man whose wife already owns a house and its furnishings for any reason decides he no longer wishes to live with her, he takes his personal belongings and returns to the home of his mother or goes to live with a female relative. The wife, if she wishes to rid herself of her husband, may, in a fit of anger, throw out or burn his belongings—or, in a more placid mood, make a bundle of them and place it outside the door. He has no recourse but to leave.

The Kickapoos, and particularly the women, look askance at a wife who lives with her mother-in-law or who builds her house in the compound of the latter; for, if separation occurs, the wife is forced to take down her house and move it to the compound of a female relative. Among the eighty-three households in the 1960's, three women were living in the same compound with their mothers-in-law, in separate houses. Of these, one had a legal Mexican marriage; another had to dismantle her house and move it to the compound of a female relative when her marriage floundered; and the third has a nip-and-tuck marriage—married today, separated tomorrow.

The role of the father is much diluted among the Kickapoos, for the children call and treat as *father* not only the man who sired them but all his brothers and the husbands of their mother's sisters. The real disciplinarians are the uncles (mother's brothers), inasmuch as this relationship remains constant no matter what happens to the marriage. When a marriage breaks up, the wife usually keeps the children, except in rare cases where the in-laws step in. She is certain that female relatives will assist her, and she can depend on her sons, brothers, mother's brothers, and nephews to supply her with venison and rescue her from any difficult situation. Ownership of the house gives a woman not only status among the men but also an advantage, since she is not the one put in the awkward position of having to leave.

With the changing economic role the Kickapoo woman plays today, where she earns as much as a man in the harvests, she is even more independent and finds less need to rely on a man or subject herself to his whims.

Infidelity, mistreatment, drunkenness, nonsupport, prolonged illness, a woman's failure to meet the standards of a good mother and housekeeper, and sterility seem to be the main causes for separation; however, for every case in which a separation has occurred for any of the stated reasons, there exists another case in which the same reasons prevail and yet the couple does not separate.

Infidelity is apparently a very strong reason for separation, but this occurs mostly among the younger couples; it is an infrequent cause among the older ones. Husband stealing is a sport common among the women and one from which they seem to get special pleasure. One woman, confronted with the observation that so-and-so had been formerly married to so-and-so but was now *her* mate, went into a prolonged guffaw and bragged, "Se lo robé [I stole him from her]." There have been many cases of women enticing husbands from their wives, with resulting fights in which no holds were barred.

Some couples lead placid lives and enjoy mutual respect and affection for each other and their children; but not infrequently reports arrive of a violent quarrel, with either the husband or wife beating the other.

Often, in cases where the husband has beaten the wife, a bout of drinking is responsible. This treatment sometimes results in a temporary or permanent separation; but, as often as not, these couples go back together.

Drunkenness is probably one of the greatest causes for separation, as this weakness exists not only among the young men, but also among the old ones, and among the women as well. As was stated earlier, a certain amount of drinking is tolerated by the majority of the wives and husbands; but, when a man spends the greater part of his earnings on alcohol and abuses his wife and children, the wife usually sends him on his way. When a woman, because of her drunkenness, fails to perform her wifely duties, her husband leaves her.

Nonsupport goes hand in hand with drunkenness. A shiftless husband who fails to provide his family with the necessary sustenance is not supported for long. The wife's family urge her to rid herself of the culprit, as they are the ones who have helped support him.

One of the most tragic causes of separation is a prolonged illness, particularly on the part of the wife. If the woman becomes incapacitated, the burden of maintaining the house, collecting material for its construction, and building it annually, and the chores of cooking, washing, marketing, gathering firewood, and carrying water to the house—all woman's work—fall on the man. He may receive some assistance from relatives, but the burden is, nonetheless, severe. If the woman cannot contribute her labor as a migrant worker and there are large medical bills to pay, the man may simply not be able to support the stress; in such a case, he leaves his wife to be cared for by her relatives. However, this does not always happen. The marriage of one couple, he a heavy drinker and she crippled by arthritis, has endured thirty-six years. Many gossip that he gets drunk so that his wife will leave him, and yet she bears with him; he complains that all of his wife's duties fall on his shoulders, but he does not leave her.

Kickapoo men tolerate much sloppy housekeeping from their wives. Some of the women are models, while others are dirty and untidy, keep their houses and children likewise, and apparently have few, if any, of the qualities a Kickapoo man expects of a wife; yet the husbands continue to support them.

One man complained that his wife did not stay in the cook house as was expected of her and, furthermore, was jealous; his wife told us that he "admired the ladies" too much. He claims to have packed up his possessions and left; she claims to have told him one day, "Get out and stay out!"

Although the Kickapoos insist that the inability of a wife to have children is just cause for separation, we have known of few cases where this occurred, as the wife is not solely blamed for childlessness. In the sixties there were five couples who had been married over twenty years without having children. Two couples had children from former unions and seemed satisfied with the status quo; two others adopted children of relatives; one couple had none and seemed not to miss them.

Old Age

The Kickapoos keep neither family records nor a tribal roll, and only a few are registered in the office of vital statistics in Múzquiz. Consequently, it is difficult to know the exact age of any Kickapoo, and it is especially difficult to ascertain the age of an old person whose memory has become hazy. We were able to calculate the approximate ages of the old people for the tribal roll that we compiled by matching an important event or rite of passage in their lives with such occurrences as the arrival of the 1907 group from Oklahoma, the Mexican Revolution of 1910, the influenza epidemic of 1918, and the visit of President Cárdenas in 1936. In 1969, when Chief Papícoano casually mentioned that at twenty-four he had married one of the young women who came with the 1907 group from Oklahoma, we were able to reckon his age as eighty-six. Prior to this admission his age had been estimated as between seventy-five and ninety-five.

Some Kickapoos have told us that their grandparents lived far into the nineties and that some were over one hundred before death overtook them. Constant exposure to the elements in the semiarid region where they live tends to age the skin of the Indians prematurely. On the other hand, their many outdoor activities, the clean air of their isolated village, the leisurely pace of their lives, and their serene faith in the Great Spirit, with whom they live in harmony, all contribute to make the group uniquely healthy and long-lived in spite of an inadequate diet, unsanitary conditions, and lack of modern medical care.

In theory, among the Indians old people are revered, humored, tended, respected, and feared; but in reality, and particularly during an old person's final illness, the opposite is true. However, although general hospitality among the Kickapoos is a thing of the past, old people are never denied food when they arrive at a home, as the fear of the old, because of their supposed ability to transform themselves into witches, is much engrained among the villagers.

Old men are usually treated with more indignities than old women, as the latter, in most cases, own their homes and, with the aid of female relatives, continue to construct them annually. Thus they live independently, though this may necessitate going from the home of one relative to that of another for handouts. By the time an old man reaches his seventies, he either is a widower or is separated from his wife; and, unless he has a son or daughter with whom he lives, he is shunted from one house to another seeking shelter. If he has a small income from an Oklahoma land lease, he is happily received in the house of a relative because of his contribution to the maintenance of the household; but, if he is not a provider, he is subjected to many slights and abuses.

Occasionally, relatives tire of constructing the Kickapoo type house for an old relative and settle for a Mexican jacal which does not have to be rebuilt annually. One woman in her nineties, the oldest female in the village, had lived for many years in a jacal because she was too feeble to build her own house and her daughters had tired of helping her. One night her grandson, who shared her home and who was an alcoholic, must have dispersed the central fire when he arrived, for, during the night, the house went up in flames, charring both occupants. The body of the old woman was found near the locked door, which she had tried in vain to open. This tragedy stirred the village, causing much soul searching. Many believed they had been punished for the neglect of the two daughters toward their old mother. Later, when her son, who had been out of the village when the house burned, built a new house in the same compound, helped by his sisters, it was not a jacal, but a Kickapoo wigwam.

We have heard of sick old people being beaten by their daughters and mistreated by their grandchildren. Often, these individuals are denied food and water. It is then that a niece or nephew steps in and supplies them with little delicacies.

In spite of these inequities, with old age come many privileges and a status not enjoyed by the young. The old people are the repositories of the tribal wisdom and knowledge; it is they who know the myths, legends, and stories and can recall the war exploits with the corresponding tales of Kickapoo bravery. It is also to them that the younger people appeal during a crisis.

We were told that once, when the cavalry regiment stationed in Múzquiz arrived at night in the village during a bivouac and camped near the springs in the pecan grove, the women were thrown into a near panic. Many of the men were hunting and, because of this or for some other reason, Chief Papícoano had failed to notify the villagers of the expected arrival of the troops. When the women, during the night, heard the hoofs of many horses pass through the lanes, their first fear was that the game wardens had come to arrest the men. Our informant, while vividly describing the event, told how she and her female kin ran to the home of their oldest aunt (father's sister) for advice and comfort, as they were ready to flee to the *monte*. Rather than panic, the old aunt sent a niece to the home of the chief for advice. When the women learned the actual situation they were reassured; nonetheless, they spent the night with their aunt, a bastion of strength and wisdom.

All of the clan leaders, who are highly respected, are men in their sixties or older, for it takes a lifetime to learn the ritual associated with the ceremonies. Members of the Berry clan have expressed fear that no young man is learning the ritual of their clan and ask themselves what will happen at the death of their present leader. The chanters are also older men, who see with pleasure the young men and boys gather around them during a ceremony with the purpose of learning the songs. Although they make no overt effort to teach, they welcome those interested in learning.

Herbal societies, while admitting young persons as neophytes, do not allow them to handle medicinal herbs until maturity. For a woman, this means past her climacteric. It is the old women with many years of experience who are called in a difficult delivery, since it is only they who own and may prescribe the indicated herbs for such an emergency.

When a woman's dance for an adoption ceremony is held, no matter what the age of the deceased, one old woman, at least, heads the dancers, since she has the experience to lead the others and the stamina to dance long hours.

When a Kickapoo is interred, an old woman is asked to carry the deceased's possessions to the cemetery. She is the only female who accompanies the cortege and is privileged to select any or all articles for herself before she offers them to the gravediggers. (In practice, she always leaves some for the gravediggers.)

During each naming ceremony, it is the chief's prerogative to be present in order to acquaint himself with the name of a new member of the tribe. Two old women are also invited to be the sponsors of the child.

At a boy's first-hunt ceremony and feast, twelve old people are the ones invited to witness the boy's accomplishment.

Old people are not expected to work, but they are charged with the care of children while the able-bodied members of the family engage in many tasks. When the Kickapoos are working in the harvests near Eagle Pass, they set up their camps under the international bridge. While the younger members of the family are in the fields, the old women, each ensconced in her own camp, ride herd on the toddlers and look after the babies.

Children are frequently given to an old person to name, or an old person asks to name a child in the belief that the longevity of the name will rub off on the child. Often children are adopted by childless old women and are a source of great comfort and company to them.

Death and Burial

A Kickapoo faces death with acceptance. He believes that the Great Spirit, Kitzihiat, put him on this earth, and only he has the power to call him at will. He is confident that when his spirit is dispatched to the hereafter he will leave a trusted friend to replace him in the role he formerly occupied among his consanguine relatives. As the last act on earth, his spirit will witness the game or dance of his choice. Upon arrival in the spirit world ruled by Pepazcé, the first Indian to have died, he will be received by the spirits of his forebears, who will entertain him with his favorite game or dance. Thereafter, his life in the spirit world, free from the cares he left behind, will be a continual round of games, dances, and hunts; but should he find the spirit world not to his liking, by asking permission, he may return to this world in the body of a newborn child from two to four times. Three times a year his living kin will hold a ceremony in which his spirit will be invited to join them. Here he will be given earthly food, Indian tobacco, and the reassurance that he is remembered and cherished.

This reconciled acceptance of death is further reflected in the attitudes and manners of the deceased's relatives. Although they observe a four-day period of mourning, except for widowers or widows, whose term of mourning is imposed by the consanguine relatives of the deceased spouse, the family do not wear mourning apparel and do not visit the cemetery or care for the grave—allowing nature to take its course instead. Neither do they indulge in exterior demonstrations of grief or permit death to interfere in the execution of their daily routine. If their grief is difficult to bear, they may cry quietly in the privacy of their homes, or they may fast to assuage the pain.

Although we never attended a Kickapoo wake, we were told that, even there, it is considered improper for the bereaved to weep. A few tears quickly wiped away may be shed, but no other demonstration of grief is shown. If the sudden death of a dear one has not given the family time to control their sorrow, the leader who officiates at the ceremony held during the wake fills his ceremonial pipe with Indian tobacco and passes it to the relatives, who take a few puffs. So profound is their faith in the benefits to be derived from this tobacco that this small act suffices to calm their emotions.

During our study, a child whose father was a Kickapoo and whose mother was a Mexican was buried in the village. We were told that the grief of the child's mother and grandmother, accompanied by wailing and cries, was a shocking experience. To make matters worse, the female relatives of the child accompanied the body to the grave—a practice unheard of among the Indians. The leader who officiated called attention to the fact that the Mexican relatives of the child acted in the way that was customary to them and said that the Kickapoos should take this into consideration.

When a Kickapoo senses that his death is imminent, he begins to make preparations while his mind is rational. If he chances to live in a jacal, he asks to be taken to die in the wigwam of a relative. Should he die away from the village, either in Mexico or in the United States, he requests that his body be taken for burial either to Oklahoma or to Mexico, to be interred in a Kickapoo cemetery. One Kickapoo man died while his family were working in Lupton, Colorado; and, rather than bury him in a non-Kickapoo cemetery, the family paid a funeral home to transport his body to Oklahoma. Much fear was expressed by the Indians when a member died in Texas and it was not possible to bury him in a Kickapoo cemetery. One woman remarked when this occurred, "That one will not get there," explaining that his chances of arriving in the spirit world had been jeopardized by the failure to bury him properly.

A Kickapoo makes verbal disposition of his material and ceremonial property. He leaves his allotment of irrigable land and his horses, mules, donkeys, and cattle to whomever he pleases. Though he is under no obligation to leave these things to his consanguine family, he usually does. He designates which of his grandsons or nephews will receive his firearms and his saddle. Nowadays, since many Kickapoos own automobiles, this property also has to be considered. If he has money, he will leave it to a relative—not his widow—or will designate it for use in the expenses incurred for his adoption ceremony. If he has no money but owns livestock, he states which animal is to be sold for the expenses of this ceremony. All small property, such as bedding, personal clothes, and small tools, will be distributed in three equal parts: one for those who prepare his body for burial, one for those who dig his grave, and one for the man who will represent him at the adoption ceremony. If he owns ceremonial property, such as a bundle, chants, or a dance, he leaves it to a man who he believes will endeavor to continue the ceremonies involved with such property, preferably to one who has shown this interest during the owner's life. If he is the leader of a clan, he passes his authority to the man of his clan who has shown the greatest interest in learning the ceremonies connected with the bundle.

A woman who owns a house usually leaves it to a daughter, niece, or other consanguine female relative who will continue to build and care for it; but, in rare instances, a woman may pass her house to a son.

Every adult man or woman has his or her new burial clothes in readiness. For a man this means a new Indian style hand-sewn shirt, a buckskin breechcloth, an undecorated pair of buckskin moccasins, a kerchief for his neck, a feather for his head, and a blanket in which he is carried to his grave. A woman will have in readiness either a hand-made dress or a dress length with which a dress may be made while the body is being prepared. She will also have a new petticoat, a pair of undecorated moccasins, a green or blue ribbon for her hair—red is taboo—a new blanket, and, if she can afford it, a shawl.

Every adult makes known to his consanguine relatives the game or dance he wants performed at his adoption ceremony and in which of the three cemeteries he wishes to be buried, always near the graves of relatives. He also designates the relative who will assume the responsibility of having the three annual ceremonies for his spirit.

If a Kickapoo dies before noon, prayers are said by the leader of his clan and relatives pay their condolences, but there are no chants and the body is buried in the early afternoon of the same day. If he dies after midday, a wake, during which both prayers and chants take place, is held, lasting from the time of his death until sunrise. Burial occurs by midmorning.

When a family estimates that death is impending, the leader of the dying person's clan is called and takes the bundle of his clan to the house; if the leader is absent, any of several men who know the prayers for this occasion can be called. All consanguine relatives are notified immediately, and the children are sent to stay with one of the relatives until after the burial.

If the dying person leaves a spouse, the first duty of the clan leader is to announce to the survivor that death is imminent and he or she must leave the home to stay with the relative whose home is the farthest east. The spouse is notified when the deceased is being taken out of the hole in the west side of the house, at which time he or she must return to begin the mourning period. The leader tells the mourners to select a consanguine relative—a brother, uncle, or nephew, for a man; a sister, aunt, or niece, for a woman—to be the person who will sponsor the surviving spouse during the mourning period and eventually release him or her from further obligations to the family.

The second duty of the clan leader is to take back the Indian tobacco of the deceased and return it to the clan bundle from whence it was first given.

Then the leader of the clan sends a consanguine relative to call a waiter of the proper reciprocal clan, who, in turn, calls an assistant. These two men are told to ask six to eight men of the deceased's clan to assist the leader in the chants and also call two to four chanters of the proper reciprocal clans to be guest chanters. These bring their clan bundles and use the two gourds in each bundle to accompany the chanters, since four gourds are an indispensable adjunct in a wake. The waiters call two or three men or women of the proper reciprocal clans to prepare the body for interment. They also call an older female to be the "old woman" who sorts the personal belongings of the deceased into three piles.

When the chants are underway, the leader orders those who have arrived to prepare the body to begin their work. If a person died on the south bench (or the west bench), he is moved to the north bench and placed with his feet to the west, near the west end of the house. In order to provide privacy to the body, two of the mourners, of the same sex as the deceased, shield the bench with a blanket.

In the meantime, the entire body is washed with a cloth and plain water. The hair of a man is combed, a new queue is made, the end finished with a new ribbon, and an eagle feather inserted at the crown where the braid begins; if a man has no braid, a white band is tied around his forehead to hold the eagle feather. Kickapoo men believe that it is important for them to use a queue, not only so that the feather may be inserted in it, but also in order that Pepazcé, ruler of the hereafter, will recognize them as Kickapoos when they ask admittance to the spirit world.

The body is dressed in new apparel, taking care to use no garment that is adorned with glass or metal or that has belonged to another deceased. The leader takes purple dye kept in the clan bundle for this purpose, paints a streak on the man's face from the outside corners of his eyes to his ears, and daubs the insteps of his moccasins with the same color. The purple streaks on his face and moccasins will further help Pepazcé to identify him as a Kickapoo.

The last act of the leader is to place a bit of Indian tobacco in each hand of the deceased with these words, "You are now on your way to the spirit world of the Kickapoos." After this preparation, the body is wrapped in a new blanket. The left side is folded over first, and then the right side, while the ends, first at the head and then at the feet, are folded under the body. An old blanket is wrapped over the new one, and the corpse is tied with a new rope provided by a consanguine relative.

A dead woman is dressed in new garments, her hair is parted in the center, brought to the back, woven into a long braid, and tied with a blue or green ribbon. Two purple circles are painted on her face, one on each cheek, and her moccasins are daubed with the same purple dye.

If the deceased was a member of the Buffalo clan his body, once it is wrapped in the blanket and tied with the rope, is propped against the pile of clothing which goes to the cemetery. Either or both of those who prepared him sit by his side during the chants, which terminate at sunrise, when the body is returned to the north bench.

The clan leader comforts the mourners by telling them not to lament the death of their kin, since all must eventually go the same path; he reminds them that the loved one will join relatives soon and live a life of joy with no earthly pains or cares. Sometimes, he tells little jokes to lighten their spirits. During the chants and prayers, friends of the mourners, all of whom sit quietly on the west bench, come to express their condolences, but no one present nods in recognition. In the event any of the mourners become sleepy, they retire to the cook house, where one of the female relatives prepares coffee, with which callers and mourners may refresh themselves. If they are still sleepy, they may step outside for a short nap, but sleeping indoors on this occasion is taboo.

During the wake, the waiters have been tending two kettles of purple corn and squash or pumpkin. The larger kettle, presented to the supervisor of the grave upon termination of the interment, is taken to his home, where he shares it with his helpers. The smaller kettle is given to the waiters to share in their home.

With the approach of dawn, one of the waiters is dispatched to call a man from one of the proper reciprocal clans to dig the grave, while the other waiter calls a man to gather the stone slabs necessary to line the grave. These two men call others to help them. The grave supervisor cuts a long sand-bar willow at the river, with which he arrives at the home of the deceased to measure the length and width of the body to determine the size of the grave. The men who dig the grave and gather the stone slabs depart for the cemetery in the company of the "old woman," who carries in her hand an enameled-ware dish, the last one used by the deceased. When they arrive at the cemetery, the supervisor carefully selects a site, making sure that no other grave is disturbed. (The Kickapoos use no grave marker other than the protruding east-west ends of the pole on which the body was carried to the grave.) With gunny sacks flung over their shoulders, the men go in search of stone slabs.

In the meantime, the "old woman" chops by hand-ax any brush growing on the site and scrapes the topsoil with the enameled-ware dish. After this preliminary step, the men dig the grave with picks and use the enameled-ware dish to empty the soil to a depth of about three feet. When the other men return with the stone slabs, the supervisor enters the grave and lines the bottom and sides, without using mortar. Upon completion of this task, but leaving one man in charge of the empty grave, all return to the home of the deceased to announce that the grave is ready.

While the grave is prepared, other activities are taking place at the house. One of the relatives has provided a one-seed juniper pole, which is brought into the house through the hole two female relatives have opened from the outside on the west of the north bench. The pole is inserted beneath the rope used for tying the corpse in the blanket and serves to carry the body to the grave over the shoulders of the men who have prepared its resting place. Another female relative has pounded some purple Indian corn in the wooden mortar, winnowed it, cooked it with a bit of salt and water in a small brass ceremonial kettle, shaped the small cake, and browned it on the *comal*. While preparing the corn she takes the deceased's ceremonial spoon, scrapes off the patina, and later places the small cake on it.

If the deceased leaves a spouse, a waiter is dispatched to tell him or her that the cortege is about to begin. The widow or widower, accompanied by the relative with whom he or she has been staying, returns to the house but does not enter. As the bereaved spouse stands on the east side, the sponsor unravels the spouse's braid and places a bit of tobacco in his or her hands. Accompanied by the relative, the widow or widower walks toward the river while the body is being taken out of the house through the hole in the west side.

In the meantime, the "old woman" gives those who prepared the body one of the piles of clothing and personal trinkets of the deceased, while the body is received by the six men who carry it on their shoulders to the grave. A female relative hands the supervisor of the grave the ceremonial ladle with the small corn cake, and another relative hands the "old woman" the second pile of clothes, which she carries to the cemetery on her back.

Immediately after the body leaves the house through the hole, the mourners pour outside through the door, while two female relatives close the hole from the outside in order that the spirit may not find his way back into the house. After this, relatives may again enter the house.

The cortege, led by the supervisor of the grave and accompanied by several men to alternate carrying the corpse, begins the trip to the cemetery. Following the men goes the "old woman," the only female who may go to the cemetery.

Preadolescent children of the deceased's clan blacken their faces from the time of death and fast until after the funeral. All children are kept out of sight of the cortege, for fear the spirit of the deceased might become lonely and take a child's spirit to accompany him until he is dispatched to the hereafter.

Upon arriving at the graveside, the rope, old blanket, and pole are removed, and the body is carefully lowered into the grave in an east-west position. The ladle with the corn cake is placed on the chest, the body is covered with stone slabs, and the pole is placed on top of the shallow grave in an east-west position. All of those present turn toward the east, while the supervisor of the grave pronounces these words to the deceased: "Go willingly to Pepazcé; do not molest those of us who stay behind."

The "old woman" has spread the second share of the deceased's possessions on the old blanket, including the rope with which his body was tied to the pole. She first selects the articles she wants, invites the two men responsible for digging the grave and gathering the stone slabs to take their choice of articles, and offers the remainder to the assistants. What no one wants is piled on the stone slabs and pole and covered with sod, brush, and cactus. The only markers will be the two protruding ends of the pole and the enameled-ware dish, which the "old woman" places on top of the mound. Those present take off their shoes or moccasins and shake off the dust before returning to their homes. The supervisor goes to the home of the deceased, where he is given the brass kettle of purple corn to share with his helpers.

While the cortege is on its way, the men who prepared the body take their share of the deceased's possessions and wash them in the river. These articles have to sun four days and later be smoked with cudweed before they may be used. The "old woman" and any of the men at the graveside who take articles have to do likewise with them.

If death occurs in the winter, when the wigwam is occupied, relatives help dismantle it and move it elsewhere in the compound, where it is rebuilt; if death occurs in the summer house, it is not moved until spring, when summer houses are either refurbished or rebuilt. Moving the house serves to prevent the spirit from finding his family, for the Kickapoos believe that, when the spirit leaves the body, it visits familiar places.

Just before sunset on the day of the interment, the house is circled with ashes, beginning at the south side of the door, in the belief the spirit will take them for a ring of fire and not go through them. On the following morning, before sunrise, the ashes are carefully observed for any sign of disturbance indicating that the spirit tried to enter the house, in which event cudweed is burned to drive him out. The ashes are then carefully swept outward from the house, commencing at the south side of the door.

Not only do the family of the deceased have to observe a four-day period of mourning, but the entire village accompanies them in their time of bereavement, during which no games are played, no visiting between neighbors is permitted, and no radios are heard. In the late afternoon, the preadolescent children, who have blackened their faces and fasted during the day, are sent to the river to bathe before their evening meal.

The family assemble firearms, saddles, plows, tools, and other articles to be given to a designated relative or saved for the man who will represent the deceased at the adoption ceremony and smoke them with cudweed. If a man owns horses, mules, or burros, a bit of the tail and mane is cut off and buried in the *monte*. These animals will not be ridden or worked for a period of four days.

Mourning Period of a Widower or Widow

As the body of his wife is carried westward to her grave, the widower, accompanied by a male relative, returns to the front of their home, where they are met by the widower's sponsor, who places a bit of Indian tobacco in both hands of the bereaved. Escorted by his male relative, the widower walks toward the river which flows east of the village. Great restraint must be exercised by both men to avoid glancing back in a westward direction, for fear the spirit of the deceased wife may try to take her husband's spirit with her, as the Kickapoos believe that the spirits of couples are joined together at marriage. When the two men reach the river, the widower enters it, opens his hands, and allows the water to take the tobacco downstream.

Afterward, they go to the home of the sponsor, where the widower is given old, dry clothes in exchange for his wet garments. He then returns to the home of the relative with whom he spent the time between the preparation of his wife's body and the time for interment to await notification that he may return to his home. (Usually, a widower does not continue to live in his wife's home but goes to the home of a sister, an aunt, or a niece, if he no longer has a mother. He may take his children with him; he may leave them with his mother-in-law if she is living; or the children may be parceled out among the wife's sisters.)

At sunrise on the following three mornings, the widower takes Indian tobacco from his pouch, places a bit in each hand and, standing in front of the door, walks, one day to the south, one day to the west, and the last day to the north. As he returns, he throws the tobacco to the different directions as an offering to the manitous. Except for these sunrise walks he confines himself to his home and compound. During the initial four-day period of mourning he wears his hair loose and may not touch it; neither may he touch anyone else's hair. If he cannot resist scratching his head, he may use a stick. He may not participate in games, play the radio, or visit neighbors; and he may not, under any circumstances, attend any ceremony, but he may receive visitors offering him condolences.

On the evening of the fourth day, his sponsor goes to his home, braids his hair, and ties it with a buckskin thong. From this time until the termination of his mourning period his sponsor periodically takes him old clothes to wear and combs his hair, since he may not touch it.

The second mourning period is determined by the consanguine relatives of the deceased spouse. If a man is still young, an adoption ceremony, after which the widower will be released from any further obligations to his affinal relatives, may be held within days of the interment so that the widower will be free to remarry. This is usually done only if the death occurs near or within the time in which the Kickapoos hold their adoption ceremonies; otherwise, the widower has to wait until the following year to be released.

During the second period of mourning, the widower must observe many taboos. First of all, he must not, under any circumstances, show any interest in women and must avoid speaking to any woman other than his female consanguine relatives. Although there is no specified punishment for taking a mistress, the fear of punishment suffices to prevent this violation. If it is known that a man had a mistress before the death of his wife or is interested in another woman as a future wife, the adoption ceremony is hurried without consideration of the usual time for performing these.

The widower may not touch his hair or that of anyone else during the entire mourning period. He may, however, remove his facial hair, as described in Chapter 6. He may be a spectator at a ceremony during his second period of mourning, but he may not participate in one. He may hunt, work his fields, tend his stock, help with chores around the house, and pass the time at a craft.

A widow observes the same rules. Upon her return home on the day of her husband's burial, she spreads a ring of ashes around her house. (This ritual is performed by a female relative for a widower.) A widow continues her household duties, tends to her children, gathers material to build her house, and engages herself in her many household tasks. She stays strictly within her compound except while performing necessary tasks and avoids making social visits with relatives and neighbors. One day an informant arrived at our home in a fury. She was extremely upset over the conduct of one of her relatives, whom in Algonquian she calls *daughter* and whom we would call a cross-cousin. In the first place, the "daughter" had failed to smoke with cudweed the firearms belonging to her recently deceased spouse; second, she had gone to a wake while chants were being performed; third, instead of staying within her compound and minding her business, she was constantly trotting over to this neighbor or that on some flimsy excuse. Our informant bemoaned the fact that her daughter's aunts, whose obligation and prerogative it was to brief her on the proper conduct befitting a widow, had done nothing.

The Kickapoos tell that when Wisaka, their culture hero, gave them the laws by which they are to conduct themselves, the one heading the list was the prohibition of taking one's own life. Wisaka also told them that his father, Kitzihiat, the Great Spirit, gave each Kickapoo his life, and only he can take it away.

Within the memory of the old people, only two suicides are recalled: a father and, fifteen years later, his son, who, at twenty-two, took his life in 1962 during the early part of our study. This misfortune created such consternation and fear that some unusual punishment would befall the tribe that one of the most orthodox of the clan leaders considered it incumbent to move the entire village to a new location. In his mind, this young man had not only committed the most unpardonable sin, but had also defiled the village and desecrated the cattail-covered house where he took his life. The orthodox leader, in whose house a clan bundle is kept, did move his house some distance from the village, but no one followed suit. After some weeks, his isolation overcame his scrupulosity, and he returned to his old site in the village.

The Kickapoos say they possess no established procedure to cope with this rare situation; nonetheless, prayers were said asking Kitzihiat to forgive the unfortunate young man. The preparation of the body followed the same steps usually observed, but the interment was different. The "old woman" divided his possessions into only two piles, one for those who prepared the body and the other half for those who buried him. (A suicide does not have an adoption ceremony held for him, since his spirit is "nothing, only dust" and will forever stay in the ground where he took his life; by this violation, he forfeits a future spiritual life.) His face, instead of being painted the usual color, was striped from the outer edge of his eyes to his ears with hematite, while his moccasins were daubed with the same reddish powder. This was done in the hope that Kitzihiat would recognize him as a Kickapoo who had taken his life and have mercy on him.

While the body was being prepared by men from the proper reciprocal clans, the supervisor of the grave and his assistants went out a distance from the village, away from the cemeteries, and found a secluded place in a canyon, where they dug a slanting grave no longer than the lower half of the body, lined it with stone slabs, and returned for the body, wrapped in a canvas and secured with a rope. A pole inserted in the rope served to carry the suicide to his resting place on the shoulders of the gravediggers. The body was slipped off the pole and the lower part placed in the slanting grave, leaving the torso outside to lean against the wall of the canyon on a pad of honey mesquite mistletoe. The man's ceremonial spoon with a small corn cake was put on his chest. The "old woman" spread out his belongings and the rope on the blanket in which she had brought them. Those who wanted anything took it; the remainder of the articles were placed over the stone slabs, on which were piled sod and brush, leaving the torso exposed to the animals and to the elements.

Burial of a Warrior or One Who Dies from Gun Wounds While Not Intoxicated

When a Kickapoo man dies in battle or from gun wounds while not intoxicated, his body is prepared for burial in the same manner as that of any other, but his remains are not interred. His body is wrapped in a blanket, laid out on the ground in one of the cemeteries, and covered with a large pile of black-brush acacia so that animals cannot reach it. He is entitled to an adoption ceremony, but his spirit is dispatched not to the world where Pepazcé rules and where the majority of the Kickapoo spirits eventually dwell, but to the place where Mesicatuinata rules in the south, especially reserved for those who die in war or from gun wounds while not intoxicated. Women who die in childbirth also go to this spirit world, since the Kickapoos believe that the mother is "killed" by her child.

Burial of Those Who Die or Are Killed While Intoxicated

Although drunkenness is common among the Kickapoos, the fear of dying while in this condition is ever present, for Wisaka, among several prohibitions he gave them, included excessive drinking. Therefore a man who dies while under the influence of alcohol is buried in the same manner as a suicide. Sometimes the family holds an adoption ceremony for these individuals, but it is the consensus of opinion among the old that this is a vain gesture, for the victim's spirit stays in the ground where he met his death.

Burial of an Unnamed Child

An unnamed child is entitled to burial near the graves of his relatives in one of the several cemeteries. Since he has no membership in a clan and no name, no adoption ceremony is held for him. The Kickapoos believe the spirits of unnamed children automatically return to the place whence they came.

Upon the death of an unnamed child, the father notifies the leader of his own clan, who prays for the child and announces to Kitzihiat that the child is returning to his home, asking that he be received. The father of the child, after a consultation with the leader, calls a man or woman of his reciprocal clan to prepare the body for burial. No waiters are called and no food prepared. The father calls another man or woman, who, in turn, asks a helper to prepare the grave and asks a female to be the "old woman."

The body is bathed and dressed in the same manner as that of an adult; the face and moccasins are painted like an adult's, but the moccasins have small holes on the soles. This will prevent the child from being able to "walk" in the company of an adult's spirit in the event the latter tries to intercept the child's return to the place from whence he came. A bit of tobacco is placed in each hand, and the body is wrapped in a white cloth and a small blanket. Grave details are like those for an adult.

In the meantime, the family hand over to the "old woman" the child's personal possessions, which she divides into two piles. One of the two who made the grave returns to the house, stands in the doorway, and is handed the body by the person who prepared it; and, followed by the "old woman," it is carried to the grave. As the body is placed in the grave, the following words are pronounced: "For now, return from whence you came; if you loved your father and mother, come to them again." In observance of this death, only the family keeps a four-day period of mourning.

Chapter 11

Concept of Self and Others

Some Characteristics of the Kickapoos

The fact that the Kickapoo family has lived in a one-room house since time immemorial seems to have developed in the tribe the instinct of gregariousness to such a degree that it is one of the most salient characteristics of their nature. Privacy, as we know it, is nonexistent; they seem to dislike being alone, whether they are well or ailing. When we helped a family, one of whose members was so seriously ill that she should have been hospitalized, and inquired why she had not been, the response was, "Están tan solitos [they are so alone]." The patient and her kin preferred to stay in a cheap hostelry for several days during the medical examinations and tests, where she could be surrounded by family and friends day and night, rather than in a hospital, where visitors are restricted to certain hours.

The Indians are customarily casual in greeting each other and acquaintances. Most of them appear at a home, including ours, without any ado and take their leave likewise. They do not shake hands with each other, though they do with Mexicans and Anglos. Others are cavalierlike when greeting strangers or friends. On one occasion one of the men came to call, rose when Dolores entered the room, shook hands, and said, "Tenía ganas de llegar aquí [I was eager to come here]."

From the beginning of our work, the Kickapoos used the familiar second-person form in speaking to us in Spanish, a mode of address which the Mexicans of their socioeconomic class would consider lacking in respect.

In contrast to the many cases of courtesy and consideration, we were sometimes confronted with rudeness that was difficult to accept with equanimity but for the forbearance which anthropology teaches. A frequent woman visitor brought a cousin to meet us. The cousin immediately got down to the point of her visit: she had come to hear our record of Menomini songs. We played the record, and she seemed pleased to hear it while conversing with her cousin in Algonquian. When the record came to an end, we played Mexican songs, knowing that many of the Kickapoos enjoy them. She bluntly commanded us to stop the record, declaring in no uncertain terms that she was not interested in hearing it. When we tried to chat with her, she feigned not to hear us, yawned widely, slumped in her chair, and made herself generally disagreeable by constantly interrupting in Algonquian our efforts at conversation with her cousin.

At other times the Kickapoos have disarmed us with their friendliness. One evening, after a trying day, we went to the door, where stood one of the Indians who frequented our home. Although at all times we had been cordial and glad to receive him, on this occasion, we were somewhat displeased to see anyone at this late hour and simply asked what we could do for him. His reply was, "I did not get my fill of seeing you when last I was here."

Contrary to the belief that Indians are men of few words, we have heard them discourse for hours at a stretch in Algonquian, each attentively listening to the speaker without interrupting until he finished, when someone else took up the conversation.

We were the targets for more than one reprimand about our manners in the presence of Indians. One day Dolores was chided for her lack of courtesy when she interrupted one of the men, who was telling an involved story, by asking him to repeat a certain part she had not understood. The storyteller paused and refused to continue, nodding towards Dolores and addressing Felipe with the observation, "Me mochó la palabra [she cut off my word]." Only after apologies from the culprit did he resume his story.

Time and again we were startled or amused by the directness of the Indians. One extremely cold evening, after repeated visits from the same couple, during which conversation was forced and meaningless, we asked the man why they liked to come to our house. His quick reply was, "Afuera frío; aquí caliente [cold outside; warm here]." On numerous occasions the Indians frankly told us that the reason they came to our house to cash a check, exchange money, or have us write a letter was because we did not charge them a fee. Another day, one of our callers, after chatting for a while, observed, "Mis tripas están tronando [my guts are thundering]." After recovering from the startling remark, we followed it up by asking what he would like to eat. The answer: bread, with a thick layer of butter.

The Indians were forthright about their needs, not only for physical satisfactions, but also for money or favors—from us as well as from their relatives. Chief Papícoano called on us to write a letter to his daughter in Oklahoma, telling her he wanted to be picked up in Eagle Pass on a specified date. This meant a round trip of over 1,200 miles for his son-in-law. The old chief was wont to ask for dozens of favors, some of which we complied with, though many were completely out of our jurisdiction, such as intervening with the U.S. government for permission to hunt. The chief and others made frequent requests that we obtain permission from our ranching friends for them to hunt on their premises. This petition we automatically turned down because of the risk involved of injury to the ranchers' cattle or fences. The women are as prone to ask for favors as are the men. We were daily deluged with requests for dyes, beads, Lipton's tea, ammunition, and transportation. Gradually they learned that we would perform only such services as writing letters, cashing checks, exchanging money, helping someone who was critically ill, or making long-distance telephone calls to relatives and employers—things that they were incapable of doing without assistance.

The Kickapoos pride themselves on not owning material possessions, and some seem to disdain money, but not all. When we observed that few men had attended a meeting at the *ejido*, the response by one of the Kickapoo women was, "Sí, muy poca gente, pero si trata de dinero . . . [yes, few were there, but just let the word spread that money is going to be distributed . . .]."

When the Kickapoos have cash in their pockets they spend it liberally on food, trinkets, liquor, taxis, or long-distance calls with no thought of the morrow. A woman who missed the bus to Múzquiz from Piedras Negras after a short stint of work in Eagle Pass simply hired a taxi, which cost her twelve dollars for the hundred-mile drive, rather than wait a few hours for the bus, which would have cost her less than one dollar. Since she arrived on a day when the bus from Múzquiz to the village was not running, she hired another taxi there and paid an additional six dollars. This is a common practice among those who have spent the summer working, do not have their own transportation, and are anxious to get home.

We never saw a Kickapoo ill-at-ease in the presence of strangers. Their aplomb would put many more sophisticated persons to shame. When we received out-of-town friends and the Indians came to call, they were completely self-possessed, answering whatever questions were put to them by the visitors and joining in the conversation.

One year we took one of our informants to the University of Texas in Austin to record the Algonquian language in the Speech Department and afterward to the Texas Memorial Museum to show her the Indian collections. She took everything in her stride except the elevator—the first she had ridden in her life. Her feeling of panic soon left her when she saw us smiling and chatting.

Although the Indians usually appear unruffled and easy-going, they can become angered over trifles. One day, Dolores sent a message to an Indian woman, asking her to drop in at her convenience to identify a snapshot in which she appeared as a child. After she and her numerous children had been given gifts and refreshments, the woman demanded five dollars for her trouble. When her demand was ignored, she became petulant, mumbled something in Algonquian, and left in a huff. One of the other callers observed, "She left in anger."

Although the majority of the Kickapoo women have had several husbands and many, several lovers as well, they are extraordinarily shy in the presence of men, leaving it to the latter to converse or express the purpose of the visit. They blossomed out in conversation when none of their men were present, or alone with Dolores when "woman talk" was the subject of the interview.

Stoicism is undoubtedly a characteristic of the Indians. One woman informant who suffers from a heart condition was late for her appointment one day and explained that she had had one of her many small heart attacks, marked by a severe pain in her chest. She had spent a wretched night, with much discomfort interrupting her few hours of sleep. When it was suggested that the interview be postponed until another day, she would not consent, but insisted on proceeding as usual. During the entire morning of questions and answers, she did not mention her condition.

Among the Mexicans, some of the Kickapoos are believed to be dishonest in their word or dealings, but many are regarded as men of integrity. We were deceived a few times; mainly, when we tried to ask their Algonquian names, as this is an area in which they are loath to reveal information.

At other times we were astonished by the honesty of the Indians. One day the woodcarver brought two ceremonial ladles, whose workmanship we considered inferior, for our collection; nonetheless, we bought them. Our next guest saw the ladles and mentioned that he had tried to get some made by the same woodcarver but had been unable to have his order filled. We suggested that he take the ladles at the same price we had paid, to which he readily assented, promising to pay later. Busy with other matters, we failed to write down the amount in the small red book kept for this purpose. Several weeks passed before the young man came to pay for the ladles, and, since the little red book showed no entry, we insisted that he had already paid for them; he insisted vehemently that he had not paid. We finally accepted payment and complimented him highly on his honesty and determination to pay his debt.

Stealing is uncommon in the village, though some petty thievery does take place when the house owners are working in the United States and, because of the increasing number of small thefts, the Indians are now padlocking their homes, a practice unknown a few years back. We were never aware of anything being taken from our home, but we were warned by the Indians of certain individuals among them who had "sticky fingers."

Most Kickapoos have an exalted esteem of themselves as regards their place in the world, expressed by one old woman who said, "This world will come to an end when the Kickapoos no longer keep their old ways." Another man told us that his uncle, a former clan leader, was so wise that he understood the thoughts and wants of children before they could speak and likewise understood the language of animals.

On a visit to the village, out-of-town friends remarked on the good looks of one of the men, a compliment we translated. The man beamed with pride and modestly added, "I am always good; I harm no one."

All of the Kickapoos like to have their pictures taken and always expect a print. Only once did we find a girl who, although quite pretty, believed she was not suitable photographic material.

Once the ice is broken and they feel at ease with strangers, the Indians reveal a keen sense of humor, do not mind being teased or teasing, and have a quick and sometimes incisive riposte. A woman brought us some rag dolls which we had requested. Shortly after her visit, the matriarch of the rival camp came to call and inquired who had made the dolls. Her observation was short and cutting: "She can't make the other kind of babies; so she makes dolls."

Felipe established a joking relationship with several old ladies, who called him *nephew*, this teasing and joking relationship being consistent with aunt-nephew behavior in the Kickapoo kinship system, and he sometimes entertained them with his amateur legerdemain. A matriarch who weighs about two hundred pounds was extolling the kindness of one of the neighboring ranchers' wives and describing how years ago she had been able to visit her on horseback, which she could no longer do because of her rheumatic leg. When Felipe told her that the horse would break in two if she tried to mount it, everyone in the room laughed, the victim enjoying the joke as much as anyone else. On another occasion when Felipe teased this woman about her "friend" whose horse had died and inquired how he was going to take her for an outing, her quick retort was, "On foot!" In return she teased Felipe and blamed him for the coffee bean she had recently discharged during a nosebleed, explaining, "A man who can swallow a coin and take it out through his navel must be able to put a coffee bean in my nose." Whether she was only teasing Felipe or whether she believed him to be a witch she never disclosed.

The Kickapoos say that they have few words in their own language with which to express profanity, the worst being words that mean "whore," "dog," and "ill-bred." Their use of the word *dog* to designate a despised person is strange when one remembers that they revere the dog and think of it as a manitou. On the other hand, though they may not have learned all of the fine nuances of the Spanish language as spoken in Mexico, they have learned all of the swear words employed in the Múzquiz area and use them liberally in their speech.

Kickapoo Attitudes toward Their Own People and Culture

Attitudes toward the Culture

Like many other peoples, the Kickapoos believe that they are the center of their universe and that their Indian world is different in every way from the world of others. Kitzihiat, the Great Spirit, created them to live in this world, made by their culture hero, Wisaka, who brought them the knowledge they possess. As long as they exist, their world will last; and, as long as they follow their old ways, they will continue to live. When a Kickapoo is asked if he is content with his life in the village or would rather change for that of a Mexican or an Anglo, his immediate reply is that he prefers his own life.

The Kickapoos resent having outsiders visit the village and act as though no one but a Kickapoo is entitled to use their lanes. Early in our work, after calling on the chief, we strolled through a lane, looking at the houses and the people. We had walked only a short distance when one of the Indians demanded our business in the village. When we told him we had been to see the chief and were now merely looking around, he did not seem satisfied; but when we asked him if anyone in Múzquiz ever asked him what he was doing on their streets, he quietly left.

Our arrival in Múzquiz and subsequent interrogations elicited many threats from the elders to those who were "teaching us their ways" and selling us artifacts. At first, informants and sellers had to do both things surreptitiously. Obtaining a name or any personal information from a Kickapoo was always an uphill job, forcing us to resort to our regular informants or other members of the family. Information about the religion continued to be even more jealously guarded until the end of our stay.

The Indians were interested in learning more about their own history, as evidenced by their conversations with us. Although some of the men were curious about artificial satellites, whether the world was round, or the first moon landing, the majority of their questions were concerned with their ancestors' life in the United States or when they met the French and other Europeans. All were interested in the prints of Indians we had in our "gallery," but the one that drew the most attention was a color enlargement of Yacapita, the old Comanche woman who had gone to live with them as a girl and had left many descendants. Of even greater fascination were the pictures of Indians in issues of *Arizona Highways* and those of themselves in *The Mexican Kickapoo Indians* by Ritzenthaler and Peterson.

The objects which most attracted the women in our house were two small brass kettles that had been manufactured in the United States and used by the Indians for the ceremonial meal at the adoption ceremony. The second item of interest was the Mexican fiber furniture, which the women scrutinized carefully, curious to know if another nation of Indians had made it.

Attitudes toward One Another

The old people told us that the Kickapoos, before they began going abroad to work, were more cooperative than today, helping each other in communal tasks, such as road, irrigation-canal, and fence maintenance and tending herds and farms, while the women helped each other to gather material for the construction of their houses and in the actual building, mat making, and harvesting of wild herbs; the old people were looked after by the younger ones if they lived alone or were unable to care for themselves.

A more Mexican-oriented man said that the men did not do their share of work in the winter, leaving much of it to their wives. In his role as a contractor, he paid the women separately because, in his opinion, the men were spendthrifts. Another old Kickapoo man thought his peers spent too much time drinking, gambling, and loafing, and attributed the squabbling and drunkenness to idleness.

One old woman, after watching Dolores paint the doors of our rented house in Múzquiz, inquired, "Ese hombre, ¿no pinta [that man, doesn't he paint]?" pointing to Felipe by raising her chin in the air. When Dolores explained that Felipe let her do the painting, she grumbled and remarked, "¡Como un Kickapoo [just like a Kickapoo]!"

The old people were as concerned over the new ways and manners of their young as are old people the world over. They deplored the fact that young people were separating themselves more and more from their customs and traditions, fearing that this could be the eventual end of the Kickapoos. On seeing a beautiful wool yarn sash purchased from an old Oklahoma woman, a young Kickapoo matron admitted that she did not know its use. Her mother exclaimed, "See, these young people are not like us!" Then she glanced in the direction of her son and remarked, "He has no queue." What would her son do, she asked, when he died and was not recognized by Pepazcé because he was not wearing his hair in the traditional way of his people?

In spite of all these opinions, the Kickapoos are still cooperative (though perhaps not to the degree they formerly were, or are thought to have been, in retrospect) and still have qualities which make them a cohesive group. For example, on one occasion, when money was being distributed to the Indians by the local *municipio* out of funds from the *ejido*, an event which attracted the whole village into Múzquiz, a small child became seriously ill. Fearing that the child might die in town, the Kickapoos tried to get him to the village as fast as possible but discovered that the bus was waiting to depart until after the payments had been made and no one with a car wished to risk forfeiting his share of the money. Immediately, several Indians took up a collection for a taxi to return the child to the village, where he died shortly after arriving.

In another case, a woman who was building her house fell from the roof to the ground, breaking an arm. The word spread like wildfire through the village, bringing many offers of help. Again, money was collected to defray the expense of taking her to the physician who set her arm, plus accommodations for her family, all of whom accompanied her.

On two occasions during our study, Kickapoo houses burned to the ground. In a matter of a few hours, the owners had been supplied with timber, mats, bedding, clothing, and cooking utensils, and volunteers had rebuilt the houses and carted off the charred remains. During a third fire, when an old woman and her grandson were trapped inside a jacal by a locked door, the whole village formed a fire brigade in an unsuccessful effort to extinguish the flames and reach the victims.

We witnessed several instances of cooperation among the women at mat making and house construction, and we agree with the local Mexicans that the road through Kickapoo land is the best-maintained section of the trail to the village. Although they sometimes hire Mexican helpers for fence building and maintenance or other urgent repairs to be done while the bulk of the men are away, the Indians, when home, work gratuitously at their communal chores.

Of particular interest was the Kickapoo attitude toward the afflicted. The one mentally retarded Kickapoo was treated with great kindness and consideration and was a ready and eager helper at the ceremonies. However, the fear that he was capable of turning into a devil may have colored this tolerant and kind attitude toward him.

Certain individuals in the village, because of their conduct, are the victims of scorn. Almost all Kickapoos indulge in gossip about one another; but some are the butt of a greater share of the gossip than others.

At the time of our study, one man in particular—who should have been highly regarded because of his skills—was often derided because he enjoyed the companionship of young girls rather than women of his approximate age. A second reason for disliking him was that he lived *apartado* (to himself) and did not participate in the drinking, gambling, and gossiping parties. The Kickapoos also claimed that he was lazy and disliked all work except that which required his particular specialized skills —a complaint that seemed unreasonable to us, considering that he was the only remaining Indian skilled in his type of craft. This man had had a strong attachment for his mother during her lifetime and seemed lonely after her death. His first wife had died early, and his second marriage had been a total disillusionment to him, so that he did not want to remarry again. His mother, in an unusual procedure, left her house to him rather than to a female relative.

Another person in the village who was much criticized was a woman who had many liaisons with Mexicans rather than settling down with a Kickapoo man. She also lived apart and was seen at dances, not mingling with the others but to one side with her numerous brood, the majority of whom had no Kickapoo name. When a local physician examined her, he found her beset with anxieties.

As our friendships increased among the Kickapoos, many family feuds rose to the surface. There were two families in particular who, although they participated together in ceremonies, dances, and games, since members of each belonged to the same clans, did not see each other privately, perform community tasks together, or visit each other's homes. We have had two members of these families meet in our home; one always had to leave, since no house is large enough to hold them at the same time.

After some inquiries, we discovered that the basic reason for these family feuds was husband stealing. The women apparently enjoy this game, for they roar with laughter when the subject is brought up; however, it is really no laughing matter, as it creates more "bad blood" than any other single factor.

The Kickapoos had an ambivalent attitude toward Chief Papícoano, one moment resenting many of the things he did or failed to do, and at other times fearing all would come to an end when his death occurred. Villagers were indignant that the chief rented their communal lands, pocketed the money, and seldom, except in an emergency of great magnitude, shared the income with an unfortunate member of their group. They took umbrage at the fact the chief no longer surrounded himself with the Council of Elders, but handled what matters came up for solution without their advice, consulting only his aide.

One woman, in a moment of resentment, told us she wished the old chief would stay in Oklahoma with his daughter and never return to the village, as he was the cause of much bad blood. A few days later, the same woman was delighted to have him back in time to observe the ceremony granting women permission to gather construction material.

Once, during a long conference in our home, when the old chief fell asleep in a comfortable armchair under the warmth of a winter sun, his companions were reluctant to awaken him when it came time for departure, rehashing the exhausted topic under discussion until he awoke of his own accord.

Not once during the many visits we enjoyed with the chief, both in the village and in our home, did we hear him say anything derogatory about any of his people or anyone else.

Attitudes toward Other Peoples and Cultures

Kickapoo Attitudes toward Other Indians

Several items held special interest for the Kickapoo visitors in our home. The chief never came to call without remarking on the beauty of the Zuñi rug used as a wall hanging and on the ability of the women who made it. Indians of all ages enjoyed the issues of *Arizona Highways*, not for the scenes of natural beauty (although a few did comment on these), but for the photographs of Indians, whose similarities and differences with their culture fascinated and intrigued them. A print of Sequoyah, inventor of the Cherokee syllabary used by the Kickapoos, was popular with the men who read and wrote in it. Prints of Gauguin's Tahitian period created much interest, and they were curious to know if these people were also Indians.

Although many of the Kickapoos are descendants of a Comanche couple, those not related to them have a low opinion of them, believing them to be tricky, untrustworthy, unreliable, and crooked. It is said that the reason these persons are drunkards is their Comanche ancestry. The women are reputed to smell foul.

In telling us of the Lipans, whom the Mexican government in the nineteenth century settled on Hacienda Patiño between Morelos and Zaragoza, Coahuila, in an attempt to pacify them and teach them agriculture, one informant reported that they soon reverted to their old ways of pillage and raiding and added, "Esa gente no tiene buen corazón y por eso los matamos [those people were not good of heart; so we killed them]."

During their journeys through the United States, the Kickapoos have visited museums in various places and have encountered many Indians, among them the Menomini, Winnebago, Potawatomi, Sauk, and Fox. They have noticed the similarity of their cultures but, unable to recognize the diversity of language among these people and themselves, they are annoyed at their inability to communicate with any but the Sauk and Fox, concluding with the observation, "Esa gente muy serios [those people are very close-lipped]."

One man who worked in Arizona met the Navajos and the Zuñis and noted that they were heavy drinkers. He had hoped to buy a beaded belt from them, but balked at paying fifteen dollars. If only he could have found a drunk Navajo, he fantasied, he could have gotten one for one dollar, as he claimed that the Navajos literally give things away when drunk in order to continue the spree.

Another Kickapoo, leafing through *Arizona Highways*, commented, "Many ugly Indians on the other side; they do not bathe and they smell bad; Indians who are ugly should not have their pictures taken."

Kickapoo Attitudes toward the Mexicans

Some of the Kickapoos maintain friendly relations with the Mexicans— one woman stating that her Mexican acquaintances in Múzquiz would never let her die from lack of attention, whereas no one in the village would offer help—but the general attitude toward the Mexicans is one of covert hostility, at times breaking out into the open when the provocation is sufficient. Even the woman already mentioned was so annoyed by a Mexican spectator who shoved a Kickapoo during a drunk-man's dance that she threw a dish at him, with such perfect aim that the result was a nasty gash on the man's head.

The Kickapoos are both afraid of the Mexicans and disdainful of them. We were told by a clan leader that all skinny Mexicans were witches, and, if ever one came to our door, we should give him anything he demanded, for he was out to kill. All merchants, in their eyes, are *puro robo* (nothing but thievery), and one in particular is the special butt of such criticism, as he is happy to greet them with a broad smile when they return from the United States with money but, at the end of spring, when funds are low and they need to charge their provisions, is difficult to find, sending his wife, with no authority to extend credit, to wait on them.

One day the chief's mother-in-law came to call late in the evening, and we put her up in our guest room, which opened on the street. The following morning she reported that she sat up all night for fear Mexicans might break down the door and walk into her room, since she could hear them passing on the sidewalk.

The three groups of Mexicans who are the target of the deepest resentment are the consorts of Kickapoo women, the renters, and those hired as house tenders during the Kickapoos' absence.

The consort on whom most of the antipathy was vented during our study was accused of illegally selling mescal to the Indians, thus adding to the drunkenness and creating hard feelings between himself and the old people, who resented this flagrant disregard for their laws. Many efforts were made to evict him, but he countered that he had the right to live in the village, like other Mexicans with Kickapoo wives, and would leave only if he was guaranteed support for his Indian family.

The helpers, workers, and house tenders, who build small jacales in the village and are thereafter hard to evict, are a necessary evil which the Kickapoos have brought on themselves—for, when they work in the United States, they must leave someone in charge of their houses, compounds, and livestock. When they return with money, they want to have wood cut, water hauled, wells dug, and Mexican houses constructed, and the women often have the wives of the tenders wash, iron, and cook for them. But if one of these Mexicans does the least thing to offend a Kickapoo, then the village, in a body, wants to evict him immediately, appealing to the authorities in Múzquiz, Saltillo, or Mexico City.

Mexican Attitudes toward the Kickapoos

The Mexicans, in general, have a paternalistic attitude toward the Kickapoos, using the diminutive, *los inditos*, when speaking of them. In addressing a Kickapoo woman, they use the term *comadre*, a euphemism for *india*, which carries a certain derogatory implication. Most Mexicans, however, differentiate between the "good Indians," meaning the Kickapoos, and the "bad Indians," referring to the Comanches and others who captured residents of Múzquiz or stole from them before the Kickapoos arrived to protect them.

Children are frightened with tales of Indians, and small girls sing a ditty to their dolls which goes like this: "Hay vienen los indios por el chaparral. [Repeat.] ¡Ay, nanita, ay, tatita, me quieren matar! [There come the Indians through the brush. Oh, mama! Oh, papa! they want to kill me!]"

Although the lower-income Mexicans invite Indians to their houses, the middle and upper classes transact whatever business is at hand with the Indians at the gate. Only one well-to-do matron receives an Indian woman, a relative of her son-in-law, in the kitchen.

The Mexicans say that the Kickapoos believe everybody owes them money, food, and favors. If they are invited to eat one time, they are likely to return again, much too soon. One family who ranched near them and also rented their land put chili in the food offered the Indians to discourage their return, since many do not eat hot food.

Another renter complained that the Kickapoos were mean and vengeful. More than once, he had found his cattle shot through an eye with an arrow or crippled by blows, not for food, but because the Indians resented his renting their land.

The Mexicans believe that the Indian men are lazy, letting the women perform the major part of the chores during the winter months, and that they are improvident and spend their money on food, liquor, or trinkets. They say that the men spend too much of their time, as well as money, on ceremonies, leaving the women to make moccasins, peddle used clothing, and dress hides for the local saddlery shops in order to support their families.

When the Kickapoos are drinking, the Mexicans fear being around them, as they become belligerent and hit with anything at hand, such as a stick, rope, or rifle butt, or use knives, which they handle with dexterity. Kickapoo women are considered *muy livianas* (unchaste) and easily picked up by Mexicans, who reward their favors with a meal, a few bottles of beer, or a dress length.

One Mexican, who claims that President Cárdenas placed the Kickapoos under his care, stated at a municipal meeting we attended that the Indians have good minds until puberty, but that after this they begin to deteriorate and thereafter have to be treated like children.

A Mexican general who had a dozen or more Indians under his command during the Mexican Revolution found them invaluable, as they knew the countryside like the palm of their hands, easily located springs and places to hide, and, above all, were good marksmen and hunters.

Kickapoo Attitudes toward the Negroes

By 1861, the Seminoles who had settled near the Kickapoos had moved to Oklahoma, leaving the Negroes behind. The Negroes soon mixed with the Mexicans, became Catholics, allowed schools, learned to speak Spanish, and built their homes in the style of low-income Mexicans. In sharp contrast to this, the Kickapoos pride themselves on their resistance to miscegenation, have allowed neither schools nor evangelization, have learned only enough Spanish to meet their needs, and have adhered to their traditions with a perseverance which is astonishing.

The Mexican government continues to recognize the Negroes as rightful claimants of the Seminole portion of the original grant; not so the Kickapoos, who are convinced that, after the Seminoles left, they fell heirs to this land and that the Negroes are mere squatters. This attitude has given rise to numerous disagreements between the two groups.

This posture was brought to our attention when we drove through the Negro village in the company of an Indian who maintained that the Kickapoos did not want mixed blood among them and therefore had nothing to do with the Negroes. One of the Kickapoo women, married for thirty years to a Mexican with one-quarter Negro blood, is considered *muy mala* (very bad) by the opposing camp because of this marriage. Although this couple have lived in the village for many years, the first years of their marriage had to be spent outside. He is a cooperative and helpful man, never argues, falls in with any plans of the Indians, and is a first-rate hunter; but, in spite of these qualities and his eagerness to fit into the Kickapoo way of life, he is discriminated against and is not allowed to witness any of the indoor ceremonies.

The Indians' grudge against the Negroes has a historical background, for Seminole Negro scouts accompanied Mackenzie in his 1873 raid on Remolino. Charles Daniels, one of these scouts, is quoted by Frost Woodhull:

Well, in 1873 we cross the Rio Grande at de mouth of Las Moras Creek and went across to a little town dey call Remelino; well, this Injun camp was about one mile from Remelino Mountains; dem wuz de Kickapoo Injuns, and de Lipans dem wuz about half mile from de Kickapoo Injuns but we went and struck de Kickapoo camp fust. Dat were de Fourth Cavalry, Mackenzie wuz in comman den. General Shafter were second with his Scouts from Eagle Pass, too, you see, but we all jined together. Well, after de fight was over we had capted squaws and children, dey wuz sixteen all together, and nineteen dead ones, no bucks would be capted.[1]

Two further sore points between the Kickapoos and the Negroes are the matter of irrigation water, which was allotted in greater proportion to the Negroes than to the Kickapoos, and the dividing line between their properties, never clearly surveyed and marked with a fence.

Although the Kickapoos secretly believe that all Negroes are witches, especially the tall, skinny ones, not all has been fear and animosity between them. In the past, the Negroes held an animated "June'teenth" celebration on the river in honor of the Negro emancipation date in Texas (June 19, 1865), with barbecued beef and goat, roasting ears, tamales, watermelon, and beer free to all comers. These events were attended by many Kickapoos. Hard times and the exodus of many Negroes into Texas have made these picnics a thing of the past, but the date is still remembered and celebrated on a smaller scale.

Today, young and not-so-young Kickapoos attend the dances, weddings, and jamborees held in the Negro village, where beer is plentiful, Mexican food is available, and Mexican-style dancing is enjoyed.

Kickapoo Relations with Neighboring Ranchers

The Kickapoos resent the Anglo ranchers, who lock their ranch gates, and cannot understand why they are denied permission to hunt on the ranches. As a rule, the Mexican ranchers are more willing than the Anglos to allow them to hunt.

Not all the ranchers lock their gates or prohibit the Indians from entering their premises. Dr. Mike Long Galán befriended the Indians during his lifetime. An old Indian today often reminisces that he and Dr. Long were like brothers and enjoyed hunting together. The Robert Spences allow certain Indians in small groups to hunt on their ranch and one particular Indian, Dr. Long's friend, is befriended in the home of the Spences for having discovered a rich spring on their land. Mrs. Sarah S. McKellar, whose family owned La Mariposa, adjoining the Kickapoo grant, befriended Yacapita, the Comanche woman, whose family, on arriving at ranch headquarters during a hunting expedition, were given supplies from the Mariposa Company's store.

Kickapoo Attitudes toward Anglos

The Kickapoos have not, after living in Mexico over one hundred years, forgotten the former treatment meted them by the Anglos. One old woman bitterly related how the Indians had been forced to relinquish their lands in the United States because the Anglos tried to take their religion away from them and placed their children in Indian boarding schools in order to extirpate their Kickapoo ways.

They have not forgotten the 1865 encounter with the U.S. Cavalry near Dove Creek, nor the attack on the Tankersley Ranch in 1862; and still less have they forgotten the Mackenzie raid of 1873 at Remolino and the subsequent forced return to the U.S. Indian Territory, where they were given a reservation, only to have part of it soon divided into allotments and the remainder sold for a pittance to Anglos.

Today, they work amicably with their many U.S. employers. The missions still try to take their religion away from them, but their children are no longer forcibly placed in schools. They continue to be harassed by Anglos in more subtle ways, such as extremely low wages in the Southwest and ghetto housing on farms and orchards. There is an apparent awakening to the injustice of these conditions, as Indians are demanding better housing on threat of not returning. Because the labor supply is at a premium, farm owners are improving housing and protecting workers with Social Security and Workmen's Compensation.

Kickapoo Attitudes toward Religions

Had the Kickapoos been as diligent about keeping renters off their land as they have been about proselytizers, they would have been spared much misery and hard feelings between themselves and the Mexicans. They have clung fanatically to the stipulation in their contract with the Mexican government when they first went to Mexico that they would be allowed to follow their own customs and practices[2] and have seldom permitted either Catholic or other missionaries to preach on their land.

Several years ago, two Mormon missionaries from Oklahoma, accompanied by two converted Indians, a Pima and a Kickapoo, arrived to proselyte in the village after obtaining permission from Chief Papícoano. According to the reports we heard, no one attended their meeting. Instead, the converted Kickapoo got a resounding tongue-lashing from his relatives for bringing "hallelujahs," as missionaries are called by the Kickapoos, to the village to take the people's religion away from them.

In Oklahoma and Texas, missionaries do work with the Indians. What purpose this serves, except to confuse them, we have never been able to ascertain. The greatest benefit reaped by the Indians by attending the meetings is the large quantity of clothing given them, which is passed to their Mexican Kickapoo relatives to sell among the miners and low-income workers.

One old woman, whose son married a Mexican girl, felt very put upon because she had to look after her daughter-in-law and grandchildren while her son worked in Texas, since the young wife had no papers to cross the border. But the drop that caused her cup of indignities to overflow was being urged to attend the christening of one of her granddaughters. She stated emphatically that she was not, under any circumstances, going to enter the church.

The Catholic church has made some surface inroads among the Kickapoos, if not actual conversions. A clan leader christened his last child in the local church on the insistence of a Mexican friend, who feared the child would die a "Jew," that is, without benefit of the holy sacrament. Some weeks later, the clan leader proudly showed us his daughter's christening certificate, observing that, in this way, his child had double insurance. The oldest daughter of this same man, legally married to a Mexican, held a religio-social celebration observed for Mexican girls reaching their fifteenth birthday for one of her daughters, and later her son married a Mexican girl in the church.

If we found the customs and ways of the Kickapoos fascinating and novel, they, in turn, were equally curious and baffled by Western culture.

One man told us that in a discussion with a Mexican on their respective religious beliefs, the latter had questioned the Kickapoos' reason for offering three annual feasts to the spirits, when these cannot eat. Having noticed that Mexicans place flowers on graves, the Indian retorted, "Why do you take flowers to the dead when they cannot see or smell?"

Our home gradually became a headquarters of sorts for the Indians, where they found a warm welcome, a good market for their crafts, and encouragement in the improvement of their articles. Gift exchange became an important part of making friends, and for this purpose we had at hand dress lengths, beads, canned fruit, simple medications, and hearty meals.

Our constant interrogation annoyed many Indians, while making others suspicious of our intentions. Dolores received the nickname *esa mujer preguntona* (that woman who asks too many questions). One man was particularly piqued with her for inquiring about his mother's adoption ceremony, telling her in no uncertain terms that this was part of his "inheritance" and she was not to pry into it. He further lectured us on how the Mexican customs and beliefs had been destroyed by the Spaniards, who told the Mexicans to believe everything out of books and nothing from the stones where their "inheritance" was pictured. He ended with this remark: "Look at the *preguntones;* they are like birds who have left their nest to seek more food. Where are their fathers and mothers and their children, and why are they not staying together?"

The men were also wary of giving certain information, especially that dealing with myths, for fear our young woman servant might be having her period.

One old woman during her first luncheon with us continuously looked under the table. Understandably curious, we asked the reason for her interest. She replied that she was noticing how the table was made in order to have one like it made for herself. When we told her not to have a table made for future visits from us, she retorted that she wanted the table for Mexican callers.

Our home and manners were a source of surprise and puzzlement to the Indians from the beginning. When Chief Papícoano came to call for the first time, he found us in the midst of painting some furniture. He immediately inquired if we had set up a furniture or paint store. Later, as we acquired more and more books, they asked if we were opening a bookstore. After we accumulated a number of artifacts, they told an American linguist visiting the village that we bought and sold Kickapoo objects for a living.

When a weather station was located in the village by the Federal Department of Meteorology, it was we who were accused of placing the contraption there in order to "take their songs and ceremonies." Endless explanations were needed to convince them of the actual function of the station and of our total detachment from it.

The Kickapoos had a boundless curiosity about us, wanting to know what we were doing, why we had left our country, whether we liked Indians better than gringos, where we had been born, how we had come to Mexico, how we had found them, why we spoke Spanish when we were not Mexicans but gringos, and so on.

The tape recorder had to be taken out of the living room, as they feared we might "take their talk" and, consequently, some of their spirit. One visitor who sometimes prolonged his calls beyond our endurance we learned to dispatch with ease by bringing the recorder into the room. He would instantly pick up his hat, having suddenly remembered an important errand.

There was much jealousy among the Kickapoos over our friendship. It was some time before we were allowed to meet other Indians besides the chief's extensive family, and we were later told by more recently made friends that they had been warned not to visit us because we were "taking their inheritance," we were making a movie of them, we had a vicious dog that ate Kickapoos, and the Indian dresses and shirts in our small museum had once held Indians that we had devoured.

One man became so piqued with us when we rejected a piece of work we had ordered that he went to the *municipio* to report us, asking that we be ejected from Múzquiz. He was crestfallen when told that the reason we were in Múzquiz was because of the Indians and that we had done nothing to merit being run out of town. Two days later he returned with the finished object, and we made our peace by giving him a string of Ecuadorian beads, embellished with feathers and a shell. Had we searched high and low we could not have hit upon a more appropriate gift. His eyes opened in wide surprise, and he explained that his father had once owned a similar necklace, which he hung around his neck when praying. He returned a few days later with a minuscule obsidian mask he had found among his trinkets with the simple statement, "I bring you this."

One day a woman came to the house for the first time in the company of another, whose friendship we treasured. The first-time visitor was vexed when we inquired her name and replied that it meant "pig." Aware that she had fibbed, we let the issue drop and pursued another subject. Either her relative or her conscience caused her to have a change of heart; for, in a few days, she called again, bringing as a gift a German-silver bracelet, and telling the true meaning of her name.

Many were the gifts we received during the years we stayed in Múz-quiz: moccasins, baskets, bows and arrows, artifacts to add to our collection, pieces of jewelry, clothing, fresh venison, jerky, fresh and pickled *chilequipín*, oregano, specimens of medicinal plants, pinto beans, squash, dried pumpkin, fresh watercress, hominy, a bearskin, and, one day, a live rooster.

Chapter 12

Knowledge and Tradition

Records and Communication

When we inquired about registrations of Kickapoo births, the office of vital statistics in Múzquiz reported that Oscar Sukwe's twelve children were registered but not their descendants. To these may be added one other Kickapoo woman. It is evident that the Indians, for the most part, do not register births and deaths. In addition, the Mexican federal census has never been able to make a thorough enumeration of the Kickapoos—first, because the Algonquian names are difficult to understand; second, because any stranger in the village asking questions receives little cooperation and information; and, third, because few, if any, Kickapoos keep records of the important events of their lives. Neither Chief Papícoano nor anyone in the village maintained a tribal roll when we were there. One clan leader kept a record of his extensive family in Ba-Be-Bi-Bo for many years; but, unfortunately, one of his several wives burned his papers when he left her.

After much work and patience, and in the face of much resistance from the Indians, we compiled a tribal roll during two summers and kept it up-to-date while our research was in progress. Although the Kickapoos resented having their names *en esa caja* (in that box), many finally accepted the practicality of the tribal roll when dealing with the Bureau of Indian Affairs in the United States and their employers, to whom we wrote letters for them.

According to Forsyth, the Sauk and Fox believed that "To the white people the Great Spirit gave the book and taught them the use of it, which the Great Spirit thought absolutely necessary for them to guide them through life."[1] The Kickapoos repeated practically the same words and added that they do not need books, since, by fasting and consulting Grandmother Earth and Grandfather Fire, they gain the knowledge they seek. Furthermore, they are able to retain this knowledge in their hearts—

the Kickapoos' seat of knowledge, thought, and feeling—and can, by word of mouth, pass their *herencia* (culture) to their children.

Nevertheless, they are beginning to realize that "writing things down," as they express it, has value. One older and unusually observant man noted that "The Mexicans and people in the United States write down everything in order to remember their old ways, whereas the Kickapoos do not; thus, when something is no longer done or the way of doing something changes, it is soon forgotten." He was one of the few who approved of our "writing their history." This declaration came about one day when he noticed a print of Chief Mató Tope of the Mandan tribe hanging in our "picture gallery." The old man wanted to know to which nation the chief belonged. When we showed him Lewis Henry Morgan's *Indian Journals*,[2] he inquired whether anything about the Kickapoos was included. When we referred to the index and found nothing about his people, he was crestfallen. This brought forth his admission that, in spite of the fact that many Kickapoos resented our being "taught their ways," these should be written down so that their children might know the old ways and others could learn about them.

Forsyth made a further observation about the Sauk and Fox which is typical of the Kickapoos: "They have many papers among them of sixty and seventy years old—they take great care of old papers, without knowing anything of the purport of them."[3] Out of the many old papers they brought us to read, we found less than half a dozen of value.

Since only a few of the Indians write, the usual way of signing documents is by fingerprinting. When Chief Papícoano needed to send a message to someone in the village, he called on his aide, or anyone available, to deliver it by word of mouth. Formerly, there had been a special person appointed by the chief who was the town crier and whose duty it was to announce news, meetings, or special messages in the village. This crier no longer exists. When ceremonies are held, the planning is done by word of mouth, except for the adoption ceremonies, when the selected performers are presented with invitation sticks delivered by the waiters.

Until around 1915, young men used to call their sweethearts to the trysting place by means of a flute, widely used as a courting instrument by all the Algonquian Indians. A young man would go into the hills or climb a tree to serenade his sweetheart until she joined him. Each flute had a distinctive tone, and each flutist had his own melodies, known to the girl, who thus recognized the player.[4] Today, sweethearts have a special whistle, known only to themselves, which they use to call each other. While spending a brief time with the Kickapoos in 1953, Ritzenthaler and Peterson noted: "The whistling . . . is done by young people of either sex. The hands are cupped and air blown into the cavity between the knuckles of the thumbs placed against the lips vertically. Three fingers of the right hand are cupped so that the ends rest near the base of the index finger of the left hand. The fingers of the left hand control the aperture at the back of the hand, opening and closing to further control the tone produced by the oral cavity and lips."[5]

Reckoning and Measurement

Among the Kickapoos the magical number is four, found repeatedly throughout every phase of their culture. They have names for numbers in Algonquian from one to ten; after this, they count ten and one, ten and two, ten and three, and so forth. Although all recognize the values of both Mexican and U.S. currency, they are unable to calculate the exchange of one into the other.

Long distances, such as those between towns or cities, formerly were measured by the day or portion of the day it took a man on horseback to cover them. Although today many of the Indians travel by automobile, they continue to measure long distances in the same manner; it is not how many kilometers they travel, but what portion of the day it takes them to travel the distance. Short distances, such as the dimensions of their houses, are measured by the number of steps, either in "short steps" or in "long steps."

Large land areas in Coahuila formerly were measured in *sitios de ganado mayor*—literally, places for raising large stock, such as cattle, horses, mules, and burros. One *sitio de ganado mayor* is equivalent to 1,755.61 hectares. A place for raising small livestock, such as sheep or goats, was called a *sitio de ganado menor* and was equivalent to 780.27 hectares. The Kickapoos know about these measurements since their land grant was ceded to them on this basis.

When the Kickapoos use water from their own dam for irrigation, they agree among themselves who is to use it according to the urgency of the crop. But, when they use water from the irrigation canal which also serves the Negro village, they accommodate to the amount allowed them, which is four *días de agua*, an old Spanish measure. This water is then divided among individuals by the measurement known as a *claro de agua*, as explained in Chapter 8.

A hole dug in the ground to stake a post, whether for a house, a fence, or the goals used in games, is considered deep enough when a man can no longer reach the bottom to take out the soil with his hands.

A man who is asked what part of a hectare he can plow in a day will answer that he does a *tarea*. This old Spanish measure is approximately the equivalent of 2,500 square meters.

In buying or selling corn, wheat, or beans among themselves, the Kickapoos use one of their large oval baskets as a measure; but, when selling to the Mexicans who use scales, they buy or sell by the kilo. Although the metric system has been in use in Mexico for many years, some of the old measurements persist, such as the *bulto*, approximately five hundred liters of dry material. Staples such as flour are still sold by the *bulto* in Múzquiz.

When buying meat at the butcher's the Kickapoos do not order by the kilo but ask for five or more pesos' worth, depending on the amount they can afford to spend. Neither are exact quantities used in cooking. For breadmaking, they use hands and fingers as cups and spoons with which to measure out the flour and baking powder, add a "pinch" of salt, and add water until the dough is of the right consistency.

From childhood, Kickapoos are taught not to measure each other. This is only done when the length and breadth of the corpse is taken in order to know the size of the grave. Thus, a woman who wants to sew a new dress for herself takes no measurements but uses an old one as a model; if she makes a dress for a relative or a friend, she borrows a used one as a guide for cutting out the new one.

Some buy piece goods in Mexico by the old Spanish linear measurement of *vara*, which varies from thirty-two to forty-three inches, but when they purchase cloth in the United States they use the term *yarda* (yard). A man buying a pair of trousers does not bother to try them on but inserts his clenched fist and forearm in the waist to estimate the fit. This suffices to give him the approximate waist measurement. Shirt sizes are only guessed at.

When sewing for non-Kickapoos, the Indians are willing to take measurements. When we asked an old woman to make a man's traditional shirt for Felipe, she called for a piece of string. First she measured him for shirt length to the fingertips. Satisfied with this measurement, she tied a knot in the string and did likewise for the arm length and the shoulders. When she finished, she rolled up the string and handed it to her teen-age son. For several days we had misgivings about whether she would remember from which end of the string she had begun the knots, but when she brought the shirt, it was an approximate fit—with a few inches in every direction to grow into.

When we ordered moccasins we drew the outline of the foot. The paper usually was lost, and the size was usually wrong.

Time and Weather

The Kickapoos divide the day in two parts: from sunup to sundown, which is day, or white; and from sundown to sunup, which is night, or black. The hours of the day have little meaning to them. When a local physician prescribed a medicine to be taken at 6:00 A.M., noon, and 6:00 P.M., the only way we could get the message over to the patient was by pointing to the east, the zenith, and the west.

As will be explained in Chapter 15, the Kickapoo New Year has no definite date. Although it usually falls in February, it sometimes comes in January. The wild black cherry must bloom, the thunderers must pass over the village, and the Pleiades must be in the zenith at the time of sunset. Since the Kickapoos do not use the Gregorian calendar, except in their contacts with Mexicans and Anglos, they have little concept of the week and do not have Algonquian names for the days; when talking to Mexicans or Anglos, they simply refer to "the first day of the week," "the second day of the week," and so on. Neither are they much aware of the months of the year of the Gregorian calendar. Formerly, they had names for the twelve moons of the year; today, the only one they know is the moon of February, in which their New Year usually falls.[6] They do, however, still use the moons as a division of time; but now they call them "the first moon after the New Year," "the second moon," and so on. One old woman told us they could not gather material for the construction of the summer house beyond the second moon after the New Year.

The most meaningful divisions of time for them are the four seasons: fall, "the time when the cattails are ready to be cut"; winter, "the time of cold"; spring, "the time when plants begin to bud"; and summer, "the time of heat." There are variations on these names. Some call winter "the time when the bear cubs are born," and summer "when the crops are ready to be harvested"—both possible remnants of the former names of the moons.

Today, they tend to associate time with events in their lives, such as the season when they occupy the summer or winter house, when a certain plant, such as corn, has two leaves, or when the cactus fruit is ripe. If one asks a Kickapoo, "Will you be going to work in April?" the reply will be, "I go when the summer house is ready." (The summer house is readied during April and May.)

When leaving for the United States to work, an old woman told us she would be returning to the village "en el tiempo de calor [in the time of heat]." Not satisfied with this unspecific time, we asked her the month, and her answer was, "When the cactus fruit is ripe, I come back." We consulted our Mexican laundress, a well of wisdom regarding plants; she informed us that the prickly-pear fruit ripened in July.

The weather in northern Coahuila is variable, and extreme for the latitude. Some winters may be mild, but during others temperatures drop into the twenties (Fahrenheit). The summer days are hot, but evenings are usually cool because of a breeze that descends from the nearby mountain range, Sierra Hermosa de Santa Rosa.[7]

No rain record was made available to us in Múzquiz, but the American Smelting and Refining Company in Nueva Rosita, which had assumed the rain record begun by Hacienda Sabinas in 1902 and kept it up-to-date, gave us a copy of their chart.[8] In Nueva Rosita, some twenty miles east of the Kickapoo village, the rainfall shows an annual average of 16.99 inches during the period between 1902 and 1970. Two rainy seasons can usually be expected in the area, one in the spring and one in the fall; but in many years there is so little rain that the springs dry up, forcing the villagers to dig wells near the river in order to obtain water. In these years the crops are nonexistent. At other times, rains, frequently triggered by tropical storms in the Gulf of Mexico or the Caribbean, inundate the area, causing rivers to rise, washing out bridges, and stopping communications, not only from the village to Múzquiz, but from Múzquiz to neighboring cities and towns. The Indians are frequently isolated for a week or longer, when transportation on horseback is the only means of traveling.

Fabila states that as many as twenty freezes, with frequent snow, occur during the year in the village.[9] During the ten years of our study, we knew of only one time when snow fell in the village; however, snow frequently falls on the sierra to the west at altitudes of four to five thousand feet. Dust storms and high winds are a frequent occurrence, but the most devastating phenomenon is the hailstones, some the size of grapefruit.

The Kickapoos are exceptional prognosticators of rain. One day, after a severe period of drought when not a cloud had been in the sky to dim the intense heat, an Indian friend returned hurriedly from a shopping spree to announce that she was leaving immediately for the village, as it was going to rain. Incredulous, we wanted the signs pointed out to us. In the southeast, thunderheads were beginning to form; and by five that evening the rain did come, lasting several days. On another day when we inquired what the Indians were doing for water, as the river was dry and wells had had to be dug, one of the women, with an assurance that was eerie, said that they were not worried, since it was going to rain. That evening, a drizzle began to fall, which turned into a heavy and welcome rain. Had the magic rhizome, Solomon's seal, become damp and told her the change in the weather? The Kickapoos say that this is one way of knowing when it is going to rain.

Chapter 13

Disease, Medicine, and Intoxicants

Disease and Its Causes

The concept of germs or the transmission of disease by man and other organisms is unknown to the Kickapoos; instead, they attribute disease to foreign objects placed in their bodies through witchcraft, the breaking of laws given them by their culture hero, failure to observe the required ceremonies, disregard of food taboos and those associated with the forty-day period of involution, disregard of the diet prescribed by their own curers, handling of curative herbs without sufficient knowledge of their power, excess sexual activities, or having one's blood extracted for an examination or a transfusion; they also believe that some diseases are sent by other nations. To these causes can be added the many folk causes of diseases and conditions they have learned from their Mexican neighbors.

Some, however, do recognize that venereal diseases and tuberculosis are contagious. A man, for instance, came to call complaining that he had a kidney disorder, accompanied by much pain and frequent urgency to urinate. Although he first attributed his illness to a soaking he had received while perspiring, he also feared he might have a venereal disease, but explained, "Hace muchos años que no ocupo mujer [it has been many years since I have lain with a woman]." Another informant came to us, saying she had left the room assigned to her in a local hostelry because her bedfellow was a Kickapoo woman who is emaciated, coughs constantly, and is suspected of having tuberculosis. She refused to sleep in the same room for fear she might catch the woman's sickness.

Witchcraft, which the Indians fear as the most real and prevalent cause of illness and death, is treated in Chapter 16. The Kickapoos also believe that breaking any of the laws given to them by their culture hero can cause illness or death. Of course, the first law, which states the Kickapoos may not take their own lives, cannot bring disease; but the act itself is the greatest punishment that can be meted to a Kickapoo, as has already been shown. Murderers are constantly exposed to having disease descend on them; those who fail to comply with their ceremonial obligations are particularly subject to disease; those who steal, drink to excess, commit adultery, accumulate wealth, commit incest, gossip maliciously, or do evil through witchcraft may all be punished by disease, disaster, or death.

Breaking food taboos is considered a certain way to court illness, as is failure to observe the special taboos connected with childbirth. For example, an informant came one day with the news that one of the Kickapoo women, who had given birth to a child in a hospital in the United States, was seriously ill with a disease that made her look as yellow as a ripe pumpkin. (Later, through a local physician, we learned that she had hepatitis.) Our informant was certain that the illness had been caused by the woman's failure to obtain the necessary herbal teas to drink during her stay in the hospital. Not only must the drinking of certain teas be strictly adhered to, but failure to observe complete sexual abstinence for forty days after childbirth may also bring illness.

When a Kickapoo curer takes a case, he prescribes a rigorous diet for the duration of his four-day cure. Anyone breaking this diet exposes himself to a continuation of the illness. One day, a Kickapoo man came to call, looking haggard, thin, and unkempt, complaining that he had been in bed with influenza for a week. Noting no improvement, his mother had called one of the curers to attend him. He was progressing nicely, but instead of waiting the four days, in which he was to stay on a diet of corn gruel, he had arisen and eaten beef. He had also been given an herb which would cause the influenza to return whence it came; but, since he had disobeyed orders, the influenza had returned to punish him further.

The handling of curative herbs is not to be taken lightly, and anyone who does take it lightly subjects himself to disease. One old man who became senile (which, to the Kickapoos, meant that he was insane) was thought to have brought this condition on himself in two ways: first, though he was a member of the Berry clan and should have devoted himself to Berry ceremonies, he seldom attended them after being cured by one of the herbal societies, to which he then turned his attention; second, he was learning to handle certain herbs whose power he underestimated.

The Kickapoos believe that a person may wear himself out, age prematurely, and be prone to various illnesses if he indulges in excessive sexual activity. One of the Kickapoo women, who is constantly under the care of a curer or a Mexican *curandera* because of her numerous ailments, is thought to have brought them on herself through licentious acts in her youth. Another woman, prominent in the village, who has had many lovers, is considered by her peers to be doomed for her overindulgence.

The Kickapoos are extremely reluctant to have blood extracted, either for a test or for a transfusion. One man told us that many years ago a physician at the American Smelting and Refining Company's hospital at Nueva Rosita extracted some of his blood for a test. He had never felt quite the same from that day and had often asked the physician to return his blood. This same man was alarmed when he heard that the Kickapoos were having their blood tested on crossing the border at Eagle Pass. The thought of having any more of his blood extracted frightened him; but, since it was supposedly being done to discover if the Kickapoos had any Mexican blood and he was pure Kickapoo, he was willing to undergo the ordeal. We checked the matter at the border on our next trip to Texas and found that all persons crossing had to undergo smallpox vaccinations unless they had a recent certificate. When we informed our friend of the actual situation, he was much relieved.

During a serious illness a Kickapoo woman, who was losing large amounts of blood due to a uterine disorder, needed transfusions. A request went out among the Kickapoos for a donor, but no one was willing to give blood. Finally, the woman's brother, whose blood type fitted hers, volunteered for the transfusion, but he became so ill that he had to keep to his bed for several days. On other occasions when transfusions were needed, an outside donor—usually a young enlisted man from the local cavalry regiment—was solicited and paid sixteen dollars rather than have a Kickapoo submit to the extraction of blood.

There are various other accepted causes of disease. Reading is believed to cause insanity. Conversing with the spirit of a departed relative, in particular a spouse, can also bring insanity. This was thought to be the case with an old, senile woman who began to wander around the village talking to herself. The Kickapoos believed that the departed spirit of her Mexican spouse had come to annoy her, causing her to become insane. Anger may cause the heart to burst, bring about a cerebral hemorrhage, or cause paralysis. Being inactive and thinking too much weighs down the heart and makes it hurt, causing heart trouble. A person who deeply feels the death of a loved one can become ill, lose his appetite, and finally die of grief. Drinking coffee and cold water before dawn may be the cause of kidney trouble. Drinking cold water may bring mumps. Snow and severe cold weather can bring bronchitis. Eating too much beef forms cataracts, believed to be a cloth that veils the eyes. Taking aspirin causes a ball to form in the stomach, necessitating massage and certain herbs to dislodge it.

The moon is often blamed for the slow progress of a boil or carbuncle. When Chief Papícoano developed a carbuncle on his face which did not respond sufficiently to the medication of a curer, he confided that that particular moon was very bad for curing cuts, sores, boils, and other skin infections.

One man was convinced that disease in general and influenza in particular were sent by other races, who were cooking a mixture of garlic, chili, soap, marijuana, and an acid—all things to which the majority of the Kickapoos have an aversion. The acrid smoke from this mixture hit the dome covering this world and bounced toward the Kickapoo village, bringing disease to all. To prove his theory, he brought out a couple of pages of a comic strip, written in English, showing a Neanderthal sort of individual preparing this noxious mixture in an elaborate, Rube Goldberg–type machine. When we asked him to give us the strip, he refused, but requested that we read it to him. The captions explained that the character was making war on disease—not sending out noxious gases—but our visitor would not be convinced. He emphasized that the Kickapoos would never lend themselves to such evil doings, that is, sending out disease to others.

Kickapoo Medical Practices

Kickapoo medicine today is primarily based on plants and prayers, with the addition of a number of animal and human products, cupping horns, other paraphernalia, and several patent medicines.

In making a survey of the Kickapoos' use of plants, we discovered that they are familiar with eighty-four native plants; eighteen cultivated or imported plants, either from other parts of Mexico or from abroad, a few of which they purchase in local *hierberías* (herb shops); twelve animal products; two human products; and fifteen patent medicines, bought in local drugstores. This number of plants and other products cannot pretend to be all-inclusive, since the Kickapoos guard their medical practices with an extreme secretiveness. It represents only the ones about which we were able to elicit information. The botanical names of the plants mentioned in the text appear in the index. This section will be devoted to general information on Kickapoo medical practices.

It is interesting to speculate on how the Kickapoos, a people from the northern forest regions of Wisconsin, learned the use of the plants found in the semidesert of northern Coahuila. Did the Kickapoos learn from other Indian tribes with whom they came in contact on their long trek to Mexico and during the period when they helped to subdue the Comanches, Lipans, and Apaches, or from their Mexican neighbors? We asked ourselves this question and concluded that the way to discover the answer was to learn the plants used medicinally by lower-income local Mexicans and those used by other Indian groups with whom the Kickapoos had been in contact.

Fortunately, the Mexicans are much more generous with information about medicinal plants than are the Kickapoos. Our maid, laundress, gardener, friends, neighbors, and even strangers in Múzquiz were all willing informants, as was the goatherd of a nearby rancher, who was famous for his knowledge of native plants. We easily collected a large number of plants and learned their uses. Comparing these to a list of plants found in Fray Juan Agustín Morfi's *Excerpts from the Memorias for the History of the Province of Texas*,[1] which described a trip to inspect the presidios in Texas and Sonora in 1777–1778, we discovered that, of 172 plants mentioned by Morfi, 133 were still in daily use in Múzquiz two hundred years later. Of this number the Kickapoos use 75; they also use 27 other plants which, as far as we can determine, the Mexicans do not use.

Among the present Kickapoos are descendants of the Comanche couple who came to live with them when young. During her lifetime, the Comanche woman, Yacapita, was a famous curer. She could have brought knowledge of some plants. We also know that the Kickapoos captured other Comanche, Lipan, and Apache Indians, and it could have been from them that they learned the use of plants unknown to the local Mexican people. However, of a list of fifty-eight plants used by the Comanches and collected by Gustav G. Carlson and Volney H. Jones in Texas,[2] only ten were found to be utilized by the Kickapoos for medicinal purposes, and not always for the same ailment as in the Comanche list.

Also among the Kickapoos are descendants of other Indians, including Shawnees, Potawatomis, and Cherokees. For a number of years, the Seminoles and some Biloxis, with their Negro friends, were neighbors of the Kickapoos. Among the Negroes who still live in the village vacated by the Seminoles are several *curanderos*. These could all have contributed to the Kickapoos' herbal knowledge. It is evident, however, that during the period of residence in Mexico they have learned the use of the majority of their medicinal plants from the Mexicans.

Knowledge of plants is usually derived from an older kinsman, such as a grandparent, parent, uncle, or aunt—or sometimes from a Mexican. Some Kickapoos, however, acquire their knowledge through dreams. One woman, a member of two herbal societies and more generous than most with her knowledge, explained how she had received a cure through a dream. Many years before, her older brother, to whom she was devoted, had been stiff-jointed to such a degree that he was unable to walk. Having exhausted those she knew without the desired effect, she thought at length about the remedy she should use. She prayed to the Great Spirit that she might receive the power to cure her crippled brother. During the night she dreamed where she would find a certain juniper, whose branches and leaves she was directed to use. Arising at daybreak the following morning, she went to the exact spot she had seen in her dream and found the tree, from which she prepared hot baths for her brother which proved so beneficial that he completely recovered.

Four types of cures are practiced by the Kickapoos: those performed by the clan leaders, who employ the clan bundles; those performed during the ceremony in connection with the two buffalo dances; those performed by members of herbal societies; and those undertaken by what might be called free-lancers, who are neither clan leaders nor members of an herbal society but have learned the use of a few plants, either from a Kickapoo, from another Indian, or from a Mexican. It would be difficult to find a mature Kickapoo man or woman who does not know the use of some plant.

Any illness not suspected of being a punishment sent to a patient for failing to comply with the laws, taboos, and responsibilities of the tribe may be treated by one of the clan leaders. The clan leaders are entitled to gather certain plants which no one else would dare touch. For instance, only the clan leaders and owner of one of the two buffalo curing ceremonies may gather wild black cherry branches or wild iris rhizomes. Only clan leaders may gather Solomon's seal, the magical plant used for myriad ailments.

Faith in the medical powers of a curer is indispensable; without faith, the curer will not treat a patient. Once we asked a woman member of an herbal society why she had not treated a certain woman, and her reply was, "She has no faith in the medicine I use."

The Kickapoos have a deep and unwavering faith in their own medical abilities. One day a man with a highly irritated eye condition came to see us. The irritation had apparently been caused, according to his description, from a pesticide used in a cotton field where he had worked. Since we could not convince him to visit one of the local physicians, we gave him a vial of boric acid solution and an eye dropper. A few days later he returned, completely recovered, telling us that it had not been our medicine which had cured him, but one he had concocted with Texas prairie acacia.

When we first began our study, we financially aided a woman whom the physician diagnosed as suffering from an incurable cancer of the uterus; believing her condition hopeless, he sent her home to die. By some miracle, the woman is still living. A member of an herbal society confided that it was she who cured the woman. After her return to the village, she offered to cure her with certain herbs which she would not disclose. A large lump in her abdomen disappeared after massage, and the woman gradually recovered.

When a person is ill, the family members have a consultation and decide on the curer whom they consider most capable of restoring the patient's health. A relative, or the patient himself, if he is able to walk, takes a small gift of Indian tobacco, no more than a thimbleful, wrapped in a clean white cloth, to the clan leader or the member of the herbal society under whose care he wishes to place himself. In the case of a free-lancer, no tobacco is sent as a gift, but his treatment is similar to that of the other two types of curers, and payment is optional. The clan leader, curer, or free-lancer visits the patient, appraises the situation, and, if he believes he can handle the case, assumes charge of the patient for a four-day cure.

In former times, the curer prayed for wisdom to heal the patient and took him to a secluded place in the *monte*, where he was isolated in a temporary shelter. If the patient was female, the curer, whether male or female, was accompanied by a woman who was undergoing an apprenticeship or some female relative who was versed in the care of the sick. The cure lasted until the patient recovered or died.

Now, the curer sees his patient in the latter's home but secludes him from the family and visitors by placing blankets around the portion of the bench where he sleeps. He takes the clan bundle—in the case of a clan leader—to the house and uses the herbs and paraphernalia kept in the bundle for this purpose. He prays that he may be successful and continues to pray for the following three days. He establishes rules to be followed by the patient, family, and visitors. Before the cure commences, fire from the bundle house of the patient's clan must be brought and kept burning continuously. No food or beverages may be taken by the patient other than those which the curer prescribes, usually consisting of freshly killed squirrel or skunk soup, freshly made hominy, potatoes baked in the coals, and herbal teas. No one except the patient is allowed to eat in the house while the cure is in progress. No one who has eaten pork, beef, or bear meat may enter the house unless he first bathes in the river. No widow, widower, or pregnant woman may enter the house.

After the fourth day, the curer stops whatever medication he has been prescribing and terminates his services. The patient, whether completely well or not, bathes in the river. If the patient or family wishes the treatment to continue, a new offer of Indian tobacco is made to the same curer or to another. The family compensates the curer with a gift of a dress length, a pair of unsewed moccasins, and a kettle of Indian corn gruel. If the cure has been particularly successful, the curer may be given a little feast after the New Year ceremonies.

The leader of the Berry clan is particularly proficient in treating female disorders, such as repeated abortions and difficult deliveries. Ordinarily, a woman is attended in childbirth by a midwife, who prescribes herbal teas to effect a quick delivery, in the *monte* or in the menstrual hut. If labor lasts more than thirty-six hours, one of the attendants is dispatched with a gift of tobacco to call on the leader of the Berry clan, who takes the Little Rabbit bundle, builds a protected shelter near the place of delivery, and performs the ritual associated with this bundle until the child is born.

Whereas cures by the clan leaders, members of the herbal societies, and free-lancers may be performed at any time of the year, the cures effected by the two leaders who officiate at the buffalo dances are done only at the time of the dance. Any person who is ill is invited to submit to treatment during the ceremony held before the dance and to participate in the woman's dance, if a female patient, and in the buffalo dance itself.

Gathering information on the five existing herbal societies was one of the most difficult parts of our study, since the members are secretive about their activities and nonmembers know few details. In questioning others, one receives bizarre descriptions of the activities of the herbal-society members. Time and again we were told that the members of these societies were synonymous with *brujos* (witches). On the other hand, when a Kickapoo becomes ill, he often appeals to the services of a member of an herbal society. When a woman is ready to deliver, her close female relatives call on one of the herbal-society curers, some of whom are midwives.

Four of the herbal societies include both men and women, while the fifth has only male members. Membership is inherited from either a grandparent, a parent, an uncle, or an aunt. As members age, they look around for younger relatives who have the disposition and qualifications to undergo the long apprenticeship. Women are not allowed to handle curative herbs until their climacteric, for, prior to this event, the illness of the patient might transfer itself to the curer.

Before herbal societies hold their New Year ceremonies, which take place after those of the clans, they discard all old herbs and replace them with new ones, all of which are taken to the house where the ceremony is held and smoked with cudweed to purify them and improve their potency. Chants, accompanied by a rattle, are sung by the leader of each herbal society, always a man. They invite those they have cured during the year to prepare a kettle of venison, pumpkin, and Indian corn, served after the ceremony of purification. One of the societies serves duck, since it derives its name from this fowl. At this ceremony members are given the protective rhizome, Solomon's seal. An herbal-society curer may not treat himself with his own herbs, but must go to another Kickapoo curer or to a Mexican *curandero*.

Herbs, roots, and barks, whose source and application are jealously guarded by each member, form the basis of their cures. Specific plants and the knowledge of how to administer them are the private domain of each member, and both members and nonmembers respect this proprietary right.

Having learned from a Mexican the use of the native *Polianthes maculosa*, known in Múzquiz as *zábila*, we suggested its application to a Kickapoo woman for a swollen knee caused by a fall. She immediately informed us that only a member of a certain herbal society could handle this plant; and, in order to receive treatment, she would have to make her an offer of Indian tobacco. Unfortunately, the curer was out of the village.

Not all members of a given society know the total number of plants used by the group, by any means. Ownership of a cure has not only prestige value but also an economic value, since the curers are paid for their services, first by an offer of Indian tobacco and, after the four-day cure, whether the patient recovers or not, by the conventional dress length, moccasins, and corn gruel.

Besides plants, curers use other products and objects, such as minerals, cupping horns, and heated stones. Herbs are used both as teas and for bathing the patient. Massage is employed extensively to extract foreign objects or lumps. Some apply red-hot bits of a certain fungus to rheumatic joints; others are experts in the use of diuretic herbs; certain ones treat sterility in both men and women; some prescribe contraceptive herbs; there are those who know how to treat swellings with certain plants. Still others know how to extract foreign objects (placed in victims by witches) through massage and sucking, and how to extract blood clots resulting from a blow by the use of cupping horns.

The collecting of medicinal plants or roots involves a ceremonial procedure. One day, a member of an herbal society allowed us to accompany her to gather a certain root on condition that we drive her to the location where it was to be found, some forty miles from Múzquiz. As we approached the area, our informant began to have misgivings about her generosity for fear of reprisal from a number of sources: Kitzihiat, the Great Spirit; Grandmother Earth; the plant itself; and her colleagues; but we urged her on, minimizing her fears until at last she found the plant for which we were searching. She did not touch this specimen. First, a prayer to Kitzihiat, Grandmother Earth, and the original owner of the plant (he who had discovered its curative powers) had to be made. After this prayer, an offering of Indian tobacco was made to the first plant and permission asked of it to gather others for medicinal purposes. We walked ahead and exclaimed, "We see several plants all around us now!" She followed with the confident words, "Oh yes, now that I have given tobacco to the first one, we shall find many others."

The curers, whether they are clan leaders, members of the various herbal societies, or free-lancers, feel no sense of inadequacy if they do not cure the patient; instead, they blame the failure on several factors: the patient perhaps did not have sufficient faith in the medication and the administrator; the patient and family did not carry out the instructions concerning taboos, isolation, and diet as prescribed; or the patient and the family failed to reveal the symptoms to the curer.

A Kickapoo seldom considers interrupting the four-day cure prescribed to him. If he does not recover after this time, he repeats the cure, calls in another curer, visits a Mexican *curandero*, or, as a last resort, calls upon a local physician.

The Kickapoos not only have learned the application of many plants from the Mexicans but have also incorporated into their medical practices many of the most common Mexican folk diseases and conditions, such as *chípil* (sibling jealousy), *empacho* (indigestion), *frialdad* (excessive and prolonged discharge after parturition), *latido* (throbbing sensation in the pit of the stomach), *mollera caída* (fallen fontanelle), *mal de ojo* (evil eye), *mal puesto* (witchcraft), *punzada* (sharp pain in the eyes or ears), *susto* (fright or spirit loss), the conditions and diseases associated with heat and cold, and those resulting from *aire* (a cold blast of air). These diseases or conditions are not attended by physicians; the low-income Mexicans believe that the physicians are unable to cope with them.

Though the Indians have, in most instances, learned to deal with these Mexican folk diseases or conditions, they sometimes differ from the Mexicans in the way they handle the same ailments. For example, they have a different explanation of fallen fontanelle, the result of diarrhea during which a child loses body fluids, causing the fontanelle and eyes to appear sunken. The Mexicans believe that this results when a child suckles greedily, the breast is withdrawn too quickly after feeding, or the child hits his head when allowed to fall from his bed or while being held. The Kickapoos believe in all these causes but have also added another cause: if an expectant mother sees a Mexican kill a snake, her child will be born prone to suffering from fallen fontanelle. A child with the fallen-fontanelle symptoms is taken to the only Kickapoo woman qualified to cure the condition or to a Mexican *curandera*.

Empacho, which a local physician described as an inflammation of the stomach with loss of appetite, epigastric pain, and occasional vomiting, is believed by the Mexicans to be the result of ingesting certain foods, including chewing gum, which stick to the stomach and will not pass. Mexicans have various remedies to cure this condition, including a number of decoctions made from local or imported herbs. However, the treatment always includes massaging the abdomen and the back of the patient with pork fat and pinching or lifting the skin over the vertebrae from the waist to about eight inches above it. The Kickapoos attribute *empacho* to the eating of wheat tortillas, beans, or pork. One informant told how his grandmother made a small pillow of *té de sen* (a Cassia specimen), on which the patient laid his head after drinking a decoction of the herb. A few minutes later, the *empacho* was cured. Another Kickapoo cure for *empacho* is the application of red-hot bits of fungus to the abdomen. One day a woman curer, member of an herbal society, brought her grandson for us to see. The child had difficulty in walking and a high fever and had not eaten in five days. The woman explained that he had *empacho* and a fever in the pit of his stomach; she had attempted to cure him with red-hot bits of fungus, but the illness had not responded. When we looked at the child's abdomen, we saw marks where he had been burned.

Latido, another common Mexican condition, is described by one of the local physicians as the discovery of the descending aorta, more noticeable in thin or weak persons. It is a throbbing sensation, and the Mexicans believe that it occurs after a person has not eaten a meal at his usual schedule or has eaten without the accustomed pleasure and satisfaction. The pit of the stomach jumps, and the patient breaks out in a cold sweat and has a sensation of general debility. The patient is put to bed, and a *confortativo* (comforter) is made from a hard bread roll, which is split in two, sprinkled with alcohol, and filled with peppermint and nasturtium leaves, a few slivers of stick cinnamon, a few macerated cloves, and sliced onions. The roll is wrapped in a clean white cloth, placed over the pit of the patient's stomach, and bandaged in place. The Kickapoos recognize the same symptoms and treat the condition similarly. Since no bakeries exist in the village where one may purchase a hard roll, they forego it, using slices of onion, some bicarbonate of soda, alcohol, and peppermint leaves on a tortilla. The stomach is first rubbed with vegetable fat; then the *confortativo* is secured in a clean white cloth and snugly bandaged to the abdomen. The Kickapoos have gone the Mexicans one better on the cure for this ailment, as they also apply red-hot bits of fungus and administer herbal teas or a bowl of bean soup seasoned with onions and chili.

The belief in *chipil* is widely extended among the Mexicans and is associated with sibling jealousy. When a woman has a new child, an older one may feel neglected and unloved, mope, and begin to lose weight. The Mexicans treat this condition by hanging a coral necklace with an even number of beads, from four to sixteen, around the child's neck. They say that, if the child is actually suffering from *chipil*, the coral loses its bright color. The child is then bathed in a decoction of Texas silver-leaf. If no coral is available, an even-numbered necklace of garlic pods is used.

The Kickapoos handle *chípil* by hanging around the afflicted child's neck a tuber of wine-cup on which the child chews to dispel his sadness.

Although some of the Mexican folk diseases or conditions may be cured by Kickapoo curers, often those suffering from them prefer to be attended by a Mexican *curandero*. There are several famous ones, both men and women, in Múzquiz, the Negro village, and surrounding towns and cities.

One Kickapoo woman, who weighs over two hundred pounds and suffers from a heart condition and edema, stayed with a *curandera* several weeks. With the *curandera's* special diet and teas, she lost twenty-five pounds and her edema was reduced markedly. The *curandera* extracted a worm from the Kickapoo woman's body, which seemed to be the cause of her extreme obesity, but the real cause, the woman explained, was that she had been *salada* (hexed). Someone in the village was envious of her ability to speak Spanish fluently and of her large number of Mexican friends. She concluded by saying that envy was at the root of all hexing, a common Mexican belief.

The Kickapoos differentiate, as do the Mexicans, between God-sent illnesses and *mal puesto*, or witch-sent illnesses. The treatment for each differs. One day, a Kickapoo woman told us she had cured a man in the village of a severe diarrhea by administering a decoction of *manzanilla* (camomile tea). She warned him, however, that, if the illness was witch-sent, the cure would be of no avail and he would have to seek help elsewhere.

Mal de ojo, another Mexican folk belief, although translated as "evil eye," is caused not by an intent to harm an individual, animal, or object, but by failure to pat or touch the object of one's admiration. It is believed that all individuals possess a mysterious power, which must be discharged on the admired person, animal, or object by touching in order to forestall harm. Failure to touch may bring disease or death to an individual, wilt and kill a plant or animal, or break an object. If afflicted by *mal de ojo*, the Kickapoos do not attempt to cure themselves, but go to a Mexican *curandero*. It usually affects children; the more attractive they are, the more prone they are to *mal de ojo*. To ward it off, the Mexicans and some of the Kickapoos use either a coral necklace or a buckeye seed tied around the neck or wrist. Since the Kickapoos customarily wear beads around their necks, they seem to have a preference for coral rather than buckeye; and, as coral is expensive and hard to find, any string of red beads suffices to ward off the effects of *mal de ojo*. Though many of the Kickapoos do not believe in using either the buckeye or the coral necklace, all want strangers to pat their children on the head, the technique which discharges the mysterious power of the person who looks at a child admiringly.

The belief among the Mexicans is that anyone is capable of giving the *mal de ojo*, but some persons, those with blue or blue-green eyes, are particularly dangerous. Some of the Indians who have light eyes, and one in particular who has blue eyes, a gift from a European ancestor, are much aware of this involuntary faculty. They avoid looking at a child and, if they must do so, immediately pat him on the head. The Kickapoo with the blue eyes told us that even a glance from him at a child makes the victim become sleepy and listless.

One day we took an American pediatrician and his wife to visit the village. While there we called on several of our friends, among them a clan leader whose young wife had recently presented him with a beautiful, cherubic daughter. Minutes after our return to Múzquiz, the clan leader, his wife, and child came to see us, the father asking, almost indignantly, "Where is that blue-eyed gringo who gave my child *mal de ojo*?" We explained the situation to our friend, suggesting that he hold the child in his arms and pat her head. He went one step further: he took out his medical kit and gave her a thorough examination. While this was taking place, the father explained that, shortly after our departure, the child became listless and developed a fever. After further questioning, it was found that the mother was menstruating. The physician explained that, during this period, the milk becomes more concentrated and is therefore richer. The richness and abundance of the mother's milk had made the child sick. The young mother was advised to drink large quantities of liquid during these periods to avoid a recurrence of the malaise. We gave the parents and child a few gifts and they departed happily. When we saw the child again, she was wearing not one buckeye but two around her wrists as double insurance.

Susto, meaning fright or soul loss, is a widely spread Mexican folk belief that has popularized itself among the Kickapoos; but they do not attempt to treat it themselves—understandably, since treatment involves the recitation of Catholic prayers. It is a condition which any adult Mexican can cure at home if he or she knows the accompanying prayers.

One young Kickapoo mother came to see us with her seven-year-old daughter, whom she had taken to a Mexican *curandera* to be treated for *susto*. The day before, the child had gone to the *monte* on her burro to gather firewood. While she was riding home, the burro became alarmed and ran away, kicking its heels in the air until the child, unable to control it, fell off. The child was frightened to such a degree that, when she arrived home in tears, she went to bed, became sleepy and loose-jointed, and was so fatigued that she had no energy to rise. The mother, distressed over her child's condition, at once took her to a *curandera*, who, through prayers, pleas, and "sweeping" the child with the branches of certain herbs, restored her lost spirit, which was thought to have fled from her body during the extreme fright.

The Mexicans believe that if *susto* is not treated promptly—that is, the spirit brought back into the body—it may develop into *susto frío* or *susto meco* (cold spirit fright), a condition which can be easily treated at its incipience but which, if neglected, may develop into a serious illness, difficult or even impossible to cure. An older Kickapoo whom we had befriended during a long illness was believed to be suffering from *susto meco*. At the time we knew him he had several illnesses: an inguinal hernia, malfunctioning of the kidneys, and a coronary condition, all resulting in his opinion from his failure to submit himself to the ritual in which his spirit would be invited to re-enter his body after a *susto* that resulted from a terrible nightmare, in which he found himself surrounded by Indians from other nations, pointing their bows and arrows at him. He had awakened in a sweat, but at the time had dismissed the nightmare as of no consequence. A few months later he began to have difficulties of one sort and another, until eventually he was a bedridden man. He insisted that he was suffering from *susto meco*.

A widely spread Mexican belief in the practice called *salar* (hexing) has also become prevalent among the Kickapoos. It is understandable that this concept has gained popularity among them, as it closely parallels their own concept of witchcraft. As was mentioned above, the basis of hexing is envy. One person may envy another because he is happily married, has a good income or a pleasant home, is lucky, or has a spouse that the envious person would like to win away from him. In order to hex him, the envious person secures some excrement of the intended victim and mixes it with salt (hence the term *salar*, literally "to salt"). The mixture, in the form of a dry powder, is then sprinkled on the victim's clothing, in his house, or on his belongings.

The Kickapoos are staunch believers in hexing, and we have been told of several incidents supposedly resulting from this practice. For instance, an older Kickapoo woman who had formerly prided herself on her ability and stamina to dance for many hours told us she never goes to the dances any more, since someone hexed her at one of these affairs and she developed a sore leg, which now hinders her once-agile dancing.

The Kickapoos have adopted many of the Mexican beliefs concerned with heat and cold, whether in food, beverages, medicine, or the state of the body. In the winter, a Kickapoo will not drink a cold soda but wants it at room temperature, since he fears it will cool his body and cause him to have a cold. He will not bathe when he is perspiring for fear of catching a cold or pneumonia. A woman will not wash her hair without getting her feet wet, believing that otherwise she will catch a cold. Like the Mexicans, the Kickapoos consider certain diseases "hot" and others "cold," and take the corresponding herbs, some of which are thought to be hot and others cold.

Another condition now taken over by the Kickapoos, though of Mexican origin, is the effect of an *aire*, a cold blast of air which one may encounter when going from a warm house to the cold outdoors. The *aire* is considered the cause of many diseases, including colds, pneumonia, earache, and pains in general. The Indians use a deer or bovine horn as a cupping instrument to extract the *aire* and thus relieve the patient of his pain or illness. If no cupping instrument is available and the *aire* is lodged in the ear, causing it to ache, the blowing of hot smoke from a cigarette may alleviate or even cure the condition.

When the Kickapoos break an arm or a leg, they have it set by a physician, but for backache, sacroiliac strain, bursitis, sciatic pains, or muscle strains of any nature, they visit Don Juanito, a former coal miner, now retired and turned *componedor* (folk chiropractor). Though an amateur, he has considerable skill in this field and now dedicates his time to treating both the poor and many of the well-to-do Mexicans. Don Juanito does not charge a set fee but accepts whatever remuneration the patient is able to contribute. Although some of the Kickapoos have gone to him with broken bones, the man has the judgment and discretion to recognize that this matter is out of his line and refuses to treat them, insisting that they see a physician.

A Kickapoo woman came to see us with a severe pain in the lower region of her back and with the typical walk of a person suffering from sacroiliac strain. We sent her to a physician, who gave her pain-killing tablets and Bengué balm to massage her back; but, in spite of this treatment, the pain persisted. A few days later she returned, still suffering intense pain, but refused to go back to the physician. She asked us to take her to see Don Juanito. After his treatment, she felt much relief and was well in a few days.

The Kickapoos are strong believers in mineral baths. Formerly, the old people suffering from rheumatism and other ailments went by wagon or horseback, skirting the Sierra Hermosa de Santa Rosa and the Sierra Capulín, to the sulphur springs of Baños de San Blas, some sixty miles from the village, near the city of that name. Today, the Kickapoos are frequent visitors to the hot springs located in Hermanas, a railroad stop about fifty kilometers north of Monclova, Coahuila, easily accessible by Highway 57.

Contact with Modern Medicine

In order to gain a more complete picture of the diseases affecting the Kickapoos, we made arrangements with one of the local physicians, who had shown understanding of and empathy toward the Indians, to relay the diagnoses of the patients we sent him. We offered to pay the doctor's fees for a limited time as a way of encouraging the Kickapoos to see us about their illnesses. It was one of the most successful techniques for bringing the Indians to our home, and we chalked up the cost as part of our payment for the information we were able to elicit from and about them. Before long we were seeing four to five Indians a week and sending them with a note to the physician. With the bill, the physician sent the diagnosis, thereby supplying, in modern medical terminology, the names of the diseases which affect the Indians.

The time was ripe for this venture. Had we arrived before the forties, when the Kickapoos began working in the United States and, through their kinsmen in Oklahoma, were introduced to modern medicine in the outpatient clinics connected with public health hospitals, we probably would have had little response, since, prior to that time, the Kickapoos depended almost entirely on their own medical practices and those of the Mexican *curanderos*.

Don Aurelio Vázquez Hidalgo, justice of the peace for the Kickapoo and Negro village district for many years, told us that a hospital was built in the Negro village to care for the surrounding inhabitants during 1938–1940, while President Cárdenas was in office. Some 134 families registered as potential patients, including a few Kickapoos, but the hospital had so few patients that it soon closed.[3]

A nurse who lived in the Negro village was once sent to the Kickapoo village to treat the Indians suffering from trachoma, which, according to Fabila, was widespread among them at the time.[4] This nurse was still in the Negro village at the time of our study, and the Indians often called on her to administer injections to them.

Many factors which still exist have deterred the Indians from availing themselves of modern medicine in Mexico, the most evident being lack of confidence in and communication with the physicians, whose terminology is foreign to them; fear of the hospital, operations, injections, and transfusions; and, last but not least, the high cost of a visit to the doctor. Some Kickapoos, particularly women, are also afraid of being alone with the physician in his office. Unfortunately, at the time of our study, no female medical assistants were in attendance in Múzquiz. One woman bolted out of the physician's office when she surmised that he wanted to do a vaginal examination.

Typical of the lack of communication is the following incident. An older man who suffered from a severe inguinal hernia, malfunctioning kidneys, and a coronary condition was brought to Múzquiz, where he was lodged in one of the cheap local hostelries. He had been seen months earlier by the same physician, who had recommended an operation to correct the hernia. The Kickapoo had balked because of fear and had gone to a Mexican *curandera*, who prescribed herbs and a support. On this last occasion, the man's wife came to us for help, unable to understand why the physician who had seen the patient had not yet prescribed medication two days later. When we visited the patient, he was in great discomfort and puffed up like a toad. Felipe paid a call on the physician to clarify the situation and was informed that a urine specimen had been requested, and, until it came, no prescription could be issued. When Felipe asked him the word he had used for urine, the physician, looking surprised, said he had used the word he always used—*orina*. Then Felipe realized why the Indian had not sent a specimen. The Spanish word *orina* is foreign to the Kickapoos, who use instead the onomatopoetic word *chi*. The word *orina* and many others used by the physicians are incomprehensible to the Indians, whose knowledge of the Spanish language is limited and who use few euphemisms; furthermore, a Kickapoo will never admit that he does not understand what is being said to him. When Felipe returned to the hostelry with the information that the physician needed a specimen of *chi*, the patient exclaimed, "Is that what he wants, *chi!*" On the street a few days later, Felipe was stopped by the physician, who begged him to inform the patient that one specimen sufficed, for the family, in the meantime, had obtained many empty bottles and were sending specimens several times a day.

Another example of the lack of communication concerns a woman whose life was at stake. The family did not understand the physician's orders to supply a donor for a blood transfusion before he could prescribe medication, because of the woman's precarious condition. The family was ready to return the woman to the village, for, according to them, the physician had done nothing for her. When we explained the need of a transfusion, the family hurriedly sought a donor and the woman's life was saved.

The Mexican Public Health Service maintains the small hospital in Múzquiz, where each morning one or another of the five local physicians attends patients in the outpatient clinic for a nominal fee, depending on the family's ability to pay, while medicines are free to the most needy. As far as we know, none of the Kickapoos went to the clinic during the period of our study. The Kickapoos fear the hospital, believing that those who go in will never come out alive, that the physician will "cut them up," and that the nurses will run off the family, leaving the patient alone and at their mercy during the night. (When we were in Múzquiz it was against hospital policy to allow relatives to stay with a patient overnight.)

There is one exception to the general rule of avoiding the hospital. Young mothers are availing themselves of the Múzquiz hospital for childbirth with increasing frequency—especially those who have previously delivered in hospitals in the United States. Their stay is of short duration, as they return to the village within twenty-four hours to retire to the menstrual hut and put themselves under herbal medication.

While we were in Múzquiz, private physicians frequently prescribed injections of penicillin and other potent drugs for Kickapoo patients, but since they did not administer the injections and had no attending nurses, the entire responsibility rested on the patient or his family. They had two recourses: if they were in Múzquiz, staying at a hostelry, they could call the local male nurse, who administered injections; or they could take the prescription to the woman nurse in the Negro village, who was also qualified to give them.

One of the strongest deterrents to seeking a physician is the cost. Though the local physicians charged only the equivalent of $1.50 for an office visit in the 1960's, the patient generally left with a number of prescriptions to be filled as well. On the basis of a sample of fifty cases, we estimated that the average cost of a visit to the doctor plus the resulting prescriptions was $6.38. For the Kickapoos, whose earnings amount to only a few hundred dollars a year, such a visit is made only after much consideration. Consequently, we urged the Indians to avail themselves of the public health hospitals in the United States and the outpatient clinic in Múzquiz.

Although the Kickapoos live—at least in the winter—in an unpolluted environment, spend much of their time in the sunshine, and participate in many physical activities, they fall prey to numerous diseases, a situation which seems inconsistent with their primitive setting and tranquil existence. The high incidence of disease can probably be attributed to ignorance about communicable diseases, lack of hygiene, the persistent use of their own empirical cures and those of the Mexican *curanderos*, ignorance of preventive medicine, an unbalanced diet which leans heavily on carbohydrates and fats, an almost total absence of fresh fruits and vegetables, and, as venison becomes scarcer, a very low protein intake. Their nomadic summer life, which contrasts sharply with the peaceful existence in the village, may also be a contributing factor.

Probably as the result of the unbalanced diet and lack of oral hygiene (except for the use of homemade toothpicks), the Indians suffer from a high incidence of tooth decay and the consequent complications. None employ toothbrushes, toothpaste, dental floss, or antiseptic mouthwashes. They do have one herbal decoction for washing out the mouth when the odor is foul. They also have an herb for deadening toothache, but they never extract a decayed tooth, allowing it to fall out in its own time. They are extremely careless with their teeth, using them to crack pecans; break off twine, sewing thread, or twigs; and pry off tops of soda pop bottles. Many of their illnesses are related to decayed teeth, and some have been convinced of the wisdom of having such teeth extracted by a local dentist. Only two Kickapoos, a man and a woman, have had all of their teeth extracted. Both were fitted with dentures in a public health hospital in Oklahoma. It is a miracle how the Kickapoos live to a ripe old age, considering that, by the time they reach their forties, most of their teeth have decayed. In this area, as in all others pertaining to disease, it is difficult to convince the Indians to visit a dentist because of their fear that he will kill them. After being told that tooth extraction is painless today, some reluctantly visit the dentist, but usually only as the last resort, too late for any corrective dentistry.

In questioning the local physicians about the Kickapoos as patients, they informed us that the latter go to them only as a last resort and usually fail to follow the treatment prescribed, return for further checkups, or stay in the hospital the number of days indicated. The last complaint is particularly true of women who deliver babies in the hospital or are treated after an abortion.

Diseases of the Kickapoos Diagnosed by Local Physicians

Following is a list of the diseases, injuries, and conditions whose diagnoses we were able to secure from the local physician with whom we had made previous arrangements, from physicians at the American Smelting and Refining Company hospital in Nueva Rosita, from the local dentist, and from personal involvement in some cases. In no way does this list pretend to cover all of the diseases and conditions affecting the Kickapoos; it is only a small token sampling.

Cancer: two cases, both female patients.

Diseases affecting children: suppurating ears; tuberculosis; anemia; chicken pox; impetigo; bronchitis; influenza; common cold; mumps; malnutrition; gastroenteritis; conjunctivitis; birth defects, such as clubfoot, limping, and harelip.

Blood disorders: anemia.

Heart and circulation: several cases of cardiac disorders, two of which resulted in death; five cases of hypertension, one of which resulted in death; varicose veins.

Skin: poison ivy; furuncles; sycosis; infected nails; ingrown toenails; ringworm; allergies. Although the local physician saw no cases of small-pox during the period of our study, several Indians carry the scars of former attacks.

Skeleton and muscles: bursitis; arthritis; rheumatism; sacroiliac strains; backaches from harvesting; inguinal and navel hernias; neck cricks.

Brain and nervous system: epilepsy; headaches.

Digestive system: many cases of gastroenteritis; food poisoning; liver disorders, such as hepatitis; appendicitis; gallstones.

Urinary system: malfunctioning kidneys; pyelitis; kidney stones.

Reproductive system: disorders of the uterus; irregular bleeding and discharge; miscarriages; venereal diseases. (One of the physicians consulted about the diseases prevalent among the Kickapoos stated that the three most common are tuberculosis, venereal diseases, and alcoholism.)[5]

Breast: breast abcesses; caking of the breast.

Eyes: many injuries to the eyes caused by arrows as youngsters practice marksmanship, from flying chips while chopping wood, and from thorn brush; cataracts; glaucoma. One physician believed that the blindness that exists among the Kickapoos is due to syphilis and not to trachoma.[6] Formerly, trachoma did exist among the Indians, but no cases have been seen during the past few years.[7] An ophthalmologist in Nueva Rosita stated that trachoma was negligible but that the Indians injured their eyes by bathing in the river, where there are many mineral products.[8]

Ears: suppurating ears; cerumen; deafness.

Mental problems: one woman suffering from anxiety; one case of mental retardation.

Physical injuries: eye injuries; burns from falling into the open hearths, from scalding water, and from gasoline, which ignites when cleaning clothes; heat exhaustion; broken bones; infected cuts; wounds resulting from assault and battery or automobile accidents. Children suffer burns from scalding water and food, poisoning from drinking Clorox and eating poisonous wild berries. One man suffered second- and third-degree burns on both legs when he rescued a companion who had fallen into a vat where candelilla (wax Euphorbia) was being processed in sulphuric acid.

Respiratory system: each winter, colds, tonsilitis, influenza, bronchitis, tuberculosis, asthma, and sinusitis spread through the village. If one person in the family falls ill from any of these, the entire family is exposed, since they live in close quarters. Tuberculosis takes a heavy toll among both children and adults. A few are aware of its highly infectious nature, but the majority of families continue to employ the same eating and drinking vessels used by the tubercular member, while the afflicted take no precautions about the disposal of their sputum, discharging it on the ground where small children crawl and play. A few of the Kickapoos have spent time in the tuberculosis hospitals in Oklahoma, particularly at Talihima. While working in Provo, Utah, the Indians are being asked to take the tuberculin test; some comply, but many still refuse.

Brucellosis or undulant fever: this disease is endemic in Coahuila because of the eating of unpasteurized cheese made of milk from infected goats. However, we knew of only one case among the Kickapoos.

In spite of their fear of modern medicine, each year more and more Kickapoos are availing themselves of its benefits, particularly in Oklahoma, where this service is free to them.

The Latorres as Physicians

No anthropologist who works in the field escapes becoming a physician of sorts, and we were no exception to the rule. Many illnesses are brought to the anthropologist's attention in the hope that his medicine may be more powerful than the ones already tried. It was not long after beginning our work that we realized that playing the role of physician was expected of us. After all, does not each adult Kickapoo know how to handle one or more particular herbs? Why should we not have a wide knowledge of the white man's medicine, particularly when so many books lined the walls of our office, books from which all the white man's knowledge was derived? We accepted the challenge, alive to the fact that we could not only help the Indians but also win their friendship and gain valuable information. Fortunately, both of us come from medical families, from which we had gained some practical knowledge and especially the humility to know when to send the Indians for professional help.

Our major contribution was that of being a sounding board, listening to their aches and pains and then referring them to a physician or dentist; but on many occasions when the latter were out of town or the Indians refused to be attended by a professional, we were able to administer first aid. We also served as go-betweens for the patient and the physician, since our knowledge of the Indians' vernacular and culture placed us in a position to express their needs.

Armed with a recently published medical encyclopedia, supplies furnished by our personal physician, and first-aid materials, we were able to meet many emergencies which arose during our years with the Indians. The most popular medicine in our stock was aspirin. For headaches, colds, muscle pains, and influenza, we gave a few aspirin in small labeled vials, pointing to the east, the zenith, and the west to indicate the time of dosage. Children were particularly fond of cough drops, which they took like candy. During the period of feasts, when many ceremonies are celebrated, we had numerous visitors complaining of a pain in the pit of their stomachs. Antacid tablets were given to them to relieve the uncomfortable sensation of gorging at too many feasts.

An item that we dispensed freely was vaseline. The Kickapoo women use their hands to do many rough tasks and, during the winter months, hands, lips, and faces chap easily, causing deep and painful cracks on their fingers and hands which they try to heal with lard or bear oil.

One night, as we were ready to retire, the doorbell rang. Our visitor was an Indian, accompanied by several relatives. We wondered what had brought them at this late hour, but, not wishing to hurry them, we exchanged pleasantries until the man said to us, "Felipe, I wish to bother you with something." Five nights earlier, as he was falling asleep, he had felt something crawl into one of his ears, but after trying to extract it with a wire, he had abandoned his efforts. He was certain it was a spider, which of course he could not kill. The spider, he felt sure, was still inside his ear, which by now was quite painful, and he asked Felipe to extract it. Since it was then midnight and too late to call a physician, we assembled the supplies to perform the "operation": boiled water, an ear syringe, a basin, sterile cotton, and ear drops. After the ear had been bathed with tepid water for half an hour, the spider appeared. Felipe placed some drops in the ear to sooth the injured membrane, and the family left happily.

One day, when Chief Papícoano came to call, we inquired about an injury to his foot, which had been caught in a car door. He at once wanted Felipe to look at it. Although slight, the wound was bandaged with a soiled cloth and was not healing properly. After a thorough cleansing, medication, and a new sterile bandage, the chief was pleased with the treatment. He returned a few days later, the wound completely healed, and remarked, "Tu medicina muy buena [your medicine very good]."

Children were usually stoic and willing to submit themselves readily to treatment, except injections, which they view with horror. Many were brought to us, having suffered a bruise, a cut, or a festered place where a thorn had entered the flesh. Other children came with impetigo, a common ailment. We had at hand samples of Exthalmacine, which we gave to the mothers, warning them that the infection was very contagious and thrived when children were not kept clean. Other children were brought in suffering from pinkeye; to their mothers we gave vials of boric-acid solution and sterile cotton.

A woman friend arrived one day with her face and arms swollen from poison ivy, oak, or sumac. This woman, when young and while being courted by her Mexican husband, had had his initials tattooed on her arm with the juice of poison ivy and had been unusually sensitive to it ever since. Unfortunately, she often came in contact with these plants when in the *monte* or sierra. We applied calamine lotion and gave her a bottle to continue the treatment.

Adults came in with thorns in their fingers that had festered, cerumen in their ears that caused them to be dizzy, and ingrown toenails that had festered. We extracted thorns, cleaned out cerumen, treated toenails, and taught them how to cut them to avoid further trouble.

One day an Indian brought his small granddaughter to see us. The child's spine had been injured in an automobile accident, resulting in a hump, and a fistula on one of her feet had not healed. The leg was tied with a dirty rag on which bear oil had been smeared. Felipe cleaned the fistula, covered it with a sterile gauze, and sent her to the physician, who recommended an operation to which the grandparents would not consent. Later, when they were in Oklahoma, they took the child to the Children's Convalescent Hospital in Bethany, where the girl underwent surgery to correct the hump and to cure the fistula. Unfortunately, the grandparents took the child out of the hospital before further necessary operations could rehabilitate her completely.

Several cases of limps, clubfoot, and other defects were brought to our attention which could have been corrected, but the parents' fear of hospitals and of separation from the child and their concern that the child, while in the hospital, would become a gringo and forget his Kickapoo ways outweighed the importance of improving the defect.

A mother brought her youngest child—a thin, sad little creature—to see us, complaining that the child ate nothing and was always ill. The child looked undernourished and weighed only twenty-three pounds, although she was three years old. When we suggested that the girl be given milk, the mother protested that she did not like milk and would not drink it. We brought her a glass of cool milk and a plate of cookies, which disappeared in minutes. We told the woman that a pediatrician friend would be arriving shortly and would look at the child. When he did, he found nothing wrong, except malnutrition. He recommended vitamins and plenty of milk, boiled and cooled, since pasteurization is not practiced in that area. A few months later, the mother and father returned with the child, who looked the picture of health.

Intoxicants

George Irving Quimby is of the opinion that the American Indians readily accepted liquor for religious reasons. They obtained religious experiences from dreams and visions induced by fasting and fatigue. Rum, to which they were early introduced by the French, produced dreams and hallucinations much more quickly than fasting; consequently rum and drunkenness became a prominent part of the fur trade. This was the most demoralizing effect resulting from their contact with the white man.[9]

By 1893, missionaries in Indian Territory estimated that as many as 25 percent of the Kickapoos were drunkards—the bravest and proudest warriors in North America had come to be regarded as the heaviest drinkers in the area.[10]

Through informants and from personal observation we made a list of men and women over sixteen in the village and estimated the amount of drinking of each, arriving at the figures in Table 4.

TABLE 4
Drinking Habits

	Men	Women	Total
Nondrinkers	35	72	107
Occasional drinkers	10	10	20
Moderate drinkers	17	15	32
Heavy drinkers	35	12	47
Alcoholics	18	0	18
Total	115	109	224

This poll shows that almost 48 percent of the Indians do not drink, but 29 percent are heavy drinkers or alcoholics—an increase over the estimate of the missionaries in 1893—and 22 percent are occasional or moderate drinkers.

The Indians drink a highly intoxicating distilled liquor made from sotol and related species of the plant which is called mescal or *vino* in northern Coahuila. It is manufactured in *viñatas* (distilleries) near San Blas and is sold in the saloons in Múzquiz, in the Negro village, or in Ejido Morelos, either by the drink, in a demijohn, or in liter bottles, a bottle costing about forty cents. Mescal is usually drunk straight but is sometimes combined with soda pop. Little, if any food, is consumed while drinking. Although beer is both cheap and excellent in Mexico, costing fifteen to twenty-five cents a bottle, it takes much more beer to achieve the desired result, so that there is a preference for the mescal.

Formerly, when no alcoholic beverages were permitted in the village, the Kickapoos were forced to go to Múzquiz for their drinking. Today, although the selling of liquor in any form is still illegal, a Mexican who has a Kickapoo concubine secretly supplies it to the Indians, especially when they have exhausted their supply bought elsewhere. Furthermore, several enterprising Kickapoos, under the guise of selling soda pop, are now also furnishing their peers with mescal.

Drinking in the village is usually done outdoors at the river where the young people gather to court and dance, at gambling sessions indoors or in the compounds where the older set gather, or during ceremonies. Informants told us that, since their own police system had ceased to function, drinking had increased.

Several of the heavy drinkers and those who are alcoholics customarily go to Múzquiz to drink in the saloons and stay on a spree for several days at a time. Others go to the red-light district situated about a mile from the city limits of Múzquiz. Since women are not permitted in saloons, those women who want to drink must content themselves with going to a café or restaurant for beer, the only liquor sold there. But, since mescal is cheaper and more effective and can be bought through the side door of a saloon, women who are heavy drinkers purchase a bottle or two to drink at home or in some cheap hostelry where they spend the night.

Some of those who drank heavily told us that, once they had had one drink, they were unable to stop. Others gave various reasons for going on a four-or-five-day drunk. One young man who has a large family, of which he is very proud, considers it his prerogative to celebrate the birth of each child in this way. But he does not stop at this; he also celebrates Christmas, our New Year, the Kickapoo New Year, and any other occasion he feels merits a good spree. On two successive occasions when his wife aborted and he had to spend five days in the *monte* with her, he straightway went to Múzquiz on the sixth day and stayed drunk for several days, leaving his extensive family with relatives until his wife completed her ten-day retreat. Another heavy drinker, who spends several days out of each month on a spree in Múzquiz, confided that he had once given up drinking, but when a young nephew of whom he was very fond was killed by falling from a horse, he was so consumed with *sentimiento* (grief) that he began to drink again to drown his sorrow.

With the great amount of drinking done by both men and women, it is to be expected that many misfortunes are the result of this habit. The least of these are the occasions when drinkers make a nuisance of themselves in a saloon or café, at which time the police are called and they are placed in the local jail to cool off. In the village, the nightly drunks disturb those who like order and tranquillity. At other times, drunkenness has led to wife-beating, serious injuries, and even death. Both in Mexico and in the United States, driving while intoxicated has resulted in many casualties.

But by far the most pitiful consequence is the hunger and negligence endured by the wives and children of the drunkards. Once we saw an infant in the last stages of starvation whose mother spent her money on mescal rather than on food for the child.

A few of the heavy drinkers have given up the habit for fear of being killed while drunk, since it is believed that the spirit of a man who dies or is killed while drunk stays in the ground where he dies and cannot be dispatched to the afterworld. One of the younger men who stopped drinking told us why he now takes only an occasional beer. While working in Montana several years ago, he earned enough money to make a down payment on a pickup. One Saturday evening, he took several of his Kickapoo and Mexican friends there into town for a drink; but, once in a bar, he was unable to get them to leave to go back to the farm, and he also began to drink *una cerveza más* (one more beer). Returning home in the early hours of the morning, he fell asleep at the wheel and missed a curb, causing the pickup to overturn. Fortunately, no one was killed; but some were injured, and the car, for which he had worked so many long, backbreaking hours and on which he still owed money and had no insurance, was a total loss. This experience frightened him sufficiently to cause him to abandon drinking. He ended with this reflection, "And to think if I had been killed or had my Kickapoo companions died in the accident, none of us could have reached the afterworld of our fathers."

Chapter 14

Religion

Religion is the principal force integrating all Kickapoo society. It extends from the simple duties of a woman keeping her house and compound clean to highly structured ceremonies.[1] The Kickapoos guard religious information with the utmost secrecy. When Peterson and Ritzenthaler spent two weeks in the village, the older people refused to act as informants because they felt religion would be involved in any matter discussed. One of the religious leaders held out his hand and said that each aspect of Kickapoo life was like the fingers, which are connected to the hand, implying that Kickapoo culture is so integrated and so concerned with the religious theme that it is impossible to separate facets of culture into strictly unrelated categories.[2]

The Kickapoo religion is essentially animistic, with the belief in manitous as its basic component, and most of the religious practices involve dealing with these spirits in order to keep life untroubled and serene.[3] The Kickapoos believe that everything in this world has a spirit, life, and power. At the head of this order is Kitzihiat, the Great Spirit, who created everything but this world, which was made by Wisaka.

In speaking of "this world" they do not mean the entire earth as we conceive it, but the "world of the Indians"—in other words, this continent, which in their concept is an island. This island is flat, is floating over water, and has been preceded by three other worlds, all destroyed: the first by air, the second by rot, and the third by water. When the third world was destroyed after a rain of eighty days, everyone was drowned except the Kickapoos. They are now in the fourth and last world, which will be destroyed by fire. Four worlds are above them and four worlds are beneath them; four worlds are to the right and four worlds to the left. The dome-shaped sky is composed of solid blue rock, which appears transparent from below but not from above. The moon and sun are inside this dome, but the stars, which are outside, are people and, although they cannot see the Indians in this world, the Indians can see them. On top of the dome is a big chimney, through which Wisaka departed after making this world and bringing knowledge to his people, who were placed here by Kitzihiat.

So strong is the belief that this world is going to burn that on one occasion, when we advised a young man to keep the Social Security receipts he had received for future compensation, he told us he did not believe he would live to old age, as the world was going to burn before that time.

The Kickapoos are not certain where Kitzihiat resides. Some say in the sky above; others say they do not know; and others claim he is everywhere. They do know that he dwells in a wigwam like the ones in which they live, for Wisaka, their culture hero and a son of Kitzihiat, brought back the knowledge of its construction from a visit he made to his father. There is some disagreement among the Indians as to the number of Kitzihiat's sons. Some say he had as many as thirteen, but most agree that he had four whose names they know: Wisaka, who made this world and gave them their knowledge; Pepazcé, the first Indian to be killed; Mesicatuinata, who is a war chief; and Machemanetuha, of whom some say that he is the "devil" and represents the evil in this world. Others say that the fourth son will come in another world and that his existence does not affect the Kickapoos. All assure us that the sons were born of virgin Kickapoo maidens and Kitzihiat. Whether this and other beliefs were acquired through Christian teaching, to which they have been exposed since their first contact with the French, or are native Indian beliefs, we are not in a position to say.

Kitzihiat, through his son Wisaka, sent laws by which he expects the Kickapoos to abide. He keeps a record of their conduct brought to him by the manitous, who are vigilantes and messengers. Kitzihiat can punish Kickapoos who fail to fulfill their ceremonial obligations, taboos, and laws of ethical conduct.

The Indians believe that their God is no different from the one worshipped by the Christians, but he sent one people certain things and their people certain others. They believe that God lent man his life and calls man when he judges that his time is ripe.

Kitzihiat is thought to be too preoccupied with his many duties to be specifically concerned about the Kickapoos. For this reason, he created many manitous, including his sons, to look after the Kickapoos' welfare. Notwithstanding, he can be reached by means of messengers: tobacco, fire, the sky, and the four winds—all manitous—whenever the Kickapoos wish to communicate with him by means of the prescribed ritual.

The Kickapoos, in appreciation for the bountifulness of Kitzihiat, dedicate their dances and ceremonial food, especially puppy, to him and his *familiares* (relatives) to bring them pleasure.

Wisaka made the Indian world. Just where he lived at the time is not clear, but he underwent a struggle with the evil manitous of the water, otherwise known as the underworld horned panthers,[4] who tried to kill him by various means. First they attempted to freeze him to death by sending a heavy snow which completely covered his mother's house. He covered himself with a blanket and fell asleep when the cold numbed him. He was awakened by a small bird perched in the smoke hole, who tried to warn him of his danger, but Wisaka was too weak to respond or take any action. Later another bird came to warn him, but by this time he was so weak and hungry that he gnawed the leather of his bow and fell asleep again. Soon a third bird perched on the smoke hole and, noting that Wisaka looked dead, descended to gouge out his eyes. Awakening, Wisaka frightened the bird of prey, who went to warn the evil underworld horned panthers that they had not been able to kill Wisaka by freezing him.

After this futile effort to destroy Wisaka, the panthers planned to kill him by drowning. They began to make the sea spread around him until everything was covered with water. Wisaka, however, quickly made a small skiff and saved himself. The snapping turtle appeared and offered to help. Wisaka scraped the soil from under the turtle's flippers and body each time he dived to the bottom and brought up earth. Then the dove appeared and offered to bring twigs to make a sort of tortilla (the word used by our informant to describe the world) by combining the twigs with the soil. Wisaka placed the tortilla over the water, where it spread and spread until he had locked the huge horned panthers under this world. The thunderers, who are manitous and are called *grandfathers*, help to keep these evil animals in their place. When the world comes to an end, the horned panthers will come forth and devour everyone, including the Indians.

Another myth tells that when Wisaka finished making the world he asked a spider to spin a strong web, with which he tied the world to the north so that it will not fall. This is why the Kickapoos do not kill spiders.

After he had secured the world, Wisaka went here and there, making and naming everything. He delighted in giving the mountains strange forms, since he is playful and mischievous. He brought the deer, buffalo, bear, turkey, corn, squash, and beans. One informant told us that "Wisaka also gave the Kickapoos apples, grapes, apricots, pears, watermelons, and cantaloupes. He put the rain here to water the crops every fourteen days so the Indians would not have to work. When the white men came they took back to their world the seeds of the Kickapoo products. To the whites Wisaka gave cattle, pigs, chickens, hats, money, paper, writing, and work."

Wisaka taught the Kickapoos how to build their houses, which wood to use for making bows and arrows and other artifacts, how to perform their ceremonies, how to dance, and how to use the bundles he had secured for them. He taught them how to use the ceremonial ladles, with which they eat the food at feasts, and told them they must not use any metal objects. When we reminded our informant that the Kickapoos used brass kettles to cook ceremonial food, he retorted that Wisaka had made the first one and taught them how to use them.

Wisaka brought them the laws by which they must abide. They must not:

> Commit suicide.
> Kill another Kickapoo.
> Kill an Indian from another "nation."
> Kill a Mexican.
> Fail to fulfill their ceremonial obligations.
> Indulge in excessive drinking.
> Steal.
> Commit adultery.
> Lie.
> Accumulate wealth.
> Commit incest.
> Participate in witchcraft.
> Indulge in malicious gossip.

Wisaka is not without his frailties. For instance, he likes to drink, and when he tips the bottle too much, the whole world rocks—this is what causes earthquakes. Wisaka once got into so much mischief that the other manitous held a council and decided to send him to live in the north, but Wisaka outwitted them and flew away on the legs of the water hens. Some of the Kickapoos, however, believed that he was still around in the 1960's and was helping the Americans with the Vietnam War.

Pepazcé, the second son of Kitzihiat, who is also a manitou, was the first Indian to be killed. Long ago, when he and Wisaka were strolling through the woods, a high wind came up. They decided it would be great fun to turn themselves into acorns and let the wind scurry them along. As they went bouncing through the woods, they suddenly were stopped by a huge net that the underworld horned panthers were dragging, with which they caught Pepazcé. They then clubbed him to death. From that day, Kitzihiat put the spirit of Pepazcé in the west, where he rules the hereafter and where most of the Kickapoo spirits eventually dwell.

The Kickapoos do not believe in hell, only in heaven; however, under certain circumstances already explained a Kickapoo may be unable to reach the hereafter. This is the worst punishment that can befall them. When a Kickapoo dies, provided he is not a suicide or one killed while intoxicated, his spirit lingers around the village until he is dispatched to the hereafter through an adoption ceremony. If the deceased is a member of the Buffalo clan, he will be accompanied by the spirit of the dog eaten at the ceremony. Some believe the Kickapoos ride the spirits of horses on their trip heavenward. When we inquired of Chief Papícoano if he had a horse and he answered in the negative, we asked how he planned to arrive at the hereafter. He tartly replied, "It is not mandatory to go to heaven on horseback; one may go there on foot."

When a spirit is dispatched to the hereafter, it takes the Milky Way (another manitou) and a river, until it arrives at a bridge which has a pole across it. If by chance some spirit has wandered there without previously having had an adoption ceremony, the pole shakes until the intruder falls off. Another version is that Pepazcé, accompanied by a fierce dog who is ready to devour intruding spirits, sits at the bridge.

Mesicatuinata, the third son of Kitzihiat, was in line for chieftainship; but, through envy, his youngest brother, Machemanetuha, killed him. Kitzihiat put his spirit in charge of the spirits of warriors, those who die of gunshot wounds while not intoxicated, and women who die in childbirth. Some believe that Mesicatuinata lives in the south, but others attest that he lives with Kitzihiat. The spirits in his care spend their time enjoying themselves but also look after their kin to see that no harm befalls them.

One informant told us that the nephew of a man in the village had died in Vietnam, and an adoption ceremony had been held for him in Oklahoma to dispatch his spirit to the world of Mesicatuinata. Another informant stated that Mesicatuinata no longer received spirits—perhaps because the Kickapoos in Mexico have not been warriors for several decades.

It is easy to understand why Machemanetuha is associated with the devil or is spoken of as a symbol of evil, since he committed the second worst offense, that of killing another Kickapoo—for these beings, although they are manitous, are also Kickapoos, or were Kickapoos before they became manitous. When Forsyth was agent for the Fox and was asked by Governor Lewis Cass of Detroit to fill out a questionnaire dealing with the customs of the Indians, he told of a bad spirit called Machemantitoo, who was subordinate to the Great Spirit. The Sauk and Fox thought he was allowed to revenge himself on mankind for some unspecified wrong through the agency of bad medicine, poisonous snakes, etc.: "every accident which befalls them they impute to the bad spirit's machinations."[5] C. C. Trowbridge mentioned the same bad spirit, Motshee Monitoo, among the Shawnee, with characteristics similar to those described by Forsyth.[6]

The Kickapoos attribute to this manitou similar qualities, blaming him for witchcraft, rattlesnakes, centipedes, disease, or any disaster they cannot explain otherwise. They do not believe that any Kickapoo spirits go to the realm where he reigns after death. Some of the Kickapoos called this manitou the devil, perhaps in an effort to clarify for us the evil he represents. Some have associated him with the Christian devil.

Besides the four brothers who are manitous (and perhaps the other nine, with whom we did not become acquainted), the Kickapoos believe that Kitzihiat put many others in this world to assist and protect them. Chief among these is the fire manitou, which is called *grandfather* since, without it, they could not communicate with the other manitous and get the messages on the way. In the fire they burn Indian tobacco, another manitou, offered as the first step in asking for aid and favors. So strong is their respect for fire that a man, while he is praying during a ceremony, dares not look at the fire as it is being stirred, for fear that a spark may kill him.

Since they keep no written records, their knowledge is derived from their elders or from the manitous. When a Kickapoo needs information that he deems no one can give him, he fasts, offers tobacco to the fire, and asks its spirit to reveal the knowledge he seeks.

Each New Year, all the old fires in the village are extinguished. The leader of the Thunder clan makes a new one with the bow drill, and this fire is distributed to all homes. When a fire dies out, it suffers and says to the woman tending it, "My daughter, raise me, as I am dying." When leaving the house, one should never allow it to die, but put it out so that it will not suffer. Neither do they spit in the fire or throw the most minute piece of waste into it. A woman dares not step over the fire, believing that, if she does, her next period will not cease and she will hemorrhage to death.

Since many of the women in whose houses bundles are kept, where a fire should be constantly fed, absent themselves for several months each year, there is one house owned by a woman whose name is Mechimisi-nucoa, meaning "May Kitzihiat always grant us fire," who is charged with the maintenance of a perpetual fire. She seldom leaves her home, and when she does, for brief periods, she assigns someone to replace her so that the fire may continue to be fed. Whenever a person gives an individual ceremony he goes to a bundle house—not necessarily that of his clan—or to the house of Mechimisinucoa for coals to start the fire, before which the clan leader of the host officiates and into which tobacco is placed as an offering. If an illness occurs in a home, coals from the clan bundle house are taken to make a fire, which is constantly fed while the patient is undergoing treatment.

The four corners or directions, the four winds, and the sky that watches through the smoke hole are all manitous and are called *grandfathers*. They are vigilantes and messengers who notify the manitous with whom the Kickapoos want to communicate to ready themselves. When addressing the four corners or the four winds with the flageolet, a strict order must be observed: first the manitou who lives in the east is called, then the ones who live in the west, the south, and the north; otherwise, the message will not arrive. Also helping these manitous are the trees, rocks, moon, sun, day, and night.

The thunderers are manitous and grandfathers. The Kickapoos speak of them as "those who walk above." They are four in number and are old people. Once, when a group of Kickapoos were in our home and were enjoying the photographs of Indians in *Arizona Highways*, a small girl showed a drawing of a thunderbird with a streak of lightning in its beak to her grandmother. We pointed out that it was one of the thunderbirds of the Navajo Indians. The old grandmother shook her head and corrected us by saying, "That is not what those who walk above look like; they are old people."

The Kickapoos are not frightened by thunder and lightning, since, in their minds, these were placed here to protect them. Upon showing the damage that a hailstorm had done to the cane roof over the patio of our house in Múzquiz, we asked a Kickapoo visitor if the hail had damaged the houses in the village. He looked at us complacently and said, "We never get hail there; we have a medicine Kitzihiat gave us." With this, he pulled out the tiny buckskin pouch where he kept his Indian tobacco and showed it to us, adding that, when a storm approaches, anyone, man or woman, places a bit of this tobacco in one hand, puts a light to it, and offers it to the thunderers, saying, "Go away, grandfathers; do not molest us," and the storm disperses in minutes.

One evening, while another Kickapoo was calling on us, a severe electrical storm suddenly came up. Dolores went to the kitchen to prepare tea for our visitor. Suddenly, she was blinded by a bolt of lightning which hit a nearby power pole. She ran into the living room, out of breath, and asked our visitor if he did not have Indian tobacco to offer his grandfathers. He reassured her that the thunderers would not harm her; they were put here by Kitzihiat; they brought the rain and protected us from bad animals. Dolores insisted that this was fine for the Kickapoos, but she belonged to another "nation." He interrupted by saying, "Do not say that; say you believe the thunderers are our grandfathers. They protect every nation, Russia, Mexico, China . . ." He stepped into the patio, and whether he used his tobacco to disperse the storm, we shall never know; but in minutes it was gone.

A Kickapoo woman friend came to call shortly after a severe hailstorm, frequent in the spring. The storm had passed over the village and dropped some stones; three, the size of turkey eggs, had perforated the roof of the bundle house she was tending during the owner's absence. Immediately, she had gone behind the house to make an offering of tobacco to the thunderers while muttering to herself, "What is the matter with the people in this village? They are not offering tobacco to our grandfathers so they will not molest us!" She ended her story by saying that the storm, which could have been much worse, had immediately changed direction.

Although the Kickapoos are confident that their grandfathers will not bother them, when a severe storm passes over the village and they are either sitting or lying down, they sit on the edge of their benches and put out all of the lights and the fire. If they are walking, they stop. They are afraid of window glass and mirrors during a storm—a fear shared by the Mexicans, who cover mirrors with a cloth.

To the Kickapoos, the North Star is a manitou which they call Bear; they locate it by the Big Dipper and use it to guide them when hunting. Venus they believe to be two stars and give each a separate name, one for the evening star and one for the morning star. The two stars are said to be two Kickapoos who died long ago and whom Kitzihiat placed in the heaven as the brightest stars.

There is only one constellation which the Kickapoos call a manitou: the Pleiades, closely associated with their New Year ceremonies. When the Pleiades reach the zenith and the sun sets at the same time, their New Year is imminent. They need only to have the thunderers from the four directions announce when they may begin the clan festivals.

The earth is a manitou called *grandmother* and is supposed to have reared the culture hero, Wisaka. She sustains herself by eating human beings buried in her bosom. The vegetation on the earth is her hair. She is a source of wisdom, ready to impart knowledge to young people who have fasted and prayed. Before time to plant Indian corn, squash, and beans, the chief has a ceremony in which Grandmother Earth is offered tobacco and asked to be bountiful with the crops.

The sun is a manitou called *grandfather*. He is considered the strongest of all, since he supports the world with the help of the strong web made by the spider. The sun makes the rainbow. Children are taught never to look at the sun for fear of being blinded by his strength.

The moon is a manitou called *grandmother*. The face in the moon is the face of the Indians' grandmother, who is stirring a kettle of food for her family. If she should ever stop stirring the kettle, the world will come to an end. When an eclipse occurs, the Kickapoos believe the moon is dying and discharge their rifles to revive her. It was the moon who sent women their menses, since she appears every twenty-eight days, as does the menstrual period. Children are also forbidden to look at the moon.

When gathering timber for house construction or to make an artifact, it is necessary to cut it when the moon is full, as wood at this time is mature and will not rot easily or be consumed by borers. When corn is ready to harvest, it is done when the moon is full so that it, also, will be mature and the weevils will not eat it.

To the Kickapoos, it is incomprehensible that man has walked on the moon. When shown pictures of the first landing on the moon, they seemed both indignant and incredulous. In the first place, they asked, how could man reach the moon? And who was behind the first man who walked on the moon to take his picture? They dismissed the issue by saying it was a television trick.

Comets, meteors, and showers of meteors are considered manitous and are omens of disaster. When a comet is seen with its tail up, it augurs a big war; with its tail down, it foretells a small war. Meteors spell disaster for the Indians. Recently, they point out, it was after a heavy shower of meteors that an old woman and her grandson were burned to death in their jacal. Meteors may also presage wars. Old men in the village remember that shortly before the Mexican Revolution of 1910 a great shower of meteors occurred.

Day and night are manitous called *grandfather*. It was they who gave the names to the moieties of the tribe: Kisko and Oskasa, day and night, black and white. There are two other manitous who rule during the year, decide the weather between them, and alternate the seasons. The ocean and the water and their inhabitants, water snakes and water hens, are also manitous. They own the water, and for this reason one must ask their permission before entering their domain.

The Kickapoo-style house is a manitou; only in such a house may ceremonies be held. The horse, the buffalo, the bear, the deer, the dog eaten at ceremonies, and all the foods Wisaka placed here for the Indians are manitous. So are all of their ceremonial dances and games, except the moccasin game, which they say came from the Sauk and Fox Indians.

There are also evil manitous, such as witches, centipedes, rattlesnakes, the underworld horned panthers, and sickness, but the majority of the manitous are kindly disposed toward the Kickapoos. All can be appealed to for their grace by means of ritual, in which the offering of tobacco is most important.

The central element of the Kickapoo religion is the possession and veneration of the so-called medicine bundles, or sacred packs, called *misami* by the Kickapoos.[7] Each bundle is considered a manitou and is the most sacred possession of a clan or of an individual. Three different types of bundles are used: those that belong to the clans; those that belong to an individual, such as Chief Papícoano; and those that belong to the herbal societies.

Bundles owned by the clans are not the personal property of an individual but belong to a clan as a group, since the leader is not always the son or other consanguine relative of the man who preceded him in that post. Leadership is ideally passed to a relative; but, more often than not, it is passed to a man who, because of a fine memory, interest, and dedication, is able to learn the intricacies of the ceremonies associated with the bundle. Two clan bundles, Black Bear and Tree, were inherited by sons of the men who had been leaders of their respective clans; however, the leaders died before their sons were old enough to learn the ritual, and today these clans are aligned to others who have leaders. Because the leader of the Berry clan is an exceedingly able and intelligent man who knows how to officiate with several bundles, this clan has a three-day New Year ceremony, during which these bundles are venerated.

The second type of bundle is that owned by an individual, as in the case of Chief Papícoano, who owned two bundles with which he officiated at his various *misas de capitán* (chief's ceremonies) and at the house-building ceremonies he headed.

Bundles of the third type belong to members of the herbal societies and are used in their cures.

A clan bundle is not always kept in the home of the man qualified to officiate. It happens that the leader of the Man bundle has it in his custody, but it was formerly in the custody of his mother until her death. All of the other bundles are in the custody of women; in whose houses the bundles have been kept for many years. The women custodians do not necessarily belong to the clan of the bundle; this does not diminish their solicitude for its careful preservation. It is an honor to be so distinguished, and the women sometimes make great financial sacrifices to build the bundle houses, have them enlarged for the New Year clan ceremonies, and outfit them with the new mats which such houses demand.

All of the clans represented in Mexico have bundles except Fox, Coyote, Fire, and Eagle. Why these clans have none we have not been able to determine. One of the clan leaders explained that, when a clan is becoming extinct, leaving no member to officiate, the bundle is taken into the *monte* and carefully hidden. Others say that some of the bundles were burned in the Mackenzie raid of 1873 at Remolino. It is also said that, during the Mexican Revolution of 1910, Gen. Venustiano Carranza's men sacked the village and burned it, with consequent losses to the Indians.

It could also be that some of the individuals named in the Fox and Eagle clans were originally from Oklahoma, where these clans are also represented,[8] and later went to Mexico where no bundle exists. The Coyote clan may be the same as the Wolf clan, which also exists in Oklahoma. One clan leader told us that those individuals who now belong to the Fire clan, which is not represented in Oklahoma according to our sources,[9] were once members of the Eagle clan. Finally, it could well be that these bundles do exist but that their existence was carefully concealed from us for fear we might attempt to buy them.

The Kickapoos keep all information related to the bundles with the utmost reserve. When shown photographs of Indian bundles in various museums, some stared blankly at the pictures and said they had never seen anything like them. They are hesitant to speak of the source of their bundles and told us that they had always had them in their possession and that they were things of "the old people." But, according to a myth they told us, it was Wisaka who originally secured the bundles for them.

Skinner says of the Prairie Potawatomi: "If any Mascoutens is interrogated as to the origin of the sacred bundles of his tribe in general, the answer is invariably, 'They were invited [invented] by Wisaka' the culture hero who gave them to mankind."[10]

Many taboos are associated with the bundles, in particular for menstruating women, whose presence is thought to deplete the bundle of its power.

Although the clan bundles are kept in special houses in the custody of certain women, and those belonging to individuals are kept in their homes, either can be taken to the home of any Kickapoo living in a Kickapoo house (but not to a Mexican house) when ceremonies held there call for the use of a bundle. All the clan leaders know how to officiate during the ceremonies of their clan, but other men have also learned some of the minor ones and may be called upon in the absence or illness of the clan leader.

The bundles, approximately two feet in length and six inches in thickness, covered with a clean white cloth to protect them from dust and insects, are kept in the highest rafters on the west end of the house. Besides the white cloth wrapping, the contents are enclosed in the finely dressed skin of a two-point buck killed by a member of the clan and prepared by a girl before her menarche or a woman past her climacteric. This work is done in the *monte*, in a well-hidden spot, away from curious eyes. The entire bundle is secured with strips of buckskin.

It has been difficult to discover the contents of the bundles, since the men will give little, if any, information, and the women are not permitted to view them. We have, by dint of patience and putting bits of information together, ascertained some of the objects. For one thing, we know that parts or all of the taboo animals are preserved in the bundles. This is also true of other Indian bundles now in museums.

To begin with, every bundle contains a small sack of Indian tobacco, a pipe wrapped in a fine cattail mat and kept in a casing of fawn skin, two gourd rattles, a flageolet, a bow and drill, hematite, and commercial dyes to paint the faces and moccasins of the deceased. In some bundles are to be found human skulls; scalps; desiccated fish; human effigies; desiccated parts of mammals, birds, and reptiles; tails and hairs of buffaloes, coyotes, and cougars; claws of bears and cougars; parts of the prairie dog; rattlers, horned toads, humming birds, owls; and feathers of the golden eagle and the sparrow hawk—all of these items containing magical powers and kept in finely tanned fawn skins, tied with thongs of the same material. In the bundles are also kept certain dried plants and roots owned by the various clans and often strictly taboo to others. These are used for medicinal, ceremonial, or magical purposes. Of these we have been told of the wild cherry branches and wild iris rhizomes. Two others, common to all of the clans, are cudweed, used in the purification of bundles and houses, and the rhizome of Solomon's seal, a plant of many magical properties.

For excellent photographs and descriptions of the contents of the Sauk and Fox bundles bought by Mark R. Harrington, see his monograph, *Sacred Bundles of the Sac and Fox Indians*.

Chapter 15

Rituals and Ceremonies

Ceremonial Calendar

Kickapoo ceremonies may be divided into four general categories: the New Year clan festivals, the chief's ceremonies, individual ceremonies, and adoption ceremonies. The calendrical schedule of ceremonies is as follows.

Ceremonies that take place between late January and May:

New Year clan festivals
Naming ceremonies of the Berry and Tree clans
Herbal societies' New Year ceremonies
Adoption ceremonies
Spring feast for the dead
Nekanesheka's woman's dance and Menaquah's buffalo dance
Naming ceremonies of the Man, Water, Eagle, Fire, Raccoon, and Buffalo clans
Temporary chief's ceremony returning authority to the tribal chief
Chief's ceremony permitting women to gather construction material for the summer houses
Chief's ceremony granting permission to plant
Chief's ceremony for women to move into summer houses
House-dedication ceremonies
Ceremony for the French medal
Menaquah's woman's dance and buffalo dance
Little Rabbit ceremony
Tobacco planting ceremony
Feast of the first fruits
Departure ceremonies

Midsummer ceremonies:

Arrival ceremonies

Chief's ceremony to lift his food taboo
Rain-dance ceremony
Summer feast for the dead
Clan bundle purification ceremonies
Departure ceremonies

Ceremonies held between October and December

Arrival ceremonies
Chief's ceremony appointing a temporary chief to direct construction of the winter houses
Temporary chief's ceremony permitting women to gather construction material for the winter houses
Temporary chief's ceremony permitting women to gather cattails
Temporary chief's ceremony permitting women to move into the winter houses
House-dedication ceremonies
Winter feast for the dead
Naming ceremonies for the Bear clan
Fasting ceremonies

Ceremonies that do not follow a set calendrical schedule:

Hunters' ceremonies
Ceremony for a boy's first hunt
Ceremonies for interment (described in Chapter 10)
Murderer's ceremony
Curing ceremonies
Ceremony for borrowing tobacco
Rain ceremonies
Buffalo dance of the Bear clan

Ceremonial Music

Before describing the ceremonies, we should mention the music and musical instruments. Kickapoo music, except for lullabies and love songs formerly played on the lover's flute, is of a religious or at least ceremonial nature.

It is regrettable that we were not allowed to record their music. We took a tape recorder in hopes we might be able to use it; but, when we were flatly denied the privilege, we gave up the idea rather than use some subterfuge and risk their confidence in other areas.

We discovered that a few of the ceremonial songs they use are also those of the Menomini. These had been recorded and edited many years ago by Frances Densmore and are now available in a record entitled *Songs of the Menominee, Mandan and Hidatsa*, which may be purchased from the Music Division of the Library of Congress.[1] It is our understanding that Helen Blotz of the Music Department of the University of Wisconsin also recorded music of the Central Algonquian Indians, but we were not successful in obtaining this music. Lucille Birdscreek of Shawnee, Oklahoma, a Kickapoo, has recorded most of the music used by her tribe.

On hearing the songs obtained by Frances Densmore, the Kickapoos were able to recognize only three of them: "I Paint My Face Red," played during an adoption ceremony for a woman "Moccasin Game Song," played during the game by the same name; and "Manubus Tells the Ducks to Shut Their Eyes," played during a man's dance.

The drum is by far the most important of the musical instruments used today. It is made from a short three-legged iron kettle from which the handle is removed. The kettle, fourteen inches in diameter and ten inches deep, is partially filled with water. For each occasion it is covered with a new buckskin, stretched over the top and fastened with a new rope. Under the skin and at the top edges of the kettle are placed several pieces of corncob, around which the rope is twisted to keep the skin taut when it is moistened by shifting the kettle back and forth. A long loop or harness is left with the remaining rope so that a man carrying the drum can hang it around his neck while he supports it with both hands. We were allowed to look at the drum, but not to photograph it.

The gourd rattle which accompanies the drum we saw only at a distance and were never able to obtain one for our collection. These are kept in the bundles and are, therefore, extremely sacred objects.

The European traders introduced the Algonquian Indians to brass bells and tinkling cones.[2] The Kickapoos still use sleigh bells, but the shakers formerly made from tin are no longer in vogue. The flute or flageolet is used to alert the manitous that a ceremony is about to take place. It is used indoors during the ceremony preceding a dance or game or at any time that the manitous must be alerted to prepare themselves for a Kickapoo ceremony.

New Year Clan Festivals

The Kickapoo New Year does not occur on a fixed date but takes place at some time during the last days of January or the first two weeks of February. Before the New Year can be celebrated, certain phenomena must be observed. First, the clan leaders watch for the flowering of the wild black cherry (*Prunus serotina*). Second, they observe the constellation of the Pleiades; when it approaches the zenith approximately at sunset, the New Year is imminent. Third, the clan leaders spend their nights watching for lightning from the four directions. This is the last sign sent by the grandfathers, the thunderers, to notify them that the day has arrived to celebrate the New Year and hold their clan festivals. If the thunderer from the north is the first to be seen as he flashes across the sky, it is taken as a good omen, but the New Year does not arrive until lightning from the other three directions is also sighted. The Kickapoos consider themselves uniquely blessed if a heavy rain with much lightning comes over the village on this occasion, as this signifies that the thunderers have taken special pains to notify them. The Kickapoos then say, "It is as though they themselves had come to tell the people."

As soon as lightning from the four directions has been seen, the clan leaders, carrying their gourd rattles, go into the *monte* to chant and offer Indian tobacco to the thunderers, thanking them for the message that the New Year has arrived. In the meantime, the women who own the five bundle houses extinguish the fire, take out the ashes, and clean the hearth. Throughout the village, all radios are turned off, all games are stopped, and the canvas flap over the door of each wigwam is pulled down. Those in possession of Indian tobacco return their portions to the clan leaders. The men return to the village, while the leader of the Thunder clan goes to the Thunder bundle house to make the new fire with the bow drill. This is done secretly, but the zooming of the drill can be heard from the most distant house. As soon as the fire is made—a prerogative of the Thunder clan—the other leaders go to receive the new fire for the other bundle houses.

The New Year Clan festivals initiate the calendar of ceremonies. During the fall months, much preparation has taken place: each household has moved from the summer house into the new winter wigwam; the summer house has been unroofed and old discarded cattail mats have been burnt; and the compounds have been carefully swept to the edges. Now the bundle houses where the festivals will be held need to be enlarged to accommodate the participants. The first of these houses to be enlarged each year is the home of the temporary chief—the clan leader who assumed the command for supervising the construction of the winter houses from the permanent chief in the fall.

The men have been on numerous hunts to supply the necessary deer and bear ribs and tongues, which the women have smoked. The members of the Thunder clan have killed wild turkey—indispensable for their feast. Women have made braids of thinly sliced squash or pumpkin and dried them in the sun. Many puppies have been specially fattened, and the necessary amount of white Indian corn has been stocked. Women have been busy sewing and richly embroidering moccasins as gifts to their uncles and nephews to wear to the festivals, and those who are entitled to attend the festivals have readied new clothes. As each clan holds its festival, each person attending bathes in the river.

A none too rigid order in the sequence of the clan festivals is followed. Thunder and its two smaller associated clans are usually the first to hold their festival, although in some years Buffalo No. 1 may be the first, depending on which of the leaders saw the first lightning. Berry, however, must never be first. After Thunder, Man and its four smaller associated clans follow; Buffalo No. 1 and its two associated clans usually follow Man; then come Berry and Tree; and, last, Buffalo No. 2.

As the day for each clan to hold its festival approaches, the leader invites two leaders of the proper reciprocal clans to be the clan's guests. The leader also calls a waiter of the proper reciprocal clan to take charge of the food. The latter calls one waiter for each kettle of food he judges will be available. Early on the day of the festival, the waiters call on all members of the celebrating clan to collect food contributions. This may be venison or bear ribs and tongues, turkey, white corn, pumpkin braids, or a fat puppy. (The puppies are killed by the waiters the day before and are hung in the wigwam overnight.)

Children from about seven to adolescence, who have blackened their faces with charcoal and fasted until noon for periods of from two to three days in advance, bathe in the river at dawn on the day of their clan festival and continue to fast until festival time.

On the appointed day, the invited leaders arrive with their pipes and are presented Indian tobacco by their host. Each prays and sings three songs and puffs his pipe, blowing the smoke in the four directions, east, west, south, and north—always in the same order. They pray to Kitzihiat that he bless their hosts on this occasion and throughout the year. They smoke and pray again just before the feast and afterwards are the first to take their leave, with these words, "We give thanks to those who held this ceremony."

In the presence of the guests, the host opens the clan bundle, passes its contents through smoke, and offers Indian tobacco to the bundle and the fire. The leader beats the kettledrum four times and plays the flageolet in the four directions to alert the manitous. The leader and the guests thank Kitzihiat for all of the blessings enjoyed, ask for continuous grace throughout the year, health and long life for their people, wisdom for their chief, protection for their village, and weakness for their enemies.

They call to the attention of the manitous the fact that they are performing the ceremony they were commanded to hold and are serving the food they were commanded to eat.

A new buckskin is placed on the ground, and pieces of the rhizome of Solomon's seal are laid on it. Each piece is smoked with Indian tobacco and given to an adult. This rhizome is carried by each qualifying Kickapoo and is considered a potent deterrent against witches. Members who receive a piece of the rhizome also receive a new quota of Indian tobacco. At the termination of the festival the women who attend may take coals to start a new fire. Women who do not attend go to the houses after the ceremony to receive their new fire.

There are differences in the way each of the clans conducts its New Year festival. Thunder, Black Bear, Brown Bear, Fox, Man, Fire, and Raccoon permit only males to attend, but Water allows its only woman member to be present. (The one Coyote member is a man; we don't know whether a Coyote woman could attend.) These must arrive at the bundle house with faces painted in stripes, either black or white, depending on the moiety to which each belongs. On entering, the Kisko (white) sit on the south bench, and the Oskasa (black) sit on the north bench. Sometime during the festival, the leader selects two youths or men, approximately the same age, one from each moiety, who are presented a bowl of boiling food each. At a given signal, they begin to dip their ceremonial ladles into the bowls, and, without stopping, each consumes the contents. The one who finishes first is hailed as the winner. Members of each division, amid much joking and teasing, urge their representative to a quick finish.

Berry clan members, who are all Kisko, and Tree members, who have both Kisko and Oskasa in their clan, allow women and children over seven to attend the clan festival and invite guests from other clans to the third day of the festival. (This is the only clan festival that lasts three days.) Hosts and guests arrive with their faces painted—men streaked on the forehead, women daubed on the cheeks. No food race is held by these clans. On the first and second day all Berry members attending may eat, as well as anyone from other clans who wishes to attend the feast (but not the ceremony). Berry members eat indoors while guests eat outside. On the third day, only guests eat, while Berry members abstain.

The ceremony for the second day of the three celebrated by the Berry clan, called the Little Rabbit, is attended exclusively by women, except for the leader. Women members of the clan and all of those who have been cured of female disorders, such as abortions, difficult pregnancies and deliveries, or excessive bleeding, are expected to be present and contribute provisions. The leader gives the women information on various plants used for female disorders, intended to be used personally; but if a member of the Berry clan sees another in need of healing, she may prescribe the plants about which she has knowledge.

Throughout the ceremony, during which herbs and paraphernalia of the bundle are smoked in cudweed and offered tobacco, the women kneel on the mats and may not lift their eyes. After the ritual, a feast is served. Before eating, the women dip their index fingers in the dishpans containing the food and await a signal from their leader to begin. At the end, the house is cleared of serving utensils, and all rise and form two lines, one in front of each bench, where they stand in position to dance, shuffling their feet and swaying their bodies to the rhythm of a gourd played by the leader.

On the third day of the Berry clan festival, children are named.

Buffalo clan members are extremely reluctant to reveal anything about their ceremonies, and we were unable to obtain any specific information about them.

Naming Ceremony

When a Kickapoo child is born, he is called *not-yet-named* until his parents have a ceremony in which he receives a name for the duration of his life. There is no specified age at which a child must be named. Naming usually takes place when he is a few months old, but this depends mainly on two factors: the time when the clan of the namer is permitted to have the naming ceremony, and the time when the father or other namer is able to provide a sufficient number of deer ribs for the feast.

In the majority of cases, the father names the child, but there are several exceptions. If the father belongs to a clan whose number is greatly reduced and which no longer has a leader and has had to associate itself with a larger clan, the mother may name the child if her clan is strong. For various reasons the parents may offer the child to a relative to be named. If the husband, for any reason, is unable to provide the necessary deer ribs, the wife may ask a relative or someone else who is a good hunter to name the child. If a man dies or leaves his wife before a child is born, she is entitled to name the child or offer it to a relative. If a couple have a child named by the father and the child dies, the father passes the privilege of naming the second child to his wife or any consanguine relative of either parent. In special situations, if a woman has no spouse, the leader of her clan may allow her to name the child when another for whom the required number of ribs have been provided is named; however, if a man tries to name his child when another has provided the ribs, he is apt to be publicly scolded during the ceremony, and the leader may refuse to name the child.

It is up to the parents or namer to decide on a name for the child. Ideally, there should be no other Kickapoo in the tribe carrying the same name, an eponym of the namer's clan totem; however, this is not always the case. In a tribe of approximately four hundred there are presently fifteen duplicated names, and one name belongs to four females.

The family or namer must wait until the time when the namer's clan is permitted to have a naming ceremony. The Bear clans may name only during cold weather, when bear cubs are born. Man and Thunder may name at any time except during cold weather. Berry and Tree must name on the third day of their three-day New Year festival. Coyote names at the same time as Thunder. Buffalo, Water, Eagle, Fire, Raccoon, and Fox may name at any time.

When the time for naming approaches, the namer procures a specified number of deer ribs for the feast. Berry, Tree, Thunder, Bear, and Fox require two pairs of smoked ribs, which must be in one piece each and must include the shoulder but not the backbone, and two pairs of ribs from freshly killed deer; thus, a total of four deer are required. Man, Fire, Water, and Raccoon require four pairs of ribs from freshly killed deer; Buffalo and Eagle require two pairs of smoked ribs and one whole freshly killed deer. Buffalo must also provide puppy.

Until the father or namer is able to secure this number of ribs, he cannot hold the ceremony. Sometimes, this creates unusual expense for the namer, as hunters, because of the scarcity of deer, may make several dry trials before bagging them. Each time they go to hunt, a small feast asking for luck must be observed, as well as another upon their return, whether they have been successful or not—all this at the expense of the namer.

When the namer has been decided on, the name for the child has been chosen, the time for naming is in order, the proper number of deer have been killed, and enough Indian corn has been stocked, the namer calls on the leader of his clan or another leader who knows how to officiate at this ceremony to discuss plans for the ceremony. The child may be named in his own home or in the bundle house of his namer's clan.

The leader calls upon the chief to invite him as a witness, since it is his prerogative to be present at all naming ceremonies and to know new additions to the tribe. The leader also invites two other leaders of the proper reciprocal clans to be witnesses. The leader calls the headwaiter of the proper reciprocal clan, who, in turn, calls others to assist him with the kettles of unsalted venison and purple corn cooked indoors. The number of kettles depends on the amount of food available. The headwaiter calls two women of the proper reciprocal clans, past their climacteric, to be the child's sponsors.

About midmorning of the appointed day, the parents take the child to the bundle house of the namer, if the ceremony is to be held there. They are the only blood relatives present. If the child is named in his home, all other members of the family are dispatched to relatives. If the mother is ill or in the menstrual hut, a female relative takes the child to the ceremony.

When the ceremony is to commence, the namer and child sit on the west bench; the clan leader sits on the southwest corner of the bench; Chief Papícoano sits to the right of the leader; and the two invited leaders sit in the other corners of the house. The two female sponsors sit on the floor on either side of the door. These participants and the waiters are the only ones permitted in the house during the ceremony (except in the case of the Berry clan; see below).

The clan leader asks the namer if he has decided on a name for the child, to which the namer answers in the affirmative. Then the leader asks for the name of the child, which is given by stating, "I want to name this child————." The leader opens the bundle, offers tobacco to it and the fire, and asks these to alert the other manitous. The leader prays, announcing to Kitzihiat the name of the child and the moiety to which the child will belong—that of the namer. After this, the leader says to the child, if a boy, "If Kitzihiat grants you life, may you be a good hunter." In the case of a girl he says, "If Kitzihiat grants you life, may you be able to build your house."

After the leader finishes the prayers, the child is passed to each of the three witnesses and the two sponsors, who hold him briefly and speak thus, to a boy, "Now you are named————. May you be a good hunter, and may Kitzihiat bless you with a long life and health." If the child is a girl, they say, "Now you are named————. May you be able to build your house, and may Kitzihiat bless you with a long life and with health." When all have held the child and wished him well, the chief prays.

If the child is named in the Berry clan, he is named on the third day of the New Year festival. Everyone present—all Berry members over seven years old attend this festival—is passed the child to hold for a few minutes after he receives his name and says, "You are no longer 'no-name'; you are now called————."

At noon after a naming ceremony, all but one of the waiters go into the village to invite those who qualify for the feast to bring their wooden ladles. All may attend the feast except the blood relatives of the child and the members of his clan. One waiter remains in the house to serve the food into the enameled-ware dishpans around which the guests gather. He also announces to children who may have gathered that no blood relative of the child nor anyone of his clan may taste the food.

The leader invites all qualified guests to the feast, which is served outdoors if the weather permits. The waiter serves the leaders and the women sponsors first. Parents or namer abstain as do hosts at all ceremonies except the adoption ceremony. If any food remains, it is taken home by the guests if they do not have members of the child's clan in their home; otherwise, the food is thrown into the river.

Adoption Ceremony

Some writers have tended to emphasize only one phase of the Indian adoption ceremony. J. N. B. Hewitt states that "In the primitive mind the fundamental motive underlying adoption was to defeat the evil purpose of death to remove a member of the kinship group by actually replacing in person the lost or dead member."[3] This description, however, serves to explain only half of the intent of the ceremony. Frank G. Speck, writing about the Tutelo Indians, gives the second reason:

> The avowed purpose of the ceremony is to bring back the soul of the defunct Tutelo tribe member who has died recently, within approximately a year, into association with the living for the space of one night. The ritual reinstates the deceased among the living by the appointment, through adoption, of a beloved one in his or her place as an earthly representative. At its conclusion with the approach of daylight a final adieu is formally enacted to the departed spirit, sending it upon its final journey over the pathway of the rising sun's rays to the permanent celestial abode of the spirits.[4]

Likewise, with the Kickapoos, the adoption ceremony serves not only to adopt another person into the family to take the place of a lost member but also to send the spirit, hovering nearby from the time of death, to the spirit world.

The Kickapoos translate the adoption ceremony into Spanish as "the ceremony for bidding the spirit farewell" or "the ceremony in which the spirit retires." The person "adopted" is not so called but is known as "he or she who represented the deceased"; but since the term *adopted* is so widely used elsewhere, we shall continue this form.

In describing the adoption ceremony the Kickapoos use the term *fiesta*, which means a festive occasion. This term is not used by them for any of their other ceremonies except the feast of the first fruits, also an occasion of rejoicing.

During the adoption ceremony the wandering spirit is invited, by means of prayers, chants, and the drum, to witness his favorite dance or game and by the same means is finally admonished to join the spirits of his kin in the hereafter. At the end of the ceremony, he is given a final feast which suffices until he arrives in the spirit world to be greeted by another feast and game or dance. This is a day of joy. Every effort is made to "please the spirit" on this occasion. The person representing the deceased is treated with deference; he is the "top man on the totem pole" for a day; he is plied with ceremonial food and showered with gifts.

During the weeks in which the adoption ceremonies may be held, from the termination of the New Year festivals until the last buffalo dance in March, no one eats outdoors while the spirits are waiting to be dispatched, since these may see their living kin and become hungry and unhappy as they did during their earthly lives. All pails of water are covered at night, or the spirits may dip their fingers in them; no dishes with food are left overnight, for the spirits may become hungry and try to eat the food. Since the dishes are too heavy for the spirits to lift, they may rattle them. None of the games, such as the bowl and dice, may be played during this time.

The person who is adopted will, after the ceremony, assume the same kinship role in relation to the family which the deceased held, except in the case of a spouse. He will, at the same time, assume the dead person's social privileges and responsibilities, but only to a degree. A person replacing the parent of a child does not assume the financial responsibility of rearing the child, since this is taken care of by the surviving parent and the consanguine relatives; but the child and the adopted parent exchange gifts, observe special considerations for each other, and assume greater responsibility in times of need. The child of the deceased calls the adopted one *father* or *mother* and the adopted one reciprocates with the terms *son* or *daughter*. The adopted one may also engage in a joking behavior with those members of his adoptive family with whom this was permitted to the deceased. Later, the person adopted is the first invited to attend the feast for the dead held three times a year by the family of the deceased.

The adoption ceremonies are held immediately after the New Year clan festivals, while the people are still occupying the winter wigwams. No further ceremonies are held once they occupy the summer houses, except in rare instances. (For example, if a young man is left a widower after the summer houses are occupied, an adoption ceremony is held for his deceased wife to release the young husband from the mourning obligations to his affinal family and thus avoid the temptation to take a new wife or mistress before his release.)

Much shuttling between the Oklahoma and the Mexican Kickapoos takes place in order to participate in each other's adoption ceremonies. At times, if an Oklahoma Kickapoo dies and leaves no close consanguine relatives there, those in Mexico assume the responsibility of giving the ceremony. This works both ways.

Adoption ceremonies are not held by the surviving spouse but by the consanguine relatives of the deceased. An adoption ceremony may also be held by proxy; that is, if the person chosen by the family of the deceased to be the adopted one is absent, someone else may take his place during the ritual.

All members of the tribe carrying a Kickapoo name except suicides and those who die while intoxicated (sometimes there are exceptions to the latter) are entitled to an adoption ceremony. Those born from the union of a Kickapoo woman and a Mexican whom the clan leaders have refused to name and children who die before being named are excluded because they are not considered tribe members.

An adoption ceremony must be held within four years of the death of an individual to be effective. Some clans, such as Man, must have the ceremony within two years of death. The Kickapoos believe that, if no ceremony is held within this specified time, the spirit turns into a moth and dies of hunger. Several years ago a woman from Mexico went to Oklahoma and discovered that, through an oversight, no adoption ceremony had been held for an old uncle, who had died some twenty years before. She and other kin held the ceremony in spite of this lapse of time —not, however, without encountering difficulties, since none of the leaders would lend themselves to such a useless ritual. One of the less orthodox leaders finally consented to officiate, much to the annoyance of the others.

A few years ago a woman whose uncle had died four years earlier was confronted with the obligation of having a ceremony or suffering not only ridicule but possible punishment. She had not had the foresight to save the necessary funds and, although she was helped by another relative, she was forced to ask nonrelatives to assist her. The village immediately dubbed this ceremony as *la fiesta de caridad* (the charity adoption ceremony).

This same woman had already created for herself a distressing situation the year before, when she spoke of giving the ceremony but did not carry out her plans. To talk of giving a ceremony and then renege is considered a dangerous thing, as Kitzihiat punishes those who talk but do not act. No one in the village is safe when a member fails in his duties in this way. This belief in punishment spreads a mantle of secrecy over the date of an adoption ceremony, and only members of the family financially involved and the clan leader of the deceased who has been consulted know exactly when the ceremony will take place. As a whole, the village is not aware that a fiesta is imminent until they see the house enlarged to accommodate the mourners and performers.

All Kickapoos, including those who do not have a Kickapoo name, may attend an adoption ceremony, except the spouse of the deceased and menstruating women. The adoption ceremony is one of the three ceremonies to which visitors from outside the village are welcomed; that is, they may witness the dance or game; but they are not allowed to see the indoor ritual which takes place beforehand.

The consanguine relatives of the deceased, on the day of interment, set aside articles owned by the latter to be given to the adopted one. These are usually new clothing, bedding, jewelry, tools, saddles, a plow, and firearms.

The relatives on whom the obligation falls to give an adoption ceremony discuss the details and agree which part of the financial burden each shall assume. They begin to save money, buy dress lengths while working, and prepare the necessary buckskin articles. Each fiesta requires about one hundred dollars' worth of provisions; several deer; a pig, goats, or kids; three to ten dress lengths for the performers in a dance or game; special gifts for the adopted one, which consist of a pair of buckskin leggings, a pair of unsewed moccasins, a Kickapoo-style shirt, a woven wool sash, a breechcloth, an eagle feather, a shawl or blanket, and a silk kerchief filled with jewelry belonging to the deceased, cigarettes, candy, and small trinkets, if the adopted one is a man. If the adopted one is a woman, she is given a buckskin, a pair of unsewed moccasins, a comb with brilliants for her hair, ribbons, nylon stockings, a shawl or blanket, a silk scarf containing the deceased's jewelry, and a small blue enameled-ware kettle filled with candy, cookies, chewing gum, and fruit. If the deceased left money, part of it is spent for this occasion; if he had livestock, one or two animals are sold to buy provisions. The family also provides a large pile of firewood and large quantities of water from the springs. If the deceased was a member of the Buffalo clan, puppies fattened by the family or relatives are provided. Also provided are a new buckskin and rope for the water kettledrum.

When the family members are ready to give the adoption ceremony, they discuss plans with the clan leader of the deceased. The choice of a dance or game left by the deceased is respected; but if the deceased left no choice—the usual case when a child dies—the family and clan leader decide on the dance or game which would best please the spirit.

If the deceased was cured in a clan ceremony other than the one in which he was named, he may have asked that the clan leader who cured him officiate at his adoption ceremony. In this case, the family carries out his wishes.

There is considerable leeway in the type of dance or game performed in a fiesta. If the deceased was a man, he may have a man's dance—held only during daytime—or, if he was a heavy drinker, he will be given a drunk-man's dance, a two-day dance, a dance followed by a moccasin game or lacrosse game, or only a moccasin game, the latter always played at night. Occasionally, a man may ask that a bow and arrow game be played, but that game is usually reserved for a boy. If the deceased was a woman, a day or night dance may be held or a double-shinny ball game. Sometimes a woman may ask for a bowl and dice game; but this is reserved in most cases for a girl under seven. Dances have become so popular that today even a small girl may have a dance given for her, but in this case it must be a day dance.

If the host family have good hunters, they select a chief of the hunt, who asks two or three others to accompany him. He holds a small ceremony on the day prior to the hunt, at which his clan leader officiates. The latter asks a member of the proper reciprocal clan to perform the duties of waiter. Tobacco is offered to the manitou of the deer while prayers for a successful hunt and for the safety of the men are recited. Indian corn, pumpkin, and venison ribs are served; as usual, the chief of the hunt, as host, abstains. If the host family do not have good hunters, they ask any man in the village who is noted for his prowess to act as chief of the hunt. The family provide the feast, gasoline, and ammunition. They also provide another feast when the hunters return, whether they are successful or not.

At most, three days are spent on the hunt; then, whether or not deer have been bagged, the hunters return to the village, where a ceremony is held—if they have been successful, to give thanks; otherwise, to ask for luck on the next try.

In the meantime, the consanguine relatives of the deceased enlarge the house to accommodate all the mourners and the personnel who participate in the ceremony. All household articles except the bench mats are removed to the summer house for the day of the fiesta.

When the above details have been taken care of, the family members go to Múzquiz for the necessary provisions: flour, lard, sugar, rice, coffee, canned fruits, beans, squash or pumpkin, cabbage, potatoes, macaroni, candy, soda pop, cookies, and several cartons of cigarettes.

The selection of the leader for a dance (who is the adopted one) or the two leaders for a game (one of whom will be chosen as the adopted one at the conclusion of the game) is left to the consanguine relatives, with prior consultation with the deceased's clan leader. The adopted one must be a friend of long standing of the deceased, of the same sex and approximately the same age. If the deceased had a "declared friend," he is the first choice. His qualifications as a dancer or player are not uppermost in the choice, for he selects among his assistants some who are highly proficient in order that the dance or game may be well performed. In case a dance is followed by a moccasin game, or in case only a game is played, two leaders are chosen, both friends of the deceased, one to head each team.

When the dance leader has been chosen, the clan leader asks a man whose clan enjoys reciprocal obligations with that of the deceased to be the headwaiter. The pattern, adhered to strictly in all ceremonies, is shown in Table 5.

TABLE 5
Reciprocal Clans

Main Clans & Associates	Men Waiters	Women Cooks
Thunder Black Bear Fox	Man (headwaiter) Berry Buffalo Tree (taster)	Man (head cook)
Buffalo (No. 1 and No. 2) Eagle Brown Bear	Berry (headwaiter) Man Thunder Fire (taster)	Berry (head cook)
Man Fire Water Coyote Raccoon	Thunder (headwaiter) Berry Tree (taster)	Thunder (head cook)
Berry Tree	Buffalo (headwaiter) Thunder Fire (taster)	Buffalo (head cook)

In the event of a game or a dance followed by a game, there are two headwaiters and two women head cooks, one from each moiety, while the other waiters and cooks belong to the same moiety as the headwaiter but comply with the reciprocal clan pattern. The headwaiter asks a woman of his clan to be head cook. In choosing waiters other than the headwaiter, the affiliated clans are considered in the same capacity as the main clan, so that Berry can ask Black Bear and Fox to be waiters, as well as Thunder; but, in this hypothetical case, the headwaiter must be Buffalo.

The headwaiter and head cook assign the various tasks to the others. Two or three waiters clear the area in front of the house of rocks, vegetation, or litter, and carefully sweep this to the edges of the compound. Another waiter sprinkles the space to keep the dust down during the dance. To provide easy access and ventilation, waiters move the cattail mats to widen the entrance to the house. Some go to relatives and friends to borrow brass kettles to cook the food, large enameled-ware dishpans in which the food is served, and large coffeepots and teapots.

If the day is extremely sunny or rain is imminent, they build protective canopies for the chanters and dancers and spread out tarpaulins for them to rest on. Two waiters make the required drum and drumstick, alternate in carrying it, and, at the end, loosen it. Another waiter is placed in charge of the cigarettes spread on a new buckskin at the foot of the westernmost post of the crossbar where the gifts are hung. The supply is constantly replenished, since anyone, regardless of age or participation, is entitled to help himself.

One waiter, serving as a policeman with a wand in his hand, keeps children in order and off the dance floor and runs off stray dogs. Children are usually well-behaved, but much chatting and giggling takes place during the intermissions. Formerly, before the Kickapoos began calling upon the Múzquiz police or local regiment to keep order, it was the duty of this waiter, with the assistance of others, to tie up anyone disturbing the peace to a large pecan, to which the Kickapoos still point as the castigating tree.

The waiter assigned to be taster (only those belonging to the Fire and Tree clans have this privilege) checks to see that the food has sufficient salt—little is used—and that the coffee and tea have plenty of sugar.

The hunters deliver the venison to the headwaiter, who assigns others to cut it with knives that they carry in scabbards hung from their belts and distribute it among the several kettles, frequently stirred with a ladle. One waiter gets coals from the bundle house of the deceased's clan, with which all the fires except that in the cook house are lighted.

Others serve the dishpans of food and the coffee, tea, and fried bread. They dispose of the bones in a special place allocated to them on the western edge of the compound, where they are quickly snatched by hungry dogs. One waiter serves the performers refreshments and cigarettes during intermissions and takes them a burning stick from the ceremonial fire to light the cigarettes.

Having selected his helpers judiciously and assigned them their duties (several days before the fiesta is scheduled to take place), the headwaiter proceeds to make or have made ten invitation sticks—twenty in the event of a game or a dance followed by a game—from carefully peeled branches of lime prickly-ash, cut into ten-inch lengths. These sticks are used only for the adoption ceremony. They are taken to the house of the host family, where the clan leader is present. The latter hands one stick to the waiter and tells him to present it to the person chosen by the family as the adopted one (or the two leaders, if a game is to be played). This takes place two or three days prior to the fiesta to give the chosen one, or ones, time to prepare. The adopted one presents himself to the clan leader and the assembled family, to whom he gives his invitation stick, and is told by the clan leader that he is the one selected to lead the dance. He is instructed in his duties and is given one invitation stick for himself and nine others to give to persons he considers can help him give a good performance.

If there is to be a man's dance, each of the ten male dancers may, if he chooses, pass his invitation stick to an aunt (father's sister) or a niece (sister's daughter). During the dance, these women stand at the sides of the area and mark time to the music while performing a slow shuffle in place. They are the recipients of the ten dress lengths which hang on the crossbar. For a woman's dance, each of the ten female dancers may ask anyone she wishes to be her guest at the first feast.

There is no fixed number of chanters; the leader calls those available. Each of these men may ask an aunt or niece to be one of the second chanters, whose duty is to accompany the men as they circle the dancers at a woman's dance or chant standing in one place at a man's dance. Each receives a kettle of food cooking outdoors to take home and share with family and friends.

The women cooks' duties begin the day of the ceremony. To them falls the task of preparing the vegetables for the *nepupe* (stew) which is the ceremonial meal. They make the fried bread, coffee, and tea indoors where the ceremony is being performed. This food is served to the dancers and their guests. If a woman taster is called, as is frequently the case, she checks the proper amount of salt and sugar used. One of the cooks pounds and winnows the purple Indian corn used in making the corn gruel given to the dance leader or winner of the game at the end of the ceremony. The cooks carry wood for the inside fire and water for the coffee and tea. It is the duty of the cooks, on the day of the dance, to make the crossbar or bars on which are draped the gifts for the dancers or players, and it is also their duty to dismantle it or them as soon as the gifts have been removed.

Ten kettles of food cooking indoors is the ideal amount for a feast at a man's adoption ceremony. The one nearest the entrance, reserved especially for the first feast served to the adopted one, his companions, and their guests, contains two sets of smoked deer ribs, Indian corn, and squash or pumpkin. The one farthest west is the small brass kettle filled with corn gruel called in Spanish *el lonche pa'l espiritu* (the lunch for the spirit) taken by the headwaiter to the house of the adopted one after the dance or game. The other eight kettles, containing venison, corn, squash or pumpkin, beans, potatoes, cabbage, rice, and macaroni, are reserved for the other three feasts served during the day. Three large enameled-ware dishpans of food are served from the first kettle, one for the dancers and their guests, the second for the chanters and their guests, and the third to be placed outdoors for anyone who is hungry and wishes to eat. This pot is refilled three more times with venison and the other ingredients but not with smoked ribs. Since venison is not as plentiful as it formerly was, the ideal ten kettles are not always present. Today, perhaps there will be only four, depending on the luck of the hunters and the largesse of the hosts. Bear and javelina may be substituted for venison.

For the feasts during a woman's dance, fewer kettles cook indoors, but ever present are the ones for the adopted one and her companions and guests, and the small kettle with the *lonche* for the spirit. The number of kettles which cook outdoors depends on the number of second chanters invited. The usual number is two to five. These contain the same ingredients as the kettles indoors, except for the smoked venison ribs.

Any affinal relative, other than the surviving spouse, of the deceased may be served the food in the ceremonial house, but the consanguine relatives and the clan leader who officiates eat the food prepared in the cook house. If venison is plentiful, they are served the same type of stew as the others, minus the smoked ribs; but, if it is scarce, goat, kid, or pork is substituted. Coffee, tea, and fried bread are also served those who eat in the cook house. Visitors from outside the village are served in the cook house. This food is prepared by a woman friend of the host family who is not a consanguine relative and therefore not a mourner. She usually volunteers for this task and asks another woman to help her. Today, often a neighboring Mexican woman is hired to make wheat tortillas. At the end of the ceremony any remaining food that no one else wishes to take home is taken by the waiters and cooks.

Not infrequently, a family needs to have an adoption ceremony for a child but is unable to to bear the cost alone and therefore waits until some relative or friend has one for an adult; then, if agreed, they have both on the same occasion and share the expense. Such a case may occur when a man's dance is held. At sundown upon termination of the dance, a second ceremony, a game, may be held if the child belonged to the Man clan or one of its associates, Water, Raccoon, Fire, and Coyote, since all other clans must play games just before daybreak; however, if a man's dance which lasts until sunset is followed by a moccasin game which lasts until sunrise, the second ceremony can be adjusted for a child who belonged to any but the Man clan and its associates. The second game is played just before sunrise.

If a game follows a dance, the number of waiters is increased from six to eight, and the number of cooks from four to six. On this occasion, not only is the reciprocal clan pattern followed, but also half of the waiters and cooks must belong to each moiety. The reciprocal clan pattern takes into consideration the clans of both persons for whom the ceremonies are being held, should they belong to different clans. For instance, if the man for whom a dance is being given is Buffalo and the child is Thunder, the proper reciprocity can be achieved by calling waiters and cooks from the associated clans of both.

Man's Dance

In the event the deceased man for whom an adoption ceremony is held left a widow, certain precautions must be observed on the morning of the fiesta. The widow, accompanied by a female relative of the deceased who has earlier been designated as her sponsor for the duration of her widowhood, leaves the village. Today, it is customary to drive by car to the nearby Negro village or into Múzquiz while the ceremony takes place. Formerly, in the days of horses and wagons, the widow rode with the relative far into the *monte* in an easterly direction, out of earshot of the drum. If too feeble or ill to travel, she stays in the home of the relative who lives in the most easterly house. This precaution is based on the belief that the spirits of a couple travel together after marriage, and, since the drum calls the spirit of the deceased to appear at his adoption ceremony, it is unsafe for the widow to be within range of the drum, for fear the deceased's spirit might attempt to take her with him.

After the widow departs, the consanguine relatives clear the previously enlarged house of its furnishings, except for the bench mats. The waiters since dawn have been clearing the compound and attending to the many tasks involved in the preparations. The clan leader arrives with the deceased's clan bundle. The clan leader sits on the south bench, near the western one already occupied by the mourners. He begins the long prayers in which he announces to Kitzihiat and Pepazcé the purpose of the ceremony. In his prayers he includes words of hope and comfort for the mourners. The spirit of the deceased is called with the drum to witness and approve of this rite given to please him. Visitors offering condolences sit briefly near the mourners but exchange no words. Waiters and cooks snatch short rests on the south bench near the opening, while the chanters sit in the center of the south bench.

After two or three hours of prayers and chants and when the first feast is to be served, the men dancers and invited kinswomen, gathered at the home of the head dancer, are notified by a waiter or a cook that they are expected. They enter the house by the south side—as for all ceremonies—and approach the hosts sitting on the west bench, to whom the men return their invitation sticks, unless they have passed them to kinswomen, in which case these return them. They circle to the north and sit in the center of the north bench, reserved for them.

The area cleared in front of the house for a man's dance is a rectangle of approximately sixty by thirty feet. About forty feet from the front of the house and directly in line with the door, the cooks stake a crossbar for the gifts. In the center of the area east of the crossbar they build a small fire brought from the deceased's bundle house and constantly fed by one of the waiters. Some fifteen feet from the entrance and directly in line with the door, a long sapling is staked in the ground. If it is an extremely warm day, a canopy supported by staked saplings, under which the chanters sit, is built directly in front of the door.

After the first feast, the waiters clear the area in front of the house. At once, the dancers, followed by their kinswomen, pour out of the house and sit on a tarpaulin on the north edge of the dance area reserved for them during intermissions. As the chanters leave the house, they sit on another tarpaulin placed directly in front of the entrance and behind the tall sapling. Last to leave the house is the clan leader, who sits with the chanters. When all the performers are outside, a relative of the deceased leaves the house, arms laden with dress lengths and gifts for the adopted one and his companions, and drapes them over the crossbar, placing the adopted one's special gifts on the west end of the bar.

A waiter leaves the house with a carton of cigarettes and a new buckskin, which he lays on the ground at the foot of the westernmost upright of the crossbar and on which he empties the cigarettes. These will be replenished as needed until the end of the dance.

The Kickapoo men do not dress uniformly for the dances and certainly have nothing approaching a costume. The ideal is to wear the Kickapoo traditional dress.

Formerly, dancers wore only a breechcloth, leggings, and moccasins. Below their knees they tied rattles made with fringed strips of buckskin about three inches wide, on the end of which they secured triangular pieces of tin. They wore long German-silver earrings dangling from pierced earlobes, heavy silver bracelets around the upper arms, and several strings of glass, bronze, and bone beads. Below their knees they placed handsomely beaded garters.

In those days the adopted one, on arriving at the home of his hosts, was immediately dressed in a totally new outfit, consisting of a pair of moccasins with delicately beaded insteps and flaps, leggings, a breechcloth, a beribboned shirt, beaded garters, a vest decorated with beads and German-silver buttons and brooches, several strings of beads, bracelets, earrings, and a fine Indian blanket. He was dressed in new clothing three times annually thereafter at the feasts for the dead held by the family for the spirit of the deceased he had represented.

Today, the adopted one is usually the only dancer who appears in the traditional Kickapoo dress—and his own, at that—while the other dancers wear what they please, usually tan drill shirts and trousers, with shoes, boots, or moccasins. Some wear the frontier-style shirt, while occasionally one sees an old man wearing broadcloth leggings with ribboned edges. The Indian blanket has lately been replaced by a fringed shawl worn by both men and women. Some of the men throw it over their shoulders in a coquettish manner, while others tie it around their waists. Occasionally, an old man appears with a feather in his queue, either perpendicular or slanting, depending on his ability as a warrior. Some dancers wear sleigh bells around their ankles. At a dance we witnessed, one of the dancers wore a three-inch safety pin on his vest and an old mink fillet around his head, the tail dangling down his back. Another dancer cut a particularly bizarre figure, wearing a frontier-style shirt, no trousers, a breechcloth, a fringed shawl around his waist, western-style socks which reached midway up his calf, and oxfords. The clan leader and the chanters wear everyday work clothes, a pair of drill trousers, a shirt, and shoes or moccasins. The aunts and nieces, invited kinswomen of the dancers, do not usually wear the traditional dress seen at a woman's dance, appearing in anything that strikes their fancy.

Although moiety affiliation plays no part in a man's dance, unless it is followed by a game, some men streak their faces with their color. Others display Indian souvenirs, such as pendants, moccasins, and feather headgear, purchased in the United States.

As the clan leader beats a staccato on the drum, the dancers take their places. The kinswomen form lines directly on the south and north edges of the dance area, where they shuffle in place, swaying their bodies to the rhythm of the drum and the chants. Any female who wishes may join the two lines of women and accompany them as long as she wishes, in the belief that participation in the dance pleases the spirit of the deceased.

The male dancers move back and forth between their female kinswomen in a loose north-and-south movement. Three different steps are used at various times. One consists of two steps on one foot, repeated on the other foot and followed by a short walk of several steps. The second consists of two steps on one foot, repeated on the other foot, with a pause while the dancers emit a short whoop. The third is the same as the first, with the dancers crossing each other back and forth from north to south. Twice during the dance, once halfway and once toward the end, the kinswomen enter the dance, following their hosts around the crossbar with a simple trotlike step.

At the end of each round of dances, the performers and guests rest on the tarpaulins and are served refreshments. If dancers go to the *monte* to relieve themselves, they must go in an easterly direction so as not to meet the spirit, who is hovering in the west watching his favorite dance.

During the short intermissions, lasting no more than fifteen minutes, one of the old men privileged to wear a feather in his queue in a perpendicular position approaches the staked sapling in front of the chanters and taps it with a short wand. We were told that these men pray, asking Kitzihiat and Pepazcé to assist the spirit to find his way to the dwelling place of his kin. The spirit is told not to mind dying, not to mind leaving, not to turn or look back upon his relatives, but to continue on his way. If the deceased was a warrior and killed others, the old man prays that he may be forgiven and find the road easily. The old man, while admonishing the spirit, points to the four directions, telling him not to take the road to the east, or to the north, or to the south, but the road to the west, which leads to the spirit world. After each tap made on the post, the drummer echoes with a few beats. After these admonitions, the old man passes the wand to another, who is entitled to use it during the following intermission.

As the sun begins to set behind the nearby hills, a long pole is placed to the east of the crossbar where the gifts are draped. The waiter who made the drum takes over and moves it back and forth to moisten the buckskin and give it resonance. There follows a brief dance. The fire in the center of the area is allowed to die slowly. One of the waiters loosens the dress lengths, while another gathers the buckskin where the supply of cigarettes has been spread.

At this moment, the invited kinswomen join the dancers, each to the left of her host, and they dance in an ellipse around the crossbar and the pole recently placed to the east. As each man passes near the crossbar, he picks up a dress length and hands it to his kinswoman. In the meantime the buckskin over the drum has been loosened and the beat becomes weaker and weaker, finally dying out. The dancers and their kinswomen go to the home of the adopted one, where they pile the dress lengths on a bench.

Trailing the dancers go the four cooks. One of them picks up the long pole placed east of the crossbar and hoists it on one shoulder, while the other three dismantle the crossbar and follow the dancers now leaving the compound and going up the lane to the home of the adopted one. As the four cooks pass south of the house, they throw the saplings to one side. The headwaiter, carrying the small brass kettle of corn gruel, follows the dancers. As soon as the drum is heard no more, all of the mourners and others indoors file out quickly.

After arriving home, the adopted one invites his companions and guests to share with him and the spirit the *lonche* prepared for them. The dancers sit to the north, east, and south of the fire, while the host places a bit of the gruel to the west of the fire. This is the offering to the spirit to sustain him until arrival in the hereafter. When every grain has been eaten, that portion served to the spirit is carefully gathered into the fire and burned. During the night this fire is allowed to die, and in the early morning the ashes are deposited on the west edge of the compound where ashes for ceremonies for the dead are piled.

After the meal, the adopted one redistributes the dress lengths to the dancers' kinswomen. Before retiring, all must bathe in the river. Later, that same evening, a relative of the deceased takes one-third of the possessions left by the former to the adopted one.

In case a widow has left the village for the duration of the ceremony, her sponsor takes her home, where she finds that her consanguine relatives have replaced the furnishings and the waiters have restored the entrance to its usual width. Four days later, the widow begins the ritual of being released from any further obligations to her affinal relatives.

Man's Dance followed by Moccasin Game

Occasionally, a family decides to hold a man's dance followed by a moccasin game—the latter always played at night. In this case, the moieties, which usually play no role in the choice of the dancers and waiters in a man's dance, become of the utmost importance. Instead of one individual being chosen to be the adopted one, two are selected, one from each moiety, to head the teams playing the moccasin game after the dance. Only after termination of the game does the family know which of the two friends will be the adopted one. There are twenty dancers, rather than the ten for a regular man's dance.

The number of men waiters and women cooks is the same as for a dance; but for this occasion there is one headwaiter and one head cook from each moiety, still taking into consideration the reciprocal pattern of the deceased's clan. The first task of the headwaiters is to make the invitation sticks, now twenty, ten covered with white clay from the river and ten smeared with soot. These are brought to the clan leader and hosts, who send out the first headwaiter with one stick to invite the team captain who belongs to the moiety of the deceased. The second headwaiter takes another invitation stick to the captain of the opposite moiety designated by the family. The captains appear at the home of the host, where they are instructed as to their honor and duties and are given the remaining sticks to invite nine others of their moiety, regardless of clan affiliation, to be dancer-players.

The second task of the waiters is to make a short board, two by six inches, smeared white on one side and black on the other, which the clan leader, who is the referee in games, throws into the air to determine which team begins the game. After this, the headwaiters make twenty slender scoring sticks of sticky Baccharis about two feet long and eight others, somewhat longer, to stake in the ground each time a team wins twenty points.

When a game follows a man's dance, so that moieties are important, the waiter who makes the drum must belong to the moiety of the deceased and be assisted by a waiter from the opposite moiety. The waiter belonging to the deceased's clan carries the drum on the first round, alternating with the second waiter. The first waiter loosens the drum at the end of the dance.

Each member of each team may invite a kinswoman, either an aunt or a niece, of the opposite moiety, who must appear at the dance-game with her face smeared with the color of her host—not hers—creating considerable hilarity among the spectators, who all know one another's moiety affiliations. During the dance, the guests form a line on either side of their hosts, the Kisko on the south, the Oskasa on the north. Chanters may be of any moiety or clan; the important requirement is that they know the songs.

Dancer-players arrive at the home of their host with faces streaked in their colors and sit on benches on their respective sides of the house, Kisko on the south, Oskasa on the north. A man's dance followed by a moccasin game ends differently from one in which only the dance is held. In this case, when the sun begins to set behind the hill, the drum is not loosened, the fire is not allowed to die, the dancers do not depart, and the mourners remain in the house. The dancers disappear for a few minutes while preparations are made for the game to begin. Waiters shake out the tarpaulins where the chanters and the dancers had been seated; although they create a veritable dust storm, no one seems to care. One canvas is placed in front of the house, one on the north edge of the dance area, and another on the south edge. In the meantime, other waiters take armloads of firewood, with which they replenish the small fire and build it into a huge bonfire. It and a few kerosene lanterns placed here and there provide the only illumination.

While these preparations are taking place, the clan leader stands before the entrance to the house holding the small black and white board, while the players line up on their respective sides. The clan leader announces to Kitzihiat and the spirit of the deceased that this game is being played to please him and hopes it is agreeable. He ends by warning the teams to play fair.

Spectators, players, and scorekeepers are all intently watching the clan leader as he throws the board into the air and it falls on the tarpaulin. The team to begin the game and win the first four points will be indicated by the color revealed. There follows a mad scramble to gather up the drum and receive the four pieces of buckskin—moccasins are not actually used—and the small bell and take them to the scoring side.

Players of the scoring side and others, not on the team but of the same moiety, form a tight circle around the four pieces of buckskin. A member of the scoring side shields the manipulation of the skins by spreading his shawl or blanket, wing fashion, in front of the players. The drum is beaten by one of the players on the scoring side with a lively and inviting rhythm while members of the opposing team line up on their side.

Suddenly, the scoring side is alive with excitement as it incites and invites the opposite team to discover under which skin the bell is hidden. A member of the opposing team, half dancing, half shuffling, approaches the scoring side. Much teasing goes on at this moment from members of the team that has the skins, bell, and drum, who repeat, ''First one, first one!''

Although the man selected to try his luck attempts to look serious, so much laughter and teasing is taking place that he cannot keep his face straight. He shuffles to the tight little group, whose members make a small opening for him and continue to dare him to find the bell under the first skin he turns over. Should he score, he takes the skins and bell to his side, while another player on his team picks up the drum. If he loses, he returns to his side, followed by louder teasing and laughter while another member of his team tries his luck. In the meantime the bell has again been reshuffled. The first team has four chances to score before the two teams change sides.

The clan leader, who is also the referee, and the two scorekeepers, who must be uncles or nephews of the captains, sit cross-legged on the tarpaulin in front of the house, the scorekeepers on their respective sides of the referee, with the twenty small scoring sticks and the eight large ones in front of the referee. When a team scores four points, by finding the bell under a skin during the four permitted tries, the referee passes a slender stick to that team's scorekeeper.

The game is played from sundown to sunup, with time out for two feasts, one held at midnight and the other shortly before the termination of the game. At this feast, any spectator who is hungry may eat.

The team scoring the majority of points by sunrise is the winner and receives the ten dress lengths; the captain of the winning team will be the adopted one. The losing team's members return to their homes, while the winners, followed by the headwaiter of their moiety, go to the home of the captain, where they share the corn gruel with the departing spirit and where the kinswomen receive the dress lengths, redistributed by the captain.

Formerly, it was thought that, if the spirit of the deceased enjoyed the game played to please him, the team carrying his moiety always won; if he was not pleased, his moiety lost. This, it was believed, showed the family whether they had chosen the right game, specifically in cases where the deceased left no previous instructions. However, the Kickapoos are no longer sure that this is true.

Drunk-Man's Dance

If a man has been a heavy drinker, the members of his family feel obligated to hold a drunk-man's dance to please his spirit, regardless of their personal feelings about drinking. This dance follows the same pattern as the regular man's dance except that the person selected to be the adopted one must be a recognized drunkard. If he is a lifelong friend of the deceased and of approximately the same age, so much the better; but these qualifications are not as important as the first. As many drunkards as possible are invited, but also included are two or three old men qualified to admonish the spirit.

We had the opportunity to witness this dance during our study. When we received the invitation, we were not told of its particular nature until we arrived at the home of our host. One of the waiters, a personal friend, came to explain that, since the deceased, who was an Oklahoma Kickapoo, had been a drunkard, a "bit of mescal" in soda pop would be served the dancers.

On this day, any drunkard, whether invited or not, may enter the dance; in fact, one might say that this is Drunkard's Day. Taking advantage of this opportunity, two of the most notorious drunkards, who were not invited as dancers and do not live in the village, showed up.

The dance had begun at noon, and by 4:00 P.M. the participants were more than somewhat unsteady on their feet. At this moment, three waiters appeared, each with an enameled-ware dishpan, the first filled with ceremonial ladles, the second with stew, and the third with chunks of fried bread. A fourth waiter, carrying a large soot-covered pot and several bowls, poured steaming hot coffee to the dancers, who were taking their rest period. Not only the dancers but all who were hungry were urged to take a ladle and dip into the dishpan of stew.

The intermission lasted about twenty minutes, during which we were invited to the cook house for a stew of goat meat, accompanied by bread and coffee. When we returned to the front of the house, where we had been sitting, the drum called the dancers back into the dance. Some had sobered up a bit with the food and coffee, but they soon began to make further trips to the house where the mescal was kept, returning to the dance with partially filled bottles and bowls, dancing and drinking at the same time, offering sips to their companions, and with each swallow becoming more and more unsteady on their feet.

An old man dancer, one of the two nondrinkers, approached the sapling staked in the ground in front of the chanters and, with a wand in his hand, tapped it. The chanters and dancers stopped while the old man, gesticulating and pointing the wand in the four directions, admonished the departing spirit not to look back, not to feel bad because he had to leave his beloved kin, but to take the road to the west which would lead him to Pepazcé. Each time the old man finished a recitation, he struck the sapling and the clan leader beat the drum as in an echo. During this time even the children were hushed. After this, the chanters began a new song and the dancers a new dance.

Suddenly, one of the two uninvited drunkards, who is clubfooted, went into the dance. His clubfoot did not permit him to compete with the others, but his enthusiasm made up for his handicap. As he beat his arms on his sides, much as a rooster flaps his wings when he crows, all of the spectators burst into laughter at his antics. Apparently pleased with himself, he stood in front of the chanters and began to admonish and gesticulate in imitation of the old man who was entitled to hold the wand. One of the Indian women next to us looked chagrined. We inquired, "What is he doing? He does not have the wand." She replied, "That one does not know the dance."

With this, one of the waiters hoisted the culprit on his back, marched out to the middle of the field, and dumped him, much to the hilarity of the spectators. The man picked himself up unconcernedly and, without apparent resentment, returned to the dance.

A child of about three began to shake one of the saplings that supported the canopy over the chanters. One of the dancers, although very drunk, went to correct him. Our Indian neighbor explained that it was the young man's duty to reprove the child, as he was an uncle (mother's brother). The little tot went off to another activity, a bit crestfallen but not crying. Later, the other drunkard from out of the village took the child by the hand and led him in a dance, to the amusement of the onlookers.

The dancers continued to become more and more unsteady. The young man who had corrected the tot began to reel; it looked as though it was the end for him. One of his aunts (father's sisters) shouted at him; the young man straightened his shoulders and resumed the dance. Prior to this incident, the same young man, who is an outstanding performer, had been very active and vociferous in demanding that the chanters not stop the songs, as he wanted to continue dancing. In spite of the warning from his aunt, he walked off the dance area and went behind the house, where he stumbled and fell to the ground. Another aunt went to his side and tried to unbuckle the jingle bells around his ankles, but he resisted her help. After this, his brothers and his mother went to take him home, but again he refused. He was left alone, but, instead of stretching out on the ground and falling asleep, he pulled himself together and resumed dancing.

Another Indian friend came to sit by our side and reported that the host of the dance was out dead drunk and that several others were imbibing more than was good for them. We saw one old man reeling out of the house where the mescal was kept and could hear small boys and girls squealing with laughter as they dashed in and out of the house, amused at the capers of their inebriated elders.

One of the dancers had found a long lariat, which he waved around his head like an animal trainer. The spectators gasped for fear he might hit someone; but luckily he did not touch any of the dancers, even with a tiny flick. The waiter in charge of the crossbar holding the gifts looked stern and serious, while another waiter ordered all the small fry out of the area.

A few minutes before the dance was to end, we heard a commotion from the direction of the cook house. We, as well as many others, stayed in our places. Shortly, we saw three men carrying one of the Indians, frantically struggling to free himself, across the field in the direction of his home. When they arrived at the barbed-wire fence of the compound, nothing seemed more difficult at the moment than to get a drunk, gesticulating man over, between, or under the wires. As he was carried to his home, the chanters stopped.

Suddenly, the chanters began another song and the dance was resumed. One of the cooks placed a long sapling east of the crossbar which held the gifts. The sun quickly began to set behind the hill, while the fire was allowed to die. The waiter who had made the drum loosened it, and the beats became more and more hollow until a hushed silence spread everywhere.

At this moment, the adopted one, who was still on his feet, followed by the four remaining dancers, and their invited kinswomen, departed. When all seemed to have come to an end, we were startled to hear a cry of "Corn gruel, corn gruel!" The adopted one had forgotten to wait for the headwaiter to follow him to his home with the *lonche* for the spirit.

Suddenly, everyone in the house poured out. In a matter of seconds, the stage was cleared. No one remained except us, unable to bring ourselves back to reality.

We are certain that the spirit of the deceased was highly pleased. Not only had the dance been a success, but several unplanned incidents had lent excitement and amusement to the spectators and, we hope, to the spirit, as he witnessed the ceremony held for him.

Though drunkards are held in low esteem in the village, on this day all had been permissiveness; all of those who dislike mescal and its effects had been sufficiently good-natured to tolerate such a flagrant display of inebriation. The village drunks, who seldom participate in clan activities, since they are not encouraged to live in the village, were, on this day, welcomed and allowed to drink to their full capacity. The incipient drinkers, the invited dancers, could take their fill today; no one criticized; no one disapproved; they only laughed.

Lacrosse, or Man's Ball Game

Lacrosse as played today by the Kickapoos is a much watered-down version of the former game. Informants in their sixties do not recall seeing the players use the racket throughout the game; however, the rackets were still in use at the turn of the century, as attested by an old Mexican who, from infancy, lived near the Kickapoos. In 1905, when he was fourteen years old, he recalls watching the game which the Mexicans called *la chueca* (bent or crooked), possibly from the fact that the sapling used to make the racket is bent to form the loop where the net of buckskin thongs is interwoven.

At that time the game, an affair attended not only by the Kickapoos but also by the surrounding Mexican ranchers and residents of the nearby Negro village, was sometimes played on four successive days. They commenced at dawn and played until noon, took time out for a feast, and resumed the game until sundown. Much betting went on between the two moieties, for, besides the regular gifts for the adopted one and the winning team, relatives also hung such articles as blankets, saddles, deer-skins, clothes, and lariats on the crossbar and gambled horses, calves, and fat pigs.

The men wore only moccasins and breechcloths; the Kisko painted their faces and torsos with white stripes, while the Oskasa came to the game striped with black. The game was rough and resulted in many blows, attended by an old herbal curer who was at hand with his deer-horn to extract the bloodclots resulting from the unfettered use of the rackets. Today's Kickapoos declare that not a single male would be alive if they had continued to play with rackets, so heated did tempers become during the game.

The preliminaries for the game are the same as those for any game played for an adoption ceremony. Each headwaiter prepares four slender scoring sticks in the color of his moiety. The two headwaiters also make five black and five white invitation sticks and a short flat board, painted white and black which, when thrown, indicates the team to begin the game. They make the goal posts, put them up, and take them down after the game.

A member of the Eagle clan has the prerogative of making the ball, fashioned from a new piece of buckskin about eight inches in diameter. It is tightly stuffed with deer hair. The raw edge of the buckskin is folded toward the center about half an inch, basted with a stout thread, and pulled to make a receptacle for the hair. When enough hair is packed in to form a firm and semihard ball, the thread is tightly pulled until the opening is closed.

As soon as the captains have accepted the invitation to play, they seek out an uncle (mother's brother) or brother to make a racket for each. The same uncle or brother is the scorekeeper during the game. The racket, now used only as a token, is made from a peeled pecan sapling six feet long and 1½ inches in diameter, flattened the last two feet and heated to bend it enough so as to fold it over into a slightly elongated hoop secured by twelve loops of buckskin thong. The flattened end which forms the hoop has eight holes burned into the sides, through which narrow thongs of buckskin are laced in such a way as to form a net. Frederick Webb Hodge calls this racket the Cherokee type.[5]

On the day of the game, the captains of each division, decorated with their colors, arrive at the house of the host and hand in their invitation sticks, unless they have passed them to kinswomen, in which case the latter accompany the players and return the sticks to the hosts. They sit on benches on their respective sides of the house.

As soon as the indoor ceremonies have terminated and the first feast has been served, the players, followed by their kinswomen, the scorekeepers, and the clan leader, step out of the house. A woman mourner follows with the gifts, which she hangs on the crossbar. Besides the standard gifts listed in the description of the man's dance, today the host sometimes supplies a horse or a calf for the winners.

While the teams, each captain holding his racket, stand at attention on their respective sides, with the kinswomen behind them, the clan leader, with the short board in his hand, prays to Kitzihiat that the game about to be played will please the spirit. He admonishes the teams to play fair and not to hurt each other. After these brief words, he flings the board into the air. All is expectancy as it lands on the ground to reveal which team is the first to go to the field and have the first try at the ball.

We shall briefly describe a ball game which we saw one late afternoon. The game was held to please the spirit of a man who had died suddenly in Texas and was buried in Eagle Pass because the border authorities did not permit the entrance of his body into Mexico. There was some doubt in the minds of the Kickapoos whether it was worth bothering to have the adoption ceremony, as he had not been buried in the Kickapoo way— holding in his fists two bits of Indian tobacco as an offering to Pepazcé— but the ceremony was held just in case. One informant observed, "That one will never make it there." As he belonged to the Man clan, the game was played in the late afternoon, shortly before sunset.

When we arrived at the clearing where the game is played, two goals had been staked in the ground about two hundred feet apart, one on the north side, the other on the south, "as the world is made," a woman who explained the game to us said. The goals were made from two saplings of Texas persimmon, set eight feet apart from each other, with a crossbar placed about halfway up.

A large crowd of spectators was hovering around a huge bonfire in an effort to keep warm on this chilly, overcast February day and enjoying the steaming tamales with which a Negro woman from the neighboring village was doing a thriving business. Suddenly, a pickup arrived in a cloud of dust, bringing five Kisko players and their invited kinswomen, all painted in their distinctive white. Hardly had the dust settled when another pickup brought the Oskasa and their kinswomen, their faces smeared with black. After the arrival of the players, those present formed a loose circle around the field; others continued to come by foot, horseback, or car.

Each captain carried a lacrosse racket in his hand. The Kisko captain, the first to play in this case, hit the ball once with his racket in the direction of the west and leaned the racket against one of the goal posts on his side of the field. In the meantime, the ball was crazily thrown by hand among the players, while the referee and the scorekeepers ran back and forth, ready to hand the score sticks to each other in the event of a point—made by getting the ball through the two posts of the opponent's goal—while ducking the interceptors of passes. The game was fast, rough, and short.

Since the Oskasa were unable to score, the Kisko scorekeeper invited all spectators to join the game in an effort to help the losing team. There ensued a mad scramble, and in seconds the field was running over with players—women, men, and children. The game came to an abrupt end when the Kisko captain threw the eight score sticks into the air. The Kisko had won, and the Oskasa had not scored one point, even with the additional support.

The ball was thrown far into the *monte* by the captain of the winning team. This ball, if found by children, may be saved and used, without the rackets, which the captains keep, once all of the adoption ceremonies have terminated and the summer houses are occupied.

There were some ugly words exchanged between members of the moieties, as the winning team teased the other savagely. One woman picked up a stone and was on the verge of throwing it at a woman of the opposite moiety, but had second thoughts when her intended victim merely grimaced at her. Tempers cooled rapidly, as the players dispersed and everybody returned to the village. As the Kisko members left the grounds, they shouted, "How good it is the Kisko won; how good it is the Kisko won!" The losing team went home, while the winners returned to the home of their host to pick up their gifts, including the kettle of corn gruel which they shared with the spirit of the deceased.

Bow and Arrow Game

The bow and arrow game is usually played to please the spirit of a boy up to the age of seven. It is sometimes played alone; but, as often as not, it follows either a man's dance, a moccasin game, or a woman's dance. The number of players is six, three from each moiety, all young boys. The preliminaries are the same as in any other adoption ceremony when a game is played, while the number of waiters and cooks depends on whether the game is played alone or after another game or dance. An uncle or an older brother of the dead child makes the bows and arrows for each of the players. The waiters make the three white and three black score sticks and the two targets, one of each color, which are staked in small depressions approximately sixty feet from each other, the white one on the south and the black on the north of the field. Each player may invite as his guest an aunt or niece of the opposite moiety, who comes to the game with the color of her host.

Woman ready for a dance. Note the old-style blouse with German-silver ornaments.

Kickapoo maidens dressed for a dance.

304   Rituals and Ceremonies

The object of the game is to hit the target or the depression, thereby scoring a point. Scorekeepers of the opposite team stand at each target to see if an opponent hits it.

A small crossbar is built to drape the gifts for the adopted one and the dress lengths for his companions, winners of the game. The losing team members go home, while the adopted one and his team eat the *lonche* in the company of the spirit, and the leader redistributes the dress lengths.

Woman's Dance

Unlike a man's dance, always held during the day, a woman's dance may be given during the day or night, depending on which moiety the deceased belonged to. If she was a Kisko, she should have a day dance; if Oskasa, a night dance; but if the deceased left word that she preferred the alternative time to that to which she was entitled, her wishes are carried out.

If the woman for whom the dance is being held leaves a widower, he departs from the village, accompanied by a male relative of the deceased wife, who is his sponsor during his widowerhood, while the ceremony takes place.

The number of women dancers is ten, each of whom may invite anyone to partake of the first feast. Men waiters or women cooks go to notify them to take their own ladles and those of their respective hostesses to the feast and, upon termination, return them to their homes.

The number of waiters and cooks is six and four, respectively; but it increases to eight and six if a second adoption ceremony follows. The headwaiter makes the ten invitation sticks. Waiters make the crossbar to hang the kettles of food given to the second chanters, and the cooks make the crossbar to hang the gifts, a short distance to the east of the kettle bar.

After the first feast, eaten in the house, the dancers circle around the open rectangle four times while the clan leader beats the drum and, after leaving the rectangle, rest momentarily on tarpaulins on the north side of the dance area while the chanters sit under a canopy immediately in front of the house.

When all the performers are outside, the dancers promenade clockwise around the two crossbars, while a chanter, the drummer, the waiter carrying the drum, a man shaking a rattle, the clan leader, and mourners who wish to accompany them stand in a cluster on the southwest corner of the dance area near the house during the forty-five minutes of the first dance.

It is usually the prerogative of the clan leader to sing the first set of

Woman's dance, accompanied by chanters, drummer, and gourd shaker (at right). The drummer has his back to the camera. (The Kickapoos do not ordinarily allow anyone to photograph their dances and absolutely refuse to allow photographs of the drum.)

four songs, each repeated three times; if the dance is given for a daughter, the father is privileged to lead the first set of songs. When this set comes to an end, the clan leader turns the drumstick over to another chanter, goes to eat in the cook house, and returns to continue prayers in the presence of the mourners.

At this time, the woman in charge of the food in the cook house notifies the mourners that they may go to be served in small groups of three or four, first the men, followed by the women and children. Four mourners leave the house, their arms filled with gifts and dress lengths for the adopted one and her companions, and drape them on the crossbar.

In the meantime, the chanters are singing and the dance is underway. The women form a line, facing westward, and, with bodies almost touching, begin the clockwise dance, consisting of four little hops, followed by three steps; sometimes the hops are directed forward; sometimes a bit to the left or right. When the first long dance comes to an end, the dancers, chanters, and their guests sit cross-legged on the tarpaulins and are served refreshments and cigarettes lit with a piece of firewood.

During this rest, the chanter whose turn it is to beat the drum and lead in the singing sits on his heels with head bent low and eyes closed in a barely audible prayer, while the drum lies before him. When the time arrives for the second set of songs and accompanying dance to begin, the headwaiter approaches the chanter, in front of whom he lays the drum, shifting it back and forth to moisten the skin for resonance. The chanter beats a short staccato, signal for the dancers to fall in line. With this, the headwaiter or his assistant places the drum over his shoulders and begins to move slowly backward in front of the seated chanters until he reaches the northwest corner of the dance area. He is followed by the chanter with the drumstick, the chanter with the rattle, the female chanter, and anyone who wishes to join in the singing, all facing him. At the corner they stop long enough to finish the first song, repeated three times, before moving to the northeast corner, where they stop again, and so on, until they return to the house, having circled the dancers on the outside.

When eighty to one hundred are in the dance, the female mourners are told by the clan leader that they may join the dancers. The ceremonial cooks also join at this time, but not those in the cook house. At the end of the dance, the clan leader sings another set of chants, in which all the mourners join him.

In the event another adoption ceremony is held on the same day, whether for a boy or a girl, the invited players dance behind the women dancers. In the case of a night dance, the young children invited to the second adoption ceremony are sent to their homes and do not return until shortly before daybreak, in time to play the game.

Formerly, the adopted woman was dressed in an all new outfit at the dance and thereafter three times annually at the feast for the dead to which she was the first to be invited; but, as with the men, this is no longer done.

When the ceremony ends, the waiters take the kettles of food to the homes of the second chanters, who invite others to share them, while the headwaiter follows the dancers to the home of the adopted one with the small brass kettle filled with the *lonche* for the spirit. The adopted one redistributes the dress lengths among her companions, who later give them to nephews or uncles.

Woman's Double-Shinny Ball Game

Like lacrosse, today's double-shinny ball game is a much diluted version of its former self. Informants in their fifties recall seeing all the women on the two teams, each with a shinny stick, with which they threw the double ball without touching it with their hands. Today, only two sticks are made, one for each captain; the ball is thrown with the stick once, after which the stick is placed at the foot of one of the goal posts, and play is continued by hand.

The preliminaries for this game are like those for lacrosse, and the ball field and goal posts are made in the same way. The game is usually reserved for a girl under seven. Although the captains who head the players are of the approximate age of the deceased, the other four players are older girls or women who know the game.

The double ball, about four inches long and two inches wide, is held together with a piece of buckskin thong and stuffed with deer hair. It is made by a man from the Eagle clan entitled to this privilege. The sticks, made by an uncle or brother of the same moiety as the players, are about three feet long, heated at one end while still green, bent over, and tied with buckskin thong until the desired crook is obtained.

The headwaiters make the ten scoring sticks, five white and five black, and the small board painted with both colors which, when thrown, determines which side begins the game. The game consists in throwing the ball past and between the two goals, scoring one point each time. The winning side keeps the ball and the two sticks, with which the game may be played after the completion of adoption ceremonies.

Bowl and Dice Game

The bowl and dice game, though it is one of several used in the adoption ceremonies, is also popular in the village and is played the year around except during the time between the New Year festivals and the termination of adoption ceremonies. It is played by men, women, and children and is an occasion for considerable gambling.

The traditional equipment consists of a low wooden bowl and nine "dice," called "bones" in Spanish by the Kickapoos, which consist of seven flat disks five-eighths of an inch in diameter and two figures in the shape of an *i* without the dot, five-eighths of an inch high, the last two representing male turtles and the seven disks representing female turtles. The dice, made from deer antlers, are painted red on one side and left plain on the other.

A smaller wooden bowl, four inches in diameter, is used for the "kitty," in which each player antes twelve Texas mountain laurel beans. The object of the game is to shift or move the bowl in such a way that the seven disks turn over or the two *i* figures stand on their bases. The scoring consists of the assigned value given to each combination which turns up, from zero to twelve, the highest single score, which is reached when all seven disks turn up white and the two *i*'s stand on their bases.

This game is sometimes played for an adult woman but is usually reserved for a girl (occasionally a boy) under seven. It is sometimes played alone but usually follows a woman's or a man's dance. Although any number may play the game ordinarily, the number for an adoption ceremony is fixed at six, three of each moiety.

The dice and six scoring sticks, when used in an adoption ceremony, are newly made of lime prickly-ash by a waiter, who must belong to the same moiety as the deceased. Today, the bowl, instead of wood, is a new aluminum pie plate. The plate containing the dice is laid at the foot of the westernmost post of the gift crossbar until used by the players, either just before sunset or just before sunrise, depending on the clan of the deceased.

The team beginning the game, whose goal is for one side to win all six sticks, belongs to the moiety of the deceased. Each of the scorekeepers is an uncle or brother of the captains and belongs to the same moiety. The clan leader holds the six sticks and passes them back and forth to the scoring side, represented by the scorekeepers.

If the game follows a man's dance, the six girls stand on their respective sides of the dance area with the invited kinswomen of the dancers and mark time to the music by shifting the weight of their bodies from one foot to the other. They enter the dance, trailing the kinswomen, when these follow the male dancers. Later, the girls go into the dance area and perform a short, simple group dance alone.

If the game follows a woman's dance, the teams dance behind the ten invited dancers. If it is a night dance, they are sent home and return before daybreak to play their game. Besides the dress lengths and special gifts for the winning captain, today, a small blue enameled-ware covered kettle filled with candy, cookies, and other treats is indispensable. One woman who was allowed to have an adoption ceremony for her daughter following a man's dance was severely criticized when she failed to provide the small kettle; instead, she filled a silk scarf with treats for the winning captain.

Feast for the Dead

In late February or early March, after the New Year clan festivals and the adoption ceremonies have come to an end, adult men and women observe the first of three annual feasts for the dead.

The Kickapoos believe that the spirits of their dead must eat three times a year, as the living need three meals a day; otherwise, they will become hungry and be forced to eat foam off the water. The spirits do not look kindly upon their relatives when this negligence occurs and may bring them harm; therefore, after the death of a relative, it is incumbent that someone in the family assume the lifetime responsibility of having the three annual feasts. These are held only for consanguine relatives of the same generation and the generations immediately preceding and following. If the family is small, the surviving relatives may have to give the feasts for two or more spirits. It is not imperative that the feasts begin immediately after the adoption ceremony, but a lapse of more than four years must not be allowed.

The chief is the first to observe this ceremony and feast for the spirits of his kin, at which he officiates. Each person with this obligation assembles the necessary food for the feast: venison ribs, squash or pumpkin, and Indian corn for the stew, in which no salt or lard is used, flour and lard for the fried bread, and lastly, something sweet. If no venison is available, beef or pork ribs may be used. Formerly, when beaver was plentiful, this was the favorite meat served at the spring feast.

The host having the ceremony and feast ideally asks the leader of the deceased's clan to officiate, but any leader who knows the ceremony may be called. The host asks a waiter of any clan to serve the food, since no reciprocity is observed in this ceremony. The person who represented the deceased at the adoption ceremony is the first to be invited, but the remainder of the guests, six or eight, may be the waiter's choice.

This ceremony and feast is held in the home of the host. If the host is a man, he asks his wife to prepare the food; a single man asks the owner of the house where he lives to prepare it for him. A woman host prepares her own food.

At daybreak on the appointed day, the host bathes in the river and returns home, where the family members are given their breakfast and sent away for the day to the home of a relative. The house is tidied, the ashes from the hearth are removed, and fire, made with a bow drill, is brought from the host's clan bundle house. About midmorning the clan leader arrives and sits on the south bench toward the west, with the host opposite him on the north bench. The leader prays and offers tobacco to the fire, which, in turn, notifies the other manitous to carry the message to the spirit of the deceased, who dwells in the West with Pepazcé. The spirit is urged to attend the feast.

Soon the waiter arrives to see that all is in order. About noon, he notifies the guests that the feast is ready. They arrive with their ladles and sit on the south and north benches. If a game was played for the deceased's spirit at his adoption ceremony, the Kisko sit on the south side, the Oskasa on the north. Once the guests are settled, the leader prays again, asking for blessings and long lives for all those present and reminding them of their obligations to their departed kin.

The waiter takes a bit of the food from the brass kettle with his ladle and places it on the ground to the west of the fire for the spirit. After he has served the spirit, he empties the contents of the kettle into two large enameled-ware dishpans and places one in front of each group of guests, passing them broken pieces of fried bread and, later, the sweets.

Before beginning to eat, the leader places a bit of Indian tobacco near the food for the spirit and invites him to join them for this occasion by saying, "Your son (or daughter) is giving you tobacco and a feast; surely, come and join us on this occasion." After the feast, the leader prays again, asking the spirit to be kindly disposed toward his family, to look after them, and to remember that he is not forgotten.

When all have left by the north side of the house, the waiter, with the burnt end of a log, carefully rakes the food and tobacco offered the spirit into the fire, where it is allowed to burn until morning. Before breakfast is prepared, the ashes are gathered and deposited on the west side of the compound in a place specially reserved for this purpose.

In the summer, when the fruit of the cactus is ripe, the Kickapoos observe the second feast for the dead, at which only watermelon or cantaloupe is served. Since many are away at work, they must return either to the village or to Oklahoma or send money to a relative who holds the ceremony for them *in absentia*.

When they return to the village from their work, they observe the third and last ceremony for the spirits of their kin. They believe that, if the spirits have been well cared for during the year, they sleep through the cold winter and will not awaken until after the New Year clan festivals.

Nekanesheka's Woman's Dance and Menaquah's Buffalo Dance

Nekanesheka (Nicolás Elizondo), a member of the first Buffalo clan, is the owner of a woman's dance known by the Kickapoos in Spanish as Baile de Nicolás pa' las Mujéres (Nicolás's Dance for the Women). The dance is performed to please Kitzihiat and his *familiares* (relatives), to thank him for the blessings of the past year, and to ask that grace descend on the Kickapoos for another year.

Nekanesheka, a man in his sixties at the time of our study, inherited the dance from his father. He has been partially blind since youth and, since no woman marries a man unable to hunt, he lives with a female relative who, in Kickapoo terminology, calls him *son*. We would call him her cross-cousin. He holds the dance at the home of this woman. Nekanesheka received only the privilege of giving the dance and did not receive a bundle with it; therefore, he has to use the bundle of his clan. During our study, the man who owned the songs to the dance moved to Oklahoma and passed them to Nekanesheka.

Nekanesheka spends the time between one annual dance and the next collecting funds to defray the expenses he incurs. Through various

Nekanesheka on the day of his woman's dance.

means, he makes enough to buy ammunition and gasoline for the hunters to bring deer for the feast. Nekanesheka does not hold a ceremony and feast prior to the hunt, as the chief of the hunt does this himself, but he does provide the ammunition and gasoline for more hunts if the first is unsuccessful. During the dance he provides food for the invited clan leaders, who are special guests, the chanters and their female guests, the four women head dancers, the personnel who prepare the food, and any female, Kickapoo or other, who wishes to enter the dance. In addition, any man, woman, or child who wishes may partake of the ceremonial feast served at the end of the dance.

No one would ever recognize Nekanesheka as the owner of the woman's dance, when he is "king for a day," after seeing him in Múzquiz in his tattered, soiled begging clothes. On the day of the dance he wears his finest Indian dress: a long calico frontier shirt, adorned with narrow tucks and ribbons, a pair of handsome buckskin leggings, a black breechcloth which shows below his shirt, a kerchief on his neck, a feather in his neatly combed and beribboned braid, and a pair of black oxfords, recently shined.

A buffalo dance is held in the middle of Nekanesheka's woman's dance. Why these two dances are now given on the same occasion and whether this was always the case we do not know. The buffalo dance is a curing dance in which the manitou of the buffalo, credited with much mystic power, is invited to look upon the bodies of the participants and send his blessings, healing those who are ill. The dance is called "All the Buffaloes Are Running and Jumping" and is owned by Pancho Menaquah, leader of the Berry clan, who inherited it from his father. Nekanesheka and Menaquah give these dances while the winter houses are still occupied in late February or early March, after the New Year clan festivals and the first annual feast for the dead.

Both men and women may be cured during the performance of this ceremony—or, for that matter, anyone invited to be cured, regardless of whether he is a Kickapoo or not. The leading woman is one who, once unable to walk, had her health restored in this dance. Anyone who is cured is obligated to cooperate annually by participating in the dance and contributing provisions. These persons are taken into the Buffalo clan and enjoy its privileges and obligations but do not lose their affiliation with the clan in which they were named. Non-Kickapoo persons who are cured are also expected to contribute provisions but are denied association in the clan.

When it is time for Nekanesheka to hold the dance, he and Menaquah consult about details. Nekanesheka calls the leader of the first Buffalo clan to officiate. (This man was originally a member of one of the Bear clans but was cured in the Buffalo clan at this ceremony and eventually became the Buffalo leader.) The clan leader invites the leaders of the other four major clans to be special guests and to assist with the prayers. Nekanesheka calls two headwaiters, a member of the Fire clan to supervise the preparation of the food cooked indoors and a member of the Berry clan to supervise the food cooked outdoors. Other details are as for the woman's dance held in connection with an adoption ceremony. The outside headwaiter calls three to eight members of the Berry clan, depending on the number of deer available—one for each kettle—to assist him. The outside headwaiter also calls a woman of the Berry clan to prepare the food in the cook house and to get an assistant.

The food prepared in the brass kettle indoors consists of unsalted puppy, Indian corn, and pumpkin. It is especially blessed and is reserved for the five clan leaders and for anyone who may be ill and is attending the ceremony for the purpose of being cured. The food prepared outdoors consists of unsalted venison, including the head with the horns, pumpkin, Indian corn, potatoes, and rice. This food is primarily for the dancers and their guests, but also for anyone else who wishes to eat.

The women in the cook house prepare the food for the personnel, except the guest clan leaders and the dancers, make the fried bread for all, the coffee and tea, and ready the vegetables for the kettles cooking outdoors. The cook-house food contains the same unsalted ingredients as that cooked outdoors, but, if there is a shortage of venison, goat meat or pork is used.

The owner of the dance and the clan leader invite the four leading women dancers and the chanters, each of whom may invite an aunt or a niece as his guest to assist with the songs. The chanters ask men who are learning the songs to be the gourd shakers. The four leading women dancers must have been cured in this ceremony and must be proficient performers. The leading woman sits on the south bench immediately to the left of the door during the ceremony and intermissions, while the other three sit in the center of the north bench. The female guests of the chanters join their hosts in the center of the south bench.

Early, on the morning of the dance, the leader of the Buffalo clan takes the bundle to Nekanesheka's home. Sitting on the west section of the south bench and surrounded by the guest clan leaders, he opens the bundle, passes the articles through the smoke of cudweed, and places them on a fine buckskin laid over a finely woven cattail mat. A Mexican informant who was cured in this ceremony told us he had seen tails of badger and coyote, claws of badger and fox, rattlesnake rattles, a skull with an inserted feather, a tin can containing beans, a flute, a pipe, and a rattle laid out on the buckskin.

We were never allowed to witness a ceremony, but, from what we were told by our informants, we believe that this ceremony is very similar to that of the Fox Indians, described by Truman Michelson. Among the Fox, the leader takes tobacco from the bundle and goes to the fire, where he places four eagle feathers on the ground, one in each direction. He offers tobacco to the bundle and to the manitou of the fire, who is told that he has been put here by the Great Manitou, Kitzihiat, to help the people alert the manitous of the sky and the winds to notify the manitou of the buffalo that a ceremony is to be performed. When the leader estimates that rapport has been established with the manitous, he asks for blessings, health, and a long life, that the tribe's chief be protected, that their enemies be destroyed, and that they live as mortals again in the hereafter. The leader beats the drum four times, blows the flageolet four times, once in each direction, and chants a song four times.[6]

After several hours of prayers and chants, the ceremony is suspended. If a specific individual, man or woman, has been invited to be cured, he or she is requested to partake of the contents of the kettle cooking indoors and to dance later. Women suffering from female disorders may also be cured in this ceremony by drinking a decoction made from the bark of wild cherry, whose use is the exclusive property of the Buffalo clan.

Formerly, sometime during the ceremony, it was customary for the chanters to dip their hands and arms in a boiling kettle of food and extract portions, which they passed to their female guests. To avoid burning, the hands and arms were rubbed with the masticated root of Texas Hercules-club prickly-ash or similar roots. The men could also pick up hot coals after applying the root to their hands. Michelson states that the Oklahoma Kickapoos also performed this ritual,[7] but it is no longer done in Mexico.

After the midday feast, the clan leaders and chanters sit on their haunches on a tarpaulin in front of the house, protected from the sun by a temporary canvas shelter. These men continue to pray in barely audible voices, while behind them sit the female guests of the chanters.

The woman's dance is about to begin. Nekanesheka steps out of the house and, holding the drumstick in one hand, stands south of the seated men awaiting the inside waiter, who follows with the drum suspended around his neck. It is Nekanesheka's prerogative, as owner of the dance, to be the first to beat the drum for the first long dance. Upon hearing the staccato beat, signifying the start of the dance, the lead woman steps out of the house, followed by the other three, who casually line up, bodies almost touching, near the row of kettles, around which they will dance.

In the meantime, the leader of the Buffalo clan who officiated, with rattle in hand, joins Nekanesheka and the drum carrier, while one of the chanters, his female guest, and the youths learning the songs cluster around them and stand in the same location during the entire first dance. Nekanesheka, assisted by others, chants four songs, repeated four times. After these songs, the leader of the Thunder clan, who has been quietly praying, is handed the drumstick and replaces Nekanesheka. The new drummer sings four songs, repeated four times; he is followed by the leaders of the Berry and Man clans, and, finally, by the leader of Buffalo No. 2.

During the first set of songs, the four women—no others may enter this dance—staying close together, one behind the other, arms hanging limply by their sides, perform their dance, consisting of short hops alternating with a measured walk. Slowly but constantly they move in a clockwise direction around the crossbar from which hang the kettles of food. After the leader of the Man clan terminates his four songs, the first dance, lasting about forty-five minutes, comes to an end.

During a brief rest of fifteen minutes, while the dancers are served refreshments, all of the clan leaders and chanters continue to pray. Soon the outside headwaiter picks up the drum, which has been placed in front of the clan leader whose turn is next. The waiter places the rope over his shoulders; he and the drummer, a chanter and his female assistant, the gourd shaker, and the youths who are learning the songs pass in front of the seated men and stand in a cluster to their left. The leader of the Thunder clan, now the drummer, beats a quick staccato, and the four women, now joined by other women and girls, walk clockwise around the kettles while waiting for the music.

The drummer and his group, while standing in position, sing one song, repeated four times. After this, they slowly begin to move on the outside of the dancers, also in a clockwise direction, the drum carrier walking backward as the others, facing him, walk forward, while singing the remaining three songs, each repeated four times. Arriving at the northeast corner of the dance area, they stop to sing another song, repeated four times, then slowly move to the southeast corner of the area, then on to the place where they began, south of the seated men. This round of songs and dances lasts approximately the same amount of time as the first. This pattern is repeated until the end of the dance.

The men participating in the ceremony, except for the owner, are dressed in everyday work clothes. The older women, including the four principal dancers, wear somber solid or printed two-piece dresses consisting of a loose blouse and a full, tiered skirt. A bright kerchief is worn around the neck, pinned over one shoulder with a store-bought brooch. Several pieces of German-silver jewelry, including earrings, bracelets, and rings complete their adornment. Only occasionally does a woman now wear the old type of shawl-collared blouse, decorated with German-silver brooches.

The younger women and girls, ranging from matrons to toddlers, make up in brightness what their elders lack. They also wear the two-piece dress, but in bright prints or shiny, sleazy nylons. During the past few years it has become *de rigueur* to wear a small Spanish shawl wrapped around the waist, the fringe hanging over the full skirt. Around their necks they wear bright kerchiefs secured on one shoulder with brooches of brilliants. Many wear the hair pulled tightly back, ending in a braid, folded under and held in place with a large ribbon bow; others wear the hair in the latest bouffant style. All use numerous pieces of jewelry of the five-and-ten-cent-store variety; few now wear the old German-silver ornaments. The young girls paint round spots of rouge on their cheeks, and many, including the tiny ones, wear lipstick. Although the majority wear Kickapoo moccasins, the variety of footwear includes everything from U.S. Indian moccasins to cowboy boots.

After the second dance begins, many of the younger women and girls join the leading dancers. The dancers arrange themselves, bodies almost touching, in a graduated line, the end made up of three- and four-year-olds. When many dancers, from sixty to one hundred or more, have joined the group, one of the outside waiters places a long sapling east of the crossbar from which the kettles of food are hung. This lengthens the ellipse to give the dancers more room; if more dancers join, a second sapling is placed beyond the first in an easterly direction.

As soon as each dance comes to an end, the young girls dash off to play in many directions or assist each other in rewinding themselves into the Spanish shawls, which tend to droop during the dance. Others wipe off the perspiring and flushed faces of their companions while they are served refreshments.

Few Mexicans bother to witness this and other dances, but those who do are invited to participate. Usually a few cowboys and Negro visitors stand or sit on the ground at a discreet distance and refrain from making comments. Any Mexican or Negro woman or, for that matter, any female who is present and not menstruating may join the dancers.

About 6:00 P.M., Menaquah, leader of the Berry clan and owner of the buffalo dance, having just completed a round of chants, stops with his accompanists south of the seated men. The gourd shaker suddenly announces that the dance called "All the Buffaloes Are Running and Jumping" is about to begin and invites those present to participate. Menaquah begins to beat the drum in a new beat from that of the previous call to dance: two quick beats close together, repeated several times, followed by a single rapid beat, repeated several times.

At the sound of the last beat, the inside waiter, holding high above him the desiccated tail of a buffalo, followed by Menaquah, leads a line of men dancers encircling the women and children. Males of all ages, some with children in their arms, and many women not in the dance before, with babes in their arms or supporting crippled relatives, begin to form two long ellipses, loosely aligning themselves two or three abreast. Men, who take off their hats and hold them under their arms, and women and children trot during this dance rather than following a pattern as in the previous ones. There is much jostling, horseplay, and laughing, some of the older men and women moving from side to side while lowering their heads and thrusting them upward in imitation of a herd of buffaloes on the run.

Individuals go into the dance and fall out at different times. As many as two hundred participate, creating great clouds of dust, of which they seem unmindful. Guests and spectators are all urged to join. At the end of each set of quick drum beats, all of the participants emit a whoop.

At the termination of this dance, which lasts about twenty minutes, Nekanesheka's dance resumes. The men withdraw and leave the dance area to the women, who continue until eight or nine o'clock, when another feast is served. At this time, while the waiters are pouring the food into large enameled-ware dishpans, everyone who wishes to partake quickly runs home to get his ceremonial ladle. The dishpans are set on the ground and surrounded by the dancers and relatives, who ladle out the food while waiters refill the dishpans and bring pieces of fried bread.

The Chief's Ceremonies

The chief of the Kickapoos in Mexico leads an extremely busy life, giving numerous ceremonies; also, it is his prerogative to attend any ceremony, but he is particularly expected to be present at each naming and each boy's first-hunt ceremony. He holds several ceremonies related to the construction of the houses, the planting of corn, squash, and beans, and the feast of the first fruits, in which the taboo for eating the new green crops is lifted. The chief also observes his own arrival and departure ceremonies and the triannual feast for the dead.

House-Construction and Planting Ceremonies

In late October or early November, the chief takes one of his bundles to the house of a kinswoman and holds a ceremony in which he transfers his authority to one of the clan leaders to supervise the construction of the winter houses, a post which rotates annually. At this ceremony, to which all Kickapoo house owners are invited, the chief presents his new appointee, instructs those present to follow the new temporary chief's leadership, and prays that the women may have success in their search for construction material and be protected from harm. In preparation for this occasion, the chief, as his prerogative, asks a good hunter to provide a deer. Waiters from the Berry, Buffalo, Thunder, or Tree clan cook the unsalted venison with Indian corn and, when the feast is ready, go out into the village to invite all who wish to partake.

On the following day, the newly appointed temporary chief has a small ceremony at his clan bundle house, at which no women are present. He then personally calls on each of the seventy-six Kickapoo house owners and announces that it is time to gather the necessary building materials.

As soon as the women gather this material, they build the winter houses, cover them with new, double-thick cattail mats made the previous year, occupy them, and hold their individual house-dedication ceremonies. After this, the temporary chief holds a ceremony to which all Kickapoo house owners are invited, at which they are granted permission to gather cattails and served a feast of venison ribs, Indian corn, and squash or pumpkin. In case a death occurs among the house owners during the time the new appointee is in office, he returns the command to the regular chief, who names a new man.

In the early spring, after the New Year clan festivals, the temporary chief appointed in the fall has a ceremony in which he returns the command to the permanent chief. After resuming command, the chief holds a ceremony at his home, offering tobacco to the manitou of the one-seed juniper and granting the women permission to gather saplings of this tree, sotol scapes, and yucca. The chief instructs the women on the type of material to use and how to repair or rebuild the summer house and sets a time limit to ready it: two moons after their New Year; after this, they no longer may cut juniper saplings. In this last ceremony he includes prayers and a tobacco offering to Grandmother Earth so that she may yield bountiful crops. Permission to plant corn may be obtained from the chief at this ceremony, or they may wait for this until after Menaquah's woman's dance and buffalo dance are held.

When the women have refurbished or rebuilt the summer houses and all is in readiness except the mat roofs, the chief has a ceremony permitting the women to remove the mats from their winter houses, cover the summer houses, occupy them, and dismantle the winter houses. In the meantime, the chief asks a good hunter to provide a deer for the feast. While the men are hunting, the chief's wife, as her prerogative, is the first to cover her summer house with cattail mats. After the hunters return, a feast, attended only by men, is held in the chief's newly covered house. This is the signal for all other house owners to cover their summer houses.

House-Dedication Ceremony

Twice a year, in the fall, and in the spring, each owner of a Kickapoo house, after moving into new or refurbished quarters, has a house-dedication ceremony and feast to notify Kitzihiat that she has fulfilled her obligations. In preparation for the feast, the house owner may have fattened a puppy, or she may be fortunate enough to have a relative who has killed a deer and saved her the ribs. If she has no meat, she serves unsalted Indian corn and squash or pumpkin.

When her house and provisions are ready, she arranges the date and time for the ceremony with her clan leader, who calls a waiter of the proper reciprocal clan of the hostess to serve the food. Early on the morning of the appointed day, she bathes in the river before sunrise, returns home to prepare breakfast for her family, and sends them off to a relative. She tidies the house, takes out the old ashes, secures fire made with a bow and drill from her bundle house, and prepares the feast in a large brass kettle.

About midmorning, shortly before the leader arrives with the hostess's clan bundle, she throws branches of one-seed juniper into the fire to smoke out any evil forces in the house. When the leader arrives, she sits alone in the house with him: he, cross-legged on the south bench near the west end of the house; she, in the same fashion on the north bench to the right of the door.

The leader asks the occasion for the ceremony, and the hostess explains that she has finished her house and wishes to notify Kitzihiat. The leader opens the bundle, from which he extracts Indian tobacco, and, walking to the fire, kneels to make it an offering of tobacco, asking it to carry the message to the sky, to the four corners, and the four winds to alert Kitzihiat that this ceremony is about to take place. When the clan leader judges that Kitzihiat has been reached and communication established, he notifies him that the owner of the house has fulfilled her obligations in the construction of her house as he commanded and asks that the home be protected from evil and that the owner and family be blessed with a long and healthy life.

Shortly before noon, the waiter arrives to see that all is in readiness. After appraising the amount of food, he goes out into the village to invite six or eight guests—men, women, and children—carefully avoiding members of the hostess's clan and her blood relatives. The guests, arriving with their ladles, sit in the center of the north bench. Before serving the feast, the leader prays that all of those gathered to celebrate this occasion may be blessed. After the prayers, the waiter ladles out the food from the brass kettle into two large enameled-ware dishpans and sets them before the guests and the leader.

The guests, when leaving along the north side of the house, thank the hostess as they pass in front of her. The hostess allows the fire to die down until morning, when she sweeps the ashes and deposits them at a designated place in the compound.

Ceremony for the French Medal

It was brought to our attention that the Kickapoos have in their possession at least three and perhaps four medals given to their ancestors by the French, English, and Spanish during the eighteenth century. With the passing of time, the medals have acquired magical significance, so that they are now considered manitous and therefore are of sufficient importance to merit an annual ceremony and feast. In spite of our efforts to see all of the medals, we succeeded in seeing only one—that given to them by the French.

In 1756—the date shown on the medal—or thereabout, during the time the Kickapoos were allied with the French in defending from the English the Ohio-Illinois perimeter of New France,[8] one of the Kickapoo chiefs, Eh-chi-chi, received a silver medal for his participation. The present owner, after some persuasion and promise of an adequate recompense, was kind enough to bring the medal to our home for examination. He did not, however, allow us to photograph it.

Through a small loop at the top of the medal runs a green silk ribbon, green being the color which symbolizes everlasting life. The oval-shaped medal is 2½ inches long and 1¾ inches wide. The obverse side bears the head of the king, facing right. The legend to the left of the profile reads LUD. XV REX, while to the right appears the word CHRISTIANISS; in exergue is the date, MDCCLVI. On the reverse side appears the effigy of a female figure dressed in a flowing Greek robe, both arms upstretched, each holding a crown; in exergue are the words FEODERUM VENDIX.

The present owner informed us that, when the medal was presented to his ancestor, he was told that he and his people must always wear the Kickapoo dress as a means of recognition by their friends upon their return. This legend fits in with the fact that, by 1759, the French were on the retreat in America and were hard pressed to defend even the old settlements of Montreal and Quebec.[9] The Kickapoos have waited a long time for their friends, who never returned—for, by 1763, all of present Canada and the old Northwest Territory, so diligently defended by the French with the aid of the Kickapoos, had been ceded to the English in the Treaty of Paris.[10]

The widow of the medal's former owner told us that one of her daughters is the present custodian, but the medal is "owned" by a male heir, a nephew. It is customary to pass the medal and the responsibility for the ceremony to a son, but, in the event that the former owner leaves no sons, the medal is passed to a younger brother or a nephew. The widow also provided the information that Eh-chi-chi, when given the medal, was wearing a round gorget suspended from his neck. When the French inquired the significance of the gorget, Eh-chi-chi replied that it represented the "world." This recalls to mind the myth of the creation of the Indian world by the culture hero, Wisaka, in which the world was described to us as a tortilla. The French told Eh-chi-chi that the silver medal given to him, unlike the pottery gorget, would never break, would last forever, and would never change. According to other informants, the present owner also inherited a French flag given with the medal. The owner affirmed that they do not allow the medal to tarnish, since this negligence could bring disease to the Indians; however, when we inspected it, it was oxidized.

The owner invites the leaders of the clans to help with the prayers and chants on the day of the ceremony. The prerequisite is that they wear the traditional Kickapoo attire, in remembrance of their agreement with the French. The only woman present is the custodian. The ceremony, at which the owner officiates, begins at daybreak and ends at noon, when the host offers a feast of unsalted purple Indian corn gruel. Further details on the ritual of this ceremony were impossible to obtain.

Fabila states that a Kickapoo chief, Pemwetamwâ, who lent his services to Spain while that country was in possession of Louisiana, received a medal with the effigy of Charles III on a visit to New Orleans in 1784. According to Fabila, this medal is still in the possession of the Kickapoos.[11] Nothing was learned about the ceremonies associated with this or other medals.

Menaquah's Woman's Dance and Buffalo Dance

Menaquah owns both parts of the second combination woman's dance and buffalo dance observed by the Kickapoos. Except for details, the woman's dance is like the other, owned by Nekanesheka and held earlier, when the winter houses are occupied. According to some informants, Menaquah's dance is a curing dance in its entirety, the buffalo dance inserted in the middle of the woman's dance being the most beneficial part; but it is our opinion that two different dances may have been condensed and combined, the woman's dance being a fertility dance and the buffalo dance serving not only for curing but also as the remnant of a ritual formerly observed before and after the hunt in which sympathetic magic was exercised.

Menaquah's dance formerly was closely connected with the crops of corn, beans, and squash and was held twice annually, once when the corn was about two feet high and had three to four leaves and again when the roasting ears were ready.

Today the dance is held only once, in April but at no stipulated date. The time has been advanced due to the early departure of the Kickapoos to work, but the dance may not be held until the summer houses are occupied. During the ceremony today, prayers for rain are said, and permission is given to plant corn, beans, and squash to those who did not receive previous consent from the chief after his individual ceremony, held earlier.

The dance was formerly owned by an old woman, Thepahthehah, member of a Bear clan, who passed it and its bundle to a nephew, Nahmahpia, member of the Eagle clan. The bundle is known to contain a gourd, a desiccated buffalo tail, and two small human effigies, among other objects. When Nahmahpia died in 1963, he passed the dance and bundle to the leader of the Berry clan, Pancho Menaquah, who already knew the ritual connected with it. The bundle is in the custody of one of the nieces of the former owner, at whose home the dance is held.

The songs which accompany the dance were not the property of the former owner but of one of the most gifted chanters in the village. Only he could invite others to assist him, but any male wishing to learn could join them. This man moved to Oklahoma and passed the songs to the present owner of the dance and bundle, Pancho Menaquah.

The dance may not be held until a certain bird, considered a manitou and herald of the advent of the dance, is seen in the vicinity. The Kickapoos call this bird Wahpahnoah, in all probability a variant for the name of the bird the Fox Indians call Wâpanōwi, which they venerate and for which they hold a dance in conjunction with a buffalo dance.[12]

Roger Tory Peterson's *Field Guide to the Birds of Texas* was handed to two informants on different occasions: the present owner of the dance and a man from a different clan. Both were asked to identify the Wahpahnoah. Each pointed to a chat; one believed it to be the yellow-breasted chat and the other, the ground chat. These birds winter in the southern regions of Mexico to Panama and pass through Coahuila on their migratory flights to their breeding grounds in the northern United States between March and May and again on their flight south, in September and October.[13] The appearance of the chats in the area during their northern migration precedes the time when corn is about two feet high and has three or four leaves, since this stage is reached in late May or early June, and coincides with the time of planting the corn.

Middle-aged informants recall seeing, when they were children, old Thepahthehah, owner of the buffalo dance and lead dancer, holding a staff on top of which was fastened the desiccated tail of a buffalo, which she bobbed up and down as she kept time to the beat of the drum. When the dance was inherited by her nephew, no staff was used, but the tail is still held on high by the inside waiter as he joins others, preceded by the owner, in the buffalo dance.

During the buffalo dance we saw an epileptic girl, who had burned her legs after falling into a fire during an attack, brought into the dance with the help of a relative who supported her. A woman who weighs over 250 pounds, a frequent visitor in our home whom we had not seen dancing before, went into the dance to cure her rheumatic legs. She later explained that in the buffalo dance all who entered were showing their bodies to the buffalo manitou and asking him to heal those who were sick and that the waiter holding the desiccated tail on high was showing it to the manitou, who would be pleased to see the dance performed and send them blessings.

The present owner of the dance told us that, when the dancers lope from one side to the other, while thrusting their heads, it is in imitation of buffaloes attempting to rid themselves of branches which have caught on their horns as they gallop through the brush. He added that formerly this dance was performed by men who wore the heads of buffaloes upon their shoulders. Later, another informant in her sixties told us she did not remember when the men wore the buffalo heads on their shoulders but recalled seeing the dancers with branches on their heads.

Thomas Forsyth, in 1827, described the buffalo dance among the Sauk and Fox: "They are dressed with the pate of a buffallow skin with the horns, they imitate the buffallow by throwing themselves into different postures, also by mimicing his groans, attempting to horn each other, keeping exact time with the drum, the women often join in these dances, but remain nearly in the same spot (while dancing) and singing in a shrill voice above the men."[14]

Little Rabbit Ceremony

Sometime during the year each woman of the Berry clan and any other woman who has been cured by means of the Little Rabbit bundle holds a small, individual ceremony and feast in her home in honor of the bundle, during which gratefulness for the cure is expressed.

The hostess supplies the food, which consists of unsalted smoked deer ribs, squash or pumpkin, and Indian corn—enough to fill two large enameled-ware dishpans. When ready to hold the ceremony, she calls on the leader of the Berry clan, who calls a member of the same clan to be the waiter. After the ceremony, the waiter goes about the village and invites the number of men, women, and children that he estimates can be fed with the food available. All must be members of the Berry clan or have been cured by means of the Little Rabbit bundle.

Tobacco Planting Ceremony

When a clan leader wishes to plant tobacco, usually in March or April, he holds a small ceremony at daybreak. He asks a waiter of the proper reciprocal clan to prepare the feast of puppy or venison ribs and purple corn.

After the leader has finished the customary ritual to communicate with Kitzihiat and the manitou of tobacco, he tells them he is going to plant tobacco and requests that his efforts be rewarded. Shortly before noon, the waiter goes out into the village to invite a few old people, both men and women, to the feast.

After the ceremony the leader goes to a secluded and easily watered place, where he selects a small plot, fences it, cultivates it, and sprinkles it with ashes. He builds himself a temporary shelter, where he stays until the crop is ready. After planting the seeds he sprinkles them with the aid of a large leaf dipped in water and continues to irrigate them in this manner until maturity. All weeds are destroyed, and the tobacco plants are carefully cultivated.

It is imperative that the clan leader stand guard day and night over his plantation to prevent women from approaching. Sometimes, a man will ask another of his clan to relieve him for meals; but, likely as not, the planter stays at his post until the crop is ready to be harvested, depending on a male member of his family to bring what provisions he needs. Whether his efforts to grow tobacco have been successful or not, upon his return to the village he holds another ceremony and feast. Today, attempts to grow tobacco are rare and seldom successful; see Chapter 16.

Feast of the First Fruits

John R. Swanton states that the Indian ceremony popularly known to English-speaking people as "the green corn dance" might be more appropriately defined as the feast of the first fruits.[15] We shall use this term since, in translating the name of the ceremony from Algonquian into Spanish, the Kickapoos call it *la fiesta del primer helote* (the feast of the first roasting ear), which, by intimation, includes the new squash, beans, watermelon, and cantaloupe.

The Kickapoos have a myth which tells how they received the fruits and the reason for the ceremony. One day, Kitzihiat, who was the first chief of the Kickapoos, called his people together and told them he was taking pity upon them since they had so little to eat, but warned that he must die and they must bury him. After four days, corn, squash, beans, watermelon, and cantaloupe—four varieties of each—sprang up where his body lay; consequently, in gratitude, the Kickapoos have thereafter held an annual feast of thanksgiving. It is interesting to note that, in addition to the traditional corn, squash, and beans, the present Kickapoos have added two other fruits, the watermelon and cantaloupe, which were brought by Europeans but which they now believe were sent to them by Kitzihiat.

The feast of the first fruits formerly encompassed a complex of ceremonies: thanksgiving, lifting food taboos binding certain clan members and the chief, a warrior's horse parade and dance, a rain dance, and several other dances of a more secular nature; but the various dances are no longer given. The feast is supposed to be held as soon as the roasting ears, squash, and beans are sufficiently mature. This occurs in late June or July. However, because of the present migratory labor pattern, the clan feasts are now held earlier, before the people have left the village.

Before the warrior's horse parade and dance and other functions which used to follow could take place, the taboo prohibiting the eating of the new fruits affecting certain clan members and the chief first had to be lifted. This ceremony is still held. No one restricted by the taboo has eaten of these fruits since the New Year clan festivals. Any person bound by the taboo who eats of the fruits before he is released endangers his life, whether he knowingly breaks the taboo or not. This belief is widely shared by other Algonquian groups, among them the Creeks and Cherokees.[16]

Various degrees of vulnerability exist in the failure of this observance. If the chief breaks the taboo, it is thought that it will cease to rain and all plant life will wither and die; furthermore, he endangers his life and that of the tribe through a serious illness. If a member of the clans who are bound breaks the taboo, his health is endangered, and only by means of a ceremony may it be restored.

Those belonging to unrestricted clans are careful to observe the taboo as well, for fear of involving members of their families who must observe it. One day we had as our guest for lunch, at which cantaloupe was served, a member of the Berry clan. Knowing she was free to eat the fruit, we inquired why she had not touched it. She replied that her nephews and nieces, who were Buffalo, had not yet had their taboo lifted; therefore, she feared if she ate of the fruit she could bring them illness.

Unaware of the ramifications of the taboo in the early days of our study, we invited the chief's aide and his daughter to lunch. For dessert, watermelon was served; and, although the daughter warned her half-blind father, he obviously did not hear her, as he placed a piece of the fruit in his mouth. Suddenly realizing his mistake, he hurriedly rose and went to the bathroom. Returning to the table, from which by that time the fruit had been removed, he seemed much distressed, explaining that he had broken the taboo and feared he was in grave danger. This incident taught us two lessons: the importance of the taboo and the need to warn future guests about the food being served.

Another time, when Chief Papícoano was our guest for lunch, zucchini was served in combination with pork. Having been told what was being served, he pushed the zucchini aside, ate the remainder of the dish, and observed, "I do not know this squash; it must belong to your religion."

The degree of vulnerability is shown in the following anecdote told by several informants about one of the most highly esteemed men, a clan leader and former owner of the warrior's horse parade and dance. This man inadvertently drank water from an irrigation ditch in which Mexican children had thrown watermelon rinds. The man immediately sickened and died within a few days.

A member of the Buffalo clan, particularly vulnerable, told the following experience. When he was about nine, his grandmother was working in the corn patch. Momentarily forgetting that he had not yet had his food taboo lifted, he ran toward her. Terrified at seeing what he was doing, she ran forward to stop him, but it was too late. His arms and face had brushed against the leaves of the immature corn. Moments later, he became drowsy, wanted only to lie down, and refused food and water. As the afternoon wore on, he became deaf and fell into a deep slumber. Alarmed over his condition, family members gathered some corn and placed it on the ground, where a woman performed the proper ritual to undo the harm. After she had circled the corn many times while begging the manitou of the corn pardon for failing to observe the taboo, the boy began to awaken and was soon on his feet.

The first to hold the ceremony to lift the taboo is the Buffalo clan, in which a certain designated man, not the clan leader, is charged with officiating and giving the feast. He calls men of his own clan to prepare the unsalted puppy, cooked with fresh squash, corn, and beans. After the ceremony, in which thanks are given to Kitzihiat and the manitous of the first fruits, the waiters go out in the village to invite all who are members of the Buffalo clan and their affiliates, Eagle and Brown Bear, to partake of the feast. This ceremony lifts the taboo from these clans.

On the second day, a specially designated man, again not the clan leader, officiates at the ceremony and serves the feast to the members of the Thunder and Fox clans. Upon termination of this ceremony, Black Bear holds its ceremony and feast.

On the third day, the chief holds his own ceremony, using his bundle. Beforehand, he asks the men who officiated at the previous ceremonies to assist him with prayers and chants. He asks two old women, one a member of the Thunder clan and one of the Man clan to act as witnesses. He also calls on a man from the Berry clan to be the headwaiter. The latter calls a certain man from the Eagle clan, whose presence is indispensable, one from Tree, one from the Buffalo clan, and a certain woman from the Water clan. The headwaiter calls two women from the Buffalo and one woman from the Berry clans to preside over the food in the cook house. They prepare the food for the chief's guests and the personnel.

On the appointed day of his ceremony, the chief bathes in the river at daybreak, as do all others before this ceremony, returns to his home, dresses in his finest Indian clothes, and fasts until noon. He takes his bundle and officiates at a ceremony in which he thanks Kitzihiat and the manitous of the first fruits for their bountifulness, asks that they continue to bless his people, and reminds them that this ceremony and the events to follow are done to please them.

In the meantime, the waiters prepare special food for the chief. When he brings his ceremony to an end and after the visiting men have finished their prayers, he sits on the west bench directly in the center, facing the east door. This is the signal for the waiter to take him the first fruits. A member of the Berry clan, carrying a freshly boiled roasting ear in a ceremonial ladle, approaches the chief and holds up the ladle that he may take the first bite without touching the corn with his hands. The waiter retires with the roasting ear and returns with another ladle, in which a small portion of freshly cooked squash is carried. This the chief samples, and it is withdrawn. The same waiter returns with a small cake made of fresh corn scraped off the ear with a deer jawbone and cooked with fresh black-eyed peas. Finally, a woman member of the Water clan brings him water in a wooden bowl, which she holds up to him that he may take a sip. He is now free to eat of the first fruits, as is everyone else in the village.

The first fruits fed to the chief must be planted and grown by clan members not affected by the taboo, members of either the Berry or Man clans or their affiliates. The seeds are ideally descendants of those brought by their ancestors from the United States.

Today, the ceremony for lifting the taboo is only a skeleton of its former self, in part because of the severe droughts which have hampered the planting of the ancestral Indian seeds, but mostly because of the early annual migration of the Kickapoos, which precludes their presence at harvest time. Nonetheless, the ceremonies, in a curtailed way, are still observed. The chief holds his but sometimes has to content himself with just a bite of watermelon bought in Múzquiz if the ancestral seeds do not develop. The others affected by the taboo buy fresh fruits in Múzquiz to hold the ceremony. The three specially designated men of the Buffalo, Thunder, and Black Bear clans officiate and prepare sufficient food for all members of these clans before they begin their migration.

Warrior's Horse Parade and Dance

Formerly, after Chief Papícoano performed the ceremony to lift the food taboo, the women, having thoroughly swept their houses and compounds, began preparing large quantities of the first fruits: roasting ears, squash, and little cakes made of fresh corn mixed with fresh black-eyed peas. Each family ate its noon meal at home, but much of the bread was saved to take to the first dance held that evening.

While the women were preparing food, Weenkah, owner of the warrior's horse parade and dance, held a ceremony dedicated to the manitou of the horse. After lunch, early in the afternoon, the horse parade, honoring Kickapoos who had died in wars, began to assemble at his home. More than one hundred Indians, including small boys on burros, took part, riding with saddles or bareback.

Members of the Kisko moiety arrived with their faces smeared with white clay. Their only clothing consisted of a red breechcloth, moccasins, a kerchief around the neck, a feather caught in the braid, and bracelets of bells on the arms and ankles. Each carried a bow and quiver. Those whose horses were not white smeared them with white clay. The horses were adorned with collars of shells and red ribbons on tails and forelocks.

Members of the Oskasa moiety appeared with their bodies streaked with charcoal. They wore black breechcloths and rode black or almost black horses, or, if their horses were not dark, streaked them with charcoal. Their horses were adorned with purple ribbons on tails and forelocks.

After the riders assembled at Weenkah's home, he took the lead, carrying a kettledrum and stick in front of him, while one of the horsemen who flanked him carried a tomahawk and the other led the chants. They slowly rode to the edge of the village while the horses marked time to the beat of the drum, and the men joined in the chants. The boys on burros trailed behind. The parade made four turns around the outskirts of the village, went into the hills to the west, and turned south.

About six, they returned to Weenkah's home, dismounted and, after refreshments, began the warrior's dance and were greeted by the aunts and nieces they had invited, who arranged themselves in a line on either side of the dancers, one on the north, one on the south, according to the moiety of their hosts. Here, they kept time to the music by shuffling their feet and swaying their bodies while the men danced between the two lines.

Suddenly, the drum stopped. Those who had fought in wars tapped a sapling imbedded in the ground in front of the chanters with a rod while they recounted their exploits and gave thanks for their safe return. After each recounting of coups, the dance resumed, until sunset, when a feast was served the dancers and their invited female guests. After the feast the aunts and nieces went into the dance, facing their hosts.

Later, during the evening, the Kisko moiety sat on the south bench of the ramada, while the Oskasas sat on the north bench. Presently, bowls of steaming puppy stew were placed before them. At a given signal, amid much laughter and encouragement from members of the moieties, they began eating to determine which side could finish first.

The warrior's horse parade and dance is no longer held. When its owner died in the early forties, he passed it to a nephew who never gave it, but the bundle is renewed each year and offered tobacco by one of the leaders.

Rain Dance and Other Dances Associated with the Feast of the First Fruits

The rain dance was formerly the last event held during the feast of the first fruits. The origin of the dance is said to be the following: Long ago, a woman was taken prisoner and, while confined, dreamed that she should give an annual dance at which she would donate many presents. When she awoke from the dream, the door to her prison was open and she was able to walk into freedom.

The present owner of the dance has a stick which he notches each year and keeps high in the rafters of his house. Prior to the time for the dance, he takes out photographs of his father and grandfather, who owned the dance before him, and has them present during the ceremony, the purpose of which is to give thanks to the manitou of rain, which has matured the crops, and to ask for continued blessings. Informants state that rain invariably comes the same evening.

Formerly, after the morning ceremony, the dance took place. The men, wearing only breechcloths, moccasins, and a string of beads hung diagonally across their chests, and wide German-silver or tin bracelets on their upper arms, danced in the afternoon. Small boys, totally naked, joined the dancers and scrambled for coins thrown into the air by the host.

At night, sisters-in-law or nieces, with whom a joking relationship exists, faced their hosts and sang ribald songs while dancing. The women wore bright two-piece printed calico dresses with shawl collars adorned with many German-silver brooches. On their ankles they placed rattles, made of small pieces of tin entwined over buckskin.

In memory of the woman whose dream of gift-giving originated the dance, the men, when inviting their female guests, had to promise them a piece of jewelry or the privilege of entering their cornfields and helping themselves to roasting ears.

The man who owns this dance gives the following excuse for its discontinuance. The last time he gave the dance, drunken youths molested his adopted daughter, who was about sixteen at the time; and, when his wife went to her aid, the youths turned on her and beat her. Consequently, she has been ill since that time. On the following day he complained to Chief Papícoano, but the latter did not punish the culprits; thus, the owner does not feel further obligated to hold the dance. He does, however, return from the United States in July, no matter where he is working, and holds the ceremony associated with the dance. A waiter of the proper reciprocal clan goes into the village to invite men, women, and children to a watermelon feast held after the ceremony.

Among other dances once held during the feast of the first fruits was the squaw hop, exclusively a woman's dance. The owner of this dance and its accompanying bundle was a Potawatomi who went with the group of Kickapoos to Sonora in 1907. Later, the majority returned to Oklahoma; but some went to Coahuila, where a few, among them Piemaskiah, the owner of the dance, found a home. He belonged to a Bear clan and was considered a man of great integrity by both Kickapoos and Mexicans, since he did not drink or gamble, but dedicated himself to agriculture and to his ceremonies. Before his death, he passed the bundle and dance—the songs belonged to someone else—to a godchild. Since the latter was too young to know the ritual, this was taken over by the leader of the Berry clan, who continued to give the dance until a few years ago, when he passed it to a man in Oklahoma, where it is still given.

Another dance performed by the women was the turkey dance, in which they extended their skirts and emitted cries of "gobble, gobble" in imitation of the bird, while dancing around the chanters, who were seated on the ground in a semicircle.

One dance in which both men and women took part was called the "holding-hands dance," in which each woman held the hand of the man behind her with the left hand and the hand of the man in front of her with the right hand, switching hands at certain points in the music. Dillingham, who saw this dance performed in Oklahoma in 1953, says that the songs sung during the dance make fun of the Osages, who were the Kickapoos' mortal enemies.[17]

The rain dance and others of the cluster of the feast of the first fruits came to an end around 1953, coincident with the beginning of mass migration of the Kickapoos as farm laborers to the United States.

Arrival and Departure Ceremonies

No adult Kickapoo absents himself from the village on a long trip or returns from one without notifying Kitzihiat. This requires a small ceremony. A man or woman planning a trip, either for pleasure or business, stocks the necessary provisions for the feast: Indian corn and pumpkin and a fattened puppy or smoked bear or deer ribs; if there is no available meat, it suffices to serve Indian corn gruel.

To discuss the preparations, the host calls on the leader of his clan, if the latter is in the village; if not, he may ask any leader who knows how to officiate. The leader calls a waiter of the proper reciprocal clan of the host to prepare the feast.

On the appointed day the host has all in readiness in order that the waiter, who arrives about seven o'clock in the morning, can begin preparing the feast. When it is almost ready, he notifies the leader, who arrives with the host's clan bundle. The leader sits in his usual place—the south bench to the extreme west—while the host sits on the north bench near the door.

The leader inquires the occasion for the ceremony, to which the host replies, "I am going on a trip, and I wish to ask Kitzihiat to look after me, my home, and my belongings while I am away"; or, if he is having an arrival ceremony, he says, "I wish to thank Kitzihiat for my safe arrival and for the safekeeping of my home and my possessions."

The leader opens the bundle, from which he takes Indian tobacco to sprinkle on the fire, and prays that the fire will notify the other manitous to carry the message to Kitzihiat. He puffs a pipe offering tobacco to the manitous of the four directions, asking them to protect the traveler wherever he may go.

When the prayers end, the waiter goes out into the village to invite several men, women, and children, excepting members of the host's clan or blood relatives, to eat the food.

Before departing on the trip, the traveler gathers up a bit of the soil inside of his house, wraps it in a small cloth, and carries it on his person throughout the trip. If he becomes homesick, he places some of the soil in a glass of water and drinks it, thus dispelling his nostalgia.

Bundle Purification Ceremonies

During the New Year clan festivals and again in midsummer, the clan leaders and those who have private bundles open them to undergo a purification and replenishment ceremony.

Each object in the bundle is closely examined and passed through the smoke of cudweed. If such objects as feathers, claws, hairs, or other parts of animals have deteriorated, the leader offers tobacco to the animals whose parts he needs, asking their permission to kill them himself or to have someone he designates do so. The bundle is offered tobacco, the objects are carefully rewrapped in their buckskin covers, and the bundle is stored in a clean white cloth in the rafters.

The leader offers a small feast, for which he calls a waiter of the proper reciprocal clan to prepare the food. The latter may ask anyone he wishes to the feast—the number not to exceed those he can adequately serve.

Fasting

The Kickapoos, both adults and children, fast for various reasons. When a man lost his father and brother in an automobile accident, believing this double tragedy to be the result of witchcraft, he fasted to have a dream in which the responsible ones might be revealed to him.

If a person loses a dear one, he fasts several days, hoping thus to assuage his grief. One informant told how, as a child, she accompanied an aunt who had recently lost both parents to the *monte*, where they spent the day doing handwork. Both blackened their faces with a burnt piece of firewood from their clan house before leaving, ate no breakfast, and drank no water, returning at dusk for the evening meal. She does not recall having any specific dreams or visions but remembers crying of hunger and thirst, particularly the latter, which, to her, was more acute than the lack of food.

Another informant told us that, since the Kickapoos neither read nor write, whenever they seek knowledge, they fast, make a small gift of Indian tobacco to Grandfather Fire or Grandmother Earth, and question these manitous.

One of the most prominent leaders in the tribe killed a Mexican several years ago. He served a term in prison and, when released, spent a month fasting, seeking expiation for his crime. He is said to have fasted five days at a time, sitting hours on his haunches in deep and long prayers and lying down only for short periods of rest.

During our study, two sets of twins were born within weeks of each other, a most unprecedented occurrence. So concerned were the Kickapoos over the ill fate this might bring the tribe that one of the men volunteered to fast, seeking pity from Kitzihiat that no harm might befall his people, for the Kickapoos believe that either one of the twins must die or some member of the group will be taken.

Fasting and prayers can induce divination. One old man many years ago is said to have been able to prophesy our modern era of automobiles, planes, and bombs which would destroy many nations. He foretold that the oceans would ignite like gasoline and the world would end in ruins.

All Kickapoos, from the chief to a woman having her house-dedication ceremony, must fast until dusk on the day they are hosts. Other than fasting on the day of giving a ceremony, this ordeal takes place mainly during the winter and up to the New Year clan festivals. A person wishing to fast consults his clan leader about the length of time, usually several periods of two or three days in a row, and on rare occasions more, depending on the stamina and determination of the aspirant; the location of his shelter, either in a hidden place in the *monte* or near the river; and subjects on which his thoughts may dwell (not on his wife or carnal needs, but on lofty thoughts). He is then instructed on how to take the steam bath preparatory to the fast.

The aspirant kills a deer. His wife or a female relative smokes the ribs, divided into several sections and saved for the ceremonies which he will give after each period of fasting. The aspirant finds a suitable place to build a small shelter, snugly covered with canvas, near the springs or in the *monte*. He makes a round depression in the center of the shelter, sufficiently large to hold two large stones, cuts some boughs of one-seed juniper, and takes a large bucket to heat water.

When all is ready, he returns to the village to blacken his face with a burnt stick of firewood from his clan house, goes to the shelter, heats the stones and the water, in which he places the one-seed juniper boughs and, when the stones are hot, places them in the depression within the shelter. After these preparations, he undresses and repeatedly pours hot water over the stones, thus creating clouds of steam, until he is thoroughly cleansed, while rubbing his body with the boughs, but he does not cut his skin during the bath as mentioned by William Jones.[18]

He is now ready to fast and spend his time in prayer, his thoughts above worldly pleasures. He receives no visitors and looks upon no one. During this period, he neither bathes, shaves, nor changes his clothes.

By prearranged plan the leader of his clan and chanters are awaiting him when he returns home at the end of the self-imposed period to hold the first ceremony of the series. By the end of several hours of chants and prayers, in which Kitzihiat is asked to take pity on the aspirant and grant him his wishes, a waiter of the proper reciprocal clan has prepared the feast, containing one portion of the smoked venison ribs and Indian corn, and serves it. The faster spends the night in his home alone and, on the following two mornings, is given a small serving of unsalted purple Indian corn gruel. This, with the small amount of liquid in which the corn is cooked, is the only liquid he drinks. On the second morning, he again blackens his face, returns to his shelter to begin another period of prayers and fasting, and follows this schedule until he has completed the total time he imposed on himself.

Upon termination of his fast, he goes to kill the deer whose exact location was presumably revealed to him during his abstinence. He returns with his kill and makes preparations to hold a final ceremony. Having succeeded in his ordeal, he goes to the river to bathe and, returning home, shaves, dresses in his Kickapoo dress, and adorns himself with jewelry. His clan leader and the chanters hold a ceremony in which Kitzihiat is thanked for aiding him in his trial. During his fast, he kept a record of his dreams, which his leader now interprets as relevant to the reason for fasting.

After the ceremony, the waiters go out into the village to invite all who wish to partake of the feast, except clan members of the host and blood relatives.

A man who aspires to a period of fasting must be sure of himself, for, if he fails to fulfill his self-imposed ordeal, he becomes the laughingstock of the village. For instance, one young man whose leader feared he lacked the fortitude to withstand a fasting period made his plans. He completed the first period; but, after beginning the second, he returned to the village. The word spread that, instead of keeping his mind on lofty thoughts, he had become jealous of his wife, imagining so many infidelities on her part that he could not keep these out of his mind.

Fasting during Childhood

Kickapoo children learn to fast at a tender age. After a child reaches five or six and until puberty, whenever he misbehaves to the degree that the adult with whom he lives considers that his conduct merits fasting, he is smeared with soot on the forehead and on the mouth (if a girl, on the cheeks and mouth)—the latter to discern whether a child eats on the sly. He is given no breakfast but sent outdoors with the warning he is not to drink or eat or accept food or drink if it is offered to him. At noon, he returns home for his meal and water. This punishment may be extended to as much as three days if the child's misdemeanor has been severe.

Sometimes parents impose an unduly severe punishment on children for an act over which they have no control. A girl of fifteen was ordered a fast of three days without food or water by her father because she had inadvertently spilled boiling water on a younger brother. Another woman told us that, when she returned to the village from an Indian school in Kansas, her grandmother punished her often by imposing fasts, causing her to suffer so much from hunger and thirst that she forgot all the English she had learned in school.

Fasting as a punishment may take place at any time of the year; however, fasting to receive knowledge or wisdom, to receive grace or a long life, to receive protection or pity, to have a dream which will bring good luck, to have grandparents tell stories about Wisaka, or to be told stories in preparation for adulthood, is done only in the winter and until the New Year clan festivals. During these cold months, children voluntarily pick up a burnt log from a clan house, smear their faces, and fast from one to four days, depending on their fortitude. Usually girls fast only one day, returning from the *monte*, where they have retreated, for the evening meal; boys sometimes fast for as long as four days, drinking only water and staying in a small shelter in the *monte*, protected from animals. During this time, they may scratch themselves only with a stick.

One woman claimed that her children received the gift of writing Ba-Be-Bi-Bo by fasting from the time they were four or five. A male informant told us that, when he approached puberty, his grandmother informed him that, to receive wisdom, he must fast and consult Grandmother Earth, who would answer his questions. After smearing his face with soot, he left home at daybreak, not returning until noon the first day. Each day he stretched out the time for returning home, until on the fourth day he came back just in time for the evening meal.

Miscellaneous Ceremonies

Boy's First-Hunt Ceremony

When a Kickapoo boy is four years old, he is presented with a crudely made bow and a set of four bluntly pointed arrows by his father, uncle, or brother. He immediately begins to practice marksmanship, at first, with stationary objects and later with moving ones. By the time he is six, he is an expert at hitting a rolling metal hoop covered with willow withes. Soon, he begins to try his hand at killing birds, fish, or other small game in or near the village.

When he kills his first bird with his bow and arrow, he takes it to his father or other male relative with whom he makes his home. The relative hangs the bird from the rafters of the house for safekeeping and goes to kill a deer to hold a feast and ceremony for the young hunter.

Returning with a deer, the father speaks with the boy's clan leader, who calls a waiter of the proper reciprocal clan to prepare the feast and invites the chief and twelve old people, six men and six women, to witness the boy's accomplishment.

When the waiter has served the feast, consisting of unsalted Indian corn, squash or pumpkin, venison, and the bird, in two large enameled-ware dishpans, the leader asks who has killed the bird, and the young hunter answers. After the leader and old people each eat a small bite of the bird, the leader prays again, announcing to Kitzihiat that the boy has killed his first game and asking that he be granted health, a long life, and continuous success in the hunt.

When he kills his first deer, he has another ceremony and feast given for him, and a third one when he kills his first bear. He is then considered a full-fledged hunter.

Murderer's Ceremony

Second to suicide, murder is considered the worst crime which can be committed. When this occurs, the murderer holds a ceremony in which the spirit of his victim is asked forgiveness and begged not to haunt him but to stay in the abode where the spirits of those killed pass their time. He fasts and prays on many occasions during his lifetime to ask the forgiveness and mercy of Kitzihiat in order that his own spirit may someday arrive in the hereafter. In spite of lifelong prayers, it is possible that he may never attain this reward.

One informant told us that the Kickapoos of Oklahoma who have been in the armed forces and have killed in war observe this ceremony.

Ceremony for Borrowing Tobacco

On rare occasions, a clan leader discovers that his supply of Indian tobacco in the bundle is dangerously low and holds a small ceremony to borrow from all of the members of the tribe who wish to make a contribution.

The leader asks a waiter of the proper reciprocal clan to go from house to house announcing that the ceremony is being held for this purpose and asking that each individual contribute what he is able. About noon, the waiter goes out into the village to invite a few old people to the feast of venison ribs or puppy and Indian corn.

Rain Ceremonies

Prayers for rain may be included in any ceremony, but whenever an acute shortage of rain occurs, a special ceremony may be held by any Kickapoo, at which the manitous of the water are asked to be kindly disposed toward the Indians, recognize their need, and supply them with the needed rain.

One of these ceremonies was brought to our attention by the man who gave it, a member of the first Buffalo clan, who called his leader to officiate. The bundle was opened and tobacco offered to it and the fire. The pipe was puffed in the four directions and the gourd was shaken, announcing to the manitous the occasion of the ceremony. The host told us that a heavy rain fell in the village that same night.

Buffalo Dance of the Bear Clan

A third buffalo dance, no longer held and about which it was impossible to obtain much information, was owned by one of the two Bear clans and was a buffalo dance in its totality, not inserted in a woman's dance as are the two buffalo dances held today.

Before the dance began, those who were members of the Bear clan ate honey that they picked up from a bowl with their left hands. The granddaughter of the owner, a woman in her sixties, recalls that the dance was no longer performed after she was about eighteen. This would place the termination of the dance during the second decade of this century. The bundle, at the time of our study, was in the custody of the chief's wife and was kept in her home and periodically smoked and refurbished.

Preparation of Puppies for Ceremonial Feasts

The Kickapoos say that Kitzihiat loves dogs. One day he called one of his people to his abode and gave him instructions as to the preparation and the occasions when puppies were to be eaten to please him. When the Indian returned home he gathered his people around him. Soon, out of the ground, on one side of the hearth sprang a male dog; from the other side of the fire sprang a female. This is how the dogs came to be.

The Kickapoos are kind to dogs, give them names from the totem of the clan to which the owner belongs, and never speak roughly to them, use blasphemy, or mistreat them, for they believe that dogs have spirits like humans and go to the same hereafter. When puppies are cooked, Indian tobacco is offered to the manitou of the dogs.

The Kickapoos today serve puppy at the New Year clan festivals, at the Buffalo naming ceremony, and at individual ceremonies; formerly, they were served at the feast of the first fruits. One informant explained the eating of puppy at a ceremonial feast in this manner: "It is very tasty; it is not eaten like food, but to please Kitzihiat who put it here for us." She added that the eating of puppy is analogous to the wafer taken at a Catholic communion.

During the fall months, those who wish to contribute a puppy to the New Year clan festivals look around the neighboring *ranchos* or in Múzquiz to locate newly born puppies with their eyes still closed; these they buy, or merely ask for them. The puppies are bottle-fed until old enough to eat table leftovers, when they are fed twice daily, at midmorning and evening. They are bathed often, kept free of parasites, and kept in the house or ramada. They are not allowed out of sight for fear they may eat filth, particularly the discarded food of a woman occupying the menstrual hut.

When a ceremony is to be held, a waiter, by previous consent, goes to the houses where the fattened puppies have been kept and asks for them. The waiter who performs this task is usually an older man, a long-time widower or one whose wife is past her climacteric, to preclude the possibility that his wife or mistress, unknown to him, may be pregnant. Should this be the case, the child would be born defective. The waiter offers the puppy a bit of meat and *piloncillo* and, while the owner holds it on the ground, kills it by a quick blow on the head with a stick. To assure himself that the puppy is dead, the waiter turns it over on its back and places a stick across its neck on which he steps.

The dead puppy is taken to the river, where a fire is built and it is singed while held on a stick. With a sharp knife the skin is scraped well and the whole washed in the river. The entrails, ears, and eyes are allowed to float down the stream. After this thorough cleaning, the puppy is taken to the house where the ceremonial feast is to be held and hung on a rafter inside the door until needed.

Chapter 16

Magical Beliefs and Practices

Witchcraft

The fear of witchcraft, which serves as effective social control, pervades the life of every Kickapoo. Witchcraft is blamed for many abuses, accidents, mishaps, deaths, poisonings, burnings, diseases, epidemics, aches, and pains. Often conduct that would otherwise be punishable may be rationalized as being directed by witchcraft, making the person or persons involved impotent to act differently.

Fear of witchcraft is an important factor in many decisions. For example, a man owns a piece of land inherited from his grandfather; but, while he is clearing it, another family claims it. Instead of having an argument and creating bad feelings, in which case he might be bewitched, he stops working it and lets the new claimants take over. A woman asks a man who is skilled at fashioning ax handles to make one for her; but, upon its completion, she finds the price too high. Rather than hold his ground and receive the value of his work, he lowers the price to suit her for fear this woman might bewitch him.

It is a maxim among the Indians that one who has plenty of food will share it with others less fortunate. The story is told of a woman who came into some money and bought a yearling calf, which she butchered and hung to air on a tree while she went to gather firewood. On returning, she noticed that many people had gathered at her house, for news of her acquisition had spread like wildfire. Displeased with the crowd who waited to share the slaughtered animal, she exclaimed, "From a distance, I thought you were buzzards." This remark wounded the Kickapoos so deeply that someone bewitched her. While working in the United States, they say, she had an operation in which a rib of a yearling was removed from her side. How had this happened? A witch had placed it there. But this was not the end of the woman's punishment. Not long afterwards, her son suffered an automobile accident and was hospitalized for several weeks with a broken neck. His mother, impatient with his slow recovery and wishing to have a Kickapoo curer attend him, took him to the village, where, instead of improving, he died.

Repulsing a suitor can be disastrous to a girl. One informant told us that his sister was in love with a handsome young lad who courted her at the river when she fetched water for their mother. They planned to marry, but an older man set his heart on her. Her family urged her to make the more advantageous marriage, but she was adamant. It was not long before she developed a high fever and began to vomit blood, in which was found a short twig, the length of the index finger. The family were certain the girl had been bewitched by the older man, who had caused the twig to lodge in her throat, bringing her death.

We were told of another man, who had had incestuous relations with two of his daughters. A third daughter repulsed his advances and fell into the bad graces of her father. Soon after she married a fine man, they had a son who went blind. It was the father who was considered responsible for this tragedy. This man, like those in two more recent cases of incestuous relations, was believed to be under a witch's spell and unable to act differently.

A woman developed a severe pain in her neck and back and asked her husband to rub it. While being massaged, she noticed an object that struck against the canvas flap of the door, but at first thought nothing of it, believing it to be her cat which had jumped from one of the benches in the ramada. On glancing up, however, she noticed the cat peacefully asleep on the opposite bench in the house. Startled, she sat up, exclaiming, "It is a witch that passed by and entered." At the same moment she perceived a strong, nauseating odor, resembling that of a skunk, but different, something she had never smelled before. She became frightened on realizing that she had failed to place her bit of Solomon's seal over the door. She was sure that a witch had been inside the house, invisible to her, and had given her the severe pain.

A partially blind man explained how his condition had occurred. When he was about thirty-four, he began to have severe pain in his eyes and was so uncomfortable in the sunlight or around the smoke of the hearth that he had to be confined to a room without light or fire while he paced in pain. It behooved his aunt to cure him. After examining his eyes, she rubbed them and took out bits of deer and horse hairs, threads of a red blanket, and little animals with white heads. The aunt assured him that the objects had been placed in his eyes by a witch and it was fortunate she had intercepted the evil doings or he would have become completely blind.

One day a woman came to see us with a severe pain in the region of her kidneys, extending down the sides of her legs and up to her neck. She had begun to feel this pain when she leaned over a ground-level well to pull up a heavy bucket of water. We gave her a pain-killing tablet and some hot tea and dispatched her to the physician, who diagnosed her trouble as a sacroiliac strain. The woman could not believe that the simple act of pulling a bucket of water had caused her discomfort and blamed a witch as the perpetrator of her condition.

Not long afterward, this woman came with the news that, while her favorite aunt and her family were harvesting apples in Provo, Utah, one of the young Kickapoo men had suddenly lost his mind. Each afternoon about three o'clock, he discarded his clothes, much to the consternation of his peers, who are inordinately modest. They were certain he had been bewitched and needed to submit himself to a curer.

A single Kickapoo male about fifty years old, who had been absent from the village for about fourteen years, returned one day during the summer, inquiring about a saddle he had left behind, whose whereabouts no one could tell him. He arrived like an apparition and as suddenly left, causing no small amount of speculation; it was believed he had turned himself into a witch or had been bewitched to have stayed away so long.

A woman complained that "little animals" which she had swallowed while drinking water at night were eating the inside of her chest. She was certain they had been put there by a witch. We sent her to a physician, who diagnosed her case as one of anxiety—the only one of this type which came to our attention during our contact with the Indians. She and her children, born from unions with several Mexican consorts and barred from membership in the clans, play only a peripheral role in the activities of the village. Because of this, she is discriminated against by the others and, being by nature a timid and retiring woman, seems unable to cope with the display of coolness and ostracism.

Who are the witches? All the members of the herbal societies, regardless of age, are believed to be witches. These, in turn, accuse others of being witches. Any old person is considered a witch, whether man or woman. They have lived many years and are thought to have acquired the power to transform themselves into anything they wish. One never crosses old people because of this fear; instead, one gives them food when they arrive to visit. Clan leaders, though highly respected and trusted, may be witches. One became ill at the time when he was to officiate at an important ceremony. The village tongues were wagging that he was an "animal" (witch) to have become ill at such an inopportune moment.

Anyone whose conduct is in the least deviant is considered a potential witch. A couple invited a man to accompany them on a hunting trip. The companion went off by himself for several hours, returning with the complaint that a bad spirit had led him astray in an attempt to separate him from his friends. In his wanderings he had collected an herb which is used only on specific ceremonial occasions. When he burned some in camp to frighten the evil spirit that had pursued him, the couple were certain he was a witch; otherwise, why would he dare handle this herb in such an unceremonious setting?

One woman has no living children but has had eleven miscarriages. Although not a member of an herbal society, it is considered certain that she is a witch—or else how could she lose eleven children? It is said that she eats them.

Tall, skinny Mexicans are all considered witches, and all Negroes are considered potential ones. One of the clan leaders told us he had proof that Negroes are witches. He was at the river one day at dusk when he noticed a dark woman on the other side, to whom he spoke in Algonquian but received no answer; he then shouted to her in Spanish but got no recognition. Convinced that she was a witch, he threw a stone, which felled her, and went across the river to identify her, but she was no one he knew. When he returned with help to assist her, the woman had disappeared. That very evening word arrived from the nearby Negro village that a black woman had died suddenly a few hours earlier.

A witch does not have to be in the village to practice his or her evil work. A woman complained of a severe pain in her back during the summer when the village was deserted. One of her friends told her she must be bewitched to have such a severe pain. When we reminded her that the witch she feared the most was working in Utah, she replied, "That makes no difference; she can bring me pain even from a distance."

Besides the woman who has "eaten" her eleven children, there is also a man who is accused of "swallowing" his children. One of his daughters died shortly after giving birth to twins. One of the latter mysteriously fell from a car and permanently injured her back; another daughter is wasting away with tuberculosis; a child's relative died recently in a peculiar way. The man is blamed for all these tragedies; people say that he is a witch and lives off human flesh.

Witches can turn themselves into animals, such as bears and cougars, and into birds, the owl being the most dreaded. One woman said that frequently she heard a bird flying over her house, making a noise like the clinking of spurs. She was certain the bird was a witch, out on mischief. It could be, she believed, a member of one of the herbal societies, as they are given certain herbs which "allow them to fly over houses."

Once, when we took some of the clan leaders to talk with the governor in Saltillo, they spent the previous night in a cheap hostelry in Múzquiz but left by four o'clock in the morning and moved into the plaza because they had heard an owl at their window. All owls, according to these men, are witches.

A man told us he had gone out in the night to relieve himself when he was confronted by a huge, heavy bear that ambled with a limp, but he was too frightened to get his gun. The next morning one of the female members of an herbal society was seen limping on her way to the river. She was undoubtedly the witch that had frightened him.

Another man told how an old woman explained her limp to him by saying that she had fallen off her bed, but he doubted that this was the real cause of her injury on the basis of what was told him by a friend. While sleeping under a mosquito netting, his friend was awakened by the sensation that a person or animal was breathing near him but, through the netting, was unable to discern what the thing was. Frightened, he sat up, lashed out at the object, and immediately heard a loud thud on the floor. By the time he found his flashlight, nothing was there. This, then, was the real cause of the woman's injury. She had changed into an animal and had attempted to injure the man's friend. Proof of this was that she was limping the following day.

Kickapoos are exceedingly careful in the disposal of their excrement, hair, fingernails, and toenails. This is due to the fear that witches may use these personal items against them. Since they have no sewerage, they seek out secluded places in the *monte* to relieve themselves. It is taboo to comb one's hair or pare one's nails in a house with a cattail roof; therefore, they do these things outdoors and carefully collect the hair and nail parings, burying them secretly in the woodpile. A witch who acquires any of these items can use them in several ways. Excrement of the person to be victimized can be dried and sprinkled on the person, in the house, or nearby. This, combined with the proper ritual, can bring any disaster wished on the victim. Witches can insert pubic hairs, stones, twigs, or other foreign objects in their victims to injure them. They also make little dolls with rags and, if possible, with hair and nail parings of the intended victim to make the doll more realistic. They insert pins, needles, or thorns, or cut with sharp knives on the dolls on the location where they wish to hurt the victim.

One woman made a pair of dolls for us which exceeded in workmanship all of the others we had. We allowed small girl visitors to play with the other dolls, but not with this pair. Before we knew it, the Indians were calling the dolls Chief Papícoano and Nanachihah (his wife). One day, the woman who had fashioned them came with distressing news. She had been reprimanded by the chief's mother-in-law for making dolls to resemble her daughter and the chief, as the mother-in-law feared that we or others might use them to perform witchcraft. It took considerable talking to convince the maker that it was not our custom to do such things. After that, the dolls were stored away.

The Kickapoo witches have the reputation of being successful in the use of love philters. It is said that one of the leading men in the tribe returned his bride to her mother when he discovered that she was not a virgin. The mother promptly took the girl back to him, and since then he has not been able to rid himself of his wife, for he is given a potion to keep him in love with her. A certain witch owns a powder which is very pungent. When sprinkled on the side of a man or woman's heart it is supposed to cause that person to fall in love with the possessor. This same powder sprinkled on a handkerchief and spread over the face of a sleeping woman to whom a man has taken a fancy permits him to enjoy her without rousing her or having relatives be aware of the presence of a stranger in the house.

On the other hand, there is also a witch known to possess a powder which serves to alienate a husband and wife from one another.

Sometimes witches practice their magic on an animal before trying it out on an individual. We were told the following incident to prove this. The informant tethered his horse to his compound fence. Suddenly, the animal began to fret and snort and tried to break loose. He was unsaddled, taken to a field, and tied to a post; but here again, he began to snort, pulling on the post until he loosened himself. He raced through a lane and stopped at the pecan grove, where he was found dying. Our informant was much impressed that the horse had gone to die near a cemetery in the west, the same direction taken by the Kickapoo spirits as they go to the hereafter. This incident alarmed the villagers, as they detected witchcraft; but they comforted themselves that a horse was taken rather than one of them. This, however, was not the end of the episode. A few months later, one of the prominent men and his son were killed in an automobile accident. It was then that it was decided that the witches had been "practicing" on the horse for what occurred later.

All adult Kickapoos carry on their bodies a bit of the magical rhizome called Solomon's seal, a guarantee against most dangers, including witches. It can also be hung on the door of a house to prevent a witch from entering; but sometimes the owner forgets, giving a witch an opening to do his evil. A man told of an experience he had with a witch. One warm summer night he and his wife were sleeping on a bench of the ramada when he was awakened by a heavy padding on the earth floor. Glancing sideways, but not moving, he saw a large bear. He tried to awaken his wife by nudging her, but she was too sound asleep to be roused and he was too frightened to speak to her. The following morning, when he told his wife's aunt about this happening, she gave him these instructions, along with an extra piece of the magical rhizome: "If a bear shows up again, just chew a bit of this and spit it in the direction of the animal. It will immediately transform itself into the person who is the witch, for the bear is either a witch or a person he has changed into a bear. When the bear transforms into the original person, it will be stark naked and will beg you to release it." The aunt told the informant she would personally take care of the witch, who would live only four days.

Curers may be called in to remove a hex or any intended harm done by a witch. A woman, in great pain when her head swelled from a blow, called a Kickapoo curer, who extracted several "foreign" hairs from the top of the woman's head, which he said were the cause of the trouble. The swelling immediately decreased.

Beliefs and Practices concerning Animals

The Kickapoos have always depended on wildlife for food, clothing, tools, and, since contact with the white man, a source of income. They are observant of animals and their activities, depending on them as forecasters or augurs of weather, death, or the presence of a witch. The arrival of geese announces cold weather; when the cranes fly over the river, it is a sign of rain; the arrival of the starlings and swallows announces the approach of warm weather; the cry of the whippoorwill foretells the death of a member of the group; the cry of a fox in the daytime presages a misfortune; when toads are seen in large numbers, it is a sign of rain; when rattlers climb trees, it is a forecast of heavy rains; and, when an owl hoots, it tells them a witch is nearby.

Taboo Animals

Many animals are taboo to the Kickapoos; among them are the mountain lion, coyote, prairie dog, and, to the Buffalo clan, the bison; among birds, the eagle, hawk, turkey buzzard, owl, water hen, woodpecker, swallow, starling, grackle, crow, crane, hummingbird, scissortail, and yellow-breasted chat. Taboo animals must not be killed except under certain special circumstances. No snake may be killed, and neither may the horned lizard, commonly known throughout the Southwest as the horned toad; the spider, daddy longlegs, and bumblebee are also taboo.

Desiccated wholes or parts of many of these animals are kept in the sacred bundles. When more are needed for this purpose, a special ceremony is held in which tobacco is offered to the manitous of the taboo animals and explanations for killing them are given. The eagle and the hawk, however, are absolutely taboo to the Kickapoos; when they need feathers from one of these birds, they must pay a Mexican or other non-Kickapoo to kill the bird for them.

The migratory birds, which they call "Indian birds," are not killed because they are thought to spend the time during their annual absence in the empyrean regions with Kitzihiat. The Kickapoos do not understand the migration of birds; thus, the fact that many birds remain in the countryside, while the "Indian birds" leave, constitutes a mystery to them.

Sanctions for killing or disturbing taboo animals are early administered to Kickapoo children. One day a woman was sitting in our garden when a hummingbird appeared, flitting from flower to flower in search of nectar. The sight of the bird brought forth an account of an experience she had had as a child. One day, while cutting firewood in the *monte*, she came upon the tiny nest of a hummingbird, in which lay a newly hatched bird. Elated over her find and wishing to make a present of it to her grandmother, she carefully took the nest and proudly carried it home. On seeing what the child had done, the grandmother cut off a switch and punished her until the blood ran from her legs. Crying with pain, she was directed to take the nest to the exact branch where she had found it and never again to molest this bird, as it was sacred to her clan.

The switching that our friend received was mild compared to the sanctions supposedly imposed by the supernatural on adults who molest or kill taboo animals. The same informant told the story of a young man who once killed a chicken hawk by a shot through the head. An older brother who accompanied him on the hunt was indignant and alarmed and reprimanded him, saying, "Younger brother, you have indeed done a grave thing and you will be punished; perhaps not immediately, but eventually." Sometime later, the young man was thrown off a horse and hit a rock in the same spot where he had shot the bird, dying from the blow.

The spider and all other taboo animals are manitous. One large spider is thought to be holding the world, the sun, and the moon together with its gigantic web. The Kickapoos know that the daddy longlegs, a member of the Arachnida class, is not a spider, but they do not kill it either, except for curing ringworm, when it is offered tobacco and an explanation for taking its life. Only members of the Buffalo clan may kill it if it wanders into their compounds or houses.

Beliefs, anecdotes, and stories about animals are numerous. According to one story, a clan leader who had planted ceremonial corn found that, as soon as the ears began to mature, coyotes pulled down the stalks, pulled back the shucks, and ate the tender, milky kernels. Since he could not kill the taboo coyotes, he paid a Mexican to set a trap for them. When one was caught, the Mexican trapper asked if he did not want the coyote killed with his quirt. The leader emphatically shook his head, went to where the coyote lay, trapped by one paw, and gently gave him a lecture for having eaten the corn while it was still tender, telling him to wait until it was mature, when there would be enough for everybody, including the coyote. He further admonished the animal to take the message to all of his kin. After this lecture, the clan leader told the Mexican to release the animal.

Besides his ability to pull down cornstalks, the coyote is believed to be able to wipe off the thorns of the prickly-pear fruit with his tail before eating it. Coyotes, like rattlers, are highly respected and feared; it is considered bad luck to have a coyote cross one's path.

Animal behavior is often interpreted as a warning of misfortune. An informant told of an incident that occurred on a hunting expedition of several days. On the first morning, each member of the party went in a different direction. When they gathered around the campfire that evening, after arriving empty-handed, they began to swap impressions. All had sighted deer, but they had scampered off into the woods, snorting loudly. One of the older men commented that this behavior presaged a mishap in the village. To worsen matters, a fox cried out three times at daybreak. This clinched their fears. Immediately after breakfast, they broke up camp, since hunting under such circumstances was useless. Returning to the village, they found that one of the old women had suffered a paralytic stroke.

One day, a woman informant who enjoyed walking in our small garden to look at the flowers returned to the house with a broad smile on her face. She wanted to show us the "little child of a dust whirlwind." Perplexed, we followed her back into the garden to a loquat tree, where hung an insect, later identified as a caddis worm, which had cut sections of the leaves to shape itself a spiral, scaled case. The woman explained that the case held a green worm and that, when it came out of the case, it caused a whirlwind as it flew. This belief is of particular interest, as Clark Wissler found it among the Dakota Indians.[1]

The Kickapoo attitude toward snakes is one of respect, fascination, and fear. Early in our work, we were given a six-foot rattler's skin by a Mexican friend and, for lack of a better place, hung it in the entrance hall. One of our early Indian callers, on seeing the skin, shook his head in disapproval, asked why we had such a thing in our home, and remarked, "¡Muy malo [very bad]!" He was aghast when told that we wanted to have shoes made from the skin and warned us that if we wore them they would keep us jumping all the time. He also cautioned us that the Kicka-poo women, especially those who were pregnant, dared not come into our home as long as the skin was there.

Both land and water snakes are considered manitous. They own the water and the water hens. The snakes are believed to be capable of mes-merizing and drowning a man—an event which, although rare among the Indians, is thought to occur when a snake, owning the area where one enters the water, takes the person's spirit and carries it to its lair. One old woman told us the following anecdote to illustrate the belief that snakes are responsible for drownings. Her grandmother used to bathe each day at a certain place in the river. The large snake that lived in that particular spot had wanted to take her grandmother's spirit for a long time. For-tunately for her grandmother, the thunderers above (i.e., thunder and lightning, considered as manitous) realized what was about to take place and, during the night, killed the snake and hung it on a nearby tree. The next night the thunderers returned and carried off the dead snake.

It is believed that the water snakes plant the cattails; therefore, before a woman enters a swamp to gather cattails, she must make an offering of tobacco to prevent frightening or angering the snakes, who, because of this intrusion, could drag a woman's spirit to their lairs. Our informant emphasized this point by telling us that one day her grandmother went to gather cattails and, having forgotten her tobacco, did not offer it to the snakes. As she began to cut the cattails, a woman snake, showing only her shoulders and head above the water, appeared to her. With eyes steadfastly peering at the grandmother, the snake began to mesmerize her until she fled in fright, not daring to take a single cattail.

Chief Papícoano told how, in the old days, when the Indians went on annual hunting expeditions, they carried a long, black rope made from the manes and tails of horses. Before going to bed, they laid the rope in a circle around the shelter to ward off rattlers, who are afraid of black snakes.

The Kickapoos own a special medicine, the rhizome of Solomon's seal, which they carry on their persons at all times. Just the act of carrying this rhizome is considered sufficient to make a snake violently ill and power-less. A Mexican who has lived with the Kickapoos the greater part of his life told this snake story: He and a Kickapoo companion were hunting when suddenly they spied a huge, coiled rattler immediately in front of them where the Mexican was about to step. Fortunately, he saw the rat-tler in time to halt and draw back. The man's Indian wife added quickly that, by sheer luck, just before starting on the hunt, the Kickapoo friend had chewed some Solomon's seal and spit it on her Mexican spouse, exclaiming, "Now, you are safe!" The Mexican narrator was certain that what had prevented the coiled snake from striking him was the powerful medicine.

When the Kickapoos used to trap weasels, the aunt of an informant, leaving her protective medicine at home, went to check the traps one day and found a large rattler coiled over one of them. As the woman approached, the rattler hissed and blew its breath at her, frightening her to such a degree that she broke out with itching sores over her body.

Although the Indians are constantly exposed to snakes, only one case of snakebite came to our attention. Years ago, a group were on a hunting expedition. When the weather turned very warm, rather than sleep inside their shelter, a couple slept in the open. A rattler bit the woman, to whom first aid was immediately administered by pricking the area around the wound with a pita leaf and bathing it with a tincture of alcohol and snake-herb (*Dyschoriste linearis*). In spite of the treatment, she became deathly ill and was taken to Múzquiz, where a physician gave her the antitoxin and she recovered. Many believed she must have done something very offensive for Kitzihiat to punish her in this manner, particularly since only she, and not her husband, had been bitten.

Whereas snakes, spiders, and other taboo animals are never killed, the centipede is immediately attacked on sight. The Kickapoos do not believe a centipede dies when broken into several parts, as these continue to move.

Domestic Animals

Domestic animals among the Kickapoos include many dogs. These are kept as pets and treated kindly, but left to forage for themselves, with the result that they play an important role as scavengers. (Small puppies are used as sacred food in ceremonies; see Chapter 15.) Cats are also kept as pets, partly because of the belief that house rats and mice chew off human hair to build their nests, causing the victim to lose his mind. The cats are needed to keep the rats and mice under control. While the owners work in the United States, the cats forage for themselves in the surrounding *monte*, and their young often go wild.

Among work animals, the horse stands at the head of the list. The Kickapoos believe that the Indian pony, which they say is different from the white man's horse, was brought to them by their culture hero, Wisaka. They brand their own horses but do not castrate them, leaving this work to Mexicans. The men have no prejudices about riding mares, but do refrain from riding them for a month or more after they have foaled. Horses are not ridden, broken, or sold until they are at least three years old. To break a horse, a bridle of lechuguilla is used. Children are tied to the saddle when being taught to ride. Besides horses, mules are used for plowing and donkeys for hauling.

When a Kickapoo has an obligation, such as an adoption ceremony, a prolonged illness, a curing ceremony, or a debt, he sells one of his horses, mules, or cattle to defray the expense. When a young couple announce their marriage according to the acceptable Kickapoo tradition, the groom gives the bride a horse. She, in turn, gives it to a brother or an uncle. Horses are also used to pay for damages done to another's crop.

When sick, horses are treated with herbs and patent medicines. When a horse is being treated with herbs, it is considered fatal for it to be ridden by a menstruating woman. We were told about a horse that was undergoing herbal treatment. The owner, as soon as the horse had somewhat recovered, allowed teenagers to ride it, with the resulting bad luck that it stumbled and broke a shoulder blade, dying a few days later. The cause of the death was believed to have been neither the illness for which the horse was being treated with herbs nor the broken shoulder blade, but the fact that a menstruating girl had ridden it.

The Kickapoos believe that horses, as well as all other animals, have spirits and, when they die, go to live in the world of the spirits.

It is customary for domesticated animals, such as horses, mules, burros, dogs, and even the once despised pigs, to be given names that are eponyms of the owner's clan, but puppies raised for ceremonial feasts are simply called male or female dogs.

Cats are the subject of several beliefs. One woman who was caring for a setting hen told us that her cat had eaten the chicks as they hatched. Understandably irked with the cat, she picked up a stick to kill it, but her uncle stayed her, saying that, if she killed the cat, its spirit could return to harm her. Furthermore, cats sometimes turn themselves into witches and witches into cats. Instead of killing it, the woman took the cat to Múzquiz, where she turned it loose, adding to the already high cat population there.

Beliefs and Practices concerning Plants

Tobacco

Indian tobacco, like religion, permeates every phase of Kickapoo culture, as has been observed in the preceding pages. The Kickapoos believe that they did not always have tobacco. Kitzihiat, taking pity upon his children and wanting to send them a gift, called one of the Kickapoos from the spirit world and said, "Go to my children, the Kickapoos, but take care you do not frighten them with your appearance; explain to them that I send a gift, a piece of my heart, and show them how to raise the plant and how to use the plant which grows from my heart." The Kickapoo swallowed a piece of Kitzihiat's heart and went to see his people.

When he appeared, the people were greatly startled at seeing him return to this world, but he reassured them he was bearing a gift from Kitzihiat and began to vomit and retch the seeds of tobacco. Immediately, a gentle rain came down upon the seeds and they began to grow. At the same time, a voice was heard from the four corners of the world which said, "Look at me; care for me; water me!" The messenger instructed his people in the uses of the plant: it was to be employed for good and not for evil. With this, he returned to the spirit world. The Kickapoos added this plant to their pantheon of grandfathers—those manitous who take special interest in their welfare and serve to carry their supplications to Kitzihiat.

There are four different kinds of tobacco: the small-leaf variety used in prayers and ceremonies; the type used for curing; one used for gift-giving when "those of another nation come to visit"; and the one employed for everyday smoking.

Until a few years ago when the annual migration of the Kickapoos to the United States began, each clan leader raised enough tobacco for the clan members. Occasionally today, one of the leaders attempts to grow it, but seldom successfully. The Kickapoo women know they may not, under any circumstances, go near a tobacco plantation, whether menstruating or not, as the slightest whiff of a woman wilts the plants; but Mexican women, unaware of their danger, or both Mexican women and men, are thought to cast the evil eye on the plants and kill them. This constant threat has discouraged all further attempts to grow it. Because of this ever-present danger, the clan leaders in Mexico today get their tobacco from their colleagues in Oklahoma.

Tobacco, blessed by the clan leader, is distributed only to those regarded as worthy, at the New Year clan festivals. Those women who are not permitted to attend their clan festival get their portions from the leader who is the custodian for the entire village. The Kickapoos go to their clan festival with a small, circular piece of unused buckskin and a thong to receive their new issue of tobacco. Each man carries this minuscule pouch on his person, but women keep theirs hung on an upright in the house, unless they are traveling or gathering certain plants, to guard it from a sudden onset of menstruation.

To ensure the efficacy of tobacco, an appropriate prayer must accompany the offering. No ceremony can be performed without tobacco and its accompanying prayers, either as an offering to the fire or the bundle or to be smoked in the ceremonial pipe.

To the Kickapoos, tobacco is an effective solace on many occasions. Even ordinary tobacco gives gratification, relaxation, comfort, and pleasure; it erases anger, pain, and hate and drives away evil thoughts.

Whenever a Kickapoo seeks a medicinal plant in the field, he offers a bit of tobacco to the first of its kind that he finds and asks permission of this one to take others. If a Kickapoo is ill and wishes to place himself in the care of one of the curers, he or a member of his family takes an offering of tobacco to the curer who assumes the case. The women make an offering of tobacco to the one-seed juniper when cutting saplings for house construction and to the snakes and water hens who own the water before they enter to cut cattails.

Tobacco also has more utilitarian uses, as an agent against insect or snake bites, earache, nosebleed, or an aching back. To emphasize the power of tobacco an informant related the following experience: while lifting a bucket of water from a ground-level well she sprained her back and, after several days of intense pain, went to see a Mexican *componedor* (amateur chiropractor). In spite of this treatment, two days later she could not get out of bed. She recalled her leader telling the clan during the New Year festival that, when one has unsuccessfully tried a cure, one may appeal to the manitou of water by making it an offer of tobacco and bathing four consecutive days in the river at daybreak. This, the clan leader had told them, was the method used by the old Indians, who had passed their knowledge to the leaders. Awakening her spouse, she asked him to get her tobacco pouch and a stout stick to support her until she reached the river, some distance from her home. With his help, she walked to the river, each step causing her to cringe in pain. Arriving, she placed a bit of tobacco in her left hand and, addressing the manitou of the water, pronounced these words: "Help me in my affliction, I pray of you." She then threw herself into the river, in the meantime opening her hand and allowing the water to carry the tobacco to the manitou. This ritual she repeated for four consecutive days. On the second day, she no longer needed the help of her spouse to support her; on the third day she was further improved; and, after the fourth day, she had completely recovered.

To misuse Indian tobacco may bring death to an individual. Every Kickapoo vividly keeps in his memory the fate of a young man who, needing money quickly one day, sold his tobacco to a Mexican cowboy. Not long afterward, a Mexican, married to one of the Kickapoo women, heard the cowboy brag about his recent acquisition and the power associated with it. The young Kickapoo's misdeed soon became common knowledge in the village. Not long afterward, the young man went insane.

Solomon's Seal

Other than tobacco, by far the most highly regarded and magical plant among the Kickapoos is Solomon's seal, known in Algonquian to the Indians as "sweet medicine." This plant belongs to the clan leaders, and only they know where it is found in Coahuila and in Utah at altitudes above three thousand feet. An informant once accompanied a clan leader to gather Solomon's seal, observing that it greatly resembled wax Euphorbia; but when he returned the following day, hoping to find it, the plant had disappeared. Only the clan leaders or those assigned by them may gather the rhizome, and this must be done in June or July, when the moon is full and the plant's complete potency is assured. The leaders offer Indian tobacco to the first plant they see and do not take it, but ask its permission to gather others in the area.

During the New Year clan festivals, the clan leaders bless the rhizomes and distribute small pieces to the adults, giving them instruction on the plant's uses. Women are warned not to carry the root on their person until four days after menstruation.

The men carry it on their person in a small bundle of white cloth tied with a green ribbon. The women carry it in their bosom or pinned to a garment. Although this rhizome is held in great esteem, it can be given or sold to a non-Kickapoo; but it is worthless unless the appropriate prayers accompany it.

Solomon's seal is considered highly efficacious. It not only protects the carrier from numerous evils, such as poisonous snakes, centipedes, witches, thieves, harm to loved ones, and ill health, but also can keep a spouse from straying, can be used to enamor a desired person, can prognosticate the weather (becoming damp when rain is imminent), and can cure horses of snakebite. The Kickapoos claim that, while they carry the rhizome, a snake is powerless in their presence and will become violently ill. One Indian said that, if he was carrying this rhizome and performed the correct ritual, he could pick up a rattlesnake without any harm. A woman described how she and a companion slept on the ground during a recent trip to the mines where they sold merchandise. When we exclaimed, "Were you not afraid of rattlers?" she smiled at us and replied, "Con mi medicina no me hacen na'a las vívoras [with my medicine, snakes do me no harm]."

The Kickapoos believe in witches as surely as we believe the astronauts landed on the moon, and nothing fills them with more fear; but, if they have Solomon's seal, they feel secure. It is hung in the doorway at night to prevent witches from trespassing. A woman gave us a small piece of the rhizome with this information: "To'as las noches como poquito; así no entran naiden a mi casa [every night I nibble a bit; thus no one can enter my house]." When we inquired if *naiden* (no one) meant no witches, she nodded in accord.

If, for any reason, a Kickapoo leaves the village, he places several pieces of firewood in the doorway in such a manner that he can tell at a glance, upon his return, if someone has tampered with the sticks in an attempt to enter. If he is away and is told or has a premonition that his premises are being molested, he takes out his Solomon's seal and offers it Indian tobacco and prayers. This makes him confident that all is well. If he leaves loved ones at home, this same ritual protects them from harm.

The root is often used for curing purposes, not only by the clan leaders, the curers, and members of the herbal societies, but also by individuals who have been instructed in its uses by their clan leaders. One woman told us she had had a severe pain in her chest for several days and had cured herself by chewing and swallowing small bits of the rhizome.

Solomon's seal combined with the rhizome of the wild purple iris and the proper prayers can give the owner the power to do anything he wants. The rhizome is particularly effective in affairs of the heart. One woman confided that, as long as she can get a supply, the man to whom she is married will never leave her. She expressed this confidence by saying, "Ese hombre no me suelta [that man won't let go of me]."

One of the curers, who gave us a sample, explained to Dolores: four nibbles of the rhizome each day, and "Ese hombre no te deja [that man (raising her chin toward Felipe) will not leave you]." And in case she did not follow her instructions and he did leave her, or died, she could take four nibbles daily and have no difficulty finding another man.

We were told the following anecdote about a Mexican who had a Kickapoo concubine in the village. After a quarrel, she sent him away, but then she began to long for him so passionately that she was desperate. It seems that someone sold her Mexican lover a bit of the rhizome plus the prayers, and he was "making" her seek him out. If he continued in his obstinacy of not returning to her, she would become so hungry for love she might go out into the street and take up with any man who approached her. Unfortunately, her mother, who was a curer and could counteract this situation, was away at the time.

A woman related that when she was still a girl—before her menarche— she was washing clothes at the river one day when an older man began making advances. She repulsed him to the point of calling him *un viejo gastado* (an old man, sexually worn out). In spite of her disgust, a few days later she had an uncontrollable desire to see this man and went to his home. Fortunately, the man's mother was in the house and nothing happened. When the girl informed her grandmother what had taken place, the latter was understandably alarmed, especially since the girl had not had her menarche. They immediately sought a curer to negate the charm the man held over the girl; both the grandmother and the curer were sure that the old man had prayed to his piece of Solomon's seal in order to enamor the young virgin.

A Kickapoo friend presented us with a small, elaborately etched German-silver brooch with two minuscule curved projections in the shape of claws, given to her many years ago by an old woman. It was used in conjunction with the rhizome to enamor the person one desired. She had been extraordinarily successful with it on several occasions, she said, but now no longer needed it, as she had lost interest in men. When we asked if the brooch still had the power to "catch" someone, she retorted, "Have you not noticed the two little claws which serve to catch the one desired?"

As mentioned earlier, the efficacy of Solomon's seal extends into the animal kingdom. When a horse is bitten by a rattlesnake, the owner takes out his rhizome, offers it Indian tobacco and a prayer, chews off a bit and, with a sharp pin moistened with saliva, makes four stab wounds surrounding the bite, one for each time he makes a complete circle around the animal, spitting saliva at the wound during each turn.

"The Three Sisters": Corn, Beans, and Squash

Many magical beliefs and practices surround the three most important food plants used by the Kickapoos—corn, beans, and squash, all considered manitous and called "the Three Sisters." One old man told us the Kickapoos are still using the seeds of the corn originally brought by them from the Great Lakes area. This was verified by Dr. Hugh Cutler of the Missouri Botanical Garden of St. Louis, Missouri, to whom we sent samples of the corn.[2]

The Kickapoos once had four different colors of Indian corn: white from the north, black (dark puple) from the south, yellow from the east, and red from the west, but they now use only white and black. There are also four varieties of beans.

Various myths relate the source of the three plants. One version relates that an old woman found a grain of corn and, curious to see the plant, put the seed in the ground. The following year she planted the grains produced and thereafter had all the corn she needed. The same woman had a small dog who wandered off between the corn plants one day. When she missed him, she searched and discovered that the little dog's black eyes had been transformed into beans and its head into a squash. This myth was told by a woman whose maternal grandfather was a Shawnee.

Another myth tells that, when the first Kickapoo chief died and was buried, his people began to notice three different plants growing out of the ground where he lay: out of the region of the head came round squash; from the region of his teeth, came white kernels of corn; and from his fingers sprouted string beans.

The chief may not grow the Indian corn, beans, and squash indispensable to perform his ceremony to lift the food taboo during the feast of the first fruits; he assigns a man from the Berry or Man clan or one of their affiliates to perform this task. The man appointed selects an isolated place, builds a shelter, and supplies it with provisions for two moons. During this time he avoids the village and his spouse and does not bathe or change his clothes. He prepares the ground, plants the seeds, waters them by hand, and places a scarecrow among them to frighten the looting birds. Later, when the plants are maturing, they are guarded from strangers, who might kill the crop by casting the evil eye. They are particularly protected from menstruating women, whose mere odor is believed to wilt the tender shoots. As the ears of corn ripen, they must also be guarded from coyotes, who pull back the shucks to enjoy the milky kernels.

Today, Indian corn is used exclusively for ceremonial occasions; not, however, the squash and beans grown by the few who spend the summers at home. The seeds of these two plants are Mexican varieties and not descendants of ancestral seeds.[3] At present, the bulk of the Indian corn is brought from Oklahoma, where it is still grown in ample amounts, but seed is also brought from there and planted in Mexico.

Exactly when the watermelon and the cantaloupe became important ceremonial fruits for the Kickapoos, we have not been able to determine. Quimby tells us that the French, in their early contacts with the Algonquian tribes, brought them the watermelon,[4] which is of African origin. When Father Jacques Marquette visited the Indians at the mouth of the Arkansas River in 1673, he noted that "They eat no fruit but watermelon."[5] Both the watermelon and the cantaloupe are now considered Indian foods by the Kickapoos, are manitous, and have been added to the original "Three Sisters."

Dreams

The Kickapoos believe the reason a person dreams is because, while he is asleep, his spirit leaves the body and wanders, observing and watching what is occurring; at other times, it has personal experiences. It is therefore of the utmost importance that a sleeping person never be brusquely awakened; rather, his name must be quietly and gently called in order to give the spirit time to re-enter the body; otherwise, the spirit may become frightened and remain out of the body, causing the latter to sicken.

Not all dreams have significance, but certain ones have special meanings. To dream that a house has a hole in the west augurs a death.

To dream that an Indian who is ill rides a horse signifies that, although very sick, he will recover. An old Mexican renter, unaware of this belief, called on one of the Indians who was seriously ill and, as a joke, told of having seen the patient riding a horse, but about to fall because the rider was intoxicated. The family burst into smiles and commented, "He is going to get well." Indeed he did, and lived many years.

To dream that one's spouse is ill is an omen of death, since it is believed that when persons marry their spirits will thereafter be together.

To dream that the spirit of a deceased spouse has come to accompany the survivor to an adoption ceremony augurs death. When one of the most beloved old women was seriously ill, she told her nieces that she had dreamed that the spirit of her former spouse had come to accompany her to an adoption ceremony. The nieces, disturbed by the dream and the possible loss of their aunt, immediately burned cudweed, whose name means "to smoke out spirits." The smoke from the cudweed was apparently effective, as the patient dreamed no more of her former spouse.

Sometimes dreams may presage a tragedy or may be a reminder of some former trespass. A woman described a dream, prefacing her experience with the query, "Is not the spirit a wonderful thing, the way it can travel so far and wide?" One afternoon when she was sitting on a bench of the ramada, embroidering moccasins, she became drowsy and stretched out to have a short nap. During the brief rest, she saw a girl, five or six years old, running toward her, laughing and moving her head from side to side. She awoke smiling to herself over the antics of the girl; but suddenly a fear gripped her heart that this vivid dream might augur a misfortune. Later in the evening, a neighbor came with the news that her son had returned from Eagle Pass, where he had learned that a niece of our informant had died suddenly of a strange malady while her parents were working. Our friend was certain that her spirit had been to the place where the child, just prior to her death, had come running to her. Since attempts to bewitch her had been unsuccessful, she believed the child had died in her place, carrying out the plans of the witch to destroy her family.

Deaf-Mutes

The one deaf-mute youth in the village is also mentally retarded. Everyone is kind to him, giving him money, cigarettes, and food. He, in turn, does little chores, especially during the preparation of the feasts for ceremonies, such as carrying firewood and sprinkling the earth floor of the dance area. He never fails to participate in the man's dances, shuffling along like a disjointed puppet.

One day, some of his neighbors, riding on burros to their fields, observed a commotion in front of the compound where he lives. The mother of the youth was shouting that she was tired of giving him money for soda pop and cigarettes and dared him to ask the passing couple for some. At this, the youth mounted the burro of his neighbors and rode off with them. They gave the young man cigarettes and supper and made him a place to sleep in their shelter, warning him before retiring not to stray off.

When they got up the following morning, the youth was nowhere to be found. His host and hostess searched the neighborhood and concluded he had returned to his mother's home.

Later in the afternoon, when they picked up his mother to take her shopping in Múzquiz, they inquired about the youth and were told he had not returned. The couple, concerned over this turn of events for fear they might be held responsible for the boy's disappearance, quickly made the trip to Múzquiz and returned to the village, to find the youth had not yet appeared.

Immediately the couple, as well as many others, mounted on horses and burros and searched the surrounding hills for three days without finding a trace of the boy. By now greatly alarmed, Chief Papícoano went to Múzquiz to report the case to the authorities, who broadcast the boy's description over the local radio.

The following day, a truck driver, carrying a load of fluorite to the processing plant in Múzquiz, heard the news over his radio. As he was approaching the crossing, some fifteen miles from Múzquiz, which leads to the Indian village, he saw a young man on the side of the road who fitted the description of the missing Indian. The driver invited the youth to accompany him into Múzquiz and was convinced he had the right person when he noted the youth was a deaf-mute. On reaching Múzquiz, the youth was turned over to the authorities, much to the relief of everyone in the village.

When we inquired why the runaway youth had created such a commotion, we were told by one of the clan leaders that it is their belief that a deaf-mute, if lost, will turn into a devil with an insatiable hunger for human flesh. Had the youth not been found soon, he would have returned to the village to devour the Kickapoos.

Twins

Among the Kickapoos, as among many other peoples, twins are considered potentially dangerous. They are believed to be a sign of bad luck; and, unless one dies or is given away, some close member of the family is sure to meet death; on the other hand, they are also believed to be manitous.

The only twins among the Indians when we arrived were accepted because their mother had died at childbirth. Two sets of twins who were born a few years later were cause for much speculation and fear among the members of the tribe. The parents of one set gave one of the twins away, while the mother of the other set allowed one to die of malnutrition, hoping by this expedient to circumvent the death of a close relative.

Notes

Introduction

1. Robert E. Ritzenthaler and Frederick A. Peterson, *The Mexican Kickapoo Indians*, p. 9.

2. John M. Goggin, "The Mexican Kickapoo Indians," *Southwestern Journal of Anthropology* 7(1951):314.

3. Margaret Welpley Fisher, Introduction to *Ethnography of the Fox Indians*, by William Jones, p. 1.

4. Carlos Basauri, "Los ki-ka-poos," in *La población indígena de México*, by idem, III, 643–663; Alfonso Fabila, *La tribu kikapoo de Coahuila*; Roberto de la Cerda Silva, "Kikapús," in *Etnografía de México*, by idem, Francisco Rojas González, and René Barragán Avilés, pp. 671–681.

Chapter 1. Historical Sketch

1. A. M. Gibson, *The Kickapoos: Lords of the Middle Border*, p. 3. The Old Northwest extended from the eastern Great Lakes west to the Mississippi, with the lakes on the north and the Ohio River on the south. It included the present states of Ohio, Indiana, Illinois, Michigan, Wisconsin, and part of Minnesota (*Columbia Encyclopedia*, 3d ed., s.v. "Northwest Territory").

2. Charles Callender, *Social Organization of the Central Algonkian Indians*, p. xiii.

3. Louise Phelps Kellogg, *The French Regime in Wisconsin and the Northwest*, pp. 69–70.

4. Callender, *Social Organization*, p. 3.

5. Betty Ann Wilder Dillingham, "Oklahoma Kickapoo" (Ph.D. dissertation, University of Michigan, 1963), pp. 12–13.

6. Gibson, *The Kickapoos*, p. 15.

7. Hiram W. Beckwith, *The Illinois and Indiana Indians*, pp. 119–120.

8. Gibson, *The Kickapoos*, p. 13.

9. Dillingham, "Oklahoma Kickapoo," p. 13.

10. Kellogg, *The French Regime*, p. 39.

11. Grant Foreman, *Last Trek of the Indians*, p. 38.

12. Reuben Gold Thwaites, ed., *Jesuit Relations and Allied Documents: Travels and Explorations of the Jesuit Missionaries in New France, 1610–1791*, LVIII, 329–330.

13. Gibson, *The Kickapoos*, pp. 22–23.

14. Ibid., p. 24.

15. *Columbia Encyclopedia*, 3d ed., s.v. "Paris, Treaty of."

16. Gibson, *The Kickapoos*, pp. 25–30.

17. Ibid., pp. 33–39.

18. Dillingham, "Oklahoma Kickapoo," pp. 27–28.

19. Gibson, *The Kickapoos*, p. 47.

20. Dillingham, "Oklahoma Kickapoo," pp. 30–31.

21. Beckwith, *The Illinois*, p. 133.

22. Foreman, *Last Trek*, p. 26.

23. Gibson, *The Kickapoos*, p. 71.

24. Foreman, *Last Trek*, p. 27.

25. Ibid., pp. 27–31.

26. Ibid., pp. 38–39.

27. Ibid., pp. 39, 44.

28. Gibson, *The Kickapoos*, pp. 83–84.

29. Ibid., p. 109.

30. Ibid., p. 108.

31. Ibid., p. 147.

32. Ibid.

33. José María Sánchez, "A Trip to Texas in 1832," trans. Carlos Castañeda, *Southwestern Historical Quarterly* 24(1926):280.

34. Dorman H. Winfrey and James Day, eds., *The Indian Papers of Texas and the Southwest, 1825–1916*, I, 12.

35. Ralph W. Steen, *History of Texas*, p. 190.

36. Gibson, *The Kickapoos*, p. 150.

37. Vito Alessio Robles, *Coahuila y Texas desde la consumación de la Independencia hasta el Tratado de Paz de Guadalupe Hidalgo*, II, 198–199.

38. Gibson, *The Kickapoos*, p. 153.

39. Walter P. Lane, T. H. Dixon, and John P. Cox, *Battle with the Kickapoos*, pp. 1–7.

40. Gibson, *The Kickapoos*, p. 155.

41. Ibid., pp. 156–158.

42. U.S. Congress, Senate, *Affairs of the Kickapoo Indians*, Sen. Doc. No. 215, 60th Cong., 1st Sess. (1908), III, 1907.

43. Dillingham, "Oklahoma Kickapoo," p. 50.

44. U.S. Congress, Senate, *Affairs of the Kickapoo Indians*, III, 1912.

45. Gibson, *The Kickapoos*, p. 158.

46. Ben E. Pingenot, ed., *Paso del Aguila: A Chronicle of Frontier Days on the Texas Border as Recorded in the Memoirs of Jesse Sumpter*, p. 4.

47. Kenneth Wiggins Porter, "Seminole Flight from Fort Marion," *Florida Historical Society Quarterly* 22, no. 3(January 1944):129.

48. Edwin C. McReynolds, *The Seminoles*, p. 263.

49. Mrs. William L. Cazneau (Cora Montgomery), *Eagle Pass, or Life on the Border*, ed. Robert Crawford Cotner, pp. 73–74.

50. There has been much confusion in the spelling of the names, tribes, and languages of the Indians who went to Mexico and, in particular, of the term *mascogo*, frequently used by Mexican authorities. The best interpretation we have been able to find is that the term derives from the word *Muskogean*, an Algonquian term referring to a linguistic family, one dialect of which was spoken by the Seminoles and, probably, by the slaves and freed Negroes who accompanied Wild Cat to Mexico.

As far back as October 18, 1850, when the Inspector General of the Eastern Military Colonies, Don Antonio María Jaúregui, and Wild Cat signed an agreement admitting the "Seminoles, Quikapus and Mascogos, the last consisting of freed

Negroes," to Mexico, the Negroes have been called *los negros mascogos* by the Mexican authorities. When the Seminoles returned to the United States in 1861 and earlier, the Negroes, uncertain of their status in the land they had left, remained in Mexico. Their descendants are today called *negros mascogos*.

51. *Informe de la Comisión Pesquisidora de la Frontera del Norte*, p. 257.

52. Pingenot, ed., *Paso del Aguila*, p. 12 n. 11.

53. Antonio María Jaúregui, Inspector General of the Eastern Military Colonies, and Wild Cat, Chief of the Seminole Tribe, Agreement of June 27, 1850; *Informe*, p. 258.

54. José María Lacunza, Minister of Foreign Affairs, to Antonio María Jaúregui, Inspector General of the Eastern Military Colonies, Resolution of October 18, 1850. This and all subsequent translations from Spanish are ours, except where otherwise indicated.

55. Juan Vicente Campos, Governor of Coahuila, Decree of the Legislature of the State of Coahuila, September 25, 1850.

56. Kenneth Wiggins Porter, "The Seminole in Mexico, 1850–1861," *Hispanic American Historical Review* 31, no. 1(February 1951):7.

57. *Informe*, p. 260.

58. Pingenot, ed., *Paso del Aguila*, p. 126.

59. Porter, "The Seminole in Mexico," p. 8.

60. Pingenot, ed., *Paso del Aguila*, pp. 69–72.

61. Gen. Alberto Guajardo Papers, Notes, p. 6.

62. *Informe*, pp. 260–262.

63. Gen. Alberto Guajardo Papers, no. 139.

64. Kenneth Wiggins Porter, Vassar, Poughkeepsie, New York, Letter, March 23, 1947, to Mrs. Sarah S. McKellar, Eagle Pass, Texas. This source is in conflict with the report of Chief No-ko-aht, who claimed that when his followers arrived in El Nacimiento in 1865 they found no other Kickapoos there. (See below, following note 78.)

65. Alfred Barnaby Thomas, ed., *Teodoro de Croix and the Northern Frontier of New Spain, 1776–1783*, pp. 3–17.

66. Ildefonso Villarelo, "El centenario de la fundación de la Ciudad de Piedras Negras," *El Nacional* (Mexico City), May 29, 1949.

67. Gen. Alberto Guajardo Papers, no. 139.

68. U.S. Congress, Senate, *Explorations of the Red River of Louisiana in the Year 1852*, by Capt. Randolph B. Marcy and Brevet Capt. George B. McClellan, Sen. Exec. Doc. No. 54, 32d Cong., 2d Sess. (1853), p. 105.

69. *Informe*, p. 266.

70. U.S. Congress, Senate, *Affairs of the Kickapoo Indians*, III, 1886.

71. Ibid.

72. Gibson, *The Kickapoos*, p. 201.

73. Robert E. Ritzenthaler and Frederick A. Peterson, *The Mexican Kickapoo Indians*, p. 19.

74. Gibson, *The Kickapoos*, pp. 202–203.

75. George A. Root, ed., "No-ko-aht's Talk—A Kickapoo Chief's Account of a Tribal Journey from Kansas to Mexico and Return in the Sixties," *Kansas Historical Quarterly* 1(1932):155.

76. Harry Wood, "Battle of Civil War in Concho Country," *San Angelo Standard Times*, January 10, 1965. Different versions of this story are given by J. Evetts

Haley, in *Fort Concho and the Texas Frontier*, and by Gibson, in *The Kickapoos*, pp. 204–207. Both Haley and Gibson give Fossett's name as Henry.

77. J. N. Gregory, *Fort Concho: Its Why and Wherefore*, pp. 31–32.

78. Root, ed., "No-ko-aht's Talk," pp. 156–157. No-ko-aht's version is closer to Gibson's account of the battle than to that of Wood.

79. Ibid., pp. 157–158.

80. Gen. Alberto Guajardo Papers, no. 61.

81. Gibson, *The Kickapoos*, p. 201. Later, some of these Mexican Kickapoos were forced to relocate in Oklahoma (see below).

82. Ibid., p. 210.

83. Ibid., pp. 222–223.

84. Ibid., p. 226.

85. Martha Buntin, "The Mexican Kickapoos," *Chronicles of Oklahoma* 11, no. 1(1933):695–697.

86. Gibson, *The Kickapoos*, p. 229. Gibson gives Miles's name as Jonathan B. Miles. The U.S. Interior Department's *Biographical and Historical Index of American Indians and Persons Involved in Indian Affairs* lists him as John De Bras Miles. Foreman, in *Last Trek*, gives John D. Miles.

87. Buntin, "The Mexican Kickapoos," p. 698. Gibson, in *The Kickapoos*, gives Henry M. Atkinson and F. G. Williams; Foreman, in *Last Trek*, gives Harry M. Atkinson and Thomas G. Williams; the Interior Department index cited in note 86 gives H. M. Atkinson and Thomas G. Williams.

88. Buntin, "The Mexican Kickapoos," p. 699.

89. Gregory, *Fort Concho*, p. 31.

90. Frost Woodhull, "The Seminole Scouts on the Border," *Frontier Times* 15, no. 3(1937):120.

91. Foreman, *Last Trek*, pp. 210–211.

92. Buntin, "The Mexican Kickapoos," no. 2, pp. 700–703.

93. Ibid., p. 703.

94. Gibson, *The Kickapoos*, p. 269.

95. Kenneth Wiggins Porter and Edward S. Wallace, "Thunderbolt of the Frontier," *The Westerners* 8, no. 4(1961):84.

96. R. E. Moffitt, Santa Rosa, Coahuila, Letters, January 19, 1879, and February 9, 1879, to Lt. John L. Bullis, Fort Clark, Texas.

97. John Willet, land entrepreneur, Statement of June 17, 1895.

98. Interview with Chief Papícoano, Múzquiz, August 7, 1967.

99. Willet, Statement of June 17, 1895.

100. Kenneth Wiggins Porter, "Farewell to John Horse: An Episode of Seminole Negro Folk History," *Phylon* 8, no. 3(1947):272 n. 3; 273 n. 5.

101. Interview with Kaizatoa (Víctor Flores), Múzquiz, March 19, 1966.

102. Interview with Menichika (Benito González), Múzquiz, January 12, 1967.

103. Interview with Pancho Menaquah, Múzquiz, February 22, 1971.

104. Interview with M. K. Foster, Nueva Rosita, Coahuila, October 1, 1965.

Chapter 2. Setting, Language, and Transportation

1. Alfonso Fabila, *La tribu kikapoo de Coahuila*, p. 8.

2. President Lázaro Cárdenas, Decree of September 21, 1938.

3. Ibid.

4. Ibid.

5. Interview with M. K. Foster, Nueva Rosita, Coahuila, October 1, 1965.

6. *Informe de la Comisión Pesquisidora de la Frontera del Norte*, pp. 277–278.

7. Fabila, *La tribu kikapoo*, p. 32.

8. Truman Michelson, "Preliminary Report on the Linguistic Classification of Algonquian Tribes," in *Twenty-eighth Annual Report of the Bureau of American Ethnology*, p. 229.

9. Cecilio A. Robelo, *Diccionario de Aztequismos*, 3d ed., p. 338.

10. *Columbia Encyclopedia*, 3d ed., s.v. "Sequoyah."

11. W. P. Clark, *The Indian Sign Language*, p. 315.

12. Ibid., p. 213.

13. William Whistler, Major of the Second Infantry Regiment, Safe-conduct issued to a band of Kickapoos, September 28, 1832.

14. Interview with Dorothy Ostrom Worrell, Eagle Pass, Texas, July, 1960.

15. Amounts of money are given in U.S. dollars except where otherwise stated.

Chapter 3. Habitation

1. Robert E. Ritzenthaler and Frederick A. Peterson, *The Mexican Kickapoo Indians*, pp. 81–89.

2. George Irving Quimby, *Indian Life in the Upper Great Lakes*, p. 134.

3. John M. Goggin, "The Mexican Kickapoo Indians," *Southwestern Journal of Anthropology* 7(1951):319.

Chapter 4. Food and the Quest for Food

1. President Lázaro Cárdenas to Chief Papíkuano, Directive of September 22, 1938.

2. Interview with Charles Downing, Eagle Pass, Texas, June, 1960.

3. George Irving Quimby, *Indian Life in the Upper Great Lakes*, p. 112.

Chapter 5. Crafts

1. Robert E. Ritzenthaler and Frederick A. Peterson, *The Mexican Kickapoo Indians*, p. 76.

2. George Irving Quimby, *Indian Life in the Upper Great Lakes*, p. 138.

3. John C. Ewers, *The Horse in Blackfoot Indian Culture*, pp. 90–91.

4. Alanson Skinner, *Material Culture of the Menomini*, p. 356.

5. Quimby, *Indian Life*, p. 151.

Chapter 6. Dress, Personal Care, and Adornment

1. Mark R. Harrington, "Too Much Hominy," *The Masterkey* 18, no. 5(1944): 156.

2. John M. Goggin, "The Mexican Kickapoo Indians," *Southwestern Journal of Anthropology* 7(1951):321.

Chapter 7. Economy

1. Charles Callender, *Social Organization of the Central Algonkian Indians*, p. 3.
2. George Irving Quimby, *Indian Life in the Upper Great Lakes*, p. 133.
3. Callender, *Social Organization*, p. 12.
4. Quimby, *Indian Life*, p. 134.
5. Ibid.
6. Ibid., p. 111.
7. Ibid., p. 112.
8. Houston Clyde Wilson, "The Ethno-history of the Kickapoo Indians" (M.A. thesis, University of Texas, 1953), p. 160.
9. Charles M. Gates, ed., *Five Fur Traders of the Northwest*, p. 41.
10. Emma H. Blair, ed., *The Indian Tribes of the Upper Mississippi Valley and Regions of the Great Lakes*, II, 148–150.
11. Louise Phelps Kellogg, *The French Regime in Wisconsin and the Northwest*, p. 196.
12. Callender, *Social Organization*, p. 5.
13. Ibid. p. 6.
14. U.S. Congress, Senate, *Explorations of the Red River of Louisiana in the Year 1852*, by Capt. Randolph B. Marcy and Brevet Capt. George B. McClellan, Sen. Exec. Doc. No. 54, 32d Cong., 2d Sess. (1853), p. 105.
15. Interview with Aldon McKellar, Múzquiz, August 10, 1962.
16. Interview with Robert Spence, Sr., Sabinas, Coahuila, January 18, 1970.
17. Mark R. Harrington, "Too Much Hominy," *The Masterkey* 18, no. 5(1944): 156.
18. Alfonso Fabila, *La tribu kikapoo de Coahuila*, p. 14.
19. Interview with M. K. Foster, Nueva Rosita, Coahuila, October 1, 1965.
20. José María Lacunza, Minister of Foreign Affairs, to Antonio María Jaúregui, Inspector General of the Eastern Military Colonies, Resolution of October 18, 1850.
21. All information regarding wages and working conditions is from the decade 1960–1970 and is based on the reports of our Kickapoo informants and, in some cases, on our own observations.
22. Fabila, *La tribu kikapoo*, p. 20.
23. Ibid.

Chapter 8. Political and Legal Organization

1. Grant Foreman, *Last Trek of the Indians*, p. 216.
2. Robert E. Ritzenthaler and Frederick A. Peterson, *The Mexican Kickapoo Indians*, p. 41.
3. President Lázaro Cárdenas, Decree of September 21, 1938.

4. *Código Agrario y leyes complementarias*, in *Leyes y códigos de México*, 11th ed., Book 3, Article 140.

5. Cárdenas, Decree of September 21, 1938.

6. To confirm our deductions, the plats that show landmarks and boundaries would be indispensable. Several efforts to see the one drawn up in 1892 by Engineer Luis Mijar y Haro, which exists in the Agrarian Department, were unsuccessful. We were equally unsuccessful in attempts to inspect or obtain the Pastor plat and another "formed" or "made up" by a commission from the Secretariat of Agriculture and Development in 1923, the plat utilized by Engineer López Moctezuma when he divided the *colonia* El Nacimiento into three sections, and the plat drawn up by the Agrarian Department in 1938, when President Cárdenas expropriated land from La Mariposa and Las Rusias to give to the Kickapoos and the Negroes.

7. Gen. Alberto Guajardo Papers, no. 139.

8. Interview with Chief Papícoano, Múzquiz, February 25, 1962.

9. Gen. Alberto Guajardo Papers, no. 61.

10. President Venustiano Carranza, Decree of October 25, 1919.

11. Antonio María Jaúregui, Inspector General of the Eastern Military Colonies, and Wild Cat, Chief of the Seminole Tribe, Agreement of June 27, 1850.

12. Gen. Alberto Guajardo Papers, no. 139.

13. Ibid., no. 61.

14. Ibid., no. 62.

15. Carranza, Decree of October 25, 1919.

16. Governor of Coahuila (signature illegible) to Municipal President of Múzquiz, Order of February 6, 1920.

17. See Chapter 1, note 50. The inference about types of land was reached through information from the justice of the peace, Aurelio Vázquez Hidalgo, and personal inspection in his company of the farm lands of the half-breed Mexicans, where his parcel was located.

18. Manuel López Moctezuma, Secretariat of Agriculture and Development, to Municipal President of Múzquiz, Notice of January 17, 1920.

19. Gumaro García de la Cadena, Director of Land and Colonization, to Carlos Ramos, Inspector of Colonies, Instructions of November 12, 1926.

20. Carranza, Decree of October 25, 1919.

21. Cárdenas, Decree of September 21, 1938.

22. Carranza, Decree of October 25, 1919.

23. Cárdenas, Decree of September 21, 1938.

24. Interview with Robert Spence, Sr., Sabinas, Coahuila, January 18, 1970.

25. Interview with Aurelio Vázquez Hidalgo, Múzquiz, February 18, 1964.

26. Cárdenas, Decree of September 21, 1938.

27. Ibid.

28. Ibid.

29. Interviews with Aurelio Vázquez Hidalgo, Múzquiz, May 4, 1966; May 6, 1966.

30. President Lázaro Cárdenas to Citizens Papikuano and Mi-nu-mi-ma, Agreement of July 20, 1936.

31. Interview with Aurelio Vázquez Hidalgo, Múzquiz, May 4, 1966.

32. Ibid.

33. Vito Alessio Robles, "Kikapus y mascogos," Mexico City newspaper (name not annotated), September 21, 1936.

34. President Lázaro Cárdenas to Lic. Gabino Vázquez, Director of the Agrarian Department, Instructions of May 29, 1937.

35. President Lázaro Cárdenas to Prof. Graciano Sánchez, Director of the Department of Indian Affairs, Instructions of May 30, 1937.

36. President Lázaro Cárdenas to Chief Papíkuano, Directive of September 22, 1938.

37. Alfonso Fabila, *La tribu kikapoo de Coahuila*, p. 17.

38. Ibid.

39. Ibid., p. 16.

40. Ibid., pp. 18–19.

41. *Código Agrario*, Book 3, Title 1, Ch. 3, Article 169.

42. Ibid., Ch. 1, Article 144.

43. Ibid., Book 1, Ch. 1, Articles 22–31.

44. Interview with Robert Spence, Sr.

45. Fabila, *La tribu kikapoo*, p. 16.

46. Typescript copies of contracts and agreements between ranchers and Indians, 1951–1954, Múzquiz Municipality; interview with Oscar Sukwe, Múzquiz, January 1, 1962.

47. *Ejidatario* enrollment, 1955.

48. Fabila, *La tribu kikapoo*, p. 20.

49. Chief Papícoano and Oscar Sukwe, Termination of authority and acknowledgment of same, April 10, 1958.

50. Interviews with Dr. Jesús Pader, Múzquiz, May 30, 1961; with Papícoano, Múzquiz, April 4, 1961; with Pisacana, Múzquiz, April 4, 1961.

51. Interview with Jesús Garza Salazar, Múzquiz, May 3, 1964.

52. Julio Ogarrio Daguerre, Consulting Attorney, Department of Water, Land, and Colonization, to Menouninia, Chief Papícoano's Aide, Notification of August 16, 1932.

53. Interview with Jesús Garza Salazar, Múzquiz, May 2, 1964.

54. Papícoano, Chief of the Kickapoos, Nanamakia, and Sukwe, and Jesús Garza Salazar and others, Agreement of May 25, 1954.

55. Kaizatoa and others, representing the Kickapoos, to the Municipal President of Múzquiz, Petition of March 5, 1964.

56. Kaizatoa and others, representing the Kickapoos, to the Agrarian Department, Petition of March 13, 1964.

57. Adolfo Anico, President of Ejido, Notice of June 3, 1967.

58. Miguel Rodríguez González, Livestock census of October, 1967.

Chapter 9. Social Structure

1. Lewis Henry Morgan, *Systems of Consanguinity and Affinity*.

2. Betty Ann Wilder Dillingham, "Oklahoma Kickapoo" (Ph.D. dissertation, University of Michigan, 1963), p. 104.

3. Charles Callender, *Social Organization of the Central Algonkian Indians*, p. 18.

4. Sol Tax, "Social Organization of the Fox Indians," in *Social Anthropology of North American Tribes*, ed. Fred Eggan, p. 264.

5. Truman Michelson, *Fox Miscellany*, p. 63.

6. William Jones, "Kickapoo Ethnological Notes," *American Anthropologist*, n.s. 15, no. 2(1913):335.

7. Tax, "Social Organization," p. 268.

Chapter 10. Life Cycle

1. Martha Buntin, "The Mexican Kickapoos," *Chronicles of Oklahoma* 11, no. 2(1933):827.

2. Betty Ann Wilder Dillingham, "Oklahoma Kickapoo" (Ph.D. dissertation, University of Michigan, 1963), p. 247.

3. Sol Tax, "Social Organization of the Fox Indians," in *Social Anthropology of North American Tribes*, ed. Fred Eggan, p. 264.

4. Charles Callender, *Social Organization of the Central Algonkian Indians*, p. 24.

5. Dillingham, "Oklahoma Kickapoo," pp. 132–133.

6. Ben J. Wallace, "The Oklahoma Kickapoo: An Ethnographic Reconstruction," *Wisconsin Archeologist* 45, no. 1(1964):58.

7. Emma H. Blair, ed., *The Indian Tribes of the Upper Mississippi Valley and Regions of the Great Lakes*, II, 216.

8. Callender, *Social Organization*, p. 63.

9. Dillingham, "Oklahoma Kickapoo," p. 132.

10. Ibid.

11. Blair, ed., *Indian Tribes*, II, 216.

12. Alanson Skinner, *The Mascoutens or Prairie Potawatomi Indians*, p. 35.

13. Blair, ed., *Indian Tribes*, II, 214.

14. Ibid.

Chapter 11. Concept of Self and Others

1. Frost Woodhull, "The Seminole Indian Scouts on the Border," *Frontier Times* 15, no. 3(1937):121.

2. José María Lacunza, Minister of Foreign Affairs, to Antonio María Jáuregui, Inspector General of the Eastern Military Colonies, Resolution of October 18, 1850.

Chapter 12. Knowledge and Tradition

1. Emma H. Blair, ed., *The Indian Tribes of the Upper Mississippi Valley and Regions of the Great Lakes*, II, 221.

2. Lewis Henry Morgan, *The Indian Journals, 1859–62*, ed. Leslie A. White.

3. Blair, ed., *Indian Tribes*, II, 221.

4. Robert E. Ritzenthaler and Frederick A. Peterson, "Courtship Whistling of

the Mexican Kickapoo Indians," *American Anthropologist*, n.s. 56, no. 6, pt. 1(1954):1088.

5. Ibid.

6. Both Truman Michelson, in *Fox Miscellany*, p. 73, and Thomas Forsyth, in *Indian Tribes*, ed. Blair, II, 220, give lists of Fox and Sauk moons, with the meanings of the names. It seems probable that the old Kickapoo names were similar. According to our informants, Kickapoos, Fox, and Sauk speak mutually intelligible dialects.

7. Alfonso Fabila says that the average temperature is 76° F., with a maximum of 120° and a minimum of 32° (*La tribu kikapoo de Coahuila*, p. 10). However, while we were in Múzquiz, the temperature sometimes dropped as low as 20°.

8. Hacienda de Sabinas and American Smelting and Refining Company, Rain record, 1902–1970.

9. Fabila, *La tribu kikapoo*, p. 11.

Chapter 13. Disease, Medicine, and Intoxicants

1. Padre Fray Juan Agustín Morfi, *Excerpts from the Memorias for the History of the Province of Texas*, ed. Frederick C. Chabot, Appendix, pp. 70–71.

2. Gustav G. Carlson and Volney H. Jones, "Some Notes on Uses of Plants by the Comanche Indians," *Papers of the Michigan Academy of Science, Arts, and Letters* 25(1939):517–542.

3. Interview with Aurelio Vázquez Hidalgo, Múzquiz, May 4, 1966.

4. Alfonso Fabila, *La tribu kikapoo de Coahuila*, p. 24.

5. Interview with Dr. Jesús Pader, Múzquiz, May 30, 1960.

6. Interview with Dr. Jacobo Chapa Long, Múzquiz, June 24, 1960.

7. Ibid.

8. Interview with Dr. Régulo Zapata Múzquiz, Nueva Rosita, Coahuila, May 26, 1961.

9. George Irving Quimby, *Indian Life in the Upper Great Lakes*, p. 154.

10. A. M. Gibson, *The Kickapoos: Lords of the Middle Border*, p. 283.

Chapter 14. Religion

1. Ben J. Wallace, "The Oklahoma Kickapoo: An Ethnographic Reconstruction," *Wisconsin Archeologist* 45, no. 1(1964):34.

2. Robert E. Ritzenthaler and Frederick A. Peterson, *The Mexican Kickapoo Indians*, pp. 45–46.

3. Betty Ann Wilder Dillingham, "Oklahoma Kickapoo" (Ph.D. dissertation, University of Michigan, 1963), p. 143.

4. See Alanson Skinner, *The Mascoutens or Prairie Potawatomi Indians*, p. 48.

5. Emma H. Blair, ed., *The Indian Tribes of the Upper Mississippi Valley and Regions of the Great Lakes*, II, 223.

6. Vernon Kinietz and Erminie W. Voegelin, eds., *Shawnese Traditions: C. C. Trowbridge's Account*, p. 41.

7. Dillingham, "Oklahoma Kickapoo," p. 150.

8. Ibid., p. 123.

9. Ibid.; Frederick Webb Hodge, ed., *Handbook of American Indians North of Mexico*, I, 685; William Jones, "Kickapoo Ethnological Notes," *American Anthropologist*, n.s. 15, no. 2(1913):335.

10. Alanson Skinner, *The Mascoutens or Prairie Potawatomi Indians*, p. 56.

Chapter 15. Rituals and Ceremonies

1. Frances Densmore, collector, *Songs of the Menominee, Mandan and Hidatsa* (L.P. record).

2. George Irving Quimby, *Indian Life in the Upper Great Lakes*, p. 151.

3. J. N. B. Hewitt, "Adoption," in *Handbook of American Indians North of Mexico*, ed. Frederick Webb Hodge, I, 15.

4. Frank G. Speck, *The Tutelo Spirit Adoption Ceremony*, p. 10.

5. Frederick Webb Hodge, ed., *Handbook of American Indians North of Mexico*, I, 127.

6. Truman Michelson, *Contributions to Fox Ethnology*, pp. 9–35.

7. Truman Michelson, *Notes on the Fox Wâpanōwiweni*, p. 13.

8. A. M. Gibson, *The Kickapoos: Lords of the Middle Border*, p. 24.

9. Ibid.

10. Ibid.

11. Alfonso Fabila, *La tribu kikapoo de Coahuila*, p. 25.

12. Michelson, *Notes*, p. 7.

13. Roger Tory Peterson, *A Field Guide to the Birds of Texas*, pp. 209, 223, 224.

14. Emma H. Blair, ed., *The Indian Tribes of the Upper Mississippi Valley and Regions of the Great Lakes*, II, 230.

15. John R. Swanton, *The Indians of Southeastern United States*, pp. 256–257.

16. John Witthoft, *Green Corn Ceremonialism in the Eastern Woodlands*, pp. 49–55.

17. Betty Ann Wilder Dillingham, "Oklahoma Kickapoo" (Ph.D. dissertation, University of Michigan, 1963), p. 190.

18. William Jones, "The Algonkin Manitou," *Journal of American Folk-lore* 18(1905):184.

Chapter 16. Magical Beliefs and Practices

1. Clark Wissler, "The Whirlwind and the Elk in the Mythology of the Dakota," *Journal of American Folk-lore* 18 (October–December 1905):256–268.

2. Dr. Hugh Cutler, Missouri Botanical Garden, Saint Louis, Letter, April 10, 1970, to authors.

3. Ibid.

4. George Irving Quimby, *Indian Life in the Upper Great Lakes*, p. 112.

5. Reuben Gold Thwaites, ed., *Jesuit Relations and Allied Documents: Travels and Explorations of the Jesuit Missionaries in New France, 1610–1791*, LIX, 159.

Glossary

affinity: the status of being related by marriage.
aficionado: buff, fan, enthusiast.
ahuacacuahuitl (Nahuatl): avocado.
ahuacate or *aguacate* (Spanish): avocado.
ahuacatemisi: Algonquianized word for *avocado*.
Algonkian, Algonkin, Algonquin: variants of *Algonquian*.
Algonquian: a family of North American Indian languages; an Indian of an Algonquian-speaking tribe.
andar: to live together without being married in the acceptable Kickapoo way.
Ba-Be-Bi-Bo: Cherokee syllabary used by the Kickapoos.
bayo: a beige bean.
bracero: a Mexican agricultural or industrial laborer permitted to enter the United States to work for a limited period of time.
brujo, bruja: witch.
bulto: an old Spanish dry measure comprising approximately five hundred liters of material, such as beans or corn.
bundle: a package of objects that have special magical or ritualistic properties.
café: coffee.
cafti: Algonquianized word for *coffee*.
callejón: a public alley between ranches.
campaña: former two-to-three-month hunt.
casco: headquarters of a ranch.
chi: the word used by the Kickapoos for *urine*.
chicales: dried corn kernels.
chiche: breast.
chichero: brassière.
chilepiquín: bush pepper (*Capsicum annum*).
chípil: sibling jealousy.
clan: a group of individuals, not necessarily kin, whose names are eponyms of the same totem and who share the ritual, teachings, and protection associated with a sacred or medicine bundle.
claro de agua: the amount of water that passes through an irrigation ditch approximately two feet wide by two feet deep from sunrise to sunset or vice versa.
Código Agrario: Agrarian Code.
colonia: a colony; a group of persons who settle and cultivate land in a new area. This was the term used for the Kickapoo settlement at El Nacimiento until the establishment of the *ejido* there.

colonia militar: a garrison established to protect civilian *colonias*.

comadre: name given and used reciprocally by the mother and godmother of a child. As used by the Mexicans in addressing Kickapoo women, it is a condescending and paternalistic term.

comal: a griddle for cooking tortillas; the lid of a wood stove.

comerciar: to engage in commerce; to trade.

componedor: folk chiropractor.

confortativo: comforter; specifically, a loaf of bread condimented with herbs and placed on the abdomen when suffering from *latido*.

consanguine: related by blood.

cuarterón: literally, a person who has one-quarter Negro blood; in Múzquiz, a person with any mixture of Mexican and Negro blood.

curandero, curandera: a folk healer or curer.

día de agua: the amount of water that passes through the main irrigation canal from sunrise to sunset or vice versa.

ejidatario: a person entitled to use *ejido* land.

ejido: communal land.

empacho: a condition in which ingested food adheres to the stomach and will not pass.

endogamy: the practice of choosing a mate inside one's clan.

enfermedad: sickness; menses.

exogamy: the practice of choosing a mate outside one's clan.

familiares: relatives.

family, extended: a family consisting of the father, mother, children, and other relatives.

family, nuclear: a family consisting of the father, mother, and children.

frialdad: a condition said to occur in women who fail to observe the forty-day period of abstinence after the birth of a child, characterized by a yellow discharge.

fritada de cabrito: a fricassee made with the entrails of a kid.

herencia: an individual's heritage.

huaraches: leather sandals.

jacal: hut.

jarrito: earthenware jar in which beans are cooked.

Kisko: Algonquian word signifying "paints with white clay"; one of the two moieties of the Kickapoo tribe.

latido: a throbbing in the pit of the stomach with accompanying pain and discomfort.

liviana. SEE *muy liviana*.

lonche: lunch.

los de la casa: kinsfolk.

lotería: a form of bingo.

luna: the moon; menses.

macho: a male who is considered or considers himself manly, brave, and sexually attractive to women.

mal de ojo: evil eye.

mal puesto: witchcraft.

mano. SEE metate and mano.

Masarina: brand name for a prepared cornmeal used for making tortillas.

matrilocal: having reference to a married couple residing with the wife's mother.

menarche: the first menses.

mescal: a potent distilled liquor made, in Coahuila, from sotol and related species.

metate and mano: a curved stone on which grain is ground and the cylindrical hand stone which accompanies it.

migas de tortilla: a Mexican dish prepared with pieces of fried tortillas and a tomato and onion sauce.

misami (Algonquian): sacred pack or medicine bundle.

misas de capitán: the chief's ceremonies.

moiety: one of the two primary groups into which the tribe is divided. The Kickapoo moieties are called Kisko and Oskasa.

molcajete: volcanic rock mortar and pestle.

mollera caída: fallen fontanelle.

monte: brush country.

morcilla: blood sausage.

morral: an istle or plastic bag for carrying objects.

mujer nueva: a woman interested in sex.

mujer vieja: a woman no longer interested in sex.

municipio: city hall; unit of local government, similar to an American county or township.

muy liviana: a woman easily persuaded into a dalliance.

muy troteadora: a woman who changes husbands and lovers frequently.

nana: grandmother.

nekanaki (Algonquian): reciprocal clan friends.

nepupe (Algonquian): stew.

ocotillo: Jacob's staff (*Forquieria splendens* Engelm).

Oskasa: Algonquian word signifying "paints with charcoal"; one of the two moieties of the Kickapoo tribe.

paco: a variety of poker.

partido: team or division; used by the Kickapoos to refer to the moiety.

patrilineal: determining the transmission of name, property, or authority through males.

pavé: a setting of stones placed together so closely that no metal shows; used to describe the manner in which beads are sewed on moccasins.

petate: straw mat.

picadillo: ground meat seasoned with onions, tomatoes, and spices.

piloncillo: brown sugar cone.

pinole: toasted and ground dry corn.

pita: various yucca species.

Plan de Guadalupe: the Plan of Guadalupe, signed at Hacienda de Guadalupe, Coahuila, March 26, 1913, in which the government of Victoriano Huerta was disregarded and the leadership of Venustiano Carranza recognized in its place.

pochismos: Castilianized words, such as *lonche* for "lunch."

policía judicial: federal police.

quiote: the tender, roasted end of the century-plant scape.

ramada: a shelter made with branches of trees or shrubs; the porch in front of a Kickapoo summer house.

resguardo forestal: game and forest wardens.

señorita: an unmarried woman; among the Mexicans and Kickapoos, a girl who has had her first menses.

sentimiento: grief.

sitio de ganado mayor: an old Spanish measure of land comprising 1,755.6 hectares.

sopa de helote: stewed fresh corn.

sororate: the custom in which a man marries his wife's sisters, either during her life or after her death.

soyate: the dry leaves of various species of yucca used for roofing.

susto: fright or spirit loss.

susto frío: an old spirit loss not attended to immediately.

susto meco: same as *susto frío*.

tarea: an old Spanish measure of land, the amount a man can plow in one day with a team of mules or horses; approximately 2,500 square meters.

tortilla de harina: wheat-flour tortilla.

traer: to bind; to be wed in the approved Kickapoo way.

transvestism: wearing the clothing of the opposite sex.

trastero: a kitchen cupboard.

troteadora: SEE *muy troteadora*.

vara: an old Spanish linear measure, varying between thirty-two and forty-three inches.

viejo gastado: a sexually used-up man.

viñata: a place where mescal or wine is made.

vino: wine; in Múzquiz and among the Kickapoos, used as a substitute for the word *mescal*.

yarda: yard.

zona de tolerancia: red-light district.

Bibliography

Archival and Unpublished Material

Anico, Adolfo, President of Ejido. Notice to renters to sign acknowledgment that they have been given a ninety-day period of grace in which to find other pastures. El Nacimiento, June 3, 1967. Photocopy in collection of authors.

Campos, Juan Vicente, Governor of Coahuila. Decree of the Legislature of the State of Coahuila ordering the Indian immigrants to evacuate the land on the headwaters of the San Rodrigo and San Antonio rivers. Saltillo, September 25, 1850. Photocopy in collection of authors.

Cárdenas, President Lázaro. Decree of September 21, 1938, assigning 4,335.28 hectares of land, expropriated from La Mariposa, to the Kickapoos. Published in the *Periódico Oficial*, Saltillo, June 1, 1940. Typescript copy in collection of authors.

――――. To Chief Papíkuano. Directive instructing the Kickapoos to observe the closed season on deer and notification that restitution of land is being resolved. Presidency of the Republic, Mexico City, September 22, 1938. No. V 542. Original in collection of authors.

――――. To Citizens Papikuano and Mi-nu-mi-ma. Agreement reiterating the traditional right of the Kickapoos to hunt and use the natural resources on their land unrestrictedly. El Nacimiento, July 20, 1936. No. 1432. Photocopy in collection of authors.

――――. To Lic. Gabino Vázquez, Director of the Agrarian Department. Instructions to supply the Kickapoos with twenty mules. Presidency of the Republic, Mexico City, May 29, 1937. No. 1121V. Original in collection of authors.

――――. To Prof. Graciano Sánchez, Director of the Department of Indian Affairs. Instructions to supply the Kickapoos with a sewing machine and wheat or other needed seed. Presidency of the Republic, Mexico City, May 30, 1937. No. 1120 V. Original in collection of authors.

Carranza, President Venustiano. Decree recognizing that the lands owned by the Seminoles, Kickapoos, and Mascogos, called Hacienda El Nacimiento, comprising 7,022.44 hectares, have left the dominion of the nation. Querétaro, October 25, 1919. Sección de Agricultura y Fomento, Dirección Agraria, Departamento de Colonización, Mexico City, no. 6067. Also in Múzquiz Archives. Typescript copy in collection of authors.

Cutler, Dr. Hugh, Missouri Botanical Garden, Saint Louis. Letter, April 10, 1970, to authors.

Dillingham, Betty Ann Wilder. "Oklahoma Kickapoo." Ph.D. dissertation, University of Michigan, 1963.

Ejidatario enrollment, 1955. Transcript copy in collection of authors.

García de la Cadena, Gumaro, Director of Land and Colonization. To Carlos Ramos, Inspector of Colonies. Instructions to fix boundaries and erect landmarks in Colonia El Nacimiento. Mexico City, November 12, 1926. Secretaría de Agricultura y Fomento, Dirección de Aguas, Tierras y Colonización, Sección Técnica, No. 014460. U 1.71. Typescript copy in collection of authors.

Governor of Coahuila (signature illegible). To Muncipal President of Múzquiz. Order giving *cuarterones* (half-breeds) 429 hectares of land from Colonia El Nacimiento. Saltillo, February 6, 1920. Secretaría de Gobernación y Fomento, Sección 11, no. 538. Typescript copy in collection of authors.

Guajardo, Gen. Alberto, Papers. Pages 6, 39, and 66 of General Guajardo's notes; documents nos. 61 (November 29, 1866), 62 (February 20, 1867), and 139 (August 18, 1852). Beinecke Rare Book and Manuscript Library, Yale University. Photocopies in collection of authors.

Hacienda de Sabinas and American Smelting and Refining Company. Rain record, 1902–1970. Nueva Rosita, Coahuila. Photocopy in collection of authors.

Jaúregui, Antonio María, Inspector General of the Eastern Military Colonies, and Wild Cat, Chief of the Seminole Tribe. Agreement in which eight *sitios de ganado mayor* at the headwaters of the San Rodrigo River and eight at the headwaters of the San Antonio River are assigned to the Seminoles, Kickapoos, and free Negroes. Villa de San Fernando, Coahuila, June 27, 1850. Inspección de las Colonias de Oriente, Mexico City. Typescript copy in collection of authors.

Kaizatoa and others, representing the Kickapoos. To the Agrarian Department. Petition that Chief Papícoano and others desist from renting communal lands. Múzquiz, March 13, 1964. Carbon copy in collection of authors.

———. To the Municipal President of Múzquiz. Petition asking that Chief Papícoano and others desist from renting Kickapoo land to ranchers. Múzquiz, February 12, 1964. Carbon copy in collection of authors.

———. To the Municipal President of Múzquiz. Petition asking that Chief Papícoano, his aide, Pisacana, and Sukwe desist from renting the pastures of El Nacimiento to Mexican ranchers. El Nacimiento de los Kickapoos, March 5, 1964. Typescript copy in collection of authors.

Lacunza, José María, Minister of Foreign Affairs, to Antonio María Jaúregui, Inspector General of the Eastern Military Colonies. Resolution admitting the Seminoles, Kickapoos, and Mascogan Indians as colonizers, subject to the laws of colonization and federal lands. Mexico City, October 18, 1850. Código de Colonización y Terrenos Baldíos, no. 144, pp. 474–478, Archivo del Estado, Saltillo, Coahuila. Typescript copy in collection of authors.

Lewis, Mrs. J. H. "Interview on the Kickapoos of Oklahoma." Interviewed by Amelia F. Harris, February 18, 1938. Typescript. Indian-Pioneer History Foreman Collection, Indian Archives, vol. 61, pp. 233–264. Oklahoma Historical Society, Oklahoma City.

López Moctezuma, Manuel, Secretariat of Agriculture and Development. To Municipal President of Múzquiz. Notice that Hacienda El Nacimiento has been divided in three sections: one for the Kickapoos, one for the Mascogan Negroes, and one for the *cuarterones* (half-breeds) and Mexicans married to women descendants of the colony's founders. Múzquiz, January 17, 1920. Múzquiz Archives. Typescript copy in collection of authors.

Moffit, R. E., Santa Rosa, Coahuila. Letters, January 19, 1879, and February 9, 1879, to Lt. John L. Bullis, Fort Clark, Texas. Received by the Adjutant General's office, 1871–1880; File 1653 (Mexican Border Troubles). National Archives, Washington, D.C. Microfilm copy 666, roll 208, in collection of authors.

Ogarrio Daguerre, Julio, Consulting Attorney, Department of Water, Land, and Colonization. To Menouninia, Chief Papícoano's Aide. Notification that petition to evict non-Kickapoos from Hacienda El Nacimiento must be done through local judiciary rather than administrative channels. Mexico City, August 16, 1932. Typescript copy in collection of authors.

Papícoano, Chief, and Oscar Sukwe. Termination of authority and acknowledgment of same. Múzquiz, April 10, 1958. Original in collection of authors.

Papícoano, Chief of the Kickapoos, Nanamakia, and Sukwe, and Jesús Garza Salazar and others. Agreement to rent Kickapoo pasture lands for a period of ten years. Múzquiz, May 25, 1954. Múzquiz Archives. Typescript copy in collection of authors.

Porter, Kenneth Wiggins, Vassar, Poughkeepsie, New York. Letter, March 23, 1947, to Mrs. Sarah S. McKellar, Eagle Pass, Texas. Original in collection of authors.

Rodríguez González, Miguel. Livestock census in El Nacimiento de los Kickapoos. El Nacimiento, October, 1967. Carbon copy in collection of authors.

Whistler, William, Major of the Second Infantry Regiment. Safe-conduct issued to a band of Kickapoos. Fort Dearborn, Illinois, September 28, 1832. Photocopy in collection of authors.

Willet, John, land entrepreneur who arranged sale between the Sánchez Navarro estate and David Harkness McKellar and J. W. and A. E. Noble. Statement, asserting that no Indians or Negroes were living on Hacienda El Nacimiento in 1879 when he inspected the land and that, to his knowledge, the Seminole Indians, Negroes, and Kickapoos were mere squatters. San Antonio, Texas, June 17, 1895. Typescript copy in collection of authors.

Wilson, Houston Clyde. "The Ethno-history of the Kickapoo Indians." M.A. thesis, University of Texas, 1953.

Published Works

Alessio Robles, Vito. *Coahuila y Texas desde la consumación de la Independencia hasta el Tratado de Paz de Guadalupe Hidalgo*. 2 vols. Mexico City: Talleres Gráficos de la Nación, 1945–1946.

———. "Kikapus y mascogos." Mexico City newspaper (name not annotated), September 21, 1936. Clipping in collection of authors.

Basauri, Carlos. "Los ki-ka-poos." In *La población indígena de México*, by idem, III, 643–663. Mexico City: Secretaría de Educación Pública, 1940.

Beckwith, Hiram W. *The Illinois and Indiana Indians*. Fergus Historical Series No. 27. Chicago, 1884.

Bennett, M. K. "The Food Economy of the New England Indians, 1606–75." *The Journal of Political Economy* 63, no. 5(October 1955):369–397.

Blair, Emma H., ed. *The Indian Tribes of the Upper Mississippi Valley and Regions of the Great Lakes*. 2 vols. Cleveland: Arthur H. Clark, 1911.

Blumensohn, Jules. "The Fast Among the North American Indians." *American Anthropologist*, n.s. 35(1933):451–469.

Buntin, Martha. "The Mexican Kickapoos." *Chronicles of Oklahoma* 11, nos. 1 and 2(1933):691–708, 823–837.

Callender, Charles. *Social Organization of the Central Algonkian Indians*. Milwaukee Public Museum Publications in Anthropology. Milwaukee, 1962.

Carlson, Gustav G., and Volney H. Jones. "Some Notes on Uses of Plants by the Comanche Indians." *Papers of the Michigan Academy of Science, Arts, and Letters* 25(1939):517–542.

Cazneau, Mrs. William L. (Cora Montgomery). *Eagle Pass, or Life on the Border*. Edited by Robert Crawford Cotner. Austin: Pemberton Press, 1966.

Cerda Silva, Roberto de la. "Kikapús." In *Etnografía de México*, by idem, Francisco Rojas González, and René Barragán Avilés, pp. 671–681. Mexico City: Universidad Nacional Autónoma de México, Instituto de Investigaciones Sociales, 1957.

Clark, W. P. *The Indian Sign Language*. San Jose, Calif.: Rosicrucian Press, 1959.

Código Agrario y leyes complementarias. In *Leyes y códigos de México*. 11th ed. Mexico City: Editorial Porrua, 1964.

Columbia Encyclopedia. 3d ed. New York: Columbia University Press, 1963.

Croix, Teodoro de. *Teodoro de Croix and the Northern Frontier of New Spain, 1776–1783*. Translated and edited by Alfred Barnaby Thomas. Norman: University of Oklahoma Press, 1941.

Densmore, Frances, collector. *Songs of the Menominee, Mandan and Hidatsa*. L. P. record. Washington, D.C.: Library of Congress, Division of Music, n.d.

Diccionario Porrúa de Historia, Biografía y Geografía de México. Mexico City: Editorial Porrua, 1964.

Douglas, Fredric H., ed. "Beadwork History and Technics." Denver Art Museum, Leaflet 117. Denver, 1957.

Eggan, Fred, ed. *Social Anthropology of North American Tribes*. Chicago: University of Chicago Press, 1955.

Emmart, Emily Walcott, ed. and trans. *The Badianus Manuscript*. Baltimore: Johns Hopkins Press, 1940.

Ewers, John C. *The Horse in Blackfoot Indian Culture*. Bureau of American Ethnology, Bulletin 159. Washington, D.C.: Smithsonian Institution, 1954.

Fabila, Alfonso. *La tribu kikapoo de Coahuila*. Biblioteca Enciclopédica Popular, no. 50. Mexico City: Secretaría de Educación, 1945.

Farmacopea mexicana de la Sociedad Farmacéutica Mexicana. Mexico City: Editorial Botas, 1952.

Fisher, Margaret Welpley, ed. SEE Jones, William.

Font Quer, Pío. *Plantas medicinales*. Mexico City: Editorial Labor, 1962.

Foreman, Grant. *The Five Civilized Tribes*. Norman: University of Oklahoma Press, 1934.

———. *Last Trek of the Indians*. Chicago: University of Chicago Press, 1946.

———, ed. SEE Marcy, Randolph B., and G. B. McClellan.

Gates, Charles M., ed. *Five Fur Traders of the Northwest*. Saint Paul: Minnesota Historical Society, 1965.

Gibson, A. M. *The Kickapoos: Lords of the Middle Border*. Norman: University of Oklahoma Press, 1963.

Goggin, John M. "The Mexican Kickapoo Indians." *Southwestern Journal of Anthropology* 7(1951):314–327.

Goodman, Sula Saltsman. "Visit with the Kickapoo of Oklahoma." *Talking Leaves* 5, nos. 4 and 5(1960):2–6.

Gregory, J. N. *Fort Concho: Its Why and Wherefore*. San Angelo, Tex.: Newsfoto Publishing Company, 1957.

Hagan, William T. *The Sac and Fox Indians*. Norman: University of Oklahoma Press, 1958.

Haley, J. Evetts. *Fort Concho and the Texas Frontier*. San Angelo, Tex.: San Angelo Standard Times, 1952.

Harrington, Mark R. *Sacred Bundles of the Sac and Fox Indians*. Anthropological Publications, vol. 4, no. 2. Philadelphia: University of Pennsylvania, 1914.

————. "Too Much Hominy." *The Masterkey* 18, no. 5(1944):155–156.

Harris, Charles H., III. "Empire of the Sánchez Navarro." *Américas* 24, no. 4(1972):12–18.

Hewitt, J. N. B. "Adoption." In *Handbook of American Indians North of Mexico*, edited by Frederick Webb Hodge, I, 15–16. New York: Pageant Books, 1959.

Hickerson, Harold. "The Feast of the Dead Among the Seventeenth Century Algonkians of the Upper Great Lakes." *American Anthropologist*, n.s. 62, no. 1(1960):81–107.

Hilger, Sister Inez M. *Chippewa Child Life and Its Cultural Background*. Bureau of American Ethnology, Bulletin 146. Washington, D.C.: Smithsonian Institution, 1951.

Hodge, Frederick Webb, ed. *Handbook of American Indians North of Mexico*. 2 vols. New York: Pageant Books, 1959.

Hoffman, Walter James. *The Menomini Indians. Fourteenth Annual Report of the Bureau of American Ethnology, Part I*. Washington, D.C.: Smithsonian Institution, 1896.

————. "The Midē'wiwin or 'Grand Medicine Society' of the Ojibwa." In *Seventh Annual Report of the Bureau of American Ethnology*, pp. 143–300. Washington, D.C.: Smithsonian Institution, 1891.

Houck, Louis, ed. *The Spanish Regime in Missouri*. 2 vols. Chicago: R. R. Donnelley and Sons, 1909.

Hunter, John D. *Memoirs of Captivity among the Indians of North America*. London: Longman, Hurst, Reese, Orme, Brown and Green, 1823.

Informe de la Comisión Pesquisidora de la Frontera del Norte. Mexico City: Imprenta del Gobierno en Palacio, 1877.

Jones, William. "The Algonkin Manitou." *Journal of American Folk-lore* 18(1905):183–190.

————. "Algonquian." In *Handbook of American Indian Languages*, Part 1, pp. 737–873. Bureau of American Ethnology, Bulletin 40. Washington, D.C.: Smithsonian Institution, 1911.

————. *Ethnography of the Fox Indians*. Edited by Margaret Welpley Fisher. Bureau of American Ethnology, Bulletin 125. Washington, D.C.: Smithsonian Institution, 1939.

————. "Kickapoo Ethnological Notes." *American Anthropologist*, n.s. 15, no. 2(1913):332–335. [Published posthumously by Truman Michelson.]

————. *Kickapoo Tales*. American Ethnological Society, publication no. 9. New York, 1915.

Kellogg, Louise Phelps. *The British Regime in Wisconsin and the Northwest*. Madison: State Historical Society of Wisconsin, 1935.

———. *The French Regime in Wisconsin and the Northwest*. Madison: State Historical Society of Wisconsin, 1925.

Kelly, Isabel. *Folk Practices in North Mexico: Birth Customs, Folk Medicine, and Spiritualism in the Laguna Zone*. Latin American Monographs, No. 2. Austin: University of Texas Press, 1965.

Kinietz, Vernon, ed. *Meearmeear Traditions: C. C. Trowbridge*. Ann Arbor: Museum of Anthropology of the University of Michigan, 1938.

———, and Erminie W. Voegelin, eds. *Shawnese Traditions: C. C. Trowbridge's Account*. Ann Arbor: University of Michigan, 1939.

Lane, Walter P., T. H. Dixon, and John P. Cox. *Battle with the Kickapoos*. Houston: Union National Bank, 1933. [Extract from *Border Wars of Texas*, edited by James T. De Shields. Tioga, Texas: The Herald Co., 1912.]

Latorre, Dolores L. and Felipe A. "The Ceremonial Life of the Mexican Kickapoo Indians." In *Proceedings, VIIIth International Congress of Anthropological and Ethnological Sciences* (1968), II, 268–270. Tokyo: Science Council of Japan, 1969.

———. "¿Hasta qué punto los indios Kickapú se han integrado en la medicina popular y moderna de México?" *Anuario Indigenista* 29(December 1969):253–267.

Lyford, Carrie A. *Ojibwa Crafts*. Bureau of Indian Affairs. Phoenix: Phoenix Indian School Print Shop, 1953.

McDougall, W. B., and Omer E. Sperry. *Plants of Big Bend National Park*. Washington, D.C.: U.S. Department of the Interior, 1951 (reprint, 1957).

McReynolds, Edwin C. *The Seminoles*. Norman: University of Oklahoma Press, 1957.

Marcy, Randolph B., and G. B. McClellan. *Adventure on Red River: A Report on the Exploration of the Headwaters of the Red River*, edited by Grant Foreman. American Exploration and Travel Series, no. 1. Norman: University of Oklahoma Press, 1937.

Marshall, W. Taylor, and Thor Methven Bock. *Cactaceae*. Pasadena, Calif.: Abbey Garden Press, 1941.

Martínez, Maximino. *Las plantas medicinales de México*. Mexico City: Ediciones Botas, 1959.

Michelson, Truman. "The Autobiography of a Fox Woman." In *Fortieth Annual Report of the Bureau of American Ethnology*, pp. 291–349. Washington, D.C., 1925.

———. *Contributions to Fox Ethnology*. Bureau of American Ethnology, Bulletin 85. Washington, D. C.: Smithsonian Institution, 1927.

———. "Ethnological Researches Among the Fox Indians, Tama, Iowa." In *Smithsonian Miscellaneous Collections*, vol. 77, no. 2, pp. 133–136. Washington, D.C., 1925.

———. *Fox Miscellany*. Bureau of American Ethnology, Bulletin 114. Washington, D.C.: Smithsonian Institution, 1937.

———. "Kickapoo." *American Anthropologist*, n.s. 35(1933):551–552.

———. *Notes on the Buffalo-Head Dance of the Thunder Gens of Fox Indians*. Bureau of American Ethnology, Bulletin 87. Washington, D.C.: Smithsonian Institution, 1928.

———. "Notes on the Fox Mortuary Customs and Beliefs." In *Fortieth Annual Report of the Bureau of American Ethnology*, pp. 351–495. Washington, D.C., 1925.

———. *Notes on the Fox Wâpanōwiweni*. Bureau of American Ethnology, Bulletin 105. Washington, D.C.: Smithsonian Institution, 1932.

———. "Notes on the Social Organization of the Fox Indians." *American Anthropologist*, n.s. 15(1913):691–693.

———. *Observations on the Thunder Dance of the Bear Gens of the Fox Indians*. Bureau of American Ethnology, Bulletin 89. Washington, D.C.: Smithsonian Institution, 1929.

———. *The Owl Sacred Pack of the Fox Indians*. Bureau of American Ethnology, Bulletin 72. Washington, D.C.: Smithsonian Institution, 1921.

———. "Preliminary Report on the Linguistic Classification of Algonquian Tribes." In *Twenty-eighth Annual Report of the Bureau of American Ethnology*, pp. 221–290. Washington, D.C., 1912.

———. "The Punishment of Impudent Children." *American Anthropologist*, n.s. 25(1923):281–283.

———. "The Traditional Origin of the Fox Society Known as 'Those Who Worship the Little Spotted Buffalo.' " In *Fortieth Annual Report of the Bureau of American Ethnology*, pp. 497–539. Washington, D.C., 1925.

Montgomery, Rutherford G. *The Living Wilderness*. New York: Dodd, Mead and Co., 1964.

Mooney, James, and William Jones. "Kickapoo." In *Handbook of American Indians North of Mexico*, edited by Frederick Webb Hodge, I, 684–685. New York: Pageant Books, 1959.

Morfi, Padre Fray Juan Agustín. *Excerpts from the Memorias for the History of the Province of Texas*. Edited by Frederick C. Chabot. San Antonio, Tex.: Naylor Printing Company, 1932.

Morgan, Lewis Henry. *The Indian Journals, 1859–62*. Edited by Leslie A. White. Ann Arbor: University of Michigan Press, 1958.

———. *Systems of Consanguinity and Affinity*. Smithsonian Contributions to Knowledge 17. Washington, D.C.: Smithsonian Institution, 1870.

Morse, Jedidiah. *A Report to the Secretary of War of the United States on Indian Affairs*. New Haven: S. Converse, 1832.

Moseley, Edward H. "Indians from the Eastern United States and the Defense of Northeastern Mexico: 1855–1864." *Southwestern Social Science Quarterly* 46, no. 3(December 1965):273–280.

Murdock, George Peter. *Ethnographic Bibliography of North America*. 3d ed. New Haven: Human Relations Area Files, 1960.

———. *Social Structure*. New York: Macmillan Co., 1949.

Neill, Wilfred T. "Wildcat in the West." *Frontier Times* 37, no. 1(December–January 1963):16–19, 52–54.

Newcomb, W. W., Jr. *The Indians of Texas: From Prehistoric to Modern Times*. Austin: University of Texas Press, 1961.

Patton, Rev. William. "Journal of a Visit to Indian Missions, Missouri Conference." *Missouri Historical Society* 10, no. 2(January 1954):167–180.

Peterson, Roger Tory. *A Field Guide to the Birds of Texas*. Boston: Houghton Mifflin, 1960.

Pingenot, Ben E., ed. *Paso del Aguila: A Chronicle of Frontier Days on the Texas Border as Recorded in the Memoirs of Jesse Sumpter*. Austin: Encino Press, 1969.

Pope, Richard K. "The Withdrawal of the Kickapoos." *The American Indian* 8, no. 2(Winter 1958–1959):17–27.

Porter, Kenneth Wiggins. "Farewell to John Horse: An Episode of Seminole Negro Folk History." *Phylon* 8, no. 3(1947):265–273.

———. "The Legend of the Biloxi." *Journal of American Folklore* 49(April–June 1946):168–173.

———. "Seminole Flight from Fort Marion." *Florida Historical Society Quarterly* 22, no. 3(January 1944):113–133.

———. "The Seminole in Mexico, 1850–1861." *Hispanic American Historical Review* 31, no. 1 (February 1951):1–36.

———, and Edward S. Wallace. "Thunderbolt of the Frontier." *The Westerners* 8, no. 4(1961):73–86.

Quimby, George Irving. *Indian Life in the Upper Great Lakes*. Chicago: University of Chicago Press, 1960.

Radin, Paul. "Winnebago Tales." *Journal of American Folk-Lore* 22(1909):288–314.

Ritzenthaler, Robert E., and Frederick A. Peterson. "Courtship Whistling of the Mexican Kickapoo Indians." *American Anthropologist*, n.s. 56, no. 6, part 1 (1954):1088–1089.

———. "The Kickapoos Are Still Kicking." *Natural History* 64, no. 4(April 1955):200–206.

———. *The Mexican Kickapoo Indians*. Milwaukee Public Museum Publications in Anthropology 2. Milwaukee, 1956.

Robelo, Cecilio A. *Diccionario de Aztequismos*. 3d ed. Mexico City: Ediciones Fuentes Culturales, n.d.

Root, George A., ed. "No-ko-aht's Talk—A Kickapoo Chief's Account of a Tribal Journey from Kansas to Mexico and Return in the Sixties." *Kansas Historical Quarterly* 1(1932):153–159.

Sánchez, José María. "A Trip to Texas in 1832." Translated by Carlos Castañeda. *Southwestern Historical Quarterly* 24(1926):249–288.

Silverberg, James. "The Kickapoo Indians: First One Hundred Years of White Contact in Wisconsin." *Wisconsin Archeologist* 38, no. 3(1957):61–181.

Skinner, Alanson. *The Mascoutens or Prairie Potawatomi Indians*. Bulletin of the Public Museum of the City of Milwaukee, vol. 6, nos. 1–3. Milwaukee, 1924–1927.

———. *Material Culture of the Menomini*. Indian Notes and Monograph Series. New York: Museum of the American Indian, Heye Foundation, 1921.

———. *Observations on the Ethnology of the Sauk Indians*. Bulletin of the Public Museum of the City of Milwaukee, vol. 5, nos. 1–3. Milwaukee, 1923–1925.

Speck, Frank G. *The Tutelo Spirit Adoption Ceremony*. Harrisburg: Pennsylvania Historical Commission, 1942.

Standley, Paul C. *Trees and Shrubs of Mexico*. Contributions from the United States National Herbarium, United States National Museum, vol. 23, parts 1–5. Washington, D.C.: Smithsonian Institution, 1920–1961.

Steen, Ralph W. *History of Texas*. Austin: Steck, 1939.

Swanton, John R. *The Indians of Southeastern United States*. Bureau of American Ethnology, Bulletin 137. Washington, D.C.: Smithsonian Institution, 1946.

———. *The Indian Tribes of North America*. Bureau of American Ethnology, Bulletin 145. Washington, D.C.: Smithsonian Institution, 1953.

Tax, Sol. "Social Organization of the Fox Indians." In *Social Anthropology of North American Tribes*, edited by Fred Eggan, pp. 243–282. Chicago: University of Chicago Press, 1955.

Thomas, Alfred Barnaby, ed. *Teodoro de Croix and the Northern Frontier of New Spain, 1776–1783*. Norman: University of Oklahoma Press, 1941.

Thwaites, Reuben Gold, ed. *Jesuit Relations and Allied Documents: Travels and Explorations of the Jesuit Missionaries in New France, 1610–1791*. 73 vols. Cleveland: Burrows Bros., 1896–1901.

U.S. Congress. Senate. *Affairs of the Kickapoo Indians*. 3 vols. Sen. Doc. No. 215. 60th Cong., 1st Sess. Washington, D.C.: Government Printing Office, 1908.

———. *Explorations of the Red River of Louisiana in the Year 1852*. By Capt. Randolph B. Marcy and Brevet Capt. George B. McClellan. Sen. Exec. Doc. No. 54. 32nd Cong., 2d Sess. Washington, D.C.: Government Printing Office, 1853.

———. *The Report of Capt. R. B. Marcy—Route from Ft. Smith to Santa Fe—and the Report of Lt. J. H. Simpson of an Expedition into Navajo Country*. Sen. Exec. Doc. No. 64. 31st Cong., 1st Sess. Washington, D.C.: Government Printing Office, 1850.

U.S. Interior Department. *Biographical and Historical Index of American Indians and Persons Involved in Indian Affairs*. 8 vols. Boston: G. K. Hall, 1966.

Villarelo, Ildefonso. "El centenario de la fundación de la Ciudad de Piedras Negras." *El Nacional* (Mexico City), May 29, 1949. Typescript copy of original manuscript in collection of authors.

Vines, Robert A. *Trees, Shrubs, and Woody Vines of the Southwest*. Austin: University of Texas Press, 1960.

Voegelin, C. F. "North American Indian Languages Still Spoken and Their Genetic Relationships." In *Language, Culture, and Personality: Essays in the Memory of Edward Sapir*, edited by Leslie Spier, A. Irving Hallowell, and Stanley S. Newman, pp. 15–40. Salt Lake City: University of Utah Press, 1960.

Wallace, Ben J. "The Oklahoma Kickapoo: An Ethnographic Reconstruction." *Wisconsin Archeologist* 45, no. 1(1964):1–69.

Webb, Walter Prescott. *The Texas Rangers: A Century of Frontier Defense*. 2d ed. Austin: University of Texas Press, 1965.

Webber, John Milton. *Yuccas of the Southwest*. Agriculture Monograph 17. Washington, D.C.: U.S. Department of Agriculture, 1953.

Weddle, Robert S. *San Juan Bautista: Gateway to Spanish Texas*. Austin: University of Texas Press, 1968.

Wills, Mary Motz, and Howard S. Irwin. *Roadside Flowers of Texas*. Austin: University of Texas Press, 1961.

Winfrey, Dorman H., and James Day, eds. *The Indian Papers of Texas and the Southwest, 1825–1916*. 5 vols. Austin: Pemberton Press, 1966.

Wissler, Clark. "The Influence of the Horse in the Development of the Plains Culture." *American Anthropologist*, n.s. 16, no. 1, part 1(1914).

———. "The Whirlwind and the Elk in the Mythology of the Dakota." *Journal of American Folk-lore* 18(October–December 1905):256–268.

Witthoft, John. *Green Corn Ceremonialism in the Eastern Woodlands*. Occasional Contributions from the Museum of Anthropology of the University of Michigan 13. Ann Arbor, 1949.

Wood, Harry. "Battle of Civil War in Concho Country." *San Angelo Standard Times*, January 10, 1965.

Woodhull, Frost. "The Seminole Indian Scouts on the Border." *Frontier Times* 15, no. 3(1937):118–127.

Interviews

Anico, Adolfo (Pemazoa). Múzquiz, June 28, 1967.

Cadena, Padre Ernesto. Múzquiz, May 29, 1960.

Chapa Long, Dr. Jacobo. Múzquiz, June 24, 1960.

Downing, Charles. Eagle Pass, Texas, June, 1960.

Elguézabal, Juan José. Múzquiz, July, 1960.

Foster, M. K. Nueva Rosita, Coahuila, October 1, 1965.

Galán Long, Enrique. Múzquiz, July, 1960.

Garza Salazar, Jesús. Múzquiz, May 2, 1964; May 3, 1964.

Jiménez, Roberto. Múzquiz, June 25, 1960.

Kaizatoa (Víctor Flores). Múzquiz, March 19, 1966.

McKellar, Aldon. Múzquiz, August 10, 1962.

Menaquah, Pancho. Múzquiz, February 22, 1971.

Menichika (Benito González). Múzquiz, January 12, 1967.

Pader, Dr. Jesús. Múzquiz, May 30, 1960.

Papícoano, Chief. Múzquiz, April 4, 1961; February 25, 1962; February 14, 1967; August 7, 1967.

Pisacana. Múzquiz, April 4, 1961.

Spence, Robert, Sr. Sabinas, Coahuila, January 18, 1970.

Sukwe, Oscar. Múzquiz, January 1, 1962.

Urista, José María. Múzquiz, August 7, 1967.

Vázquez Hidalgo, Aurelio. Múzquiz, February 18, 1964; May 4, 1966; May 6, 1966.

Worrell, Dorothy Ostrom. Eagle Pass, Texas, July, 1960.

Zapata Múzquiz, Dr. Régulo. Nueva Rosita, Coahuila, May 26, 1961.

Index

tion by, 110, 123–124; village burned by, 269

Carson, Gustav G., 238

Cass, Lewis, 264

Catclaw (*Acacia roemeriana*), 66, 162

Cats, 339, 351, 352

Cattail (*Typha latifolia*): for bench mats, 50; for ceremonial mats, 314; for covering mats, 50; gathering, 47–48, 52–53, 319; origin of use of, 35; tobacco offering to owners of, 48

Cattle: early breeds of, 88; herds of, 96, 121, 133, 138; income from, 96, 109, 135; Kickapoos' early indifference to, 99; in payment for rental of pastures, 99, 135–136, 138; rustling, 87, 89, 117, 118, 119

Cazneau, Mrs. William L. (Cora Montgomery), 13

Cemeteries, 28

Centipede, 39, 351

Century plant agave, or maguey (*Agave americana*), 46, 89

Ceremonial beverages: coffee, 287–288, 298; mescal, 297; tea, 287–288; water, 329

Ceremonial calendar, 272–273

Ceremonial food: beans, 285, 289, 357–358; bear, 275–276, 289, 332; beaver, 310; cabbage, 285; cantaloupe, 311, 326, 358; fried bread, 287–288, 298, 310; Indian corn, 276, 285, 288, 289, 310, 314, 325–326, 328, 332, 337–338, 357–358; javelina, 289; pumpkin or squash, 275, 276, 285–321 passim, 326–330, 332, 337, 357–358; puppy, 276, 314, 325, 330, 332, 338–339; turkey, 275–276; venison, 275–338 passim; watermelon, 311, 326, 329, 358

Ceremonial paraphernalia. See Bells; Bow and arrow; Bow drill; Bowl and dice; Brass kettles; Buckskin; Buffalo tail; Cattail; Double-shinny ball game; Drum and drumstick; Flageolet; Gourd rattle; Invitation sticks; Lacrosse; Ladles; Medicine bundles; Pipes; Rattles; Scoring sticks; White and black board

Ceremonial plants. See Black-eyed peas; Cantaloupe; Cudweed; Indian corn; Indian tobacco; One-seed juniper; Solomon's seal; Texas Hercules-club pricklyash; Watermelon; Wild black cherry; Wild purple iris

Ceremonies. See Adoption ceremony; Arrival and departure ceremonies; Boy's first-hunt ceremony; Bundle purification; Chief's ceremonies; Curing ceremonies; Fasting; Feast of the first fruits; Feasts for the dead; French medal; Herbal societies; House-construction ceremonies; House-dedication ceremonies; Hunters' ceremonies; Indian tobacco; Interment; Little Rabbit bundle and ceremony; Menaquah,

Pancho; Murderer's ceremony; Naming ceremonies; Nekanesheka; New Year clan festivals; Planting ceremonies; Rain ceremonies; Rain dance; Tobacco planting ceremony

Chanters: location of, during dance, 305, 314, 315; number of, 288; as owners of songs, 323; privileges of, 288, 314, 323; qualifications of, 295, 323; reward to, for participation in dance, 301, 305, 307; role of, in dance, 305–307, 315, 316

Cherokee Indians: attack on village of, 11; descendants of, among Kickapoos, 238; under leadership of Chief Bowles, 9, 10; marriage of Kickapoos with, 184

Cheyenne Indians, 3

Chickasaw Indians, 184

Chickens, 96

Chief's aide: as chief's only advisor, 216; duties of, 100, 110; as interim chief, 108; Kickapoo attitude toward, 100. See also Nimácana; Pisacana

Chief's ceremonies, 272–273, 318–320, 327–329

Childbirth, 116, 180–182

Child labor, 91, 92, 93, 168. See also Migrant labor

Chilepiquín (*Capsicum annuum*): as condiment, 58; gathering and marketing, 97, 136, 145; skirt for gathering, 82

Chili peppers (*Capsicum* species), 61, 62

Chinaberry (*Melia azedarach*), 68, 69

Chípil, 166, 243, 244–245

Cinnamon (*Cinnamonum zeylanicum*), 58, 59

Circumcision, 182

Civil War, American, 17–20

Clan bundle houses: ceremonies held in, 275, 277, 278, 279, 318, 319; construction of, 38; custodian of bundle in, 38, 269; enlargement of, 38, 269, 275; fire in, 240, 275, 277; maintenance of, 39, 269; number of, 39; ownership of, 39; taboos concerned with, 38–39

Clans, 151–155; denial of membership in, 153–154, 157–158; names of, 151; reciprocity between, 155, 286–287. See also Berry clan; Black and Brown Bear clans; Buffalo clans; Coyote clan; Eagle clan; Fire clan; Fox clan; Man clan; Raccoon clan; Thunder clan; Tree clan; Water clan

Clark, Gen. George Rogers, 6

Clark, W. P., 31

Clark, William, 9

Class, 160

Clay, Henry, 7

Clothing, 104. See also Dress

Coffee (*Coffea arabica*): in ceremonial feasts, 285; as daily fare, 58, 60, 161; to produce milk, 182

Colonia El Nacimiento, 122, 123–131

sequence of, in New Year clan festivals, 277; time limit to hold adoption ceremony in, 283

Fox Indians, 4, 153. *See also* Sauk and Fox Indians

French medal, 5; ceremony for, 272, 321–322

Frialdad, 243

Fungus (Amanita caesarea), 244

Furniture, 41–42, 47, 101

Gallatin, Albert, 7

Games, ceremonial: bow and arrow game, 285, 303–305; bowl and dice game, 285, 308–309; lacrosse, 285, 300–303; moccasin game, 285, 294–297; woman's double-shinny ball game, 285, 307–308

Games, nonceremonial, 163–165

Garlic (*Allium sativum*), 61–62, 244

Garza, Col. Atilano de la, 24

Garza Galán, José María, 24

Garza Salazar, Jesús, 136

German silver objects: as adornment, 76, 78, 79, 284, 291–292, 317; as fetish, 357; as gifts, 225–226, 228, 284; tools for making, 70

Gestures, 30–32

Gibson, A. M., 3, 18

Goats, 96

God. *See* Kitzihiat

González, Manuel, 24

Gopher John, 12, 24

Gourd rattle, 271, 274, 275, 278, 305, 314, 316–317

Grape, cultivated (*Vitis* species), 58

Grape, wild (*Vitis berlandieri*), 58

Great Spirit. *See* Kitzihiat

Gregory, J. N., 18

Guerrero, Coahuila, 13

Guignois, Michel, 5, 6

Habitation, 35–51; adaptation of, to climate, 35; material used for building, 40, 45, 47, 50, 51; modern, 47; moving, after a death, 202; ownership of, 35; religious significance of, 37; taboos concerned with, 39. *See also* Clan bundle houses; Cook house; Furniture; Jacal; Menstrual hut; Summer house; Winter house

Hackberry (*Celtis lindheimeri*), 40, 68

Hair: care of, 57, 78; men's, 77; women's, 81–82, 173, 317

Hamilton, Henry, 6

Harrington, Dr. Mark R., 78, 89

Harris, Mr. (Moffitt's partner), 23

Harrison, Gen. William Henry, 7

Harvest, 95–96

Herbal societies, 238, 241–243, 272; members of, as curers, 239; members of, as witches, 241, 343–344; New Year ceremonies of, 241, 269, 272

Hewitt, J. N. B., 281

Hodge, Frederick Webb, 301

Hogs, 96

"Holding-hands dance," 332

Homesickness, cure for, 333

Hominy: as daily fare, 62; as food during illness, 63, 240; as gift during illness, 148; preparation of, 62

Homosexuality, 177

Honey mesquite (*Prosopis glandulosa*), 69

Honey mesquite mistletoe (*Phoradendron serotinum*), 206

Horses, 130, 133, 179; acquisition of, 86; in afterlife, 264, 352; breaking, 351–352; as compensation for damages, 116; in courtship and betrothal, 186–188; decimation of, 90, 96; disposition of, at owner's death, 197; fulfilling debts and obligations with, 352; as gifts, 130–131; as manitous, 268; naming, 352; raiding and stealing, 14, 20, 22, 23, 87; restrictions on riding, 203, 351, 352; saddle for, 68, 96; trading, 17, 87, 96; as transportation, 9, 13, 17, 19, 22, 33, 52, 53, 86, 88, 248; treatment of, 203, 351–352; Wisaka brought, 351; in witchcraft, 346; as work animals, 351–352

Hostages, 5, 6, 22

House-construction ceremonies, 319–320

House-dedication ceremonies, 272, 273, 320–321

Houses. *See* Habitation

Houston, Sam, 9–10, 11

Huerta, Victoriano, 24, 122–123

Hunters' ceremonies, 55, 57, 273, 285, 313

Hunting: beliefs associated with, 55, 57, 349, 350–351; brushes with federal police and game wardens over, 118–120; difficulties with ranchers over, 54, 88, 90, 118; and exhaustion of game, 53, 89; and game laws, 54–55, 89, 90, 130; in groups, 55; Kickapoo rationale for, 55, 118, 119

Hunting expeditions, 52, 53, 85–86, 88

Huron Indians, 4

Husband stealing, 191, 216

Incest, 113–114, 189, 342

Income: chief's, 99–100; from farming, 57, 89, 95–96; from fishing, 85; from food gathering, 58, 85, 97; from hunting, 52–53, 85; from livestock, 96; from migrant labor, 89–94; minor sources of, 96–99; from trading (with Americans), 87, (with British), 8, (with French), 4, 86, (with Mexicans), 94–95, (with prairie Indians), 17, 87; from U.S. government annuities, 7, 8, 87

Indian corn (*Zea mays*): ancestry of, 357; cake of, for burial, 201; as cash crop, 95; ceremony for planting, 358; colors of, 357; in daily fare, 60–61, 62; planting of,

Wax Euphorbia, 253, 355
Wayne, Gen. Anthony, 7
Weather, 232–233
Weenkah, 329–330
Welfare, U.S., 98, 172
Wheat (flour) (*Triticum aestivum*): for ceremonial feasts, 285–337 passim; as daily fare, 60, 61, 161, 162
Whistler, Maj. William, 90
White and black board, 295–296, 301–302
White-flowered Lippia (*Lippia alba*), 58
Wild black cherry (*Prunus serotina*): as heralder of New Year, 231, 275; medicinal uses of, 239, 271, 315
Wild Cat (Coacoochee): assigned land, 13–14, 123; leads Indians into Mexico, 12; settled in Hacienda El Nacimiento, 15, 122
Wild purple iris (*Iris hexagona*), 239, 271, 356
Willet, John, 23
Williams, T. G., 21–22
Wine-cup (*Callirhoe digitata*), 245
Winnebago Indians, 85, 218
Winter house, 35, 37, 40–42, 47
Wisaka (son of Kitzihiat): brought culture to Kickapoos, 11, 37, 206, 213, 270, 351; as helping Americans in Vietnam, 263; as manitou who looks after Kickapoos' welfare, 261; myths about, 261–263, 267; as teacher, 262–263
Wissler, Clark, 349
Witchcraft, 113, 114; animals in, 346–347; dolls for, 345; fear of, as social control, 341, 345; in illness and death, 234, 342–343; love philter in, 346; protection against, 277, 346–347, 355, 357; rape by, 346; witches and, 343–344, 346
Wolf clan (Oklahoma), 270
Woman's dance, 305–307. *See also* Menaquah, Pancho; Nekanesheka
Woman's double-shinny ball game, 285, 307–308
Woodhull, Frost, 221
Woods, Harry, 18
Woodworking, 65–70
Workmen's compensation, 98, 223

Yacapita: Cárdenas's visit to home of, 130; as *curandera*, 238; Sarah McKellar's friendship with, 222; sought asylum with Kickapoos, 158

Zábila (*Polianthes maculosa*), 242
Zona de tolerancia, 97, 258
Zuñi Indians, 217, 218